D1717482

Eike Lohde

Eine Analyse der neuesten Diem-Debatte

Über den Streit um einen der bedeutendsten deutschen Sportfunktionäre und die aus diesem resultierenden politischen Konsequenzen

Bachelor + Master
Publishing

Lohde, Eike: Eine Analyse der neuesten Diem-Debatte: Über den Streit um einen der bedeutendsten deutschen Sportfunktionäre und die aus diesem resultierenden politischen Konsequenzen, Hamburg, Bachelor + Master Publishing 2013
Originaltitel der Abschlussarbeit: Eine Analyse der neuesten Diem-Debatte: Über den Streit um einen der bedeutendsten deutschen Sportfunktionäre und die aus diesem resultierenden politischen Konsequenzen

Buch-ISBN: 978-3-95684-046-3
PDF-eBook-ISBN: 978-3-95684-546-8
Druck/Herstellung: Bachelor + Master Publishing, Hamburg, 2013
Covermotiv: © Kobes · Fotolia.com
Zugl. Humboldt-Universität zu Berlin, Berlin, Deutschland, Bachelorarbeit, Juli 2013

Bibliografische Information der Deutschen Nationalbibliothek:
Die Deutsche Nationalbibliothek verzeichnet diese Publikation in der Deutschen Nationalbibliografie; detaillierte bibliografische Daten sind im Internet über http://dnb.d-nb.de abrufbar.

© Bachelor + Master Publishing, Imprint der Diplomica Verlag GmbH
Hermannstal 119k, 22119 Hamburg
http://www.diplomica-verlag.de, Hamburg 2013
Printed in Germany

Inhaltsverzeichnis

I.   Einleitung   3

II.   Diem-Debatten im 20. Jahrhundert   6
      1. *Die erste Diem-Debatte um die Bundestagssitzung vom 23. März 1950*   6
      2. *Die zweite Diem-Debatte im Vorfeld der Olympischen Spiele 1972*   7
      3. *Die dritte Diem-Debatte - Mythos Carl Diem von 1987*   10
      4. *Die vierte Diem-Debatte - Das Gutachten von Teichler 1996*   12

III. Die neueste Diem-Debatte: Auslöser, Positionen, Gegenstände und Deutungen   14
      1. *Das Forschungsprojekt Leben und Werk Carl Diems*   14
      2. *Schäfers Diem-Eintrag im Handbuch des Antisemitismus*   17
      3. *Diskussionsgegenstände*   18
            a. *Antisemitismus*   18
            b. *Nationalsozialismus*   21
            c. *Militarismus*   23
      4. *„Kritische Historiker" gegen "Diemologen"*   25

IV.   Geschichtspolitische Konsequenzen im Zuge der neuesten Diem-Debatte   29
      1. *Zum Verhältnis von (Sport-)Geschichtswissenschaft und (Sport-)
         Geschichtspolitik*   29
      2. *Die Umbenennung der Carl-Diem-Plakette*   31
      3. *Die Umbenennungen von Carl-Diem-Straßen, -Wegen, -Sportplätzen
         und -Hallen*   32

V.   Schlussbetrachtung   35

VI.   Literatur- und Quellenverzeichnis   37
      1. *Literatur*   37
      2. *Internetquellen*   39

I.   Einleitung

Über wohl kaum einen deutschen Sportfunktionär des 20. Jahrhunderts herrscht mehr Uneinigkeit innerhalb der Sportgeschichte als über Carl Diem (1882-1962). Diem bekleidete zahlreiche sportorganisatorische Ämter in vier Epochen Deutscher Geschichte: Bereits im Alter von 22 Jahren wurde er im Deutschen Kaiserreich Schriftführer der Deutschen Sportbehörde für Athletik, zwischen 1913 und 1933 war er Generalsekretär des Deutschen Reichsausschusses für Leibesübungen, 1920 gründete er die Berliner Hochschule für Leibesübungen (DHfL) mit und nach dem Ende des Zweiten Weltkriegs war er 1947 der Gründer der Deutsche Sporthochschule in Köln (DSHS) als Nachfolgeeinrichtung der DHfL.

Doch ein Abschnitt seines Lebens wurde hierbei nicht erwähnt. Eben dieser brachte ihm noch zu Lebzeiten und weit über diese hinaus scharfe Kritik. Als Generalsekretär des Organisationskomitees der XI. Olympischen Spiele 1936 in Berlin war er maßgeblich an der Planung der vom US-amerikanischen Kultur- und Politikhistoriker David Clay Large bezeichneten „Nazi games"[1] beteiligt, die auch für viele andere Historiker eine pure Propagandainszenierung darstellten. Weiterhin wurde Diem 1939 zum Reichssportführer des Gaues Ausland ernannt und füllte damit eine offizielle Position innerhalb des NS-Regimes aus. Aber nicht nur seine sportorganisatorischen Ämter führten zur kritischen Hinterfragung. Vor allem seine Publikationen *Sturmlauf durch Frankreich* im *Reichssportblatt* von 1940 und *Olympische Flamme* von 1942 sowie seine Tagebucheinträge und Briefe, die im Laufe der zweiten Hälfte des 20. Jahrhunderts erschlossen werden konnten, brachten Politiker, Historiker und Sportwissenschaftler dazu, mit ihm härter ins Gericht zu gehen. Allerdings überwog lange Zeit für die Mehrzahl der Fachwissenschaftler und Politiker das Diem-Bild eines Mannes, der den deutschen Sport in die Moderne führte und seine Zeit im Nationalsozialismus damit verbrachte, eben diesen Sport vor der Beeinflussung der NSDAP fernzuhalten.

Es folgte ein sich über die gesamte zweite Hälfte des 20. Jahrhunderts und darüber hinaus erstreckender Streit darüber, wie Carl Diems Leben mit Berücksichtigung seines Denkens und Wirkens in der Zeit zwischen 1933 und 1945 zu deuten und schließlich mit dem Gedenken an ihn umgegangen werden sollte. So wurde schließlich der Münsteraner Historiker Frank Becker zwischen 2005 und 2007 damit beauftragt, eine, nicht nur für die Zeit des Nationalsozialistischen Deutschlands, sondern eine alle Lebzeiten Diems umfassende Biogra-

---

[1] Large, D. C.: *Nazi games. The olympics of 1936*, New York et al. 2007.

phie zu erarbeiten, die möglicherweise zu einer Konsensbildung führen könnte. Dass dieser Konsens allerdings nicht erreicht wurde, konnte der Presse entnommen werden.[2]

In dieser Arbeit soll die neueste Diem-Debatte, die von circa 2009 im Grunde bis heute anhält, analysiert werden. Dabei soll die Debatte innerhalb der deutschen Fachöffentlichkeit in den Blick genommen werden und sich folgenden Fragen unterziehen: Welche Entwicklungen führten zur neuesten Diem-Debatte beziehungsweise wodurch wurde diese ausgelöst? Welche Gegenstände wurden diskutiert und wie wurde von wem argumentiert? Im nächsten Schritt soll dann gefragt werden, welche politischen Konsequenzen die neueste Diem-Debatte nach sich zog und welchen Einfluss dabei die wissenschaftlichen Untersuchungen leisteten.

Im Kapitel II. wird zunächst ein kurzer Einblick in die vier Diem-Debatten des zurückliegenden Jahrhunderts gegeben, um mit diesem Vorwissen die neueste und deren Entstehen begreifen zu können. Diese wird im darauffolgenden Kapitel III. genauer untersucht und Auslöser, Diskussionsgegenstände sowie Positionen und Deutungen der Debattierenden aufgezeigt. Im Anschluss wird im Kapitel IV. dargestellt, welche politischen Konsequenzen der neuesten Diem-Debatte folgten. Gleichfalls wird danach gefragt, welchen Einfluss beziehungsweise welche Hilfe die neueste Diem-Debatte und aus ihr gewonnene Erkenntnisse der Sport- und (Sport-)Geschichtswissenschaft für die Politik hatte.

Eine umfassende Darstellung der Diem-Debatte mit einem parteilosen Blick auf diese liegt bisher nicht vor. Somit wurde für diese Arbeit eigentliche Sekundärliteratur, nämlich die sportwissenschaftlichen und geschichtswissenschaftlichen Darstellungen und Deutungen von Diems Denken und Handeln, für meine Fragestellungen zur Primärliteratur. Ich verfolge nicht das Ziel, Carl Diem zu bewerten und zu beurteilen. Vielmehr ist es die Aufgabe dieser Arbeit, von einem (möglichst) unabhängigen Blickwinkel die neueste Diem-Debatte zu durchleuchten und dementsprechend keine Geschichte von Carl Diem zu schreiben, sondern eher eine Geschichte der Carl-Diem-Geschichtsschreibung. Quellen, auf die ich mich beziehe, sind hierbei Fachzeitschriftenartikel, da diese Medium der Auseinandersetzungen zwischen den Sport- und (Sport-)Geschichtswissenschaftlern waren. Für das Kapitel II. werden somit die sportwissenschaftlichen Zeitschriften *Leibeserziehung* und die später gegründete *Sozial- und Zeitgeschichte des Sports* sowie die Darstellungen eines Aufsatzes von Hans Joachim Teich-

---

[2] Vgl. Leffers, J.: *Denkmalsturz: Sporthochschule verliert im Namensstreit um Carl Diem*, veröffentlicht am 22.08.07 unter :http://www.spiegel.de/unispiegel/studium/denkmalsturz-sporthochschule-verliert-im-namensstreit-um-carl-diem-a-501387.html, letzter Zugriff: 31.05.13; 14:22 Uhr oder Billig, M.: *Streit um Carl Diem. Vater des deutschen Sports als Vorbild ungeeignet*, veröffentlicht am 27.12.2011 unter: http://www.zeit.de/sport/2011-12/interview-becker-diem-nazi, letzter Zugriff: 31.05.13; 12:32 Uhr und noch einige mehr.

ler im von Michael Krüger herausgegebenem Sammelband *Erinnerungskultur im deutschen Sport* zur Beantwortung der aufgeworfenen Fragen dienen. Im zweiten Kapitel wird dann im Speziellen eine Ausgabe der *Zeitschrift für Geschichtswissenschaft* von Bedeutung sein, da diese im Mittelpunkt meiner Betrachtung steht. Ebenso wird für dieses Kapitel ein Aufsatz Krügers aus dessen bereits erwähntem Sammelband von 2012 berücksichtigt. Wichtig ist hierbei, eine kritische Distanz gegenüber den Argumentationen der einzelnen Protagonisten wahren, um sich nicht in die eine oder andere Richtung der Deutung Diems drängen zu lassen. Abschließend werden im Kapitel IV. die politischen Entscheidungen untersucht, die möglicherweise durch die neueste Diem-Debatte beeinflusst wurden. Dabei werden als Grundlage journalistische Darstellungen verwendet, um den Verlauf und die Umstände dieser politischen Konsequenzen zu schildern. Einzelne quellenkritische Überlegungen wurden stets in den Fließtext eingearbeitet, um die nötige Distanz einnehmen zu können.

II.   Diem-Debatten im 20. Jahrhundert

Ob zu seinen Lebzeiten oder über diese hinaus - wohl keine andere Persönlichkeit der deutschen Sportgeschichte wurde so kontrovers diskutiert wie Carl Diem. Im Laufe der zweiten Hälfte des 20. Jahrhunderts kam es immer wieder zu Diem-Debatten. Hans Joachim Teichler, der später noch einige Male zu Wort kommen wird, spricht davon, dass diese auf und ab in Wellen verliefen.[3] Doch abschließend konnte keine Bewertung der Person Carl Diems gegeben werden, welche sich nachhaltig unumstritten etablierte. Im folgenden Kapitel soll aufgezeigt werden, welche Diskussionsgegenstände diese Wellen kennzeichneten, wer beziehungsweise welche Gegebenheiten die „Anti-Diem-Wellen"[4] auslösten und welche neuen Erkenntnisse aus den jeweiligen Debatten resultierten. Dies kann natürlich nicht in gänzlicher Ausführlichkeit vorgenommen werden, da sich diese Arbeit auf die neueste Diem-Debatte des 21. Jahrhunderts fokussiert. Dennoch kommt eine solche nicht daran vorbei, die vorherigen Debatten zu besprechen, da sie schließlich zur neuesten Debatte führten und deren Diskussionsgegenstände schon damals in die Wege leiteten.

1.   Die erste Diem-Debatte um die Bundestagssitzung vom 23. März 1950

Bereits knapp zwei Jahre nach dem Ende des Zweiten Weltkrieges wurde die Deutsche Sporthochschule (DSHS) Köln als Nachfolgeeinrichtung der Deutschen Hochschule für Leibesübungen (DfHL), die in Berlin ansässig war, gegründet. Deren Gründungsrektor war Carl Diem, welcher bereits Leiter der DfHL und von 1936 bis 1945 Leiter des Internationalen Olympischen Instituts war. Dieser veröffentlichte während der NS-Zeit zahlreiche Schriften, darunter auch einige in nationalsozialistischen Zeitschriften. Als Carl Diem versuchte, sich in der Nachkriegszeit in den deutschen Sport zu reintegrieren, stieß er ob seines Schaffens im nationalsozialistischen Deutschland auf Widerstand. Dieser wurde ihm vornehmlich von ehemaligen Arbeitersportfunktionären entgegengebracht und hielt einige Jahre an.[5]

---

[3] Vgl. Teichler, H. J.: *Erinnerungskultur im deutschen Sport und die Diem-Debatte*, in: Krüger, H. (Hrsg.): *Erinnerungskultur im Sport. Vom kritischen Umgang mit Carl Diem, Sepp Herberger und anderen Größen des deutschen Sports*, Berlin 2012, S. 129-131.

[4] Teichler 2012, S. 129. Teichler spricht hier von einer Debatte in verschiedenen „Anti-Diem-Wellen". Mir erscheint es jedoch sinnvoll, für ein besseres Verständnis, um die zeitlichen Differenzen zwischen den Auseinandersetzungen mit Diem zu beschreiben, von mehreren Debatten zu reden, auch wenn es sich bei den verschiedenen Debatten um die selbe diskutierte Person handelte. Dabei wird das Bild des wellenförmigen Verlaufs nicht verfälscht.

[5] Vgl. Bernett, H.: *Carl Diem und sein Werk als Gegenstand der sportgeschichtlichen Forschung*, in: *Sozial- und Zeitgeschichte des Sports*, 1. Jahrgang, Heft 1, Köln 1987, S. 12.

Bei der Frankfurter Sportkonferenz am 7. Juni 1947 forderte Heinrich Sorg, der aus dem Lager des Arbeitersports stammte und zu jener Zeit Sportreferent der SPD war, von Diem, auf die Wahl ins Nationale Olympische Komitee (NOK) zu verzichten. Veranlasst zu dieser Handlung sah sich Sorg vor allem durch Diems 1942 veröffentlichtes, insgesamt 1637 Seiten starkes und drei Bände umfassendes Werk *Olympische Flamme*. Im SPIEGEL vom 16. August 1947 wurde Sorgs Behauptung zitiert, dass Diem „während der Zeit der militärischen Erfolge dieses Krieges (des Zweiten Weltkrieges; Anm. des Autors) (...) ganz den Verstand (verlor) und den Krieg in einer Art und Weise (verherrlichte), die an Verbrechen grenzt"[6]. Mit diesen Worten bezog er sich auf Diems *Olympische Flamme*, die seine „eigene Anklageschrift"[7] darstelle und von militaristischen Bemerkungen durchzogen zu sein schien. Diese Aufforderung blieb zwar wirkungslos, da Diem schließlich ins NOK gewählt wurde, kann jedoch als erste öffentlichkeitswirksame Diem-Kritik gesehen werden, die nie völlig ermattete.

Einen Höhepunkt dieser Zeit sieht Hans Joachim Teichler, der unter anderem im Jahre 1996 ein Gutachten für die mögliche Umbenennung des Carl-Diem-Weges in Köln veröffentlichte, in der 50. Bundestagssitzung am 23. März 1950. Auch hier wurde Diem erneut für den Inhalt seines Buches *Olympische Flamme* kritisiert und grundlegend darauf als Militarist betitelt. Aus den selben Gründen erhielt er über diesen Zeitpunkt hinaus Kritik aus der DDR, doch diese schadete ihm nicht, da jegliche Kommentare aus östlicher Richtung aufgrund der Spannungen des Kalten Krieges nicht als relevant gewertet und stets abgewehrt wurden.[8]

2.   *Die zweite Diem-Debatte im Vorfeld der Olympischen Spiele 1972*

Die zweite Diem-Debatte ließ knapp zwanzig Jahre auf sich warten. Im zeitlichen Vorfeld der XX. Olympischen Sommerspiele in München 1972 wurde im September 1971 im Münchener Stadtrat darüber entschieden, welche Namensträger für Straßen, Plätze und Brücken im Olympischen Dorf aufzunehmen seien. Im Laufe der Entscheidungsfindung wurde beschlossen, den Namen Carl Diem nicht zu berücksichtigen, um „politischen Komplikationen aus dem Wege zu gehen"[9]. Auf diesen Beschluss folgte am 4. Oktober des gleichen Jahres ein SPIEGEL-Artikel von Walter Goelde. Dieser befasste sich auf kritische Weise mit der Ausei-

---

[6] Ohne Autor: *Sorg-Sorgen. Unser Embryo lebt*, in: DER SPIEGEL: Nr. 33, 1947, S. 12.
[7] Ebenda.
[8] Vgl. Teichler 2012, S. 129.
[9] Hinrichsen, J. & Obieray, U. & Sonnenschein, W.: *„Der Krieg ist der vornehmsten Sport...". Geschichte und Manipulation eines Zitats von Carl Diem (2. Teil)*, in: *Leibeserziehung: Monatsschrift für Wissenschaft und Unterricht*, 21. Jahrgang, Heft 4, Schorndorf 1972, S. 127.

nandersetzung um die Sportvergangenheit der NS-Zeit und deren Funktionären. Einige dieser Funktionäre füllten über diese Zeit hinaus verantwortliche Positionen in der deutschen Sportorganisation aus – so auch Carl Diem. Im Artikel wurden die Diem-Zitate: „Die sportlichen Erfolge in Friedenszeiten haben sich in militärische Siege verwandelt" sowie „Der Krieg ist der vornehmste, ursprünglichste Sport" verwendet, wobei vor allem letzteres zu heftigem Streit führte.[10]

Die Witwe Carl Diems, Liselott Diem, reagierte mit einem Leserbrief an den SPIEGEL auf Goeldes Artikel und bezeichnete diesen als „systematischen Rufmord"[11]. Etwas später veröffentlichte der Mitarbeiter des Carl-Diem-Instituts der DSHS und Bearbeiter der 1974 herausgegebenen Autobiographie Carl Diems, Bernd Wirkus, einen Artikel in der sportwissenschaftlichen Zeitschrift *Leibeserziehung*, der gewissermaßen eine Richtigstellung des Diem-Zitats darzustellen versuchte[12]. Demnach zitiere Diem selbst nur den belgischen Schriftsteller und Dramatiker Maurice Maeterlinck aus dessen Buch *Gedanken über Sport und Krieg*. Somit ist Diem, der den Satz „Der Krieg ist der vornehmste, ursprünglichste Sport" bei einem Vortrag vor der Heeresschule für Leibesübungen in Wünsdorf im Jahre 1931 verwendete, nicht der Urheber dieses Zitates, sondern Maeterlinck – er habe dieses allerdings nicht als solches vermerkt. Weiterhin argumentiert Wirkus, dass Diem ebenso wie Maeterlinck versuche, keine positive Assoziation von Sport und Krieg herzustellen, denn Diem fuhr im nächsten Satz des Vortrags fort, dass Sport und Krieg Gegensätze seien: „Das eine ist Ernst, blutiger Ernst, das andere ist Spiel, heiteres Spiel." Mit dieser Argumentation intendierte Wirkus wohl eine Richtigstellung des Diem-Bildes, welches seiner Ansicht nach, durch Goeldes Artikel verfälscht wurde und unterstellte diesem die „Ignoranz der Herkunft des Diem-Ausspruches"[13].

Wiederum als Reaktion auf Wirkus´ Artikel folgte ein Aufsatz in der gleichen Zeitschrift nur vier Hefte später. Die Bonner Studenten Ulrich Obieray und Werner Sonnenschein sowie der Kölner Student der DSHS Jens Hinrichsen bezeichneten in ihrem Artikel, der den gleichen Namen trägt wie der von Wirkus, nur mit der Beifügung *(2.Teil)* am Ende, Wirkus´ Artikel als „offiziösen Teil einer Aktion zur Vergangenheitsbewältigung (..., der) für die Situation der Zeitgeschichte im bundesdeutschen Sport bezeichnend ist"[14] und holten zum Rundumschlag aus. Hierbei kritisieren sie nicht allein den Wirkus-Aufsatz. Auch anderen

---

[10] Goelde, W.: *Adolfs Rekruten*, in: DER SPIEGEL, Nr. 41, 1971, S. 169.
[11] Diem, L.: Schreiben an Rudolf Augstein vom 7.10.1971.
[12] Vgl. Wirkus, B.: „*Der Krieg ist der vornehmste Sport...".* Geschichte und Manipulation eines Zitats von Carl Diem, in: Leibeserziehung: Monatsschrift für Wissenschaft und Unterricht, 20. Jahrgang, Heft 12, Schorndorf 1971, S. 409-411.
[13] Ebenda, S. 411.
[14] Hinrichsen & Obieray & Sonnenschein 1972, S. 127.

Autoren, die vornehmlich in ihren angehörigen Sportfachverbandszeitschriften publizierten und „am (Liselott-)Diem-Brief orientierte Schützenhilfe leiste(te)n"[15], wurde eine fehlende kritische Haltung gegenüber Diems Arbeit im Dritten Reich vorgehalten. Ansatzpunkte der Kritik waren Fehlinterpretationen und Auslassungen von Zitaten, historischen Fakten und deren Zusammenhängen. Sie unterstellten zum Beispiel, dass Diem die von Wirkus ausgeführte positive Assoziation von Krieg und Sport eben nicht versuchte abzuwehren, da er „zeit seines Lebens die Auffassung (vertrat), daß der Sport zum Krieg gehört oder ihm dient"[16].

Letztlich sah sich Bernd Wirkus daraufhin erneut veranlasst, eine Reaktion auf den Aufsatz des Verfasserkollektivs der drei Bonner und Kölner Studenten zu leisten. Diese wurde direkt im Anschluss an deren Artikel in der *Leibeserziehung* abgedruckt. Wirkus antwortete auf die Kritik des Weglassens historischer Zusammenhänge mit dem Verweis auf den wissenschaftlichen Anspruch des Carl-Diem-Instituts: Ziel sei eine „objektive Erforschung" und nicht „die Erzeugung einer 'Legende' um eine Person"[17]. Hinzu kamen weitere Erklärungen zu den jeweils gewählten Diem-Zitaten und deren Deutungen.

Was sich aus dieser zweiten Diem-Debatte schlussfolgern lässt, ist einerseits die Schwierigkeit, mittels Sprache und dem Belegen mit Zitaten, das Denken und Handeln von historischen Personen postum zu rekonstruieren. Schließlich kann die Person, um die es geht, ebenso wenig ein Veto einlegen wie Außenstehende ein objektives Urteil abgeben können. Zweitens ist festzustellen, dass erste Zweifel an der Arbeit des Carl-Diem-Instituts aufkamen – geschehen durch Hinrichsen et al. sowie Goelde. Schließlich gab das Carl-Diem-Institut vornehmlich Schriften aus Diems Nachlass heraus, welche ein positives Bild zu erzeugen suchten.[18] Diese Zweifel wurden von der damaligen Prorektorin Liselott Diem (zwischen 1969-1971) und dem Diem-Instituts-Mitarbeiter Bernd Wirkus versucht, als falsch darzustellen. Wissenschaftliche Untersuchungen zur Organisation des Sports im Dritten Reich wurden nur marginal durchgeführt, was an der sich erst entwickelnden Sportwissenschaft sowie an der mangelhaften Quellenlage lag. Lediglich Hajo Bernett unternahm einen ersten Versuch, eine umfassendere Darstellung der *Sportpolitik im Dritten Reich*[19] durchzuführen, indem er Akten der Reichskanzlei sezierte. Der Name Carl Diem fand (zunächst) jedoch keine besondere Bedeutung. Dies sollte sich in der Folgezeit ändern.

---

[15] Hinrichsen & Obieray & Sonnenschein 1972, S. 128.
[16] Ebenda.
[17] Wirkus, B.: *In Sachen Carl Diem*, In: *Leibeserziehung: Monatsschrift für Wissenschaft und Unterricht*, 21. Jahrgang, Heft 4, Schorndorf 1972, S. 131.
[18] Vgl. Laude, A. & Bausch, W.: *Der Sport-Führer. Die Legende um Carl Diem*, Göttingen 2000, S. 204. Weiterhin: Vgl. Teichler, H. J.: *Carl Diem und sein Werk als Gegenstand der sportgeschichtlichen Forschung*, in: *Sozial- und Zeitgeschichte des Sports*, 1. Jahrgang, Heft 1, Köln 1987, S. 16.
[19] Bernett, H.: *Sportpolitik im Dritten Reich. Aus den Akten der Reichskanzlei*, Schorndorf 1971.

Eine dritte Diem-Debatte wurde durch eine sporthistorische Zeitschrift und zwei in dieser enthaltene Dokumente eröffnet. Im März 1987 gaben drei deutsche Sportwissenschaftler eine sporthistorische Zeitschrift namens *Sozial- und Zeitgeschichte des Sports* heraus. Zu diesen zählten der Hannoveraner Lorenz Peiffer, welcher sich bereits seit Mitte der 1970er Jahre in seinen Arbeiten mit Turnen und Sport im Dritten Reich beschäftigte, Giselher Spitzer, zu jener Zeit wissenschaftlicher Mitarbeiter an der Rheinischen Friedrich-Wilhelms-Universität Bonn, sowie dem Bernett-und Ueberhorst-Schüler[20] Hans Joachim Teichler. Ihrer Erstausgabe gaben sie den Titel *Mythos Carl Diem*. In jenem Titel steckt eine implizite Hypothese, nach der Carl Diem eine mythische Figur sei, die bis dato möglicherweise falsch dargestellt und interpretiert zu sein scheint. Eine Überprüfung und eventuelle Richtigstellung dessen schien den Herausgebern und Autoren wohl angebracht.

So spricht Lorenz Peiffer in seinem Aufsatz *Carl Diem und der Sport in der Zeit des Nationalsozialismus*, welcher in der oben genannten Startausgabe der *Zeitschrift Sozial- und Zeitgeschichte des Sports* erschien, davon, dass „Darstellungen von Betroffenen über eigene Erlebnisse und selbst miterlebte (...) Ereignisse und Entwicklungen (...) einer kritischen Betrachtung und Wertung"[21] bedürfen. Schließlich weisen diese durch eine persönliche Involvierung einen subjektiven Charakter auf. Jene kritische Betrachtung scheint er in den drei Quellen, die er zu Rate zieh, welche alle samt aus Diems Feder stammen und nach dem Zweiten Weltkrieg verfasst wurden, nicht zu erkennen. Deshalb liegt es nun am Historiker, eine kritische Distanz zu diesen Darstellungen einzunehmen.

Dass nun etwa 15 Jahre nach der letzten Diem-Debatte eine weitere losbrach und eine kritische (Neu-)Betrachtung und (Neu-)Wertung der Person Carl Diems nötig war, musste einen Grund haben. Diesen lieferte Reinhard Appel, der zwischen 1963 und 1991 nahezu ununterbrochen als Moderator im deutschen Fernsehen, vor allem im Zweiten Deutschen Fernsehen (ZDF), zu sehen war. Appel referierte am 28. April 1984 in der Berliner Führungs- und Verwaltungsakademie aus einem „sehr persönlichen Grund"[22] auf einer Diskussionsver-anstaltung über die Olympische Idee. Dieser „sehr persönliche Grund" war, dass Appel sich

---

[20] Hajo Bernett und Horst Ueberhorst zählen zu den bedeutendsten deutschen Sporthistorikern des 20. Jahrhundert. Bernett gilt gemeinhin als Begründer der Sportgeschichtsschreibung zur Sportpolitik im Dritten Reich. Der von Horst Ueberhorst herausgegebene Sammelband in sechs Bänden mit dem Titel *Geschichte der Leibesübungen* gilt als Standardwerk der deutschen Sportgeschichte.
[21] Peiffer, L.: *Carl Diem und der Sport in der Zeit des Nationalsozialismus – Anmerkungen zu den Schriften Carl Diems über ein von ihm persönlich erlebtes und mitgestaltetes Kapitel der jüngsten deutschen Sportgeschichte*, in: *Sozial- und Zeitgeschichte des Sports*, 1. Jahrgang, Heft 1, Köln 1987, S. 92.
[22] Appel, R.: *Aus einem Referat von Reinhard Appel vom 28. April 1984 in der Führungs- und Verwaltungsaka-demie in Berlin*, in: *Sozial- und Zeitgeschichte des Sports*, 1. Jahrgang, Heft 1, Köln 1987, S. 105.

an ein persönliches Erlebnis in seinem Referat erinnerte, in dem Diem („ein großer Mann der Olympischen Idee"[23]) im März 1945 auf dem Berliner Reichssportfeld vor der Hitler-Division Großdeutschland, der Appel zu jener Zeit angehörte, in einer „flammenden Rede, in der viel von Sparta und Opferbereitschaft vorkam, zum siegreichen Endkampf gegen die deutschen Feinde aufforderte"[24]. Diese Erinnerung gab neue Hinweise darauf, ob Diems Rolle im Nationalsozialismus die eines, wenn nicht Parteimitglieds, zumindest die eines regimezuarbeitenden Mitläufers gewesen sei. Eine solche Deutung widersetzte sich exakt dem bisherigen, von Diem selbst und durch die Arbeit des Carl-Diem-Instituts erzeugten Diem-Bild eines Gegners und Verfolgten des Nationalsozialismus.[25] Dass Diems politische Weste im Dritten Reich nicht blütenweiß sein konnte, erhärtete auch das zweite Dokument der benannten Erstausgabe der *Sozial- und Zeitgeschichte des Sports*. Dieses war die Verfügung des Nationalsozialistischen Reichsbundes für Leibesübungen (NSRL) vom 22.9.1939, in der Diem zum kommissarischen Leiter des Gaues Ausland ernannt wurde.[26] Jene Funktion Diems wurde von Liselott Diem lange Zeit bestritten.[27] Doch mit diesem Dokument verdichtete sich, dass Diem Verantwortlichkeiten im NS-Regime hatte, auch wenn er kein Parteimitglied war.

Es zeigt sich, dass nun mehr Quellen aufgetaucht sind, die nicht nur eine Würdigung Diems für seine Leistungen für die Organisation und Etablierung des deutschen Sports während der Kaiserzeit, der Weimarer Republik und der Nachkriegszeit zuließen, sondern eine kritische Betrachtung für sein Wirken in der Zeit des Nationalsozialismus notwendig machten. Doch noch war der Prozess der nötigen Quellenerschließung für eine ganzheitliche Einordnung Diems nicht abgeschlossen. So hoffte Bernett 1987, dass nach einer personellen Neubesetzung im Carl-Diem-Institut eine Forschungsstelle entsteht, die „nicht durch bestimmte Interessen der Nachlaßverwaltung eingeengt"[28] sei.

---

[23] Ebenda.
[24] Ebenda.
[25] Vgl. Peiffer 1987, S. 92.
[26] Eine ausführliche Darstellung, wie es zu dieser Ernennung kam gibt Teichler, H. J.: *Der Weg Carl Diems vom DRA-Generalsekretär zum kommissarischen Führer des Gaues Ausland im NSRL*, in: *Sozial- und Zeitgeschichte des Sports*, 1. Jahrgang, Heft 1, Köln 1987a, S. 42-91.
[27] Vgl. Teichler 2012, S. 130.
[28] Bernett 1987, S. 16.

Nachdem vor allem durch die Arbeiten von Bernett und Teichler einige neue Erkenntnisse deutlich geworden waren, nahmen sich auch die Medien wieder vermehrt der Thematik an. Anlässlich des 75-jährigen Jubiläums der DSHS Ende Oktober 1995 sah sich die Fernsehsendung *Monitor* veranlasst, die Frage zu stellen, ob sich keine anderen Vorbilder für den zeitgenössischen Sport finden lassen als Carl Diem.[29] Darin wird berichtet, dass für Diem „Olympia '36 auch als ideologisches Instrument (galt). Er stellte die Spiele uneingeschränkt in den Dienst der Nationalsozialisten und ermöglichte ihnen so diese ungeheure Propagandashow"[30]. Um Diems Zusammenarbeit mit dem NS-Regime zu unterstreichen, gaben die Reporter auch Reinhard Appel das Wort, um erneut die Durchhalterede Carl Diems auf dem Reichssportfeld zu schildern. Hier beschuldigte Appel Diem als „mitschuldig, daß (...) junge Menschen geopfert wurden, in einer Situation, die ja bereits ausweglos war."[31] Diese Kritik, die in der *Monitor*-Sendung an Diem geäußert wurde, stellt in seiner Schärfe eine neue Dimension dar, da sie nun auch weitreichendere politische Konsequenzen nach sich zog. Denn Anträge für Umbenennungen von Carl-Diem-Straßen, -Wegen, -Sportplätzen und -Hallen wurden in der Folge zahlreich gestellt.[32]

Als Konsequenz dieses nun öffentlichen Politikums beauftragte der Rektor der DSHS, Joachim Meister, den Sportwissenschaftler Hans Joachim Teichler, eine Expertise zur Rolle Carl Diems in der Zeit und im zeitlichen Umfeld des NS-Regimes abzugeben. Diese wurde dann im dritten Heft des Jahres 1996 der Zeitschrift *Sozial- und Zeitgeschichte des Sports* veröffentlicht. Für die Zeit zwischen 1933 und 1945 untersuchte Teichler sowohl Diems Tätigkeiten in der deutschen Sportverwaltung als auch seine publizierten Schriften. Außerdem nutzte er Diems Tagebuch als Quelle, mit der er belegen konnte, dass Diem „zwar ausgesprochen national, aber nicht völkisch dachte und die antisemitische Ausrichtung der NSDAP ablehnte"[33].

Mit dieser These versuchte Teichler auch die Rede Diems auf dem Reichssportfeld zu erklären. Dabei bezieht er sich auch auf verschiedene Publikationen Diems und dessen Tagebuch, in denen er „an einer Grundüberzeugung fest(hielt), die aus seiner politisch-

---

[29] Eine Transkription des Beitrags findet sich unter http://www.aussichten-online.de/diem-monitor.html, letzter Zugriff: 3.5.2013; 13:24 Uhr. Moderation: Klaus Bednarz, Reporter: Mathias Werth und Bernd Wengen.
[30] Ebenda.
[31] Ebenda.
[32] Vgl. Kluge, V.: *Zum aktuellen Stand in der „Diem-Debatte"*, in: *Kurier. Informationen der Deutschen Sporthochschule Köln*, 25. Jahrgang, Heft 2, Köln 2002, S. 2.
[33] Teichler, H. J.: *Die Rolle Carl Diems in der Zeit und im zeitlichen Umfeld des NS-Regimes*, in: *Sozial- und Zeitgeschichte des Sports*, 10. Jahrgang., Heft 3, Köln 1996, S. 61.

gesellschaftlichen Prägung in der Kaiserzeit erwachsen war"[34], welche sich auch in der Rede äußere. Diese „Prägung" sei zwar national gewesen, doch nicht rassistisch oder antisemitisch.

Im Anschluss an diesen Aufsatz folgt eine Stellungnahme der Expertenkommission zu Werk und Person Carl Diems, welche vom Präsidium des Deutschen Sportbundes (DSB) vom 3. Mai 1996 herausgegeben wurde. Dieser wohnten sowohl DSB-Funktionäre als auch der Rektor der DSHS sowie namhafte Sportwissenschaftler bei. Diese Stellungnahme schien ein Versuch zu sein, auf die aufgekommene Kritik an dem Gesamtwerk Carl Diems, die durch die Erkenntnisse über seine Tätigkeit zur Zeit des Nationalsozialismus hervorgerufen wurde, zu reagieren. Da nun wie erwähnt die Zahl der Umbenennungen von Diem-Straßen etc. stieg und auch der Name der vom DSB vergebenen Diem-Plakette für sportwissenschaftliche Leistungen zur Diskussion stand, schienen sie eine Empfehlung für nötig zu halten. Dass diese Expertenkommission mit Persönlichkeiten aus der Sportpolitik (z.B. Jürgen Baur, Vorsitzender des Bundesausschusses für Bildung, Gesundheit und Wissenschaft des DSB), der Universitätsleitung (Joachim Meister, DSHS-Rektor) und Sportwissenschaft (Ommo Gruppe, Karl Lennartz und Giselher Spitzer) bestückt war, sollte vermutlich eine Einigkeit der verschiedenen Kompetenzbereiche suggerieren. Diese empfahlen deutlich, keine Umbenennungen durchzuführen. Allerdings konnte die Expertenkommission ihre Empfehlung nur ohne eine vollständige Biographie über Carl Diems gesamtes Leben vornehmen. Diese Gesamtdarstellung, welche sowohl Diems Werk in der Kaiserzeit, der Weimarer Republik, im nationalsozialistischen Deutschland und in der deutschen Nachkriegszeit berücksichtigt, blieb bis zum Zeitpunkt jener Stellungnahme aus. Eine solche Gesamtdarstellung lies einige Jahre auf sich warten. Die Debatte, die dieser entwuchs, soll im Anschließenden dargestellt werden.

---

[34] Teichler 1996, S. 73.

III.   Die neueste Diem-Debatte: Auslöser, Gegenstände, Positionen und Deutungen

Wie die letzte Diem-Debatte des 20. Jahrhunderts zeigte, standen sowohl Sportwissenschaft als auch die sportpolitisch Verantwortlichen vor dem Dilemma, dass keine ganzheitliche Bewertung der Person Diems, welche das Schaffen seines ganzen Lebens berücksichtigt, vorlag. Zwar wurden Arbeiten über Diems Tätigkeiten für verschiedene Epochen durchgeführt, doch eine Darstellung, welche sein ganzes Leben umfasst und hilfreich für eine konsensfähige Urteilsbildung sein konnte, sucht man vergeblich. Mit dieser Aufgabe wurde nun der Münsteraner Historiker Frank Becker zwischen 2005 und 2007 beauftragt. In diesem Kapitel soll es um die neueste Diem-Debatte gehen. Hierbei waren verschiedene Faktoren ausschlaggebend, welche im Folgendem aufgezeigt werden.

1.   Das Forschungsprojekt „Leben und Werk Carl Diems"

1996 nahm eine Expertenkommission, die vom Deutschen Sportbund (DSB) berufen wurde, Stellung zu der in den 1990er Jahren geführten Diskussion über Carl Diems Handeln in der Zeit des nationalsozialistischen Deutschlands und konkret, ob es nötig sei, Diem-Straßen, -Wege, -Sportplätze und –Hallen umzubenennen. Sie kamen zu dem deckungsgleichen Ergebnis mit dem Teichler-Gutachten, dass kein Handlungsbedarf bestehe, Umbenennungen vorzunehmen, da Diems Verdienste „um den deutschen Sport insgesamt außer Zweifel"[35] standen. Dennoch gaben diese in ihrer Stellungnahme zu bedenken, dass Diems „Leben und Werk (...) Anlaß zur kritischen Auseinandersetzung, die jedoch unter Berücksichtigung des historischen Kontextes geführt werden muß"[36], geben solle. So wurde einige Jahre später auf Initiative des DSB und der DSHS eine Projektgruppe unter Vorsitz von Ommo Grupe berufen, welche aus namhaften Forschern sowohl aus der Sportwissenschaft als auch der Geschichtswissenschaft bestand. Michael Krüger agierte hierbei als wissenschaftlicher Leiter des Projekts, welches den Titel *Leben und Werk Carl Diems* trug.[37]

Deren Aufgabe war es nun, einen ausgewiesenen (Sport-)Historiker zu finden, der erstmals eine alle Lebzeiten Diems umfassende Biographie erarbeiten sollte – anders als noch 1996, als mit Hans Joachim Teichler ein Sportwissenschaftler beauftragt wurde. Maßgebliches Anforderungsprofil war, dass dieser Biograph nicht nur ausgesprochene sport- und olympiahistori-

---

[35] Präsidiumsbeschluss des DSB: *Stellungnahme der Expertenkommission zu Werk und Person von Carl Diem (1882 bis 1962)*, in: *Sozial- und Zeitgeschichte des Sports*, 10. Jahrgang, Heft 3, Köln 1996, S. 75.
[36] Ebenda, S. 79.
[37] Mitglieder der Projektgruppe waren Ommo Grupe, Christiane Eisenberg, Gertrug Pfister, Hans Joachim Teichler, Norbert Müller, Karl Lennartz und Michael Krüger.

sche sondern auch zeithistorische Kenntnisse besitzen sollte. Diesen glaubten sie im Münsteraner Professor Frank Becker zu finden, welcher vor allem in den 1990er Jahren Arbeiten zu sporthistorischen Themen für die erste Hälfte des 20. Jahrhunderts verfasste[38]. Finanziert wurde das Projekt durch ein Stipendium der Alfried Krupp von Bohlen und Halbach-Stiftung, welches für drei Jahre von 2005 bis 2007 vorgesehen war. Frank Becker hatte nun die Aufgabe erhalten, eine wissenschaftlich und methodisch fundierte Biographie zu schreiben, welche „sowohl die Tätigkeiten, Leistungen und Verdienste Carl Diems im und für den deutschen, internationalen und olympischen Sport (...) in der Kaiserzeit, der Weimarer Republik, im Dritten Reich und im Nachkriegsdeutschland"[39] einschließt. Gleichzeitig sollten seine „Tätigkeiten, Leistungen und Verdienste" in den zeithistorischen Kontext eingearbeitet werden, so dass „politische, wirtschaftliche, kulturelle und soziale Entwicklungen in den Zusammenhang der Arbeit Diems"[40] gestellt werden konnten. Durch diese Kontextualisierung wurde eine kritische Betrachtung von Diems Entscheidungen, Handlungsmöglichkeiten etc. intendiert.

Dabei sah sich der Beirat nach eigenen Worten verpflichtet, keinen inhaltlichen Einfluss auf die Arbeit zu nehmen, jedoch Unterstützung zu leisten.[41] Diese äußerte sich unter anderem in der Abhaltung von Tagungen, welche zwischen 2005 und 2007 insgesamt dreimal durchgeführt wurden, in denen verschiedene Vertreter aus Geschichts-, Kultur- und Sportwissenschaft Themen diskutierten, die einer Kontextualisierung Diems Werk Ertrag bringen und dem Biographen Anregungen geben sollten.

Schließlich teilte Becker seine Diem-Biographie mit dem Titel *Den Sport gestalten. Carl Diems Leben (1882-1962)* epochal in vier Bände ein. 2009 erschien der erste Teil (Band III), welcher sich mit Diems Leben und Werk in der NS-Zeit beschäftigt. Warum zuerst der Teilband mit dem Schwerpunkt auf die Zeit des Nationalsozialismus erschien, scheint Nils Havemann — jener hatte mit seiner Monografie über den deutschen Fußball in der Zeit des Nationalsozialismus gewisse Bekanntheit in der Fachöffentlichkeit erlangt — in der Einleitung Beckers zu lesen. In dieser problematisiert Becker die Brisanz um die Umbenennungen von Diem-Straßen aus der jüngeren Vergangenheit.[42] Entscheidend für diese Maßnahmen war

---

[38] Um nur ein paar wenige zu nennen: *Sport bei Ford. Rationalisierung und Symbolpolitik in der Weimarer Republik*, in: *Stadion. Internationale Zeitschrift für Geschichte des Sports*, 17. Jahrgang, Heft 17, Köln/Leiden/Brill/Sankt Augustin 1991, S.207-229, *Diskursanalyse des Sports*, in: Jürgen Court (Hg.), *Sport im Brennpunkt - philosophische Analysen. Schriften der Deutschen Sporthochschule Köln*, Sankt Augustin 1996, S.103-126, *Amerikanismus in Weimar. Sportsymbole und politische Kultur 1918-1933*, Wiesbaden 1993.

[39] Krüger, M.: *Leben und Werk Carl Diems – ein Forschungs- und Projektbericht*, in: Krüger, M. (Hrsg.): *Erinnerungskultur im Sport. Vom kritischen Umgang mit Carl Diem, Sepp Herberger und anderen Größen des deutschen Sports*, Berlin 2012, S. 187.

[40] Ebenda.

[41] Vgl. Ebenda.

[42] Vgl. Havemann, N: Rezension zu: *Becker, Frank: Den Sport gestalten. Carl Diems Leben (1882-1962): Band III: NS-Zeit. Duisburg 2009*, in: *H-Soz-u-Kult*, 25.09.2009, veröffentlicht unter: http://hsozkult.geschichte.hu-

Diems Handeln zur NS-Zeit und schien daher für einen Umgang mit der Diem-Erinnerung am dringensten benötigt. Ebenfalls 2009 folgte dann Band I zum Kaiserreich. 2010 erschien Band IV über die Nachkriegszeit und schließlich 2011 Band II für die Zeit der Weimarer Republik.

Bereits am 1. März 2010 gab der wissenschaftliche Projektbeirat eine Stellungnahme ab, ob eine Revision der Empfehlungen zum Umgang mit Carl Diem aus dem Jahre 1996 notwendig sei. Diese kamen zu folgendem Urteil:

> „1. War Diem Nationalsozialist, Rassist, Antisemit? Antwort: Nein. Es gibt keine Belege für diese Behauptungen. Diem war nicht Mitglied der NSDAP. Er äußerte sich im Gegenteil immer wieder kritisch über den Nationalsozialismus und die NS-Sportführung sowie gegenüber Rassismus und Antisemitismus.
> 2. Hinsichtlich der Rede Diems vom 18. März 1945 auf dem Reichssportfeld war es Dr. Becker trotz akribischer Rekonstruktion der Ereignisse nicht möglich, neue Erkenntnisse zu gewinnen. Weder Inhalt noch Umstände und Wirkung der Ansprache konnten zweifelsfrei geklärt.
> 3. Auch über diese Punkte hinaus enthält der vorgelegte Band III keine Hinweise auf moralisch verwerfliche Entscheidungen oder Haltungen Carl Diems im Dritten Reich. Die Darstellung unterstützt vielmehr insgesamt das in der neueren Forschung mehrfach geäußerte Urteil, dass Diem den ihm zur Verfügung stehenden Handlungsspielraum durchaus genutzt hat, um unabhängig von den nationalsozialistischen Machthabern zu agieren. Allerdings verhielt er sich in manchen Situationen opportunistisch."[43]

Diese Stellungnahme wurde unterschrieben vom wissenschaftlichen Beirat des Projekts *Leben und Werk Carl Diem*; der Biograph Frank Becker zählte nicht zu deren Kreis. Der Beirat sprach Carl Diem ausdrücklich von (so gut wie) jeder Schuld frei, was daraufhin zu einer heftigen Diskussion unter (Sport-)Historikern und Sportwissenschaftlern führte. Dies wird im Folgenden genauer aufgezeigt. Doch zunächst soll ein weiterer Auslöser der neuesten Diem-Debatte dargelegt werden.

---

berlin.de/rezensionen/2009-3-235, letzter Zugriff: 16.05.13; 13:33 Uhr. Die erwähnte Monografie: Havemann, N.: *Fußball unterm Hakenkreuz. Der DFB zwischen Sport, Politik und Kommerz*, Frankfurt am Main 2005.
[43] Gruppe, O. & Krüger, M. et al.: *Wissenschaftlicher Beirat zum Forschungsprojekt „Leben und Werk Carl Diems", 1. März 2010*, in: Krüger 2012, S. 219-221 sowie in Krüger, M.: *In Sachen Carl Diem – auf den Spuren der Wahrheit*, in: *Olympisches Feuer*, 59. Jahrgang, Heft 4-5, Frankfurt am Main 2010, S. 45f.

2. Schäfers Diem-Eintrag im Handbuch des Antisemitismus

Im gleichen Jahr der Veröffentlichung von Beckers Teilband der Diem-Biographie mit dem Schwerpunkt auf die NS-Zeit, erschien auch der zweite Band des vom Antisemitismusforscher Wolfgang Benz herausgegebenen *Handbuch des Antisemitismus*. Dieses Handbuch umfasst insgesamt sieben Bände (neun Teilbände) und konzentriert sich im eben erwähnten 2009 erschienenen zweiten Band auf Personen, die mit dem Begriff *Antisemitismus* in Verbindung zu bringen seien.

So fand auch Carl Diem seinen Platz in diesem. Der Historiker Ralf Schäfer, welcher beim Herausgeber des Handbuches an der Technischen Universität Berlin promovierte[44], verfasste diesen Artikel, der etwas mehr als zwei Seiten einnahm.[45] Darin stellt Schäfer zunächst in drei Absätzen in knapper Form Diems Arbeit sowohl im Kaiserreich, in der Weimarer Republik als auch im Nationalsozialismus dar. Anschließend schildert er in den letzten beiden Absätzen eine antisemitische Haltung Diems. Hierbei verpasst er jedoch „seinen Antisemitismus"[46] (gemeint ist Diems Antisemitismus) genauer zu definieren. Diese fehlende Begriffsdefinition ist laut dem Rezensenten Uwe Ullrich ein generelles Problem des Handbuchs, da eine zu weit gefasste Verwendung des Begriffs Antisemitismus eine genaue Beschreibung von Einstellungen, Denken etc. von Personen nicht möglich mache und zu Missverständnissen führen würde.[47] So scheint der allgemeine Begriff des Antisemitismus für Judenhass nicht auszureichen, um einer Beschreibung dieses Judenhasses einer Person gerecht zu werden. Dass eine Präzisierung des Begriffs jedoch noch von Bedeutung sein wird und Schäfer eine genauere Begriffsdefinition vornimmt, erhält im Folgendem noch seine Wichtigkeit.

Genauer beleuchtet wird diese Problematik noch im folgendem Kapitel III.3. *Diskussionsgegenstände*. Wichtig ist zunächst, dass die Herstellung der Verbindung der Person Carl Diems mit einer antisemitischen Einstellung neuen Zündstoff für eine Debatte gab, welche verschiedene Positionen hervorbrachte.

---

[44] Schäfer, R.: *Militarismus, Nationalismus, Antisemitismus. Carl Diem und die Politisierung es bürgerlichen Sports im Kaiserreich*, Berlin 2011.
[45] Schäfer, R.: *Diem, Carl*, in: Benz, W. (Hrsg.): *Handbuch des Antisemitismus. Judenfeindschaft in Geschichte und Gegenwart. Personen*, Band 2/1, Berlin 2009, S. 171-173.
[46] Ebenda, S. 172.
[47] Ullrich, U.: *Antisemitismus-Handbuch zum „Nachschlagen". Rezension zu Wolfgang Benz (Hg.): Handbuch des Antisemitismus. Judenfeindschaft in Geschichte und Gegenwart (Band 1-5)*, veröffentlicht unter: http://www.citizentimes.eu/2012/09/06/antisemitismus-handbuch-zum-nachschlagen/, letzter Zugriff: 13.5.13, 12:45 Uhr.

Im Zuge der Veröffentlichung der Diem-Biographie *Den Sport gestalten. Carl Diems Leben (1882-1962)* sowie des Eintrags Carl Diems im *Handbuch des Antisemitismus* durch Ralf Schäfer kam es zur neuesten Diem-Debatte. Das Medium, über welches die wissenschaftliche Diskussion ausgetragen wurde, war hierbei eine Ausgabe der *Zeitschrift für Geschichtswissenschaft* (ZfG) aus dem Jahre 2011. Diese gibt mit dem sinngebendem Titel *Erinnerungspolitik oder kritische Forschung? Der Streit um Carl Diem*[48] dem Leser die Feststellung auf den Weg, dass auch nach mehr als 60 Jahren der Auseinandersetzung über die Deutung Carl Diems Leben ein Dissens besteht – es wird immer noch gestritten. Die Autoren, die zu diesem Thema Beiträge in der ZfG veröffentlichten, sind bekannt: der Diem-Biograph Frank Becker, der Historiker Ralf Schäfer, welcher seine Dissertation zur Bedeutung Diems für die Politisierung des bürgerlichen Sports im deutschen Kaiserreich und den Diem-Eintrag ins *Handbuch des Antisemitismus* verfasste sowie der Sportwissenschaftler und Leiter des Projekts *Leben und Werk Carl Diems* Michael Krüger, welcher die Stellungnahme vom 1. März 2010 mitverfasste. Über welche Gegenstände diese gestritten haben und mit welchen Argumentationen diese gestützt wurden, wird nun folgend dargestellt.

a)   Antisemitismus

Die Frage, ob Diems Denken und Handeln mit dem Begriff des *Antisemitismus* zu beschreiben sei, war wohl die am heftigsten diskutierte und soll daher auch als erstes durchleuchtet werden. „Wer hierzulande vom Antisemitismus spricht, tut dies meist mit Blick auf den Holocaust. Unter Antisemiten stellt man sich Fanatiker wie Julius Streicher vor, brutale SA-Schläger oder sadistische SS-Schergen, die als Propagandisten, Schreibtischtäter oder KZ-Wärter ihre Untaten begingen."[49] Mit diesen Sätzen beginnt Ralf Schäfer seinen Beitrag in der dritten ZfG-Ausgabe von 2011 und bringt die Problematik eines verfremdeten Verständnisses des Begriffs *Antisemitismus*, wie er „hierzulande" typisch scheint, auf den Punkt. Dabei meint er eine Interpretation zu erkennen, in der antisemitisch nur derjenige sei, der im Sinne der nationalsozialistischen Ideologie judenfeindlich war. Diese Deutung stellt für ihn jedoch eine Verengung dar, denn bereits im wilhelminischen Kaiserreich waren judenfeindliche Haltun-

---

[48] Benz, W. & Borgolte, M. & Iggers, G. G. &Klein, F. & Schubert, E. & Steinbach, P. & Thomas, L. (Hrsg.): *Erinnerungspolitik oder Kritische Forschung? Der Streit um Carl Diem*, in: *Zeitschrift für Geschichtswissenschaft*, 59. Jahrgang, Heft 3, Berlin 2011.
[49] Schäfer, R.: *Carl Diem, der Antisemitismus und das NS-Regime*, in: *Zeitschrift für Geschichtswissenschaft*, 59. Jahrgang, Heft 3, Berlin 2011a, S. 252.

gen vorhanden. Somit war Antisemitismus keine neue Idee des Nationalsozialismus, viel mehr griffen „(a)ntisemitische Einstellungen und Praktiken (...) in Bürgertum und Adel schon im Kaiserreich um sich, prägten soziale Beziehungen, kulturelles Handeln, politische und staatliche Strukturen"[50]. Dennoch würde eine Verallgemeinerung des Antisemitismus, wie er im Kaiserreich im Bürgertum und dem Adel gedacht und praktiziert wurde mit dem Antisemitismus des Nationalsozialismus, welcher schließlich im Genozid endete, wiederum zu einer verfälschten Geschichtsdeutung führen. So nimmt Schäfer eine Trennung des wilhelminischen Antisemitismus vom „eliminatorischen Antisemitismus" des NS-Regimes vor.[51]

Einen Antisemitismus, wie er im wilhelminischen Kaiserreich in Adel und Bürgertum vorlag, erkennt Schäfer in Diems Denken und Handeln. Als Quellen zieht er dabei vor allem Diems Tagebucheinträge und Briefe heran, die er für seine Dissertation analysierte. Aus diesen liest er Diems Sympathie zur Neuen Rechten, die besonders der Annahme, dass alle Menschen gleich wären, widersprachen. So echauffierte sich Diem zum Beispiel in einem Brief an seinen Freund Franz im Jahre 1913 über die Dominanz der jüdischen Journalisten in deutschen Zeitungen, „die das Reich an der nötigen Machtentfaltung hindern (und ...) dem Arsenal des politischen Antisemitismus"[52] entstammte. Weiterhin entwickelte Diem während der Kaiserzeit eine „antisemitische Wahrnehmung des angeblich jüdischen Körpers und Habitus" und das „Feindbild 'Jude' hatte sich tief in seine Alltagswahrnehmung eingegraben".[53] Eine antisemitische Haltung Diems ist für Ralf Schäfer auf dessen Quellen basierend nicht von der Hand zuweisen. Auch für die Weimarer Zeit meint Schäfer eine antisemitische Haltung Diems zu finden, da Diem an seiner selbstbegriffenen negativ konnotierten Wahrnehmung des Jüdischen auch zu jener Zeit festhielt.[54]

Dennoch betont er, dass „sich Diems wilhelminischer Antisemitismus vom Rassenantisemitismus der Nationalsozialisten (unterschied)"[55]. Diems Judenfeindlichkeit endete, sobald sich Juden assimilierten und ihre jüdische Identität aufgaben. Schließlich war der Vater seiner Frau ein durch die Nürnberger Rassegesetze betitelter „Halbjude". Gleiches gilt für Theodor Lewald, der Diem über lange Zeit in der Weimarer Republik in der Sportverwaltung zur Seite stand. Außerdem wurden zu jener Zeit an der DHfL, an der Carl Diem als Prorektor tätig war, auch jüdische Studierende und Mitarbeiter geduldet.

---

[50] Schäfer 2011a, S. 253.
[51] Vgl. Ebenda, S. 252f., S. 257.
[52] Vgl. Ebenda, S. 255.
[53] Ebenda, S. 256.
[54] Beispiele führt Schäfer 2011a auf den Seiten 256 und 257 an: Im Olympischen Kongress 1925 wurde „gejüdelt". Der Westteil der Stadt Berlin sei „verjudet". Das „'jüdische' Aussehen" von Frauen in West-Berlin erregte Diems Abneigung.
[55] Ebenda, S. 257.

Eine ähnliche Denkweise wie Schäfer weist der Diem-Biograph Frank Becker mit seinem Beitrag *Carl Diem und der Nationalsozialismus* in der selben Zeitschrift auf. Mit Verweis auf seinen I. Teilband seiner Biographie stellt er klar, dass Diem „antijüdische Ausfälle (...) während des Kaiserreichs"[56] äußerte. Im nächsten Satz nimmt er ebenso wie Schäfer eine zeitgeschichtliche Einschränkung vor, dass sich diese vom „Vernichtungsantisemitismus des Nationalsozialismus unterschied(...)", es jedoch „keinen Grund (gibt), sie herunterzuspielen, trugen sie doch bekanntlich dazu bei, dass der Vernichtungsantisemitismus in Deutschland auf fruchtbaren Boden fiel".[57] So benutzt auch Becker den Begriff „Antisemitismus"[58], allerdings mit Einschränkung auf die Kaiserzeit. Antisemitismus sei „für Diem nur für die Zeit vor dem Ersten Weltkrieg im Rahmen seiner privaten Korrespondenz belegbar. In den Weimarer Jahren änderte sich seine Einstellung."[59] Darin unterscheidet sich Beckers Meinung von der Schäfers, der eine antisemitische Haltung Diems über das Ende des Ersten Weltkrieges hinaus zu erkennen vermag.

Eine gegensätzliche Position nimmt Michael Krüger ein, welcher die Stellungnahme des Wissenschaftlichen Beirats des Diem-Projekts mit verfasste.[60] Dieser weist jegliche Antisemitismusvorwürfe gegen Diem zurück. Dabei geht er auf einen Schäfer-Beitrag[61] in der ZfG ein Jahr zuvor ein, dessen Behauptungen den Ergebnissen der Diem-Biographie Beckers widersprächen. Dass dem jedoch nicht so ist, stellt Becker in seinem Aufsatz *Carl Diem und der Nationalsozialismus* klar. Diem vom Antisemitismus freizusprechen, wäre eine Fehlinterpretation seiner Forschungsergebnisse.[62] Somit habe Krüger fehlinterpretiert und nicht Schäfer, wie es Krüger zu glauben scheint. Des Weiteren verweist dieser auf eine fehlende Wissenschaftlichkeit in Schäfers Diem-Eintrag im *Handbuch des Antisemitismus*. Dieser verzichtet auf jegliche Quellenangaben und dies müsse „bei einer solch sensiblen Thematik als sehr fragwürdig erscheinen"[63]. Er geht sogar noch weiter. Diem als antisemitisch zu bezeichnen „ist nicht nur absurd, sondern ist auch eine Beleidigung der Familie Diem und seiner Frau Lieselott (...) ebenso bedeutet er (der Antisemitismus-Vorwurf; Anm. des Autors) eine Belei-

---

[56] Becker, F.: *Carl Diem und der Nationalsozialismus*, in: *Zeitschrift für Geschichtswissenschaft*, 59. Jahrgang, Heft 3, Berlin 2011, S. 243.
[57] Ebenda.
[58] Ebenda.
[59] Becker, F.: *Den Sport gestalten. Carl Diems Leben (1882-1962)*, *Stellungnahme, Punkt 11, Diem und der Antisemitismus*, in jedem seiner 4 Bände abgedruckt.
[60] Krüger, M.: *Zur Debatte um Carl Diem*, in: *Zeitschrift für Geschichtswissenschaft*, 59. Jahrgang, Heft 3, Berlin 2011, S. 201-209.
[61] Schäfer, R.: *Sportgeschichte und Erinnerungspolitik: Der Fall Carl Diem*, in: *Zeitschrift für Geschichtswissenschaft*, 58. Jahrgang, Heft 11, Berlin 2010, S. 877-899.
[62] Vgl. Becker, 2011, S. 243 (die letzten beiden Absätze).
[63] Krüger 2011, S. 206.

digung seiner jüdischen Freunde und Bekannten"[64]. Ob dieser Versuch, den Leser möglicherweise emotional durch eine solche Äußerung zu beeinflussen, in eine wissenschaftliche Arbeit gehört, ist vermutlich ebenso fragwürdig. Als Gegenargument, dass Diem nie Antisemit gewesen sei, führt Krüger die jüdischen Freunde und Weggefährten Diems während der Zeit des Nationalsozialismus auf.[65] Dass Schäfer dies ebenfalls tat, um aufzuzeigen, dass Diem kein Antisemit im Sinne der nationalsozialistischen Ideologie war und um ihn von dieser abzugrenzen, scheint Krügers These, Diems Denken und Handeln sei zu keiner Zeit als antisemitisch zu deuten, nicht wirklich zu stützen. Die Trennschärfe zwischen wilhelminischen Antisemitismus und eleminatorischen Antisemitismus des NS-Regimes ließ Krüger vermissen.

b)   Nationalsozialismus

Eine weitere bedeutsame Frage für die Beschreibung Diems, war die nach dessen Verhältnis zum NS-Staat. Diem war von 1933 bis 1936 Generalsekretär des Organisationskomitees der Olympischen Spiele im Jahre 1936 in Berlin, von 1936 bis 1945 Leiter des Internationalen Olympischen Instituts in Berlin und von 1939 bis 1945 Leiter des Gaues Ausland des NSRL und hatte somit Positionen in der NSDAP-eingegliederten Sportorganisation inne. Allerdings findet Becker es „unsinnig", zu fragen, um die Rolle Diems im Nationalsozialismus zu klären, ob Diem Parteimitglied der NSDAP gewesen sei oder nicht. Viel wichtiger sei es, die Frage zu stellen, „ob er den Nationalsozialismus unterstützt, ihm zugearbeitet und auch teilweise mit ihm sympathisiert hat"[66]. Eben diese „Seinsfrage"[67] meint der Wissenschaftliche Beirat nach Beendigung des *Projekts Leben und Werk Carl Diems* stellen zu müssen, um zu einer erkenntnisbringenden Deutung Diems zu gelangen. So kommen sie zur Antwort: „Nein"[68]. Schließlich war Diem tatsächlich nie NSDAP-Mitglied und habe sich im Gegenteil „immer wieder kritisch über den Nationalsozialismus (...) sowie gegenüber Rassismus und Antisemitismus geäußert" [69] – so zumindest die Stellungnahme des Beirats.
Auch hier sieht Becker seine Forschungsergebnisse missverstanden. Denn seine Diem-Biographie antworte mit: ja. Mit Verweis auf seinen III. Teilband schildert er, Diem habe sich immer wieder für neue Aufgaben im NS-Sport bemüht, sein Verhalten gegenüber dem Re-

---

[64] Krüger 2011, S. 207.
[65] Vgl. Ebenda, S. 207.
[66] Becker 2011, S. 243.
[67] Ebenda.
[68] Grupe, O. & Krüger, M. et al. 2012, S. 221.
[69] Ebenda.

gime trotz Wissens um den Holocaust nicht verändert, von dem er nachweislich spätestens seit dem Sommer 1943 informiert war. Außerdem habe er bewusst den Antisemitismus im NS-Staat dem Ausland gegenüber runtergespielt, um die Olympischen Spiele 1936 und die damit verbundene Täuschung zu sichern und um schließlich auf das Argument des Beirates zu antworten: es gab „mindestens ebenso viele positive Äußerungen über den Nationalsozialismus und die NS-Sportführung"[70] wie kritische. So sieht Becker seine Forschungsergebnisse vom Beirat und ausdrücklich von Michael Krüger missachtet, der in der Zeitschrift *Sportwissenschaft*[71] 2010 die Ergebnisse des Projekts darzustellen meint und „Zitate (...) aus dem Zusammenhang gerissen und dadurch sinnentstellt"[72] habe. [73]

Krüger wiederum verweist in der ZfG 2011, in der auch Becker wie bereits erwähnt seinen Beitrag einbrachte, dass dieser in der Diem-Biographie selbst darstelle, „dass Diem kein Nationalsozialist war und immer wieder die Politik der Nationalsozialisten im Allgemeinen und ihre Sportpolitik im Besonderen kritisierte"[74]. Dies tat er gleichfalls mit Verweis auf den III. Band der Diem-Biographie. Und so führt er fort, dass er zwar den „sportgestählten Soldaten (rühmte), nicht die NS-Politik" und Becker Diems Ämter im Dritten Reich „als politisch bedeutungslos" wertete.[75]

Krüger pflegt vielmehr eine Interpretation Diems als politisch Naiven, der „in Schuldzusammenhänge verstrickt" war, doch dies trifft „grundsätzlich auf jeden Menschen zu, insbesondere auf solche, die das Pech hatten, in Zeiten und unter Umständen gelebt zu haben wie Diem"[76]. Krüger räumt zwar ein, dass Diems „Biographie auch Makel aufweise", diese jedoch „in jedem Lebenslauf von 'großen', in der Öffentlichkeit gefeierten Persönlichkeiten leicht nachzuweisen"[77] seien. Damit löst er Diem aus seinem zeithistorischen Bezug heraus, um ihn mit anderen Persönlichkeiten, die zu anderen Zeiten und Umständen lebten, zu verallgemeinern. Eine solche Inschutznahme täuscht über historische Tatsachen hinweg, dass Handlungsalternativen bestanden und verharmlost durch die zeitliche Verallgemeinerung die NS-Verbrechen, samt Holocaust.

Ralf Schäfer vertritt eine ebenso grundsätzliche Annahme, dass Diem wie für den Vorwurf des Antisemitismus auch für den eines Nationalsozialisten schuldig zu sprechen sei – auch wenn dieser kein NSDAP-Mitglied war. So schrieb Schäfer, Diem wäre „im NS-Staat

---

[70] Becker 2011, S. 244.
[71] Vgl. Krüger, M.: *Leben und Werk Carl Diems. Ein-Forschungs- und Projektbericht*, in: *Sportwissenschaft*, 40. Jahrgang, Heft 4, Heidelberg 2010, S. 268-284.
[72] Becker 2011, S. 248.
[73] Vgl. Ebenda, S. 243-247.
[74] Krüger 2011, S. 204.
[75] Ebenda, S. 204f.
[76] Ebenda, S. 205.
[77] Ebenda.

und im Nationalsozialismus angekommen"[78] gewesen. Schäfer ging über die Meinung des Projekt-Beirats hinaus, dass Diem zwar „in manchen Situationen opportunistisch" gehandelt habe, sich jedoch keine „moralisch verwerflichen Entscheidungen und Handlungen" zu Schulde kommen ließ.[79] Diems opportunistisches Verhalten im Nationalsozialismus auf „manche Situationen" zu beschränken, reduziert für Becker seine Schuld – Diem habe ein „durchweg opportunistisches Verhalten" an den Tag gelegt.[80] Diese Reduzierung spiele „seine gestaltende Mitwirkung in verschiedenen Funktionen (in der NS-Zeit) unverhältnismäßig herunter"[81].

„Unter allen schlechten Regierungsformen ist die Diktatur aber immer noch die relativ beste"[82]. Mit diesem Zitat meint Schäfer Diems Sympathien für die NS-Diktatur zu erkennen. Weiterhin deutet Schäfer Diems Ausübung seiner Ämter im NS-Staat als willentliches Zuarbeiten für diesen: mit seiner Tätigkeit als Gauleiter Ausland wirkte er bei der „Umsetzung der NS-Herrschaft über die eroberten Gebiete mit", er „nutzt seine Handlungsspielräume im Sinne des Regimes" und wurde schließlich zu seinem 60. Geburtstag vom *Völkischen Beobachter* mit den Worten „die Bedeutung Dr. Diems" angepriesen.[83] All diese Gründe sprechen laut Schäfer dafür, dass Diem aktiv dem NS-Regime weiterhalf.

c) Militarismus

Schließlich stand der Begriff Militarismus zur Diskussion, der in den Beirats-Empfehlungen nicht berücksichtigt wurde. Dies scheint für Becker völlig unverständlich zu sein, da Diem gerade deswegen Zeit seines Lebens und darüber hinaus in der öffentlichen Kritik stand.[84]

Einen solchen Militarismus, also ein Vorherrschen von militärischen Denkkategorien, die eine Notwendigkeit des Krieges implizieren[85], glaubt Becker mit seiner Biographie nachzuweisen. Er führt zahlreiche Beispiele an, die belegen sollen, dass Diem sowohl in der wilhelminischen Kaiserzeit, in der Weimarer Zeit als auch im Nationalsozialismus stets das Soldatische glorifizierte und eine militaristische Haltung einnahm. So habe er sich schon in der Kaiserzeit im Vorstand des Jungdeutschlandbundes organisiert, welcher „eine Militarisie-

---

[78] Schäfer 2011a, S. 262.
[79] Grupe, O. & Krüger, M. et al. 2012, S. 221.
[80] Becker 2011, S. 247.
[81] Ebenda.
[82] Diem an Erich Günther Blau, 30.6.1931, CuLDA, in: Schäfer 2011a, S. 259.
[83] Schäfer 2011a, S. 261f. Schäfer wertete das letzte Zitat als Anpreisung Diems des *Völkischen Beobachters*.
[84] Vgl. Becker 2011, S. 244.
[85] Vgl. Zum Begriff „Militarismus" und dessen Ausprägung: Vgl. von Bredow, W.: *Militär und Demokratie in Deutschland: Eine Einführung (Studienbücher Außenpolitik und internationale Beziehungen)*, Wiesbaden 2007, S. 66f.

rung der deutschen Jugend im Zeichen bevorstehender totaler Kriege bezweckte"[86]. Außerdem war er, wie auch Hans Joachim Teichler nachweisen konnte, in der Weimarer Republik daran beteiligt, Wehrsportorganisationen zu gestalten und begeistert, als Hitler 1935 die Wehrpflicht wieder einführte. Becker führt auch das Beispiel der Reichssportfeldrede vom 18. März 1945, um eine entsprechende Formulierung zu verwenden, ins Feld. Der Projekt-Beirat erkennt den Augenzeugenbericht von Reinhard Appel sowie Diems Stichwort-Manuskript nicht als zuverlässige Quellen an, um nachzuweisen, dass Diem wissentlich zahlreiche Hitlerjungen in den sicheren Tod führte. „Weder Inhalt noch Umstände und Wirkung der Ansprache konnten zweifelsfrei geklärt werden."[87] Wieder sieht Becker sich und seine Ergebnisse missverstanden. Ein Befehlsnotstand, welcher Diem gezwungen hätte, diese Rede zu halten, ist „höchst unwahrscheinlich"[88]. Und auch das Argument, Diem habe auf die antiken Soldaten verwiesen, um den Bezug zum Zweiten Weltkrieg zu vermeiden, sei falsch. Er habe bewusst versucht, mithilfe des „rhetorischen Mittels der historischen Analogie"[89] eine Verknüpfung zwischen Geschichte und Gegenwart zu schaffen, um die Hitlerjungen, den Spartanern gleich, zu motivieren, ihre Heimat – das Deutsche Reich – zu verteidigen. Umstände und Inhalt seien damit für Becker geklärt. Dass Diem dies willentlich und ohne Zwang tat spreche im Sinne Beckers für Diems militaristische Einstellung.[90]

Zum Vorwurf des Militarismus nimmt Krüger nur kurz Stellung. Die Kritik Beckers, dass Diem Militarismus vorzuwerfen sei, welche er unter anderem aufgrund des Aufsatzes *Sturmlauf durch Frankreich* von 1940 vornimmt, weist er zurück. In diesem „rühmt er (...) die Leistung der sportgestählten Soldaten, nicht die NS-Politik"[91]. Ein Faible für das Soldatische kann Krüger Diem, auch wenn eben jene Soldaten durch den Sport gestählt wurden, nicht absprechen. So glaubt auch er, dass „einige militaristische und chauvinistische Äußerungen Diems"[92] bleiben. Allerdings seien diese vor dem Hintergrund zu verstehen, dass Diem „Sympathien für soldatisches Auftreten und alles Militärische" hatte, doch „kein Vertreter eines verdrillten Wehrsports gewesen sei".[93]

Auch an dieser Stelle wird uns bewusst, welche Schwierigkeit darin besteht, Personen mit Kategorien und Begriffen zu bewerten, die scheinbar unterschiedlich verstanden werden können. So meint Krüger, dass sich „aus den Studien Beckers" keine Beweise ergeben, dass

---

[86] Becker 2011, S. 244.
[87] Grupe, O. & Krüger, M. et al. 2012, S. 221.
[88] Becker 2011, S. 245.
[89] Ebenda.
[90] Vgl. Ebenda, S. 244f.
[91] Krüger 2011, S. 204f.
[92] Krüger 2012, S. 196.
[93] Ebenda.

24

Diem ein Militarist gewesen sei, um schließlich fortzufahren, dass „militaristische und chauvinistische Äußerungen Diems" nicht abzusprechen wären.[94] Die Ambivalenz dieses Ausdrucks scheint offensichtlich. Doch nicht nur Krüger, auch Becker und Schäfer verpassen es (leider), zu erklären, was sie unter dem Begriff Militarismus verstehen. Diese fehlende Definition mündet schließlich in widersprüchliche Darstellungen und einer Polarisierung.

4.   *„Kritische Historiker" gegen „Diemologen"*

Was sich schon in den Unterkapiteln *a) Antisemitismus, b) Nationalsozialismus* und *c) Militarismus* zeigte, war die Tatsache, dass zur Bewertung Diems für die Zeit bis zum Ende des Zweiten Weltkriegs ein Dissens bestand. Michael Krüger spricht gar von einem „Sporthistorikerstreit"[95], entfacht durch die Ergebnisse des *Projekts Leben und Werk Carl Diems* und dessen Begleiterscheinungen. In diesem Streit der Sporthistoriker ist eine Lagerbildung unverkennbar. Auf der einen Seite stehen Michael Krüger und dessen Projekt-Beirat. Auf der anderen sind der Diem-Biograph Frank Becker sowie Ralf Schäfer einzuordnen. Hierbei grenzen sich die beiden Lager eigenständig voneinander ab.

So bezeichnet Michael Krüger hinsichtlich einer sogenannten „Gegenveranstaltung zu dem (...) Abschlusskolloquium des Diem-Projekts am 10. Dezember 2010" deren Teilnehmer – federführend war auf dieser „Gegenveranstaltung" in Berlin Ralf Schäfer – in Anführungszeichen als „kritische Sporthistoriker".[96] Er verweist zwar darauf, dass diese sich selbst so bezeichneten, dennoch ist ein zynischer Unterton, der mit der Anführung verdeutlicht wird, wohl kaum verkennbar. Deutlich wird dies, indem Krüger wenige Zeilen weiter die „Kritiker" wiederum in Anführungen setzt. Dabei zählt er Becker zwar nicht zum „Kritiker"-Kreis, doch erscheint eine Zuteilung zu diesen sinnvoll. Schließlich decken sich Beckers Äußerungen in der ZfG größtenteils mit denen Schäfers.

Dabei vertreten jene „kritischen Historiker" laut Krüger – Becker wurde von ihm wie gesagt davon ausgenommen – die These, dass der bürgerliche Sport „im Kern faschistisch sei"[97]. Ausgehend von dieser These, schreiben die „kritischen Historiker" (Sport-)Geschichte. Sie haben gewissermaßen eine Brille auf, mit der sie in jedem Funktionär des bürgerlichen Sports der ersten Hälfte des 20. Jahrhunderts einen Faschisten sehen und so nur zu „kritischen" Äußerungen kommen können. Diese Geschichtsschreibung, vorgenommen von „Ralf

---

[94] Krüger 2012, S. 196.
[95] Krüger 2011, S. 201.
[96] Ebenda, S. 202.
[97] Ebenda, S. 209.

Schäfer und seine(n) Kollegen", speise sich „aus der neomarxistischen Frankfurter Schule",
nach der, der Marx'schen Annahme für Religion folgend, auch Sport Opium für das Volk
sei.[98] Ein solches Denkmuster scheint für Michael Krüger als Erklärung zu dienen, warum
„Schäfer und seine Kollegen" auch Carl Diem als Antisemiten, Nationalsozialisten und Militaristen deuteten. Dieses zeichnet sich stets durch eine Verabsolutierung der Sportfunktionäre
(nicht nur) im Dritten Reich als Faschisten aus.

Dieter Langewiesche, der Schäfers Dissertation *Militarismus, Nationalismus, Antisemitismus: Carl Diem und die Politarisierung im bürgerlichen Sport im Kaiserreich* rezensier-
te, glaubt, dass Frank Schäfer einen „Willen zur Eindeutigkeit"[99] des Diem-Bildes zu erzeugen versucht, was seine Quellenbefunde nicht leisten können. Somit scheint Krüger mit dem
Vorwurf, dass Schäfer ein statisches Deutungsmuster, einen „Willen zur Eindeutigkeit",bei
der Diem-Beschreibung innehabe, nicht allein zu stehen.

Gelichwohl ist für Schäfer kritisch anzumerken, dass seine Dissertation zum Zeitpunkt
der Herausgabe der behandelten ZfG-Ausgabe noch nicht veröffentlicht wurde. Somit lag
Schäfers Arbeit Michael Krüger noch nicht vor, so dass er diese auch nicht in seine Argumentation einbeziehen konnte. Ob er dies für seinen ZfG-Beitrag getan hätte, bleibt jedoch frag-
lich, da Schäfers verwendeten Quellenbelege in Krügers Aufsatz im 2012 erschienenen Sammelband *Erinnerungskultur im Sport* im Teil zu Diems Schaffen im Kaiserreich keine Berücksichtigung fanden.

Wie bereits erwähnt, zählt Krüger Becker nicht zu den „kritischen Historikern", dennoch scheint eine Zuordnung Beckers zu den Diem-Kritikern, in Anführungszeichen gesetzt
oder nicht, sinnvoll. Schließlich weist Becker mit seiner Biographie und dem ZfG-Beitrag
nach, warum er glaubt, dass eine Bezeichnung Diems als Antisemiten (mit Einschränkung auf
den wilhelminischen Antisemitismus), Nationalsozialisten (Sympathisanten, Unterstützer und
Zuarbeiter[100]) und Militaristen sinnvoll sei. Diese Zuschreibungen sind vor dem Hintergrund
zu sehen, dass Becker zwar vom damaligen DSB und der DSHS beauftragt, jedoch lediglich
von der Alfried Krupp von Bohlen und Halbach-Stiftung finanziert wurde und somit keine
finanzielle Verantwortung vom Deutschen Sportbund hatte. DSB (später DOSB) und DSHS
finanzierten zwar die Fachtagungen des Projektbeirats, jedoch nicht den Biographen. Außerdem war er als Privatdozent der Universität Münster im Zeitraum seiner Forschung selbstän-

---

[98] Krüger 2011, S. 209. Wer Schäfers Kollegen seien, expliziert Krüger nicht. Allerdings erwähnt er auf der Seite
207 Lorenz Peiffer und Dietrich Schulze-Marmeling, die im „Fußball-Historikerstreit" Anhänger der „kritischen" Sportgeschichte gewesen seien.
[99] Langewiesche, D.: *Ralf Schäfer: Militarismus, Nationalismus, Antisemitismus*, veröffentlicht unter:
http://www.sehepunkte.de/2012/06/21495.html, letzter Zugriff: 22.5.13; 13:05 Uhr.
[100] Vgl. Becker 2011, S. 243.

dig und eigenverantwortlich tätig. Zudem verwies Krüger darauf, dass sich der Projektbeirat einig war, „jede inhaltliche Einflussnahme zu vermeiden"[101]. Somit war seine Forschung das Ergebnis einer nahezu völlig unabhängigen Arbeit, die im Grunde durch keine anderen Interessen als dem Erkenntnisgewinn für die Sportgeschichte zu betrachten sind. Mit dem Wissen um die Umstände des Zustandekommens von Beckers Forschungsergebnissen gewinnen diese weitere Legitimität.

Die Benennung des zweiten Lagers nimmt Schäfer selbst vor. Diejenigen, die zu diesem gehören und „die Etablierung und Stabilisierung eines positiven Diembildes" zum Ziel haben, nennt er „Diemologen"[102].Ihnen wirft er eine Apologie Diems vor. Bereits in den 1970er Jahren habe sich „in der Sportwissenschaft eine Schule formiert"[103], die in direkter Beziehung mit dem Carl-Diem-Institut oder dem Carl-und-Lieselott-Diem-Archiv ständen.

Auch Hubert Dwertmann, der ebenfalls in der ZfG-Ausgabe von 2011 einen Artikel verfasste, erkennt einen Forscherkreis der deutschen Sportwissenschaft, der „im Sinne der NS-Sportfunktionäre argumentiert"[104]. Er scheint ebenfalls eine „Diem-Apologie" zu sehen, welche vor allem vom „Diem-Schüler Ommo Grupe" sowie vom „Grupe-Schüler Michael Krüger" tradiert wurde. [105] Eben jene waren sowohl in der Expertenkommission von 1996 sowie im Projektbeirat zu *Leben und Werk Carl Diems* vertreten. Die persönliche Nähe von Grupe und Krüger zu Carl Diem scheint eine Erklärung für die in beiden Gutachten (1996 sowie 2010) abgegebene positive Diem-Wertung zu sein. Es stecken „bewusste Verfälschungen"[106] und „interessenbezogene Einflussnahmen"[107] dahinter – eine nötige wissenschaftliche Distanz wurde demnach nicht eingenommen. Gleiches gilt für den Gutachter von 1996, Hans Joachim Teichler, der 1989/90 Preisträger der Carl-Diem-Plakette für hervorragende sportwissenschaftliche Leistungen war und deshalb laut Schäfer „Carl Diem vom Vorwurf des Antisemitismus freisprach"[108]. Jene Unabhängigkeit der Forschung wie sie Frank Becker gegeben war, fehlte laut Schäfer und Dwertmann sowohl Grupe und Krüger als auch Teichler. Aufgrund dieser Tatsache kommt Schäfer zu folgender resümierenden Erkenntnis: „Ihr Forschungsprogramm (zu *Leben und Werk Carl Diems*; Anm. des Autors) musste scheitern, weil

---

[101] Krüger 2012, S. 187.
[102] Schäfer 2011a, S. 263.
[103] Ebenda.
[104] Dwertmann, H.: *Die Beteiligung von Sportfunktionären im NS-Regime und ihr Einfluss auf die Sportgeschichtsschreibung nach 1945*, in: *Zeitschrift für Geschichtswissenschaft*, 59. Jahrgang, Heft 3, Berlin 2011, S. 230-241, Zitat: S. 241.
[105] Ebenda, S. 239.
[106] Schäfer 2011a, S. 263.
[107] Dwertmann 2011, S. 239.
[108] Schäfer 2011a, S. 263.

es auf vorgefassten Meinungen beruht, die mit der Quellenlage nicht in Einklang zu bringen sind, und sich hermetisch vor Einwänden schützt."[109]

In diesem Kapitel wurde deutlich, dass es immer noch einen deutlichen Dissens innerhalb der deutschen Sportgeschichte darüber gibt, wie Carl Diem im Allgemeinen und sein Handeln bis 1945 im Speziellen zu beschreiben sei. Dass hinter den verschiedenen Deutungen auch Haltungen, Interessen und Ziele der diskutierenden Autoren stecken, wurde ebenfalls deutlich. Es zeigte sich auch, dass diese beiden Lager unterschiedlichen wissenschaftlichen Disziplinen entstammen. Die „kritischen Historiker" waren hier ausgewiesene Geschichtswissenschaftler und die „Diemologen" Sportwissenschaftler. So möchte man möglicherweise mit einem Meta-Blick meinen, dass die verschiedenen Disziplinen um die Deutungshoheit über die Person Diems rangen.[110] Diskutiert wurde heftig und an Vorwürfen gegenüber dem anderen Lager, ob von den „kritischen Historikern" oder den „Diemologen", wurde nicht gespart. Welchem Diem-Bild man zu folgen habe, bleibt dem Leser überlassen. Ein konsensfähiges Diem-Bild blieb jedoch aus.

---

[109] Schäfer 2011a, S. 243.
[110] Vgl. Jungbauer, A.: *Die Auseinandersetzung um „Sportvater" Carl Diem - am Beispiel seiner Geburtsstadt Würzburg, die nun ihre größte Veranstaltungshalle umbenennt*, in: *SportZeiten. Sport in Geschichte, Kultur und Gesellschaft*, 4. Jahrgang, Heft 1, Göttingen 2004, S. 97f.

IV. Geschichtspolitische Konsequenzen im Zuge der neuesten Diem-Debatte

Nachdem im vorhergehendem Kapitel die Diskussionsauslöser, Gegenstände, Standpunkte und Deutungen erörtert wurden, soll im nächsten Schritt die neueste Diem-Debatte weitere Tiefe gewinnen, indem geschichtspolitische Konsequenzen im Zuge der Debatte dargestellt werden. Dabei wird zunächst geklärt, wie (Sport-)Geschichtswissenschaft und (Sport-) Geschichtspolitik zueinander stehen, um zu verstehen, welchen Beitrag wissenschaftliche Forschungen wie das Projekt *Leben und Werk Carl Diems* leisten können, um politische Konsequenzen ziehen zu können. In welcher Form sich diese (sport-)geschichtspolitischen Konsequenzen schließlich äußerten, wird dem anschließend dargestellt.

1. Zum Verhältnis von (Sport-)Geschichtswissenschaft und (Sport-)Geschichtspolitik

Zunächst scheinen einige theoretische Überlegungen notwendig, um das Verhältnis von Wissenschaft und Politik im Allgemeinen und (Sport-)Geschichtswissenschaft und (Sport-) Geschichtspolitik im Speziellen besser zu begreifen. Michael Krüger versucht dies in seinem Aufsatz *Leben und Werk Carl Diems – ein Forschungs- und Projektbericht*[111] anzustellen. Dabei spricht er von einer „maßgebliche(n) Differenz von Geschichtswissenschaft und Geschichtspolitik"[112]. In diesem Zusammenhang rezipiert er eine Annahme des bedeutenden deutschen Soziologen Max Weber, dass Wissenschaft als Ziel haben sollte, Wahrheiten und Objektivität zu produzieren, nicht moralische Urteile zu fällen. Allerdings kommt die Wissenschaft nicht umhin, auf Werturteile zurückzugreifen, da diese „Gegenstand und wissenschaftliche Fragestellungen konstituieren"[113]. Wendet man diese über Weber hinaus gedachte Annahme auf den Forschungsauftrag zu *Leben und Werk Carl Diems* an, so könne zwar keine Objektivität produziert werden – dies ist für den Historiker nicht möglich, da er als Subjekt stets in der Retrospektive auf die Vergangenheit blickt und nur die Möglichkeit hat, sich einer objektiven Darstellung dieser zu nähren – doch „gut oder besser begründete moralische Bewertungen Diems"[114] zu Tage zu bringen, liege im Rahmen des Möglichen. Diese „moralische(n) Bewertungen Diems" können als Ertrag der geschichtswissenschaftlichen Forschung schließlich als Hilfestellungen für geschichtspolitische Entscheidungen dienen.[115]

---

[111] Krüger 2012, hier konkret zu dieser Thematik: S. 176-182.
[112] Ebenda, S. 176.
[113] Ebenda, S. 177.
[114] Ebenda.
[115] Vgl. Ebenda, S. 176f.

Doch sieht sich Becker nicht der Entscheidung mächtig, eine Empfehlung auszusprechen, wie mit dem Namen Carl Diems und dessen Gedenken umgegangen werden soll. Becker stellt am Ende jedes Teilbandes seiner Diem-Biographie sein Rollenverständnis als Geschichtswissenschaftler in Hinblick, eine Empfehlung auszusprechen, klar:

> „Da die Entscheidung, wie mit dem Gedenken an Diem zu verfahren ist, letztlich durch wissenschaftliche Erkenntnisse nicht zwingend in der einen oder anderen Richtung präjudiziert wird, in der Folge also eine (geschichts-)politische und moralische ist, spreche ich die Empfehlung aus, dass sie von den jeweiligen betroffenen Bürgerinnen und Bürgern in den zuständigen politischen Gremien getroffen werden sollte. Jedes Gemeinwesen und jede Institution, die mit dem Problem konfrontiert ist, über die Beibehaltung oder Änderung einer Namensgebung zu befinden, sollte in den üblichen Prozessen demokratischer Willensbildung das Pro und Contra eines positiven Bezugs auf eine Persönlichkeit wie Diem abwägen."[116]

Er spricht sich also von der Verantwortung frei, eine konkrete Empfehlung zum Gedenken an Diem zu geben, da diese nicht der Geschichtswissenschaft, sondern der Geschichtspolitik obliege. Er gibt diese weiter an die „zuständigen politischen Gremien".

Nun forderte der (noch damalige) DSB laut Krügers Darstellung zu Beginn des Forschungsauftrages allerdings eine Empfehlung für den Umgang mit der Person Carl Diems vom Forschungsprojekt, da die öffentliche Kritik gegen diesen weiter anhielt. Schließlich wurden Namensänderungen von Carl-Diem-Straßen, -Wegen, -Sportplätzen und -Hallen bereits von immer mehr Kommunen forciert und auch die vom DSB alle zwei Jahre vergebene Auszeichnung für hervorragende sportwissenschaftliche Arbeiten hatte Diem zum Zeitpunkt des Projektauftrages als Namenspatron.[117]

Der Projektbeirat ging somit über Beckers Wahrnehmung der Grenze der wissenschaftlichen Aufgabe hinaus, die Geschichte darzustellen, jedoch nicht moralisch wertend konkrete Handlungsempfehlungen zu geben und tut eben dies: „Der Beirat sieht aufgrund dieser Befunde (der von ihnen „missverstandenen"[118] Ergebnisse von Beckers Arbeit; Anm. des Autors) keinen Anlass zur Revision des DSB-Empfehlung von 1996. Er kann auch die

---

[116] Becker, F.: *Den Sport gestalten. Carl Diems Leben (1882-1962), Band I: Kaiserreich*, Duisburg 2009, S. 323, *Band II: Weimarer Republik*, Duisburg 2010, S. 333, *Band III: NS-Zeit*, Duisburg 2008, S. 339, *Band IV: Bundesrepublik*, Duisburg 2008, S. 251.
[117] Die konsequenten Umbenennungen von Diem-Straßen, -Wegen, -Sportplätzen und –Hallen sowie der DSB-Auszeichnung wird in den beiden nachfolgenden Unterkapiteln ausführlich dargestellt.
[118] Dass diese von Becker als missverstanden wahrgenommen wurden, wurde in den Kapiteln *Diskussionsgegenstände* sowie *„Kritische Historiker" gegen „Diemologen"* mehrfach aufgezeigt.

Umbenennung von Carl-Diem-Straßen, -Sportplätzen und –Turnhallen nicht empfehlen."[119] Dies konnte und wollte Becker allerdings in seiner Rolle als (Sport-) Geschichtswissenschaftler nicht leisten, dies sollten „Bürgerinnen und Bürger in zuständigen politischen Gremien" tun, ergo die (Sport-)Geschichtspolitiker. Es zeigt sich eine verschobene Trennlinie der Aufgabe von Geschichtswissenschaft und Geschichtspolitik von den Aufgabengebieten der Wissenschaft zwischen Beckers Vorstellungen und denen des wissenschaftlichen Beirats unter Leitung von Michael Krüger, was nicht die erste Meinungsverschiedenheit zwischen diesen war.

2. *Die Umbenennung der Diem-Plakette*

Bereits 2001 sah sich der Deutsche Leichtathletikverband (DLV) veranlasst, seine Auszeichnung von Leichtathletikfunktionären für deren Verdienste umzubenennen. Diese Auszeichnung wurde seit dem Todesjahr Carl Diems, der selbst begeisterter Leichtathlet war, mit der Verleihung des *Carl-Diem-Schildes* vorgenommen und durch die Belastung Diems von Reinhard Appels geschilderter Reichssportfeldrede umbenannt in *DLV-Ehrenschild*. Da Diems Grundeinstellung nach den Angaben der DLV-Vizepräsidenten „undemokratisch, nationalistisch, inhuman und rassistisch"[120] gewesen sei, war „die Umbenennung (...) an der Zeit"[121].

Nachdem der DLV als bedeutender deutscher Sportfachverband nun von Carl Diem als Namensgeber seiner Auszeichnung verabschiedete, dürfte sich auch der DSB als Dachverband ernsthaft veranlasst gesehen haben, darüber nachzudenken, ob eine Umbenennung ihrer Auszeichnung für hervorragende sportwissenschaftliche Arbeiten nötig sei – auch trotz des Gutachtens Teichlers von 1996, welches keine Umbenennungen für nötig hielt. Am 20. Mai 2006 schlossen sich der DSB und das Nationale Olympische Komitee für Deutschland (NOK) zum Deutschen Olympischen Sportbund (DOSB) zusammen. Präsident des neu zusammengeschlossenen DOSB wurde Thomas Bach. Dieser beschloss mit seinem Präsidium in dessen 13. Sitzung am 7. September 2007, dass fortan nicht mehr historische Persönlichkeiten für die vom DOSB vergebenen Preise namengebend seien sollten. Somit wurde die *Carl-Diem-Plakette* umbenannt und stattdessen der *DOSB-Wissenschaftspreis* vergeben. Die Auszeich-

---

[119] Gruppe & Krüger 2010, S. 43.
[120] DLV-Vizepräsidenten Theo Rous und Rüdiger Nickel, zitiert in: Jungbauer A.: *Gericht bestätigt "Opfer-Rede" vor Hitlerjugend - Wird Halle umbenannt?*, In: *MAIN-POST* vom 22.01.2002, veröffentlicht unter: http://www.waechterpreis.de/s02p_diestories.html, letzter Zugriff: 24.5.13; 12:30 Uhr.
[121] DLV-Präsident Prokop zu den Umständen der Umbenennung des Carl-Diem-Schildes, veröffentlicht unter: http://www.gbg-koeln.de/diem/verbaende/dlv.htm, letzter Zugriff: 24.5.13; 12:32 Uhr.

nungen sollen „stärker mit dem DOSB in Verbindung" [122] stehen, so die Erklärung des DOSB-Präsidiums. Wenn man sich an Krügers Darstellung erinnert, dass der DSB als Vorgängerverband noch 2005 als einer der Projektgeber den Auftrag gab, eine Empfehlung für den Umgang mit dem Gedenken an Carl Diem auszusprechen, erscheint es unverständlich, dass der DOSB noch vor Abschluss des Projekts die *Carl-Diem-Plakette* umbenannt hat.[123] Allerdings wurden auch weitere Auszeichnungen des DSB nicht mehr nach Persönlichkeiten der Sportgeschichte (u.a. *Fritz-Wildung-Plakette*) benannt. Ein neuer Trend des noch jungen DOSB schien es zu sein, sich vom Gedenken an historische Persönlichkeiten mithilfe von Auszeichnungen zu verabschieden und nun diese „stärker in Verbindung mit dem DOSB" zu setzen.

Scheinbar war ein Grund für die Umbenennung, dass sich der DOSB aufgrund der öffentlichen Diskussion um Carl Diem beugte, die auch Ende der 1990er Jahre nach dem Gutachten von Hans Joachim Teichler nicht beendet war und ihn deshalb als Namenspatron für deren Wissenschaftspreis strich. Weiterhin ist es auch schwer belegbar, dass der Projektbeirat eben eine Empfehlung forderte. Krüger belegt eine „ausdrückliche Bitte des Deutschen Olympischen Sportbundes" mit einer Fußnote, in der er auf den Brief- und E-Mail-wechsel mit diesen verweist und beendet diese mit der Klammer „(beim Verfasser)".[124] Somit wurde diese „Bitte" nie veröffentlicht, sondern sei über den Verfasser, also Krüger, einzusehen. Eine merkwürdige Konstellation, welche die Frage offen lässt, ob eine Empfehlung überhaupt gefordert wurde. Man müsse Krüger hierbei auf die Wahrhaftigkeit des Beleges vertrauen. Ob man dies tut, bleibt dem Leser selbst überlassen.

3.   Die Umbenennungen von Carl-Diem-Straßen, -Wegen, -Sportlätzen und –Hallen

Nicht nur die vom DSB verliehene *Carl-Diem-Plakette* gab nach dem Zusammenschluss von DSB und NOK zum DOSB ihren Namenspatron auf, auch zahlreiche Kommunen verabschiedeten sich vom Namen Carl Diems auf ihren Straßenschildern und Sportstätten. Bereits um die Jahrtausendwende wurden Carl-Diem-Straßen, -Wege, -Sportplätze und –Hallen umbenannt – um nur einige zu nennen: Mühlheim an der Ruhr (1996 *Carl-Diem-Straße* umbenannt), Mannheim (1997 *Carl-Diem-Halle* umbenannt), Berlin-Steglitz (2001 *Carl-Diem-Sporthalle* umbenannt) und Eschweiler (2002 *Carl-Diem-Straße* umbenannt).[125] Auch Carl

---

[122] http://www.dosb.de/de/start/details/news/13_sitzung_des_dosb_praesidiums_am_7_september_2007_in_stuttgart/8773/cHash/139a6c0736, letzter Zugriff: 24.5.13; 14:00 Uhr.
[123] Vgl. Krüger 2011, S. 205f.
[124] Krüger 2012, S. 176.
[125] Vgl. http://www.waechterpreis.de/s02p_diestaedte.html, letzter Zugriff: 29.05.13; 12:51 Uhr.

Diems Geburtsstadt Würzburg sah sich im Oktober 2003 veranlasst, etwas mehr als ein Jahr vor Projektbeginn von *Leben und Werk Carl Diems*, deren *Carl-Diem-Halle* sowie die von der Stadt Würzburg verliehene *Carl-Diem-Plakette* für örtliche verdiente Sportfunktionäre Diem als Namenspatron umzubenennen. All dies geschah also bereits, bevor Ergebnisse des Projekts vorlagen. Die Beweislast schien für die genannten Kommunen zu diesem Zeitpunkt wohl bereits erdrückend genug.

Am 01.01.2008 wurde dann auch der vielleicht bedeutendste *Carl-Diem-Weg*, nämlich der an dem die Deutsche Sporthochschule Köln liegt, geändert in *Am Sportplatz Müngersdorf*. Dem ging eine „mindestens seit 1995"[126] währende Diskussion um die Umbenennung voraus. Im September 2006 hatte die örtliche Bezirksverwaltung schließlich diesen Vorgang beschlossen. Allerdings wertete dies der DSHS-Rektor Walter Tokarski als „Skandal" und so ging die Sporthochschule vor das Kölner Verwaltungsgericht, um die Umbenennung doch noch zu verhindern – man wollte noch die Forschungsergebnisse Beckers abwarten. Wie gesagt scheiterte dieser Versuch, auf Zeit zu spielen.[127]

Und auch die *Carl-Diem-Straße* wurde 2009 im Kölner Stadtteil Pulheim umbenannt. Dafür sprachen sich sowohl der Kölner Bürgermeister Dr. Karl August Morisse sowie die Grünen und die FDP aus.[128] Schließlich nahmen sich auch, ebenfalls nach langer Diskussion, „die zuständigen politischen Gremien" der Stadt Münster, an deren Westfälischen Wilhelms-Universität Michael Krüger das Institut für Sportwissenschaft leitet, im November 2010 die Umbenennung des *Carl-Diem-Weges* vor. Fortan hieß dieser *Sentruper Straße*.[129]

Zum Zeitpunkt der Umbenennung der *Carl-Diem-Straße* in Köln sowie des *Carl-Diem-Weges* in Münster lagen die Ergebnisse von Frank Beckers Forschung in Form des III. Teilbandes der Diem-Biographie, der dessen Leben und Werk in der NS-Zeit darstellt, bereits vor. Diese enthielt wie gesagt keine Empfehlung für eine Umbenennung von Diem-Straßen, - Wegen etc. – diese Aufgabe gab Becker an „zuständige politische Gremien" weiter. Dennoch stellte er dar, inwiefern Diem sich „in Schuldzusammenhänge verstrickte", welche eine Beschreibung dessen als Antisemiten, Rassisten, Nationalsozialisten und Militaristen nahelegen. Doch der Vorgang der Umbenennungen setzte bereits einige Jahre vorher ein, sodass Beckers Ergebnisse letztlich nur das zu bestätigten schienen, was vermutlich vorher schon als festste-

---

[126] Leffers, J.: *Denkmalsturz: Sporthochschule verliert im Namensstreit um Carl Diem*, veröffentlicht am 22.08.07 unter: http://www.spiegel.de/unispiegel/studium/denkmalsturz-sporthochschule-verliert-im-namensstreit-um-carl-diem-a-501387.html, letzter Zugriff: 29.05.13; 14:55 Uhr.

[127] Ebenda.

[128] Vgl. ohne Autor: *Carl-Diem-Straße wird umbenannt. Ratsbeschluss*, veröffentlicht am 23.09.09 unter: http://www.ksta.de/region/ratsbeschluss-carl-diem-strasse-wird-umbenannt,15189102,12850778.html, letzter Zugriff: 29.05.13; 14:35 Uhr.

[129] Vgl. Rüttenauer, A.: *„Krieg der Expertisen". Die Vergangenheit des Carl Diem*, veröffentlicht am 06.12.10 unter: http://www.taz.de/!62342/, letzter Zugriff: 29.05.13; 14:38 Uhr.

hend angesehen wurde. Daran konnte auch die Stellungnahme des Projektbeirats vom März 2010 nichts mehr ändern.

Es zeigte sich das, was Becker explizit ausdrückte: Die (Sport-) Geschichtswissenschaft kann lediglich Darstellungen der Vergangenheit liefern, die Entscheidung, wie mit diesen umgegangen wird, obliegt der Politik. Diese deuteten die Darstellung Beckers so, dass Diem sich des Antisemitismus, des Zuarbeitens für das NS-Regime und des Militarismus schuldig machte und somit Anlass bestand, seinen Namen von Straßenschildern zu entfernen sowie Diem-Wege, -Sportplätze und –Hallen umzubenennen. Führt man sich die Tatsache vor Augen, dass bereits vor der Veröffentlichung der Forschungsergebnisse und der Empfehlung des Projektbeirats in vielen Städten Umbenennung vorgenommen wurden, scheint die Mehrheit der „zuständigen politischen Gremien" bereits überzeugt gewesen zu sein, dass die Schuld Diems ausreichend bewiesen wäre, was Beckers Arbeit dann retrospektiv bestätigte. Dass dies für Krüger „unverständlich"[130] ist ist die eine Sache, die andere ist jedoch, dass es zeigt, wie sich die Aufgabenverteilung in der Praxis ausdrückt: Wissenschaftler liefern Forschungsbefunde, die Politik wertet diese und entscheidet.

---

[130] Chatzoudis, G.: *"Eine Art damnatio memoriae verhängt" Zur Debatte um Carl Diem. Interview mit Prof. Dr. Michael Krüger*, veröffentlicht am 26.11.2012 unter: http://www.lisa.gerda-henkel-stiftung.de/content.php?nav_id=4106, letzter Zugriff: 29.05.13; 14:33 Uhr.

V.   Schlussbetrachtung

Auch am Ende des 20. Jahrhunderts konnte mit dem Gutachten Hans Joachim Teichlers die Debatte um Carl Diem nicht beendet werden. Weiterhin wurde Diems Denken und Handeln bis 1945 kritisch reflektiert und politische Entscheidungen, wie die Umbenennungen von Diem-Straßen, -Wegen etc. um die Jahrtausendwende durchgeführt.

So kam es am Ende des ersten Jahrzehnts des 21. Jahrhunderts zur neuesten Diem-Debatte. Ausgelöst wurde diese durch Beckers Diem-Biographie, besonders durch den 2009 veröffentlichten Teilband zur NS-Zeit und den Eintrag Carl Diems im *Handbuch des Antisemitismus* durch Ralf Schäfer. In Folge dieser beiden Publikationen wurde die neueste Diem-Debatte vorwiegend in einer Ausgabe der *Zeitschrift für Geschichtswissenschaft* von 2011 innerhalb der Fachöffentlichkeit ausgetragen. In dieser diskutierten die Geschichtswissenschaftler Frank Becker und Ralf Schäfer sowie der Sportwissenschaftler Michael Krüger darüber, ob Diems Haltung retrospektiv als antisemitisch, nationalsozialistisch und militaristisch zu deuten sei. Eben dies wies Krüger eindeutig zurück. Er argumentiert, stellvertretend für den Beirat des Projekts *Leben und Werk Carl Diems*, zu dem zahlreiche Sport- und (Sport-)Geschichtswissenschaftler zählten, dass Diems Denken und Handeln nicht mit den zur Diskussion stehenden Begriffen zu beschreiben seien, vielmehr wäre Diem sogar Kritiker „der Politik der Nationalsozialisten im Allgemeinen und ihrer Sportpolitik im Besonderen"[131]. Dem Gegenüber stand Beckers Deutung, dass all dies auf Diem jedoch zutraf, mit der Einschränkung, dass Diem kein Antisemit im Sinne des eliminatorischen NS-Antisemitismus gewesen sei, sondern, wie im Unterkapitel *Diskussionsgegenstände* beschrieben, dem des im deutschen Bürgertum während der Wilhelminischen Kaiserzeit weit verbreitet gedachten Antisemitismus entsprach. Nach dem Ersten Weltkrieg änderte Diem schließlich seine Einstellung in Bezug auf das Jüdische. Ähnlich sieht es Schäfer, der jedoch eine antisemitische Haltung über die Zeit des Ersten Weltkriegs hinaus bei Diem zu erkennen glaubt. Dennoch sei diese vom Antisemitismus der Nationalsozialistischen Ideologie abzugrenzen. Es zeigte sich, dass sich gewissermaßen zwei Lager bildeten: Auf der einen Seite die Diems weiße Weste aufrecht erhalten wollenden „Diemologen", zu denen unter anderem Michael Krüger zählt, und den „kritischen Historikern", die Diems Weste als stark beschmutzt sehen, auf der anderen. Zu den „kritischen Historikern" zählte Krüger explizit Schäfer, doch auch Becker ist wohl in diesem Lager zu verorten, aufgrund der Schäfer-nahen Deutungsmuster.

---

[131] Krüger 2011, S. 204.

Schließlich wurde die Frage nach dem Einfluss der sport- und (sport-geschichts) wissenschaftlichen Forschungen für die Politik geklärt. Da bereits vor Abschluss und Veröffentlichung der Forschungsergebnisse des Projekts *Leben und Werk Carl Diems* der DOSB den wissenschaftlichen Preis für hervorragende sportwissenschaftliche Leistungen nicht mehr nach Carl Diem benannte – wie es dessen Vorgängerverband DSB handhabe – ist nicht eindeutig nachzuweisen, ob dieser überhaupt den Rat des Projektbeirats einfließen lassen hätte. Auch forcierten weiterhin zahlreiche Kommunen die Umbenennungen ihrer Carl-Diem-Straßen, -Wege etc. – wie 2009 in Köln oder 2010 in Münster geschehen. Die Darstellungen Beckers lieferten letztendlich eher finale Entscheidungsbestätigungen als Entscheidungshilfen.

Im letzten Absatz seines Aufsatzes *Diem, der Antisemitismus und das NS-Regime* fordert Schäfer einen Paradigmenwechsel von der deutschen Sportwissenschaft mit dem Ziel einer „historiografischen Neuvermessung des Sports im Nationalsozialismus, die auch die Analyse der politischen Motivation seiner Protagonisten einschließt"[132]. Doch es stellt sich die Frage, wie die Sportwissenschaft dies leisten könne. Nachdem sich die Geschichtswissenschaft innerhalb der letzten zehn, zwanzig Jahre immer mehr sportgeschichtlichen Themen angenommen hat, scheint die Sportgeschichte innerhalb der Sportwissenschaft weiter zurückgedrängt zu werden. So lief im Jahr 2011 die Professur für Zeitgeschichte des Sports der Universität Potsdam aus und an anderen Universitäten ist die Sportgeschichte anderen Teildisziplinen, wie der Sportpädagogik, angegliedert. Dies mag nicht heißen, dass eine „Neuvermessung" nicht möglich sei. Dennoch bleibt ausblickend die Frage, ob die Sportgeschichte bei sichtlich sinkender Bedeutung innerhalb der Sportwissenschaft es nachhaltig leisten kann, wissenschaftlichen Nachwuchs herauszubilden, um stetig Wissensfortschritt zu produzieren und potentiell überholte Paradigmen zu überarbeiten.

---

[132] Schäfer 2011a, S. 263.

VI.   Literatur- und Quellenverzeichnis

1. Literatur

Appel, R.: *Aus einem Referat von Reinhard Appel vom 28. April 1984 in der Führungs- und Verwaltungsakademie in Berlin*, in: *Sozial- und Zeitgeschichte des Sports*, 1. Jahrgang, Heft 1, Köln 1987, S. 105.

Becker, F.: *Den Sport gestalten. Carl Diems Leben (1882-1962). Band III. NS-Zeit*, Duisburg 2009.

Becker, F.: *Den Sport gestalten. Carl Diems Leben (1882-1962). Band I. Kaiserreich*, Duisburg 2009.

Becker, F.: *Den Sport gestalten. Carl Diems Leben (1882-1962). Band VI. Bundesrepublik*, Duisburg 2010.

Becker, F.: *Den Sport gestalten. Carl Diems Leben (1882-1962). Band II. Weimarer Republik*, Duisburg 2011.

Becker, F.: *Carl Diem und der Nationalsozialismus*, in: *Zeitschrift für Geschichtswissenschaft*, 59. Jahrgang, Heft 3, Berlin 2011, S. 242-251.

Bernett, H.: *Sportpolitik im Dritten Reich. Aus den Akten der Reichskanzlei*, Schorndorf 1971.

Bernett, H.: *Carl Diem und sein Werk als Gegenstand der sportgeschichtlichen Forschung*, in: *Sozial- und Zeitgeschichte des Sports*, 1. Jahrgang, Heft 1, Köln 1987, S. 7-41.

Dwertmann, H.: *Die Beteiligung von Sportfunktionären im NS-Regime und ihr Einfluss auf die Sportgeschichtsschreibung nach 1945*, in: *Zeitschrift für Geschichtswissenschaft*, 59. Jahrgang, Heft 3, Berlin 2011, S. 230-241.

Goelde, W.: *Adolfs Rekruten*, in: DER SPIEGEL, Nr. 41, 1971, S. 169-170.

Gruppe, O. & Krüger, M. et al.: *Wissenschaftlicher Beirat zum Forschungsprojekt „Leben und Werk Carl Diems", 1. März 2010*, in: Krüger, M. (Hrsg.): *Erinnerungskultur im Sport. Vom kritischen Umgang mit Carl Diem, Sepp Herberger und anderen Größen des deutschen Sports*, Berlin 2012, S. 219-221.

Hinrichsen, J. & Obieray, U. & Sonnenschein, W.: *„Der Krieg ist der vornehmsten Sport...". Geschichte und Manipulation eines Zitats von Carl Diem (2. Teil)*, in: *Leibeserziehung: Monatsschrift für Wissenschaft und Unterricht*, 21. Jahrgang, Heft 4, Schorndorf 1972, S. 127-130.

Jungbauer, A.: *Die Auseinandersetzung um „Sportvater" Carl Diem - am Beispiel seiner Geburtsstadt Würzburg, die nun ihre größte Veranstaltungshalle umbenennt*, in: *Sport-Zeiten. Sport in Geschichte, Kultur und Gesellschaft*, 4. Jahrgang, Heft 1, Göttingen 2004, S. 93-101.

Kluge, V.: *Zum aktuellen Stand in der „Diem-Debatte"*, in: *Kurier. Informationen der Deutschen Sporthochschule Köln*, 25. Jahrgang, Heft 2, Köln 2002, S. 1-4.

Krüger, M.: *Leben und Werk Carl Diems. Ein-Forschungs- und Projektbericht*, in: *Sportwissenschaft*, 40. Jahrgang, Heft 4, Heidelberg 2010, S. 268-284.

Krüger, M.: *Zur Debatte um Carl Diem*, in: *Zeitschrift für Geschichtswissenschaft*, 59. Jahrgang, Heft 3, Berlin 2011, S. 201-209.

Krüger, M.: *Leben und Werk Carl Diems – ein Forschungs- und Projektbericht*, in: Krüger, M. (Hrsg.): *Erinnerungskultur im Sport. Vom kritischen Umgang mit Carl Diem, Sepp Herberger und anderen Größen des deutschen Sports*, Berlin 2012, 175-216.

Large, D. C.: *Nazi games. The olympics of 1936*, New York et al. 2007.

Laude, A. & Bausch, W.: *Der Sport-Führer. Die Legende um Carl Diem*, Göttingen 2000.

Ohne Autor: *Sorg-Sorgen. Unser Embryo lebt*, in: DER SPIEGEL: Nr. 33, 1947, S. 12.

Peiffer, L.: *Carl Diem und der Sport in der Zeit des Nationalsozialismus – Anmerkungen zu den Schriften Carl Diems über ein von ihm persönlich erlebtes und mitgestaltetes Kapitel der jüngsten deutschen Sportgeschichte*, in: *Sozial- und Zeitgeschichte des Sports*, 1. Jahrgang, Heft 1, Köln 1987, S. 92-111.

Präsidiumsbeschluss des DSB: *Stellungnahme der Expertenkommission zu Werk und Person von Carl Diem (1882 bis 1962)*, In: *Sozial- und Zeitgeschichte des Sports*, 10. Jahrgang, Heft 3, Köln 1996, S. 75.

Schäfer, R.: *Diem, Carl*, in: Benz, W. (Hrsg.): *Handbuch des Antisemitismus. Judenfeindschaft in Geschichte und Gegenwart. Personen*, Band 2/1, Berlin 2009, S. 171-173.

Schäfer, R.: *Sportgeschichte und Erinnerungspolitik: Der Fall Carl Diem*, in: *Zeitschrift für Geschichtswissenschaft*, 58. Jahrgang, Heft 11, Berlin 2010, S. 877-899.

Schäfer, R.: *Militarismus, Nationalismus, Antisemitismus. Carl Diem und die Politisierung es bürgerlichen Sports im Kaiserreich*, Berlin 2011.

Schäfer, R.: *Carl Diem, der Antisemitismus und das NS-Regime*, in: *Zeitschrift für Geschichtswissenschaft*, 59. Jahrgang, Heft 3, Berlin 2011a, S. 252-263.

Teichler, H. J.: *Carl Diem und sein Werk als Gegenstand der sportgeschichtlichen Forschung*, in: *Sozial- und Zeitgeschichte des Sports*, 1. Jahrgang, Heft 1, Köln 1987, S. 7-41.

Teichler, H. J.: *Der Weg Carl Diems vom DRA-Generalsekretär zum kommissarischen Führer des Gaues Ausland im NSRL*, in: *Sozial- und Zeitgeschichte des Sports*, 1. Jahrgang, Heft 1, Köln 1987a, S. 42-91.

Teichler, H. J.: *Die Rolle Carl Diems in der Zeit und im zeitlichen Umfeld des NS-Regimes*, in: *Sozial- und Zeitgeschichte des Sports*, 10. Jahrgang, Heft 3, Köln 1996, S. 56-74.

Teichler, H. J.: *Erinnerungskultur im deutschen Sport und die Diem-Debatte*, in: Krüger, H. (Hrsg.): *Erinnerungskultur im Sport. Vom kritischen Umgang mit Carl Diem, Sepp Herberger und anderen Größen des deutschen Sports*, Berlin 2012, S. 119-135.

von Bredow, W.: *Militär und Demokratie in Deutschland: Eine Einführung (Studienbücher Außenpolitik und internationale Beziehungen)*, Wiesbaden 2007.

Wirkus, B.: *„Der Krieg ist der vornehmste Sport...“. Geschichte und Manipulation eines Zitats von Carl Diem*, in: *Leibeserziehung: Manatsschrift für Wissenschaft und Unterricht*, 20. Jahrgang, Heft 12, Schorndorf 1971, S. 409-411.

Wirkus, B.: *In Sachen Carl Diem*, in: *Leibeserziehung: Monatsschrift für Wissenschaft und Unterricht*, 21. Jahrgang, Heft 4, Schorndorf 1972, S. 131-132.

2.   Internetquellen

http://www.aussichten-online.de/diem-monitor.html, letzter Zugriff: 3.5.2013; 13:24 Uhr.

http://www.citizentimes.eu/2012/09/06/antisemitismus-handbuch-zum-nachschlagen/, letzter Zugriff: 13.5.13, 12:45 Uhr.

http://www.dosb.de/de/start/details/news/13_sitzung_des_dosb_praesidiums_am_7_septembe r_2007_in_stuttgart/8773/cHash/139a6c0736, letzter Zugriff: 24.5.13; 14:00 Uhr.

http://www.gbg-koeln.de/diem/verbaende/dlv.htm, letzter Zugriff: 24.5.13; 12:32 Uhr.

http://hsozkult.geschichte.hu-berlin.de/rezensionen/2009-3-235, letzter Zugriff: 16.05.13; 13:33 Uhr.

http://www.ksta.de/region/ratsbeschluss-carl-diem-strasse-wird-umbenannt,15189102,12850 778.html, letzter Zugriff: 29.05.13; 14:35 Uhr.

http://www.lisa.gerda-henkel-stiftung.de/content.php?nav_id=4106, letzter Zugriff: 29.05.13; 14:33 Uhr.

http://www.sehepunkte.de/2012/06/21495.html, letzter Zugriff: 22.5.13; 13:05 Uhr.

http://www.spiegel.de/unispiegel/studium/denkmalsturz-sporthochschule-verliert-im-namens streit-um-carl-diem-a-501387.html, letzter Zugriff: 31.05.13; 14:22 Uhr.

http://www.taz.de/!62342/, letzter Zugriff: 29.05.13; 14:38 Uhr.

http://www.waechterpreis.de/s02p_diestories.html, letzter Zugriff: 24.5.13; 12:30 Uhr.

http://www.zeit.de/sport/2011-12/interview-becker-diem-nazi, letzter Zugriff: 31.05.13; 12:32 Uhr.

Classical Econophysics

W. Paul Cockshott,
Allin F. Cottrell,
Gregory J. Michaelson,
Ian P. Wright

and

Victor M. Yakovenko

2009

cf. Das Argument 305

Routledge
Taylor & Francis Group

LONDON AND NEW YORK

First published 2009
by Routledge
2 Park Square, Milton Park, Abingdon, Oxfordshire OX14 4RN

Simultaneously published in the USA and Canada
by Routledge
711 Third Avenue, New York, NY 10017

Routledge is an imprint of the Taylor & Francis Group, an informa business

First issued in paperback 2011

© 2009 W. Paul Cockshott, Allin F. Cottrell, Gregory J. Michaelson, Ian P.
Wright and Victor M. Yakovenko

Typeset in Times NR by RefineCatch Limited, Bungay, Suffolk

British Library Cataloguing in Publication Data
A catalogue record for this book is available from the British Library

Library of Congress Cataloging in Publication Data
Classical econophysics / edited by Paul Cockshott ... [et al.].
    p. cm. – (Routledge advances in experimental and computable
economics ; no. 12)
    1. Economics–Methodology.   2. Economics–Research.
3. Statistical physics.   I. Cockshott, W. Paul, 1952–
    HB131.C53 2009
    330.01′5195–dc22   2008049250

ISBN13: 978-0-415-47848-9 (hbk)
ISBN13: 978-0-415-69646-3 (pbk)
ISBN13: 978-0-203-87754-8 (ebk)

Contents

List of Figures   ix
List of Tables   xv
List of Digressions   xvii
Acknowledgements   xix

Introduction   1

PART I
Work, information and value   5

1   Problematizing labour   7
    1.1   Watt on work   7
    1.2   Marx: the architect and the bee   12
    1.3   The demonic challenge   19
    1.4   Entropy   20
2   Problematizing information   30
    2.1   The Shannon–Weaver concept of information   30
    2.2   Entropy reductions in action programs   38
    2.3   Alternative views of information   38
3   Labour productivity   47
    3.1   Raising production in general   47
    3.2   Accelerated production   53
    3.3   Parallelizing production   58
4   Babbage and the birth of digital technology   74
    4.1   Copy and calculating   74
    4.2   Tables   75
    4.3   Prony, Babbage and the division of mental labour   77
    4.4   Babbage's machines   81

5 From machines to the universal machine   85

   5.1 Processing information   85

   5.2 Turing machines   89

   5.3 The universal Turing machine   97

   5.4 Decidability and the Church–Turing thesis   99

   5.5 The TM computability of markets   103

   5.6 RUR or Robots R Us   108

6 Political economy: value and labour   113

   6.1 Smith and Watt   113

   6.2 Labour commanded as a measure of value   117

   6.3 Labour time and the determination of value   119

   6.4 Ricardo: clarity achieved   121

   6.5 Marx's contribution   125

   6.6 Two challenges to the labour theory of value   130

   6.7 The probabilistic response   136

PART II

Exchange, money and capital   137

7 The probabilistic approach to economic variables   139

   7.1 Probabilistic models   139

8 The statistical mechanics of money   148

   8.1 Introduction   148

   8.2 Boltzmann–Gibbs distribution   149

   8.3 Computer simulations   150

   8.4 Thermal machine   152

   8.5 Models with debt   153

   8.6 Boltzmann equation   155

   8.7 Non-Boltzmann–Gibbs distributions   156

   8.8 Nonlinear Boltzmann equation vs. linear

       master equation   158

   8.9 Conclusions   159

9 A probabilistic approach to the law of value   161

   9.1 The law of value   161

   9.2 The model   163

   9.3 Simulation results   168

9.4   Analysis   174

9.5   Discussion   180

10   Value in the capitalist economy   184

    10.1   Farjoun and Machover's approach to price   185

    10.2   Information content of prices   188

    10.3   Prices and the rate of profit   190

    10.4   Empirical evidence for labour theory of value   192

11   Money, credit and the form of value   203

    11.1   Money and the form of value   203

    11.2   Two theories of money   206

    11.3   Monetary relations and records   210

    11.4   Money space, an illustration   214

    11.5   Commodity–money space   220

    11.6   The logical properties of financial transactions   226

12   Banking and capital   233

    12.1   Bank credit   233

    12.2   The necessity of paper money   244

    12.3   Banking technology   247

    12.4   The interest rate   254

    12.5   Dominance of the financial sector   256

PART III

Class distribution of income   261

13   A probabilistic model of the social relations of capitalism   263

    13.1   Introduction   263

    13.2   A dynamic model of the social relations of production   264

    13.3   Results   271

    13.4   A note on methodology   287

    13.5   Essential and inessential properties of capitalism   290

14   Understanding profit   292

    14.1   Sraffa: profit and the technology matrix   293

    14.2   Kalecki: profit and monetary flows   298

    14.3   Demographics and the long-run rate of profit   300

PART IV
Information and coordination   319

15   Hayek, information and knowledge   321
     15.1   Inadequacy of the price form   323
     15.2   Information flows under market and plan   332
     15.3   The argument from dynamics   337

PART V
Appendices   341

Appendix A   The law of value: proofs   343
Appendix B   The law of value: experimental details   346
Appendix C   A simple planning program   347
Appendix D   Profits in the SA model   349

     References   353
     Index   361

Figures

1.1 The Newcomen engine built by Smeaton. 8

1.2 Watt's steam engine with separate condenser. 9

1.3 Tessellation of the plane using hexagons. 15

1.4 Nature is the architect of the hexagonal columns of Fingal's cave. 17

1.5 C_{60}, a spontaneously formed dome structure. 18

1.6 Gas initially in equilibrium. 21

1.7 If there is a vacuum on the right and gas on the left the piston will move to the right, increasing the entropy of the system. 23

1.8 The molecules in a lattice gas move along the lines of a triangular grid with fixed velocities. 25

1.9 Collisions in a lattice gas. 26

2.1 A lattice gas can be built in electronic hardware. 34

2.2 In a lattice gas, Maxwell's demon can be implemented with this logic circuit. 34

2.3 The Mandelbrot set, a complex image generated from a tiny amount of information. 39

2.4 Configurations of parallel poles are unstable and tend to evolve towards the anti-parallel configuration. 43

3.1 When inserting axle A into bearing B we want to minimize the conditional information $H(B|A)$, between B and A. 51

3.2 A slice through the axle. 52

3.3 Part of a pin with a fault on its circumference. 53

3.4 The lockstitch sewing machine of Elias Howe. 56

3.5   The Lock-stitch presented in plan, elevation and perspective views, along with a generating action program.   57

3.6   Treadle spinning wheel.   59

3.7   Compton's Mule.   60

3.8   Samian ware was an advance in pottery, since moulding allowed mass production.   61

3.9   NMOS Transistor.   70

3.10   NMOS fabrication steps.   71

4.1   A Roman abacus showing the number DXXVI, or 526 in decimal notation.   75

4.2   Babbage's prototype difference engine, from his engineering drawings.   83

5.1   Turing machine.   89

5.2   (a) Circle. (b) Inverse circle.   90

5.3   (a) Circle as bitmap. (b) Inverse circle as bitmap.   90

5.4   Inverting bitmap TM.   91

5.5   Inverting bitmap execution.   91

5.6   States of the Copying TM.   93

5.7   Schema of the Copying TM.   93

5.8   Copying TM executing.   94

5.9   States of the Searching TM.   95

5.10   Schema of the Searching TM.   96

5.11   UTM with inverting bitmap TM.   98

5.12   Undecidability of Halting Problem.   102

5.13   The Unimate Robot, introduced in 1961.   109

6.1   The celebrated Marshallian supply–demand cross.   133

8.1   Histogram and points: stationary probability distribution of money.   151

8.2   Time evolution of entropy.   152

8.3   Histograms: stationary distributions of money with and without debt.   154

8.4   Histogram: stationary probability distribution of money in the multiplicative random exchange model studied by Ispolatov *et al.* (1998).   156

8.5   Histogram: stationary probability distribution of money in the model with taxes and subsidies.   157

9.1 Stationary distributions of sector sizes with fitted normal distributions collected from a random sample of a 4-commodity economy with parameter settings N:500, L:4, M:2.5×10^5, R:25, C:2. 170

9.2 Relationship between mean sector size and $\frac{Nl_i}{c_i}$ from 20 random samples of 3-commodity economies. 171

9.3 Evolution of mean commodity prices in a 3-commodity economy and stationary distribution of commodity prices with fitted exponential distributions. 171

9.4 Evolution of vector correlation of mean prices and labour values over four samples of 3-commodity economies. 172

9.5 Stationary market prices and MELT transformed labour values in a 10-commodity economy. 173

10.1 Farjoun and Machover's predicted form of ψ, the ratio of price to labour-content. 186

10.2 Farjoun and Machover's predicted ψ compared with measured ψ for the UK in 1984. 189

10.3 Relation between profit rates and organic composition, 47 sectors of the US economy, 1987. 198

11.1 Opening section of Esnunna Law Code. 214

11.2 A walk in Manhattan. 223

11.3 Points of equal net worth (isovals) in the space of commodities and money have the same form as points passed through in the phase space of altitude and velocity squared by a falling body. 225

11.4 Effect of loans in moving the relative position of agents. 229

12.1 Probability surface for a form's assets and liabilities, normalized to turnover. 241

12.2 Plot of the probability distribution for firms along the gross debt/gross credit axis with respect to commercial debts outstanding. 242

12.3 Plot of $g(D, x)$, the probability distribution for firms along the net debt/credit axis with respect to cash holdings. 243

12.4 Plot of the fraction of firms going bankrupt per period against the ratio of mean money holding. 243

12.5 Plot of the largest fraction of a bank's deposits withdrawn in a single day over a 20 year period as the number of customers rises. 245

12.6 The distribution which represents the greatest excursion from a bank's mean reserve position. 255

12.7 Flows into and out of the financial sector. 257

13.1 Class distributions: histograms of the number of actors in each economic class with a constant bin size of 1. 272

13.2 Wage and profit shares in national income. 274

13.3 The complete income distribution plotted as a ccdf in log–log scale. 276

13.4 The class components of the income distribution plotted as ccdfs in log–log scale. 277

13.5 The lower regime of the income distribution plotted in log-linear scale. 277

13.6 The power law regime of the income distribution plotted as a ccdf in log–log scale. 277

13.7 The complete money distribution plotted as a ccdf in log–log scale. 278

13.8 The class components of the money distribution plotted as ccdfs in log–log scale. 279

13.9 A section of the workers' money ccdf plotted in linear–log scale. 279

13.10 A section of the capitalists' money ccdf plotted in log–log scale. 279

13.11 Firm size distribution: histogram of firm sizes by employees in log–log scale with a constant bin size of 1. 281

13.12 Firm size growth rate distribution: histogram of the log growth rates of firms per simulated year in linear–log scale with a constant bin size of 1. 282

13.13 Firm deaths distribution: Histogram of firm deaths per simulated month in log-linear scale with a constant bin size of 1. 284

13.14 Rescaled GDP growth rate distribution: histogram of the log growth rate of GDP in linear–log scale with a constant bin size of 1. 285

13.15 Recession duration distribution: Histogram of the frequency of the duration of recessions in log-linear scale with a constant bin size of 1. 286

13.16   Capital-weighted rate-of-profit distribution: Histogram of amount of capital invested that generated a given percentage profit rate within a simulated year.   287

13.17   Firm-weighted rate-of-profit distribution: Histogram of number of firms that generated a given percentage profit rate within a simulated year.   288

14.1   How the rate of profit (dotted line) falls as the wage rises, wages being expressed in tons of iron.   295

14.2   Evolution of the profit rate under constant population growth.   305

14.3   Evolution of the profit rate given declining population growth.   305

14.4   Evolution of the profit rate given declining population growth and constant real wages.   306

14.5   Evolution of the profit rate given declining population growth and technical improvement.   307

14.6   Accumulation of capital as a percentage of profit in the UK, 1855–1969.   313

14.7   Organic composition of capital and profit rate in the UK, 1855–1969.   314

14.8   The evolution of the equilibrium rate of profit predicted by the theory in this chapter and the rate of profit observed in the UK and Japan.   315

14.9   Evolution of the profit rate in the USA.   316

Tables

1.1	Boltzmann's measure of unevenness	24
2.1	A possible code for transmitting messages that are true one-third of the time	32
2.2	The action plan of the demon	35
2.3	Tabulation of the functions x AND y, x OR y	35
2.4	Projected Landauer heat dissipation in 21st century computers operating at 300° Kelvin	37
4.1	The number of balls in pyramidal piles	80
5.1	ASCII codes	86
6.1	Differing organic composition generates differing profit rates	128
10.1	Example input–output table	193
10.2	Average percentage deviations between market prices and labour values for the USA for selected years	194
10.3	Comparing the correlation of prices to labour values in different countries	195
10.4	Price regressions for the UK in 1984	196
10.5	Profit rates and organic composition, BEA fixed capital plus one month's circulating constant capital as estimate of capital stock	197
10.6	Regressions of price on labour values and some alternative 'value-bases' for the UK	200
10.7	Regression of alternative value bases for Greece	200
10.8	Coefficients of variation for x-content per £ of output	201
11.1	Agents' holdings of money and commodities	222
11.2	Figuring agents' wealth	222

12.1   The *D* matrix stored as a ternary relation   234

12.2   A bank need only store credit information as a
       binary relation   234

12.3   Growth of the world gold stock 1840 to 2000   238

14.1   Physical input–output table of economy with a surplus   295

14.2   Example of a Sraffian Standard System   296

14.3   The rate of profit: five scenarios   309

14.4   Rising organic composition of capital, manufacturing and
       mining in Sweden)   314

15.1   Convergence of gross production on that required for the
       final net product   338

15.2   Timings for applying the planning algorithm in Appendix
       C to model economies of different sizes   339

B.1   Labour value/market price correlations from random
       samples of the **SCE**   346

Digressions

1.1	Apian efficiency	16
1.2	Boltzmann's equation for Entropy	23
6.1	Rent and Nature's Bounty	125
6.2	Interpreting Marx	131
7.1	The Boltzmann–Gibbs distribution	142
11.1	Coins and Abaci	211
11.2	Money and the illusion of Pepper's ghost	221
11.3	Relations	230–1
12.1	Paper money in socialist economies	236
12.2	A Turing machine program to update bank ledgers	252
13.1	Power-law distributions	275

Acknowledgements

We would like to thank Moshe Machover and some anonymous referees for their help in going over the book and making suggestions to improve it.

We would also like to thank Donald Knuth and Leslie Lamport, whose TEX and LATEX systems made the preparation of this book much easier than it would otherwise have been.

Section 10.4.4 reproduces results that appeared in Cockshott and Cottrell, 1997. Section 10.4.5 contains some material previously published as Cockshott and Cottrell, 2005. Chapter 15 contains some material that was previously published in Cottrell and Cockshott, 1993. Chapter 9 contains work previously published as Wright, 2008b and chapter 13 contains work previously published as Wright, 2005b. Both are the work of Ian Wright, as is chapter 7. Chapter 8 is the work of Victor Yakovenko. Other chapters are the joint work of the other three authors.

Introduction

'Classical econophysics': the title of our book is a pun on classical economics and classical physics. By classical physics we mean physics from Galileo to Bohr; by classical economics, we mean economics from Smith to Marx. Of course such intellectual traditions don't cease to exist, or cease to be studied, when new models come to prominence. To take but two examples, the recent field of complex dynamics ('chaos theory') is within the paradigm of classical physics, while the neo-Ricardian school of economics revived work in the classical paradigm in the second half of the twentieth century. What justifies our endeavor is the observation that while the intellectual tools used by the new sub-discipline of econophysics derive largely from classical physics, econophysics has failed to appreciate the breadth of issues that concerned classical economics.

Classical physics had among its great discoveries the formulation of laws of motion, the concept of energy conservation and the exploration of thermodynamics and statistical mechanics. Within this framework the concepts of energy and work played a central role. For the classical economists, work (labour) was also central. They concerned themselves with how work was done, how to make labour more efficient, and how labour's product is divided among the different classes of society. So we have Smith saying

> Labor was the first price, the original purchase-money that was paid for all things.
>
> (Smith, 1974: ch. 5)

or Ricardo saying

> By far the greatest part of those goods which are the objects of desire, are procured by labour; and they may be multiplied, not in one country alone, but in many, almost without any assignable limit, if we are disposed to bestow the labour necessary to obtain them.
>
> (Ricardo, 1951: 12)

and Babbage:

> The cost of any article may be reduced in its ultimate analysis to the quantity of labour by which it was produced.
>
> (Babbage, 1832: ch. 18, par. 210)

or Marx:

> Economy of time, to this all economy ultimately reduces itself.... [E]conomy of time, along with the planned distribution of labour time among the various branches of production, remains the first economic law on the basis of communal production.
>
> (Marx, 1973: 173)

When they made work the foundation of their analysis, the classical economists were not content just to talk about it in the abstract. They concerned themselves with with the actual work processes of the day and how and why these enhanced production, questions that have tended to slip below the horizon of later economists. In this book we take the concerns of the classical economists – Smith, Ricardo, Babbage and Marx in particular – seriously.[1] Bear in mind that Smith, Babbage and Marx are probably better described as philosophers than as economists. That is certainly how they considered themselves. We attempt to apply to these concerns, the methodological approach that has proven useful in other areas of econophysics investigation. We look at three broad areas:

(1) Work and the physical production of goods.
(2) Value and prices.
(3) The distribution of revenue between the different classes of society.

We approach all of these issues in a physical and computational way. We consider ourselves licensed to import concepts from physics, information theory and theoretical computer science to the questions under examination. In addition, but at crucial points we use the results of agent-based simulation models to attempt to uncover the minimal set of logical assumptions required to produce the economic phenomena that the classicals observed.[2]

Production

We start out by asking how work is possible. We all know it occurs, but what is it about nature that allows human beings to engage in productive activity? What, if

---

[1] For a discussion of this see Grossman (1977: 43–6).

[2] We are aware that such models are not definitive, only suggestive. You can demonstrate that observed phenomena are not inconsistent with the logically computable consequences of your model. You do not know whether your model is minimal in the sense that there is no lower complexity model that could adequately reproduce the same results. But it does tell you that a more complex model is not needed.

anything, is the relationship between work as understood by classical physics and work as understood by the classical economists?

In the course of interrogating the idea of labour we discover that the modern idea of information provides a key to understanding both human labour in general (chapter 2), and industrial mass production in particular (chapter 3). From looking at information and machinery, we progress to the notion of the universal intellectual machine foreseen by Babbage and Turing (chapters 4 and 5). The concept of universality developed by Turing provides, we think, a perspective from which the special character of human labour in the production process can be understood.

Why is labour special? Why could not electricity, steel or horsepower instead of labour time be the foundation of economic value (chapter 10)? We argue that it is a dual universality of human activity that gives it this role. It is universal in the sense that human work is needed for all productive activities, but human beings are also 'universal robots'. They can adapt themselves to to all the productive roles our society needs. Despite the fantasies of science-fiction, no mere machine yet has that universal adaptability (chapter 5).

Exchange

After examining human activity as the source of value in the classical economists (chapter 6) we examine what evidence there is to support this intuition on their part, looking at

- simulation data (chapter 7),
- empirical data (chapter 10), and
- arguments from statistical mechanics (chapter 10).

We conclude that the classical theory of value is in fact well supported on all these grounds.

Following an analysis of basic commodity exchange we go on in chapter 11 to examine money and what Marx termed 'the form of value'. Marx's work remains interesting as it attempted to apply a formal analysis to exchange and money, using the tools then available to him: Hegelian logic. We attempt to re-analyse the formal aspect of exchange value using a triad of concepts drawn from modern theories of formal systems:

(1) the concept of a metric space (section 11.5.1),
(2) the notion of symmetry (section 11.6), and
(3) the idea of a signature (section 11.4).

The first idea is borrowed from geometry. The second comes from the way physics conceptualizes conservation laws, and formalizes the notion that commodity exchange is a formally conservative system. The third idea, signature, comes from the theory of types, but it closely corresponds to the use to which Marx put such formal notations as $M \to C \to M'$. In the process of our analysis we end up rejecting a 'substance' based notion of money as something made from an inherently valuable material. This idea, which was very much part of the classical tradition, may have seemed appropriate during the days of metallic currency but is no longer helpful. Instead we elaborate a chartalist interpretation of money.

Class distribution of revenues

In chapters 7 and 8 we explain the path-breaking work on the statistical mechanics of money by Dragulescu and Yakovenko (2002) and how, assuming the conservation of money, a highly unequal Gibbs–Boltzman distribution of wealth will arise in a simple exchange economy. In chapter 13 we move on to an economy in which the buying and selling of labour is allowed. We show that in such an economy the distribution of income becomes even more unequal, characterized by what is termed a *power law* distribution. We generate these results with very simple assumptions about the nature of production relations.

In chapter 14 we look at the laws governing the level of profits in a capitalist economy, focusing in turn on input–output, monetary and demographic constraints. The background to this is the concern of the classical economists with an apparent tendency for profit rates to decline with the passage of time. We confirm that this tendency is real, and explain why the criticisms of it by Okishio were ill founded.

Planning and the market

In a final part of the book we look at the debates between socialist economists and Hayek over the role of information flows in economies. We employ the methodology of algorithmic information theory, explained in earlier chapters, to asses the validity of the arguments of the Austrian school regarding the impossibility of mitigating the effects of unfettered capitalism.

The authors

Paul Cockshott is Reader in Computing Science at the University of Glasgow.

Allin Cottrell is Professor of Economics at Wake Forest University.

Greg Michaelson is Professor of Computer Science at Heriot-Watt University.

Ian Wright is a PhD student in economics at the Open University.

Victor Yakovenko is Professor of Physics at the University of Maryland.

Part I

Work, information and value

1 Problematizing labour

1.1 Watt on work

Prior to the eighteenth century, muscles – whether of humans, horses or oxen – remained the fundamental energy source for production. Not coincidentally, the concepts of work, power, energy and labour did not exist in anything like their modern form. People were, of course, familiar with machinery prior to the modern age. The Archimedean machines and their derivatives – levers, inclined planes, screws, wheels, pulleys – had been around for millennia to amplify or concentrate muscular effort. Water-power had been in use since at least the first century A.D.,[1] initially as a means of grinding grain; during the middle ages it was applied to a wide variety of industrial processes. But water-power, and its sister wind-power, were still special-purpose technologies, not universal energy sources. Limited by location and specialized use, they did not problematize effort as such.

A note on terminology is in order here. The (admittedly not very elegant) verb 'to problematize' derives from the work of the Althusser and Balibar (1970) who coined the term *problématique* (problematic) to refer to the field of problems or questions that define an area of scientific enquiry. The term is fairly closely related to Thomas Kuhn's idea of a scientific 'paradigm' (Kuhn, 1970). So, to problematize a domain is to transform it into a scientific problem-area, to construct new concepts which permit the posing of precise scientific questions. In the pre-modern era engineers and sea captains would know from experience how many men or horses must be employed, using pulleys and windlasses, to raise a mast or obelisk. Millers knew that the grinding capacity of water mills varied with the available flow in the mill lade. But there was no systematic equation or measure to relate muscular work to water's work, no scientific problematic of effort. That had to wait for James Watt, after whom we name our modern measure of the ability to work.

Watt, the best-known pioneer of steam, did not actually invent the steam engine, but he improved its efficiency. As Mathematical Instrument Maker to the University of Glasgow he was called in to repair a model steam engine used by the department of Natural Philosophy (we would now call it Physics). The

---

[1] See Strand (1979), de Ste. Croix (1981: 38).

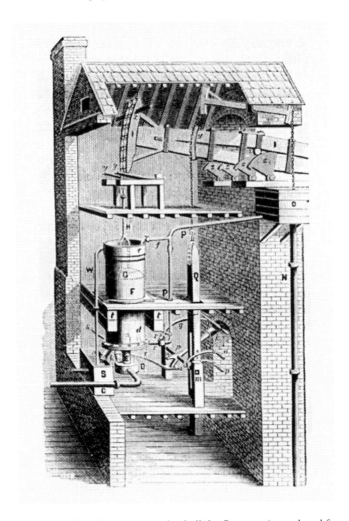

Figure 1.1 The Newcomen engine built by Smeaton (reproduced from Thurston).

machine was a small scale version of the Newcomen engine that was already in widespread use for pumping in mines.

The Newcomen engine was an 'atmospheric engine'. It had a single cylinder, the top half of which was open to the atmosphere (Figure 1.1). The lower half of the cylinder was connected via two valves to a boiler and a water reservoir. The piston was connected to a rocking beam, the other end of which supported the heavy plunger of a mine pump. The resting condition of the engine was with the piston pulled up by the counter-weight of the pump plunger.

To operate the machine, the boiler valve was opened first, filling the cylinder with steam. This valve was then closed and the water-reservoir valve opened, spraying cold water into the piston. This condensed the steam, resulting in a partial vacuum. Atmospheric pressure on the upper surface of the piston then drove it down, providing the power-stroke. The two-phase cycle could then be repeated to obtain regular pumping.

Watt observed that the model engine could only carry out a few strokes before the boiler ran out of steam and it had to rest to 'catch its breath'. He ascertained that this was caused by the incoming steam immediately condensing on the walls of the cylinder, still cool from the previous water spray. His solution was to provide a separate condenser, permanently water-cooled, and intermittently connected to the cylinder by a valve mechanism. The cylinder, meanwhile, was provided with a steam-filled outer jacket to keep its inner lining above condensation temperature (Figure 1.2). His 1769 patent was for 'A New Method of Lessening the Consumption of Steam and Fuel in Fire Engines'.

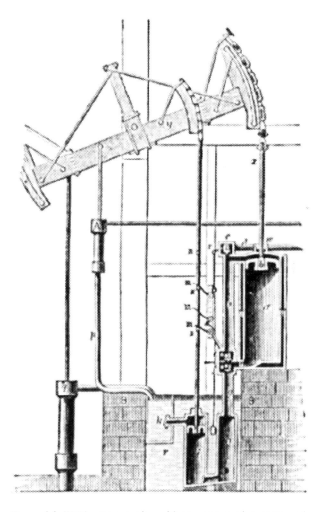

Figure 1.2 Watt's steam engine with separate condenser (reproduced from Thurston).

Watt's later business success was based directly on this gain in thermal efficiency. His engines were not sold outright to users, but were leased. The rental paid was equal to one-third the cost of coal saved through using a Watt engine rather than a Newcomen engine (Tann, 1981). This pricing system worked so long as the Newcomen engine provided a basis for comparison, but as Watt's engines became the predominant type, and as they came to be used to power an ever-widening range of machines, some system of rating the working capacity of the engines was needed. Watt needed a standardized scale by which he could rate the power, and thus the rental cost, of different engines. His standardized measure was, of course, the horsepower: users were charged £5 per horsepower year.

Watt's horse was not a real horse, naturally, but the abstraction of a horse, a standardized horse. The abstraction is multiple: at once an abstraction from particular horses, an abstraction from the difference between flesh and blood horses and iron ones, and an abstraction from the particular work done. The work done had to be defined in the most abstract terms, as the overcoming of resistance in its canonical form, namely raising weights. One horsepower is 550 ft lb/sec, the ability to raise a load of 1 ton by 15 feet in a minute.

While few real horses could sustain this kind of work, its connection to the task performed by Watt's original engines is clear. The steam engine was a direct replacement for horse-operated pumps in the raising of water from mines. But with the development of mechanisms like Watt's sun and planet gear, which converted linear to rotary motion, steam engines became a general purpose power source. They could replace water wheels in mills, drive factory machines by systems of axles and pulleys, pull loads on tracks. Engine capacity measured in horsepower abstracted from the concrete work that was being performed, transforming it all to work in general. Horsepower was the capacity to perform a given amount of work each second. By defining power as work done per second, work in general was itself implicitly defined. All work was equated to lifting. Work in general was defined as the product of resistance overcome, measured in pounds of force, by the distance through which it was overcome.

Mechanical power seemed to hold the prospect of abolishing human drudgery and labour. As Matthew Boulton proudly announced to George II: 'Your Majesty, I have at my disposal what the whole world demands; something which will uplift civilization more than ever by relieving man of undignified drudgery. I have steam power.'[2] To a world in which human muscle was a prime mover, this equation of

---

[2] Compare Antipater of Thessalonika's eulogy on the introduction of the water mill:

> Stop grinding, ye women who toil at the mill.
> Sleep on, though the crowing cocks announce the break of day.
> Demeter has commanded the water nymphs to do the work of your hands.
> Jumping one wheel they turn the axle
> Which drives the gears and the heavy millstones.

work in the engineering sense with human labour was exact. Work on ships, in mines, at the harvest, was work in the most basic physical sense. Men toiled at windlasses to raise anchors, teams pulled on ropes to set sails and hauled loads on their backs to unload cargo. Children dragged coal in carts from drift mines, women carried it up shafts in baskets on their backs. The 'navigators' who built canals did it with no mechanical aid more sophisticated than the wheelbarrow (a combination of lever and wheel, two Archimedean devices).

As horsepower per head of population multiplied, so too did industrial productivity. The power of steam was harnessed, first to raise weights, then to rotate machinery, then to power water-craft, next to trains, and eventually – through the mediation of the electricity grid – to tasks in every shop and home, while human work shrank as a proportion of the total work performed. More and more work was done by means of non-human energy, yet the need for people to work remained. A steam locomotive might draw a hundred-ton train, but it needed a driver to control it. Human work became increasingly a matter of the supervision, control and feeding of machines. Thus the identification of work with the overcoming of physical resistance in the abstract, and of human labour-power with power in Watt's sense, contained both truth and falsehood. Its truth is shown by the manifest gains flowing from the augmentation of human energy. Its falsity is exposed by the residuum of human activity that expresses itself in the control, minding and direction of machinery.

Indeed, the introduction of powered machinery had the effect of lengthening the working day while making work more intense and remorseless. The cost of powered machinery was such that only men with substantial wealth could afford it. Cheap hand-powered spindles and looms could not compete with steam-powered ones. Domestic spinners and hand-loom weavers had to give up their independence and work for the owners of the new steam powered 'mules' and looms. Steam power brought no increase in leisure for weavers or spinners. Rather, the drive to recoup the capital cost of the new machinery brought longer working hours and shift-work, to a rhythm dictated by the tireless engine. The fact that the machinery was not owned by those who worked it, meant that it enslaved rather than liberated.

A particular pattern of ownership was the social cause of machine-enforced wage slavery, but that is only half the story. We may ask why the new machine economy needed human labour at all. Why did 'self acting' – or as we would put it now, 'automatic' – machines not displace human labour altogether? A century ago, millions of horses toiled in harness to draw our loads. Where are they now? A remnant of their former race survives as toys of the rich; the rest went early to the knackers. Why has a similar fate not befallen human workers? Why has the race of workers not been killed off, to leave a leisured rich attended by their machines?

Watt's horsepower killed the horse, but the worker survived. There must be some real difference between work as defined by Watt, and work in the sense of human labour.

1.2   Marx: the architect and the bee

Karl Marx proposed an argument which seems at first sight to get to the essence of what distinguishes human labour from the work of an animal or a machine, namely purpose.

> A spider conducts operations which resemble those of a weaver, and a bee would put many a human architect to shame by the construction of its honeycomb cells. But what distinguishes the worst architect from the best of bees is that the architect builds the cell in his mind before he constructs it in wax. At the end of every labour process, a result emerges which had already been conceived by the worker at the beginning, hence already existed ideally. Man not only effects a change of form in the materials of nature; he also realizes his own purpose in those materials. And this is a purpose he is conscious of, it determines the mode of his activity with the rigidity of a law, and he must subordinate his will to it.
>
> (Marx, 1976: 284)

This suggests that animals, lacking purpose, can be replaced by machines, but that humans are always required, in the end, to give purpose to the machine. We cite Marx's statement because it articulates what is probably a widely held view, yet it has several interesting problems. This is an issue where it is difficult to go straight for the 'right answer'. It may be profitable to beat the bushes first, to scare up (and shoot down) various prejudices that can block the road to a scientific understanding.

First, are animals really lacking in purpose? The spider may be so small, and her brain so tiny, that it seems plausible that blind instinct, rather than the conscious prospect of flies, drives her to spin. But it is doubtful that the same applies to mammals. The horse at the plough may not envisage in advance the corn he helps to produce, but then he is a slave, bent to the purpose of the ploughman. Reduced to a source of mechanical power, overcoming the dumb resistance of the soil, he is readily replaced by a John Deere. The same cannot be said of animals in the wild. Does the wolf stalking its prey not intend to eat it? It plans its approach with cunning. Who are we to say that the result – fresh caribou meat – did not 'already exist in the imagination' of the wolf at its commencement? We have no basis other than anthropocentric prejudice on which to deny her imagination and foresight.

Turning to Marx's human example – an architect – his argument looks even shakier. For do architects ever build things themselves? They may occasionally build their own homes, but in general what gives them the status of architects is that they don't get their hands dirty with anything worse than India Ink. Architects draw up plans. Builders build. (In eliding this distinction Marx showed an uncharacteristic blindness to class reality).

An office block, stadium or station has, it is true, some sort of prior existence, but as a plan on paper rather than in the mind of the builders. If by collective labour civilized humans can put up structures more complex than bees, it is because they can read, write and draw. A plan – whether on paper or, as in earlier epochs, scribed on stone – coordinates the individual efforts of many humans into a collective effort.

For building work, then, Marx is partly right: the structure is raised *on paper* before it is raised in stone. But he is wrong in saying that it is built in the imagination first, and in implying that the structure is put up by the architect. What is really unique to humans here is, first, the social division of labour between the labour of conception by the architects and the work of execution by the builders, and second, the existence of *materialized plans*: configurations of matter that can control and direct the labour of groups of humans.

While insect societies may have a division of labour between 'castes' – for example between worker and soldier termites – they do not have a comparable division between conception and execution, between issuers and followers of orders. Nor do insects have technologies of record and writing. They can communicate with each other. Dancing bees describe to others the whereabouts of flowers. Walking ants leave scent trails for their companions. These messages, like human speech, coordinate labour. Like our tales, they vanish in the telling. But, not restricted to telling tales, we can can make records that persist, communicated over space and time.

Our tales are richer too. The set of messages that can be expressed in our languages is exponentially greater than in the language of bees. Each works by the sequential combination of symbols – words for us, wiggles for bees – but we have many more symbols and can understand much longer sequences. The number of distinct messages that can be communicated by a language is proportional to v^m where v is the number of distinct symbols that are recognized in the language and m is the maximum message length. If bees have a repertoire of six types of wiggles and can understand 'sentences' of three wiggles in succession, then they can send $6^3 = 216$ different messages. A human language with a vocabulary of 3000 words and a maximum sentence length of 20 words could convey about $3.486784401 \times 10^{69} = 348{,}678{,}440{,}100{,}000{,}000{,}000{,}000{,}000{,}000{,}$ $000{,}000{,}000{,}000{,}000{,}000{,}000{,}000{,}000{,}000{,}000{,}000$ distinct sentences. Of course, not all of these would be grammatically correct, and a small fraction of those would make any sense, but the number of messages is still astronomically greater than what insects can manage. And we can keep piling on the sentences until the listener loses track.

All this leaves open another interpretation of what Marx had to say. True enough, architects may not themselves build theatres, any more than Hadrian built his wall or Diocletian his baths.[3] But Hadrian caused the wall to be built and Diocletian's architect caused the baths to be built to a specific design. If the architect creates only a paper version of a theatre, can we say, at any rate,

---

[3] It was, of course, the rank and file legionnaires who built Hadrian's wall; see Davies (1989). This use of the word 'built' is common in class societies, where the actual builders get no credit for their creations; their labour contributes instead to the fame of a ruler or architect.

that he creates this drawing in his mind before setting it down on paper? This interpretation of Marx's story of the architect and the bee seems to make sense, but it's not clear that it offers a true description of what an architect actually does.

1.2.1   Emergent buildings

Some individuals – autistic infant prodigies or *idiot savants* – do seem to have the ability to hold in their minds almost photographically detailed images of buildings they have seen. Working from memory, they are able to draw buildings in astonishing and accurate detail. But it is questionable whether professional architects work in this way. Some may, but for others the process of developing a design is intimately tied up with actually drawing it. They start with the broad outlines of a design in their minds. As this is transferred to paper, they get the context within which the mind can work to elaborate and fill in details. The details were not in the mind prior to starting work, they emerge through the interaction of mind, pen and paper. In other words, pencils and paper don't just record ideas that exist fully-formed, they are part of a production process that generates ideas in the first place.

At any one time our conscious mind can focus on only a limited number of items. On the basis of what it is currently conscious of, its context, it can produce responses related to this context. In reverie the context is internal to the brain and the responses are new ideas related to this context. In an activity like drawing a plan or engineering diagram, the context has two parts

(1) an internal state of mind; and
(2) that part of the diagram upon which visual attention is fixated,

and the response is both internal – a new state of mind – and external – a movement of the pencil on the paper.[4] Where in reverie the response, the new idea, slipped all too easily from grasp, paper remembers.[5] Architecture exchanges for the fallibility and limited compass of memory the durability of an effectively infinite supply of A0. One might say that complex architecture rests on paper foundations.

If the idea of the architect as creating buildings spontaneously out of the imagination is dismissed as an almost religious myth, redolent of the Masonic characterization of the deity as the *Great Architect*, what then remains of the antithesis between architect and bee? Well, how do the bees shape their hive? We can be sure there are no drawings of hexagons, made by the 'queen', and executed

---

[4] The reader may notice that this argument is a thinly disguised version of Alan Turing's famous argument (Turing, 1937).

[5] 'Our civilization or at all events our records depend very largely on the employment of paper.' Pliny, *Natural History*, Book XIII.

Figure 1.3 Tessellation of the plane using hexagons.

by her worker daughters.[6] We are talking here of *apis mellifera* not the solitary bumble bee. The labour of the honey bees is collective, like that of workers on a building site, yet although they have no written plans to work from they create a geometrically precise, optimal and elegant structure.

1.2.2 Apian efficiency

Consider the problem to which the honeycomb is the answer: to come up with a structure that is equally capable of storing honey or sheltering bee larvae, is waterproof, is structurally stiff, provides a platform to walk on, and which uses the minimum material. Given this design brief it is unlikely that a human engineer could come up with a better structure.

The structure has to be organized as a series of planes to provide access. Within the planes, the combs, the space has to be divided into approximately bee-sized cubicles. These could be triangular, square, or hexagonal (the only three regular tessellations of the plane). Our architects have a predilection for the rectangular, but the hexagonal form is superior.

A tessellation of unit squares has a wall length of 2 per unit area, since a single unit square has four sides of unit length, each shared 50 per cent with its neighbours. A tessellation of hexagons of unit area has a wall length of $\frac{2}{\sqrt{3}}$ per unit area, a reduction by a factor of $\sqrt{3}$ (see Digression 1.1). The honeycomb structure used by bees is thus more efficient than a rectilinear arrangement in its use of wax.

The fact that hexagonal lattices minimize boundary lengths per unit area means that they can arise spontaneously, for example in columnar basalts. Here the tension induced in rocks as they cool encourages cracking, preferentially giving rise to six sided columns. We might suspect that the beehive too, gained its structure from a process of spontaneous pattern formation analogous to columnar basalts or packed arrays of soap bubbles. But this doesn't tally with the way the cells are built up, or with the uniformity of their dimensions. In a partially constructed honeycomb the cells are of a constant diameter; those in the middle

---

[6] The breeding female is no more an architect or Caesar than the Pope is the genetic father of his followers. Monarchy and patriarchy project dominance relations onto genetic relations and vice versa. Apian Mother becomes queen, the Vatican monarch, Holy Father.

Digression 1.1   Apian efficiency

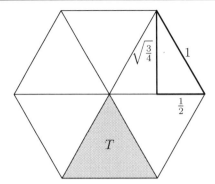

(1)   A hexagon of unit side is made up of 6 identical equilateral triangles, thus its area is $6T$ where T is the area of an equilateral triangle of unit side.

(2)   The area of an equilateral triangle of unit side is $\frac{1}{2}bh$ where b the base $= 1$ and h the height $= \sqrt{\frac{3}{4}}$. So $T = \frac{1}{2}\sqrt{\frac{3}{4}} = \frac{\sqrt{3}}{4}$.

(3)   The area of one hexagon is then

$$6\frac{\sqrt{3}}{4} = \frac{3\sqrt{3}}{2}$$

(4)   The hexagon's six sides are each shared 50 per cent with a neighbour.

(5)   Wall per unit area for a hexagonal tessellation is then $3/\frac{3\sqrt{3}}{2} = 2/\sqrt{3}$ which is better than the wall to area ratio for squares.

The Honeycomb Conjecture – namely, that a hexagonal grid represents the best way to divide a surface into regions of equal area with the least total perimeter – has been debated since 36 BC when it was mentioned by Varro in his book on agriculture, but it evaded proof until the work of Hales (2001).

of the comb are all of uniform height while towards the edge the depth of the cells falls. The bees build the cells up from the base, laying wax down on the upper margins of the cell walls, just as bricks are added to the upper margin of a wall by a bricklayer. The construction process takes advantage of the inherent stability of a hexagonal lattice, allowing the growing cells to form their own scaffolding. But the process also demands that the bees can deposit wax accurately on the growing cell walls, and that they stop building when the cells have reached the right height. That is, it depends on purposeful activity on the part of the bees.

A similar process takes place in the human construction of geodesic domes, hexagonal lattices curved through a third dimension. These have an inherent

Figure 1.4 Nature is the architect of the hexagonal columns of Fingal's cave. (Photo
  by Andrew Kerr)

stability that becomes more and more evident as you add struts to them. You
build them up in a ring starting at ground level. The structure initially has a fair
degree of play in it, but the closer the structure comes to a sphere the more rigid
it is. Human dome builders, like bees, exploit the inherent structural properties of
hexagonal lattices, but they still need to cut struts to the right length and put them
in the correct place. The bees likewise must select the right height for their cell
walls and place wax appropriately.

Spontaneous self-assembly of hexagonal structures similar to geodesic domes
does occur in nature. The Fullerenes are a family of carbon molecules named
after Buckminster Fuller, the inventor of the geodesic dome. The first of these
to be discovered, C_{60}, has the form of a perfect icosahedron (see Figure 1.5).
Condensed out of the hellish heat of a carbon arc, it depends on thermal vibrations
to curve the familiar planar hexagonal lattice of graphite onto itself to form a three
dimensional structure. No architect, or bee, is required. The atomic properties of
carbon select the strut length. Thermal motion searches the space of possible
configurations; a small fraction of the molecules settle into the local energy
minima represented by C_{60} and its sisters.

If bees can't rely upon spontaneous self-assembly to build their hives, must
they have a plan in mind before they start? Since they can't draw, 'the mind'
would have to be where they held any plans. While we can't rule this out, it
seems unlikely. The real requirement is that they can execute a program of work.
A bee arriving on the construction site must, in the darkness, find an appropriate
place to put wax, for which they need a set of rules:

If the cell is high enough to crawl into, put no more wax on it,
otherwise if the cell has well-formed walls add to their height,
otherwise if it is a cell base smaller than your own body diameter, expand it,
otherwise start building the wall up from the base . . .

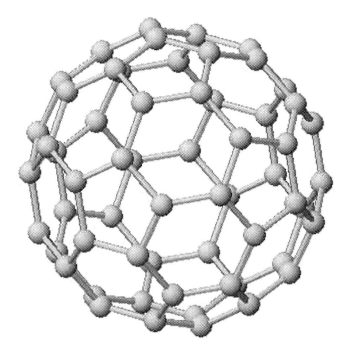

Figure 1.5 C$_{60}$, a spontaneously formed dome structure.

No internal representation of a completed comb need be present in the bee's mind. The same rules – simultaneously present in each of a hive full of identical cloned sisters – along with the structural properties of beeswax, produce the comb as an emergent complex structure. The key here is the interaction between behavioral rules and an immediate environment that is changed as the result of the behaviour. The environment, the moulded wax, records the results of past behaviour and conditions future behaviour. But for rules to be converted into behaviours by the bees, the bees must have internal 'states of mind', and be able to change their state of mind in response to what their senses are telling them. A bee that is busy laying down wax is in a different state of mind from one foraging for pollen and their behavioral repertoire differs as a result.

As we have argued above, what an architect does is not so different. Architects produce drawings, not buildings or hives, but producing a drawing is an interactive process in which the architect's internal state of mind, his knowledge of the rules and stylistic conventions of the epoch, produces behaviour that modifies the immediate environment – the paper. The change to the paper creates a new environment, modifying his state of mind and calling into action other learned rules and skills. The drawing is an emergent property of the process, not something that pre-existed as a complete internal representation before the architect put pencil to paper.

1.3   The demonic challenge

Purposeful labour depends upon the ability to form and follow goals. A goal is a representation of a state of affairs that does not exist plus a motivation to achieve it. Although bees do not have the goal-processing capabilities of the human mind, they nonetheless follow simple goals. Goal processing – from simple, reactive programs hard-wired in the neural circuitry of insects, to the much more adaptive and sophisticated rational planning capabilities of humans – is the mechanism that distinguishes the constructive activity of humans and bees from the blind efforts of Watt's engines. An engine transforms energy in one form to another, but it does not act to achieve states of affairs, unlike bees that build or humans that labour.

There is an intinguing 'hidden' connection between purposeful labour and work in the engineering sense. Any purposeful activity overcomes physical resistance and involves *work*, measured in watts, for which we must be fueled by calories in our food. The hidden connection comes from the realization that, at least in principle, purposeful labour could itself be a source of fuel.

Recall that Watt's key invention was the separate condenser for steam engines, which saved fuel by preventing wasteful condensation of steam within the cylinder of the engine. In the years after Watt's invention, it came to be realized that the thermal efficiency of steam engines could be improved by maximizing the pressure drop between the boiler and the condenser. A series of inventions followed to take advantage of this principle: Trevithick's high pressure engine, the double and then the triple expansion engine. These had the effect of increasing the amount of effective work that could be extracted from a given amount of heat. But successive gains in efficiency proved harder to come by. The amount of work obtained per calorie of heat could be increased, but not without limit.

It was understood that work could be converted into heat, for instance through friction, and heat could be converted back into work, for instance by a steam engine. But if you convert work into heat, and heat back into work, you always end up with less work than you put in. In converting work into heat, the number of calories of heat obtained per kilowatt hour of work is constant – conversion of work into heat can be done with 100 per cent efficiency. The reverse is not true. Heat can never be fully converted into useful work.[7] The practical imperative of improving steam engines gave rise to the theoretical study of the laws governing heat, the laws of thermodynamics.

One of the first formulations of the second law of thermodynamics was that heat will never spontaneously flow from somewhere cold to somewhere hot.[8] This implied that, for instance, there was no chance of transferring the heat wasted in the condenser of a steam engine back to the boiler where it would boil more water. Thermodynamics ruled out perpetual motion machines.

---

[7] Carnot was able to show that the efficiency of heat engines depended on the temperature difference between heat source, for example the boiler, and the heat sink, for example a steam engine's condenser.

[8] This formulation was due to Clausius in 1850; see Porter (1946: 8–9).

But James Clerk Maxwell, one of the early researchers in thermodynamics, came up with an intriguing paradox.

> One of the best established facts of thermodynamics is that it is impossible in a system enclosed in an envelope which permits neither change of volume nor passage of heat, and in which temperature and pressure are everywhere the same, to produce any inequality of temperature or of pressure without the expenditure of work. This is the second law of thermodynamics, and it is undoubtedly true as long as we can deal with bodies only in mass, and have no power of perceiving or handling the separate molecules of which they are made up. But if we can conceive of a being whose faculties are so sharpened that he can follow every molecule in its course, such a being would be able to do that which is presently impossible to us. For we have seen that the molecules in a vessel full of air at a uniform temperature are moving with velocities by no means uniform, though the mean velocity of any great number of them, arbitrarily selected, is almost exactly uniform. Now let us suppose that such a vessel is divided into two portions, A and B, by a division in which there is a small hole, and that a being, who can see individual molecules, opens and closes this hole, so as to allow only the swifter molecules to pass from A to B, and only the slower ones to pass from B to A. He will thus, without the expenditure of work, raise the temperature of B and lower that of A, in contradiction to the second law of thermodynamics.
>
> (Maxwell, 1875: 328–9)

The configuration of the thought experiment is shown in Figure 1.6. As the experiment runs the gas on one side heats up while that on the other side cools down. The end result is a preponderance of slow molecules in cavity A and fast ones in cavity B. Since heat is nothing more than molecular motion, this means that A has cooled down while B has warmed up. No net heat has been added, it has just redistributed itself into a form that becomes useful to us. Since B is hotter than A, the temperature differential can be used to power a machine. We could connect B to a boiler and A to a condenser and obtain mechanical effort. An exercise of purposeful labour by the demon outwits the laws of thermodynamics. It seems that the second law of thermodynamics expresses the coarseness of our senses rather than the intractability of nature.

1.4   Entropy

One perspective on the devilment worked by Maxwell's demon[9] is that it has *reduced the entropy* of a closed system. The concept of entropy was first developed by Clausius in 1865 (see Harrison, 1975) when he introduced the idea that in any machine like a steam engine a certain amount of the energy available in the fuel

---

[9] Norbert Wiener coined the term 'Maxwell demon' for the tiny 'being' envisaged in the thought experiment.

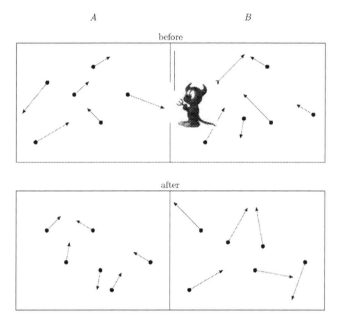

Figure 1.6 Gas initially in equilibrium. Demon opens door only for fast molecules to go from *A* to *B*, or slow ones from *B* to *A*. Result: slow molecules in *A*, fast in *B*. Thus *B* is hotter than *A*, and the difference can be used to power a machine.

was irretrievably lost. He called this unusable energy *entropy*. Clausius held that while energy itself could neither be created nor destroyed, the amount of wasted or unusable energy in the universe, or in any closed system, tended to increase. This tendency of wasted energy to rise in any physical process was the ultimate limit to the efficiency of our sources of power.

According to Clausius, adding heat to a system always increases its entropy (and subtracting heat always lowers entropy) but the magnitude of the change in entropy is inversely related to the initial temperature of the system. He expressed this as

$$\text{change in entropy} = \frac{\text{added heat}}{\text{temperature}} \tag{1.1}$$

Thus if a certain amount of heat is transferred from a hotter to a cooler region the increase in entropy in the cooler region will be greater than the reduction in entropy in the hotter, and overall entropy rises.[10] Conversely, if heat is transferred from a colder to a hotter region entropy falls. Clausius's concept of entropy as

[10] In mathematical terms: $\Delta S = \Delta Q / T$, where ΔS is the change in entropy of a system consequent upon the addition of a quantity of heat ΔQ at absolute temperature T.

an abstract quantity allowed him to give the second law of thermodynamics its canonical form: the entropy of any closed system tends to increase over time.[11]

Using (1.1) we can readily see that Maxwell's demon violates the second law of thermodynamics. Suppose the demon has been hard at work for some time, so that B is hotter than A, specifically B is at 300° Kelvin and A is at 280° Kelvin. He then transfers 1 joule of heat from A to B. In doing so he reduces the entropy of A by $1/_{280}$ joules per degree and increases the entropy of B by $1/_{300}$ joules per degree giving rise to a *change in entropy* of $\frac{1}{300} - \frac{1}{280} = -\frac{1}{4200}$. This is a net reduction in entropy, contrary to the second law.

Clausius's formulation of entropy did not depend in any way upon the atomic theory of matter. Maxwell's proposed counter-example to the second law was explicitly based on atomism. With Ludwig Boltzmann, entropy is placed on an explicitly atomistic foundation in terms of the distribution of molecules. Boltzmann said that the entropy of a system was higher when the distribution of molecules was more even. But this 'even' distribution had to be defined not just in terms of the position of the molecules, but also in terms of their movement. Taking movement into account complicates things so let us first consider the question just in terms of the positions of molecules.

Boltzmann's formula (see Digression 1.2) relates the entropy of a gas, for instance steam in a piston, to the evenness of its atomic distribution in position and movement: the less even the distribution the lower the entropy. This evenness is measured by dividing the gas up into little cells and counting how many molecules there are in each cell. If each cell of 1 cc of gas contains about the same number of molecules – that is, if the distribution of molecules is very even – then the entropy will be high. If the distribution is uneven the entropy will be low.

Suppose we have a cylinder with a moveable piston in the middle as shown in Figure 1.7. On the left of the piston we have steam at normal atmospheric pressure, on the right we have a vacuum. This is obviously a very uneven distribution on molecules, and in the normal course of events the piston will be pushed to the right performing work. This was just what Watt's 'atmospheric' engine did. As it performs work, the entropy of the system will increase. Boltzmann had to come up with a mathematical formula that would express the entropy in terms of the distribution of the atoms in the cylinder. If we apply the formula to the initial distribution shown in the top diagram of Figure 1.7 the formula must give a lower value for entropy than it gives for the distribution shown in the bottom diagram.

In this simple example we need consider just two cells in space, corresponding to the two halves of the cylinder, along with 8 atoms that can be in one cell or the other. Boltzmann's approach involved counting the number of atoms in each cell and multiplying it by the logarithm of the number of atoms in each cell. This gave him a measure of the unevenness of the distribution of the atoms. If you have

---

[11] In Clausius, the concept of entropy remains firmly linked to the sort of practical considerations, namely steam engine design, that first gave rise to thermodynamics. Later, as we shall see, it becomes generalized.

Digression 1.2   Boltzmann's equation for Entropy

Boltzmann defined entropy in terms of a summation (or integral) over molecular *phase space*. The concept of phase space is a generalization of our normal concept of three-dimensional space to incorporate the notion of motion as well as position. In a three-dimensional coordinate system the position of each molecule can be described by three numbers, measurements along three axes at right angles to one another. We usually label these numbers x, y, z to denote measurements in the horizontal, vertical and depth directions. However, each molecule is simultaneously in motion. Its motion can likewise be broken into components of horizontal, vertical and depth-wise motion which we write as m_x, m_y, m_z, representing motion to the left, up and back respectively. This means that a set of six coordinates can fully describe both the position and motion of a particle. Boltzmann's equation is then

$$S = -k \int f(v) \log f(v) dv$$

where v denotes volume in six-dimensional phase space, $f(v)$ is a function that counts the number of molecules present in that volume, and k is a constant, now known as Boltzmann's constant. By 'volume in phase space' we mean a range of possible values of the 6 coordinates. For example, a volume 1 mm cubed on the spatial axes and 1 mm per second on the motion axes. The function $f(v)$ would then specify how many molecules there were in that cubic millimeter with a range of velocities within 1 mm per second in each direction. The minus sign in Boltzmann's formula is needed to make entropy increase with the evenness of the distribution, consistent with Clausius's earlier formulation.

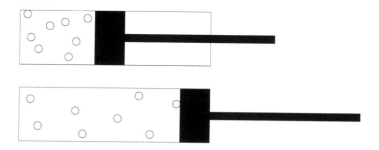

Figure 1.7 If there is a vacuum on the right and gas on the left the piston will move to the right, increasing the entropy of the system.

Table 1.1 Boltzmann's measure of unevenness. See how the unevenness score is higher when all of the atoms are in one cell. To
simplify the calculations we have used logarithms to the base 2
here. Recall that $l = \log_2(n)$ is the number l such that $n = 2^l$, so
$\log_2(8) = 3$ since $8 = 2^3$

Atoms in cells L, R	$L \log_2 L + R \log_2 R$	'Unevenness'
8, 0	$8 \times 3 + 0 = 24$	24
4, 4	$4 \times 2 + 4 \times 2 = 16$	16

not used logarithms since leaving school, it may not be obvious that this works,
so to convince you we have provided a worked example in Table 1.1.

The table shows how the Boltzmann measure of unevenness depends on the
location of the atoms, highest when all 8 are in one cell, and lowest when they
are evenly divided between the cells. Boltzmann then went on to conclude that
since the entropy of a gas was proportional to its evenness it must be proportional
to the negative of its unevenness:

$$\text{Entropy} = -k \times \text{unevenness} \qquad (1.2)$$

The constant of proportionality, k, relating unevenness to entropy is now called
Boltzmann's constant. For a more detailed explanation see Digression 1.2.

Boltzmann also showed that it is possible to reformulate the idea of entropy
using the concept of the *thermodynamic weight* of a state:

$$\text{Entropy} = k \log(\text{thermodynamic weight}) \qquad (1.3)$$

The thermodynamic weight is the number of physically distinct microscopic
states of the system consistent with a given macroscopic state, described by
temperature, pressure and volume. This concept is the key to understanding the
second law. Recall that the entropy of closed systems tends to increase, that is they
move into macro-states of progressively higher thermodynamic weight until they
reach equilibrium. States with higher weight are *more probable*. So the second law
of thermodynamics basically says that systems evolve into their most probable
state.

A simple analogy may be helpful here. Suppose a 'fair' coin is flipped ten
times. What is the most likely ratio of heads to tails in the sequence of flips? The
obvious answer, 5/5, is correct. Now, what is the most likely specific sequence of
heads and tails?

Trick question! There are $2^{10} = 1024$ such sequences and they are all equally
likely. The sequence featuring 10 heads has probability $\frac{1}{1024}$; so does the sequence
with 5 heads followed by 5 tails; so does the sequence of strictly alternating heads
and tails, and so on. The reason why a 5/5 ratio of heads to tails is most likely

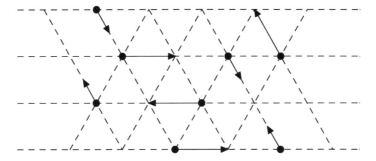

Figure 1.8 The molecules in a lattice gas move along the lines of a triangular grid with fixed velocities.

is that there are more specific sequences corresponding to this ratio that there are sequences corresponding to 10/0, or 7/3, or any other ratio. It's easy to see there is only one sequence corresponding to all heads, and one corresponding to all tails. To count the sequences that give a 5/5 ratio, imagine placing the 5 heads into 10 slots. Head number 1 can go into any of the ten slots; head number 2 can go into any of the remaining 9 slots, and so on, giving $10 \times 9 \times 8 \times 7 \times 6$ possibilities. But this is an over-statement, because we have treated each head as if it were distinct and identifiable. To get the right answer we have to divide by the number of ways 5 items can be assigned to 5 slots, namely $5 \times 4 \times 3 \times 2 \times 1$. This gives 252 possibilities. Thus the 'macro' result, equal numbers of heads and tails, corresponds to 252 out of the 1024 equally likely specific sequences, and has probability $\frac{252}{1024}$. By the same reasoning we can figure that a 6/4 ratio corresponds to 210 possible sequences, a lower 'weight' than the 5/5 ratio.

The number of possible states of a real gas in six-dimensional phase space is hard to visualize, so to explicate the matter further we'll examine a simpler system, namely a two-dimensional *lattice gas* (Frisch *et al.*, 1986). The 'molecules' in such a stylized gas move with constant speed, one step along the lattice per unit time (see Figure 1.8). Where the lines of the lattice meet, molecules can collide according to the rules of Newtonian dynamics, so that matter, energy and momentum are conserved in each collision. The different ways in which collisions occur can be summarized by two simple rules:

(1) If a molecule arrives at an intersection and no molecule is arriving on the diagonally opposite path, then the molecule continues unimpeded.
(2) If two molecules collide head on they bounce off in opposite directions, as shown in Figure 1.9.

Lattice gases are a drastic simplification of real gases, but they are useful tools in analysing real situations. The simple rules governing the behaviour of lattice gases make them ideal models for simulation in computer software or special purpose hardware Shaw *et al.* (1996).

T_0 T_1

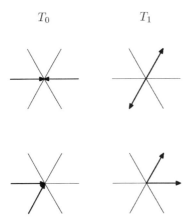

Figure 1.9 Collisions in a lattice gas: 'Molecules' colliding head on bounce off at 60°
angles (above). In other cases the collision is indistinguishable from a miss
(below). In all cases Newtonian momentum and energy are conserved.

Since the velocity of the molecules in a lattice gas is fixed, the temperature of
the gas can't change (this would involve a rise or fall in the molecules' speed). So
Maxwell's original example of a being with precise senses, able to sort molecules
by speed, is inappropriate. But we can invent another demon to guard the trapdoor.
Instead of letting only fast molecules through from A to B, this being will keep
the door open unless a molecule approaches it from side B. Thus molecules
approaching from side A are able to pass into B, but those in B are trapped. The
net effect is to raise the pressure on side B relative to A while leaving temperature
unchanged.

A lattice gas has only a finite number of lattice links on which molecules can
be found, and since the molecules move with a constant velocity, Boltzmann's
formula (1.3) simplifies to:

$$\text{Entropy} = -k \times n \times \text{the sum for all } i \text{ of } p_i \times \log(p_i) \qquad (1.4)$$

where p_i is the probability of the node being in state i and n is the number
of nodes.[12] The weighted summation over the possible states has the effect of
giving us the mean value of $\log p$. Suppose we have a pair of chambers, A and B,
each of which initially has n nodes, and each containing $3n$ randomly distributed
molecules. Then there will be a 50 per cent chance of finding a molecule on each
of the six incoming paths to a node. We have $6n$ incoming paths to our nodes, and
each of these has two equally likely states: a particle is or is not arriving at each
instant. Each incoming path contributes $k \log 2 = 0.693k$. The total entropy of the
chamber is then six time this or:

---

[12] Or in the usual mathematical notation, $S = -kn \sum_i p_i \log p_i$.

Entropy of *A* in equilibrium $= 4.158kn$.

Now suppose that our demon has been operating for some time, letting *n* particles pass from *A* to *B*, so that we now have 2*n* particles in *A* and 4*n* in *B*. In *A*, the probability of a molecule coming down any one of the paths is now only $\frac{1}{3}$. We can calculate the current entropy contribution of each incoming path as follows:

Number of particles	Probability, p_i	Log p_i	Entropy, $-kp_i \log p_i$
0	$\frac{2}{3}$	-0.405	$0.270\,k$
1	$\frac{1}{3}$	-1.098	$0.366\,k$
total			$0.636\,k$

The entropy of *A* after *n* particles have been transferred by the demon is $3.816kn$ which is less than before he got to work. By symmetry of complementary probabilities the entropy of chamber *B* will be the same,[13] thus the whole closed system has undergone a reduction in entropy.

This establishes that when an initially dispersed population of particles – the gas molecules in our case – is concentrated, entropy falls.[14] This is because there are a greater number of possible microstates compatible with dispersion than with concentration, and entropy is just the log of the number of microstates.

Consider in this light the work of the bees building their hive. There are two aspects to the work:

(1) The bees first have to gather wax and nectar from flowers dispersed over a wide area and bring it to the hive.
(2) They must then form the wax into cells and place the concentrated nectar in these as honey.

Both processes are entropy-reducing with respect to the wax and the sugar. The number of possible configurations that can be taken on by wax within the few litres volume of a hive is enormously less than the number of possible configurations of the same wax, dispersed among plants growing over tens of thousands of square meters of ground. Similarly the chance that the wax, if randomly thrown together within the hive, should assume the beautifully regular structure of a comb, is vanishingly small. That the wax should be in the hive in the first place, is, in the absence of bees, highly improbable; that it should be in the form of regular hexagons even more so.

---

[13] This will not generally be the case; we have chosen the particle densities so as to ensure this.
[14] This is true on the assumption that the potential – gravitational or electrostatic – of the particles is unchanged by the process of concentration, as in our example.

The second law of thermodynamics specifies that the total entropy in a closed system tends to increase, but the bees and their wax are not a closed system. The bees consume chemical energy in food to move the wax. If we include the entropy increase due to food consumed, the second law is preserved.

1.4.1　Men and horses

Let us return to the question we asked in section 1.1: Why did the introduction of the steam engine, which made redundant the equine workers of the pre-industrial age, not also replace the human workers? We can make a rough analogy between the work done by horses in past human economies and the work done by the bees in transporting wax and nectar from flower to hive. This is in the main sheer effort, work in Watt's sense. Horses bringing bricks to a building site or bees transporting wax are doing similar tasks. What remains – the construction of the hive after the work of transportation is done or the building of the house once the bricks are delivered – is something no horse can do. Construction involves a complex program of actions deploying grasping organs, hands, mandibles, beaks, etc., in which the sequence of operations is conditioned by the development of the product being made. Human construction differs from that of a bee or a bird in:

(1)　the way in which the program of action comes into being;
(2)　the way in which it is transmitted between individuals of the species; and
(3)　the form in which it is materialized.

Among the social insects the programs of action largely come into being through the evolutionary process of natural selection. They are transmitted between parents and their offspring, genetically encoded in DNA, and they are materialized in the form of relatively fixed interactions between components of the nervous system and general physiology. In humans, the programs of action are themselves products that can have a representation external to the organism, in speech or some form of notation. Speech and notation act both as a means of transmission between individuals, and as a possible form of materialization of work-programs while the work is being carried out – as for example, when one cooks from a recipe or follows a knitting pattern. The ability to make and distribute new work programs distinguishes human labour from that of bees and is the key to cultural evolution.

But even the work of transport requires a program of action, requires guidance if it is to reduce entropy. Transport is not diffusion. It moves concentrated masses of material between particular locations, it does not spread them about at random. Without guidance there is no entropy reduction. A horse, blessed with eyes and a brain as well as big muscles, will partially steer itself, or at least will do better than a bicycle or car in this respect. But teams still needed teamsters, if only to read signposts.

The steam railway locomotive revolutionized land transport in the nineteenth century, quickly replacing horse traction for long overland journeys. Guidance by steel track made steam power the great concentrator, bringing grain across prairies to the metropolis. Railway networks are action programs frozen in steel, their degrees of freedom discrete and finite, encoded in points. Points settings, signaled by telegraph, coordinate the orderly movement of millions of tons according to precise published timetables. Human work did not all lend itself so readily to mechanization.

2 Problematizing information

We have suggested that doing purposeful productive labour typically reduces entropy. Such entropy-reducing work requires information in two forms, an action plan or capacity for behaviour, and information coming in from the senses to monitor the implementation of the action plan. Productive labour also involves work in Watt's sense of overcoming physical resistance. As such it consumes energy and produces an entropy increase in the environment that more than compensates for the entropy reduction effected in the object of labour. We have also seen how Maxwell postulated that it should be possible to reduce the entropy of a gas if there existed a being small enough to sort molecules. In this case the being would be using information from its senses, and in its action plan, to produce an entropy reduction in the gas with no corresponding increase elsewhere.

Up to now we have not rigorously defined what we mean by information. Once this is done, we shall see the deeply hidden flaw in Maxwell's argument.

2.1 The Shannon–Weaver concept of information

> My greatest concern was what to call it. I thought of calling it 'information', but the word was overly used, so I decided to call it 'uncertainty'. When I discussed it with John von Neumann, he had a better idea. Von Neumann told me, 'You should call it entropy, for two reasons. In the first place your uncertainty function has been used in statistical mechanics under that name, so it already has a name. In the second place, and more important, nobody knows what entropy really is, so in a debate you will always have the advantage.'
> (Claude Shannon, quoted in *Scientific American*, 1971)

The philosopher Bachelard (1970) argues that the formation of a science is characterized by what he calls an 'epistemological break', which demarcates the language and ideas of the science from the pre-scientific discourses that may appear to deal with the same subject matter. May appear to deal with the same subject, but did not really do so. For one of the characteristics of an epistemological break is a change in the *problematic*, the set of questions to which the science provides answers. With the establishment of a science the conceptual terrain shifts both in terms of the answers given and, more importantly, in terms of the questions that researchers regard as valid and relevant.

The epistemological break that established information theory as a science occurred in the middle of the last century and is closely associated with the name of Claude Shannon. We saw how Watt, seeking to improve the efficiency of steam pumps, contributed not only to an industrial revolution, but also to a scientific revolution when he asked questions about the relationship between work and heat. From this problematic were born both a convenient source of power and our understanding of the laws of thermodynamics. Shannon's revolution also came from asking new questions, and asking them in a very practical engineering context. Shannon was a telephone engineer working for Bell Laboratories and he was concerned with determining the capacity of a telephone or telegraph line to transmit information. Watt formalized the concepts of power and work in an attempt to measure the efficiency of engines. Shannon (1948) formalized the concept of information through trying to measure the efficiency of communications equipment. Practice and its problems lead to some of the most interesting truths.

To measure the transmission of information over a telephone line, some definite unit of measurement is needed, otherwise the capacity of lines of different quality cannot be meaningfully compared. According to Shannon the information content of a message is a function of how surprised we are by it. The less probable a message the more information it contains. Suppose that each morning the radio news told us 'We are glad to announce that the Prime Minister is fit and well.' We would soon get fed up. Who would call this news? It conveys almost no information. 'Reports are just reaching us of the assassination of the Prime Minister.' That is news. That is information. That is surprising.

A daily bulletin telling us whether or not the Prime Minister was alive would usually tell us nothing, then on one day only would give us some useful information. Leaving aside the circumstances of his death, if an announcement were to be made each morning, there would two possible messages

0 'The P.M. lives'
1 'The P.M. is dead'

If such messages were being sent over the sort of telegraph system that Shannon was concerned with, one could encode them as the presence or absence of a short electrical pulse, as a binary digit or 'bit' in the widely understood sense of the word. Shannon defines a bit more formally as the amount of information required for the receiver of the message to decide between two equally probable outcomes. For example, a sequence of tosses of a fair coin can be encoded in 1 bit per toss, such that heads are 1 and tails 0.

What Shannon says is that if we are sending a stream of 0 or 1 messages affirming or denying some proposition, then unless the truth and falsity of the proposition are equally likely these 0s and 1s contain less than one bit of information each. In that case there will be a more economical way of sending the messages. The trick is not to send a message of equal length regardless of its

Table 2.1 A possible code for transmitting messages that are true one-third of the time

Binary Code	Length	Meaning	Probability
0	1	False, False	$\frac{4}{9}$
10	2	False, True	$\frac{2}{9}$
110	3	True, False	$\frac{2}{9}$
111	3	True, True	$\frac{1}{9}$

content, but to devise a system where the more probable message-content gets a shorter code.

For example, suppose the messages are the answer to a question which we know a priori will be true one time in every three messages. Since the two possibilities are not equally likely Shannon says there will be a more efficient way of encoding the stream of messages than simply sending a 0 if the answer is false and a 1 if the answer is true. Consider the code shown in Table 2.1. Instead of sending each message individually we package the messages into pairs, and use between one and three binary digits to encode the 4 possible pairs of messages. Note that the shortest code goes to the most probable message, namely the sequence of two 'False' answers with probability $\frac{2}{3} \times \frac{2}{3} = \frac{4}{9}$. The codes are set up in such a way that they can be uniquely decoded at the receiving end. For instance, suppose the sequence '110100' is received: checking the Table, we can see that this can only be parsed as 110, 10, 0, or True, False, False, True, False, False.

To find the mean number of digits required to encode two messages we multiply the length of the codes for the message-pairs by their respective probabilities:

$$\frac{4}{9} + 2 \times \frac{2}{9} + 3 \times \frac{2}{9} + 3 \times \frac{1}{9} = 1\frac{8}{9} \approx 1.889 \tag{2.1}$$

which is less than two digits.

Shannon came up with a formula which gives the shortest possible encoding for a stream of distinct messages, given the probabilities of their individual occurrences.

$$H = -\sum_{i=1}^{n} p_i \log_2 p_i \tag{2.2}$$

The mean information content of an ensemble of messages is obtained by weighting the log of the probability of each message by the probability of that message. He showed that no encoding of messages in 1s and 0s could be shorter than this.

The formula gave him an irreducible minimum of the number of bits needed to transmit a message stream: this minimum was, he said, the real information content of the stream. Using Shannon's formula we can calculate the information content of the data stream encoded in the example above.

$$-\frac{4}{9} \times \log_2 \frac{4}{9} - \frac{2}{9} \times \log_2 \frac{2}{9} - \frac{2}{9} \times \log_2 \frac{2}{9} - \frac{1}{9} \times \log_2 \frac{1}{9} \approx 1.837 \qquad (2.3)$$

Since our code used $1\frac{8}{9} \approx 1.889$ bits for each pair of messages, we see that in principle a better code may exist.

In his 1948 article Shannon notes:

> Quantities of the form $H = -\sum_{i=1}^{n} p_i \log p_i$ play a central role in information theory as measures of information, choice and uncertainty. The form of H will be recognized as that of entropy as defined in certain formulations of statistical mechanics where p_i is the probability of a system being in cell i of its phase space. H is then, for example the H in Boltzmann's famous H theorem. We shall call $H = -\sum p_i \log p_i$ the entropy of the set of probabilities $p_1, \ldots, p_n$.

Shannon thus discovers that his measure of information is the same as Boltzmann's measure of entropy and decides that entropy and information are the same thing. Armed with this realization we can go back to the problem left to us by Maxwell. Could a sufficiently tiny entity violate the laws of thermodynamics by systematically sorting molecules?

Physicists have concluded that it is not possible. Szilard (1964), for example, pointed out that to decide which molecules to let through, the demon must measure their speed. He showed that these measurements (which would entail bouncing photons off the molecules) would use up more energy than was gained. Maxwell's demon, to vary the theological metaphor, was a *deus ex machina* (like Newton's God), able to know by immaterial means; Szilard's advance was to emphasize that knowledge or information is physical and can only come about by physical means. Brillouin (1951) extended Szilard's analysis by pointing out that at a uniform temperature, black body radiation in the cavity would be uniform in all directions, preventing the demon from seeing molecules unless he had an additional source of light (and hence energy input).

It is possible, however, to build an automaton that acts as a Maxwell demon for a lattice gas. As we said before such gases can be simulated in software, or in hardware (see Figure 2.1), with each gas cell represented by a rectangular area of silicon and the paths taken by the molecules represented by wires. In such a system the demon himself is an automaton, a logic circuit, as in Figure 2.2. A circuit like this really does work: it transfers virtual gas molecules from chamber A to chamber B. Why does this work in apparent conflict with the laws of thermodynamics?

The behaviour of the demon is summarized in Table 2.2. Notice that while there are 4 possible combinations of input conditions, there are only 3 combinations

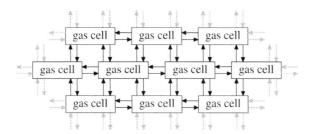

Figure 2.1 A lattice gas can be built in electronic hardware: each gas cell is represented by a rectangular area of silicon and the paths taken by the molecules are represented by wires.

of output conditions. This implies that we are moving from a system with a higher thermodynamic weight to one with a lower weight, which is what we would expect for an entropy-reducing machine. Just how much it reduces entropy depends on the probabilities of occurrence of incoming particles from each side.

Suppose that the system is in equilibrium and that the probability of occurrence of a particle on the incoming paths on each side is 50 per cent in each time interval. In that case each of the 4 possible input configurations in Table 2.2 is equiprobable and has an entropy of 2bits $= \log_2 4$. Applying Shannon's formula (2.2) to the output configurations we get

$$\frac{1}{4} \log_2 4 + \frac{1}{2} \log_2 2 + \frac{1}{4} \log_2 4 = \frac{1}{4} \times 2 + \frac{1}{2} \times 1 + \frac{1}{4} \times 2 = 1\frac{1}{2} \qquad (2.4)$$

an entropy reduction of half a bit per time step. The key to how this can happen lies in the nature of the components used, logic gates for the functions AND and OR.

Landauer (1961) pointed out that any irreversible logic gate must destroy encoded information and in the process must dissipate heat. An irreversible logic gate is one whose inputs can't be determined from an examination of their

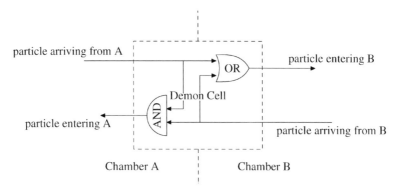

Figure 2.2 In a lattice gas, Maxwell's demon can be implemented with this logic circuit.

Table 2.2 The action plan of the demon

Input from		Output to		
A	B	A	B	Comment
No	No	No	No	No molecules involved
No	Yes	No	Yes	Door shut, molecule bounces back to B
Yes	No	No	Yes	Molecule goes from A to B
Yes	Yes	Yes	Yes	Molecules bounce off one another

outputs. Consider gates with two inputs and one output, such as the AND and OR gates whose truth functions are tabulated in Table 2.3. Roughly speaking they take two bits in and generate one bit out, thus destroying information within the system defined by the lines connecting the gates. Landauer argues that the lost information, i.e., the entropy reduction within the logic circuit, results in an increase in the entropy of the environment. Each time a logic circuit of this type operates, the lost internal entropy shows up as waste heat. By applying Shannon's formula (2.2) to the output of the AND gate we get the following:

Output	p_i	$-p_i \log_2 p_i$
false	$\dfrac{3}{4}$	≈ 0.311
true	$\dfrac{1}{4}$	0.5
	1	0.811

The output has an entropy of *less* than one bit. Given that 2 bits of information went into the gate, a total of 1.189 bits are lost in processing the inputs. Since the probability structure of OR gates is the same, a similar information loss occurs going through these.

2.1.1 Information engines as heat engines

Boltzmann's constant (see equation 1.2) has the dimension joules per log-state degree Kelvin. Landauer saw that one can use this constant to convert

Table 2.3 Tabulation of the functions x AND y, x OR y

x	y	x AND y	x OR y
false	false	false	false
false	true	false	true
true	false	false	true
true	true	true	true

entropy in Shannon's form, measured in log-states, to energy. The equation he established is

$$e = \ln(2)ktb \tag{2.5}$$

where e represents the energy-equivalent, t is temperature in degrees Kelvin, b is the number of bits, and k is Boltzmann's constant, which has a value of about 1.38×10^{-23} joules per degree Kelvin. The remaining term in the conversion is the natural log (ln) of 2, to get us from the natural logarithms used by Boltzmann to the base-2 logarithms used in Shannon's information theory.

Using Landauer's equation we can calculate the heat energy, e_{AND}, generated by a single operation of an AND gate, in which 1.189 bits are lost:

$$e_{AND} = 1.189\ln(2)kt$$

At room temperature, or roughly 300° Kelvin, this is 3.4×10^{-21} joules each time the gate switches. This is a very, very small quantity of energy which is at present mainly of theoretical interest. What it represents is the theoretical minimal energy cost of operating a two-input irreversible logic gate.

Now look again at the demon cell in Figure 2.2, which has a pair of input logic gates. The process of deciding whether to open or close the trapdoor must consume certain minimum Landauer-energy. The energy consumed by the logical decision to open or close the barrier makes the demon ineffective as a power source.

Watt started out investigating how to convert heat into work efficiently; he was concerned with minimizing the heat wasted from his engines. Since Landauer we have known that information processing, too, must dissipate heat, and that information processing engines are ultimately constrained by the same laws of thermodynamics as steam engines. We can calculate the thermodynamic efficiency of an information processing machine just as we calculate the efficiency of a steam engine. If a processor chip of the year 2000 had roughly 6 million gates and was clocked at 600Mhz, its dissipation of Landauer energy would then be $(600 \times 10^6) \times (6 \times 10^6) \times (3.4 \times 10^{-21}) = 16.3\mu w$, or 16 millionths of a watt. This is insignificant relative to the electrical power consumption of the chip, which would be of the order of 20 watts. It implies a thermodynamic efficiency of only around 0.0001 per cent. As a point of comparison, steam engines prior to Watt had an efficiency of about 0.5 per cent. The steam turbines in modern power stations convert around 40 per cent of the heat used into useful work. Two centuries of development raised the efficiency of steam power by a factor of about 100.

In thermodynamic terms a Pentium processor looks pretty poor compared to an 18th century steam engine: the steam engine was 500 times more efficient! But if compare a Pentium with the Manchester Mk1, the first electronic stored program computer,[1] we get a different perspective. The Pentium has at least a thousand times as many logic gates, has a switching speed a thousand times greater, and uses about one hundredth as much electrical power, as the venerable valve-based

---

[1]   See Lavington (1978) and Lavington (1980).

Table 2.4 Projected Landauer heat dissipation in 21st century computers operating at 300° Kelvin.

Year	Gates	Clockspeed	Landauer watts
2000	8×10^6	600 Mhz	16.3 μw
2005	3.4×10^7	1.9 Ghz	230 μw
2010	1.5×10^8	6.4 Ghz	3.24 mw
2015	6.4×10^8	21 Ghz	45.7 mw
2020	2.8×10^9	68 Ghz	643 mw
2025	1.2×10^{10}	224 Ghz	9.06 w
2030	5.1×10^{10}	733 Ghz	128 w
2035	2.2×10^{11}	2.4 Thz	1.80 Kw
2040	9.5×10^{11}	7.8 Thz	25.4 Kw

Mk1. In terms of thermal efficiency, this represents an improvement factor of 100,000,000 in fifty years. If improvements in heat engine design from Watt to Parsons powered the first two industrial revolutions, the third has benefited from an exponential growth in efficiency that was sixteen times as rapid.[2]

We know from Carnot's theory that there is little further room for improvement in heat engines. Most of the feasible gains in their efficiency came easily to pioneers like Watt and Trevithick. We're now left with marginal improvements, such as the ceramic rotor blades that allow turbine operating temperatures to creep up. In the case of computers too, efficiency gains will eventually become harder to attain. There is still, to quote Feynman, 'plenty of room at the bottom'. That is, there is mileage yet in miniaturization. We have room for about a million-fold improvement before computers get to where turbines now are. However, as we take into account the growing speed and complexity of computers, the thermodynamic constraint on data processing will come to be significant. On the one hand, if the efficiency of switching devices continues to grow at its current rate, they will be at close to 100 per cent in about 30 years. On the other hand, as computers get smaller and faster the job of getting rid of the Landauer-energy, thrown out as waste heat, will get harder. In the 27 years following the invention of the microprocessor the number of gates per chip rose by a factor of some 3000. Processor speeds increased about 600-fold over the same period. Table 2.4 projects this rate of growth into the next century.

From being insignificant now, Landauer heat dissipation becomes prohibitive in about 30 years. A microprocessor putting out several kilowatts, as much as several electric heaters, is not a practical proposition. There is a time limit on the current exponential growth in computing power.

That is not to say that computer technology will stagnate in 40 years. Landauer's equation (2.5) has a free variable in *temperature*. If the computer is super-cooled, its heat dissipation falls. But once we're in that game the rate of

---

[2] Heat engine efficiency improved about ten-fold per century. Information engines have been improving at a factor of about 10^{16} per century.

improvement in computer performance comes to be limited by improvements in refrigeration technology, and these are unlikely to be so dramatic.

2.2   Entropy reductions in action programs

Maxwell's demon cannot exist for real gases, but it can for lattice gases. If the demon really existed, he would reduce the laws of thermodynamics to the status of an anthropocentric projection onto reality. Lattice-gas devils, on the other hand, are not a threat to physics. They reduce the entropy of the gas, but only because they use logic gates with an external source of power. Nonetheless, their structure suggests something important. The demon reduces the entropy of the gas thanks to an action program which has four possible input states and only three possible output states.

We would suggest that this is not accidental: it would seem that *all production processes that produce local reductions in entropy are guided by an entropy-reducing action program.* Consider the bee once again, this time in its capacity as forager. In Maxwell's original proposal, the demon used its refined perception to extract energy from chaos. In reality a bee uses its eyes to enable it to extract energy from flowers. Were bees unable to see or smell flowers, their energy would be expended in aimless wandering followed by starvation. The bee uses information from its senses to achieve what, from its local viewpoint, is a reduction in entropy – the maintenance of homeostasis – albeit at a cost to the rest of the universe. To achieve this it requires a nervous system that performs entropy reduction on the input data coming into its visual receptors. At any given instant the bee's compound eyes are receiving stimuli from the environment. The number of possible different combinations of such stimuli is vastly greater than the number of instantaneous behavioural responses that it has while in flight – the modulation of the beat strength of a small number of thoracic muscles. In selecting one appropriate behavioural response out of a small repertoire, in response to a relatively large quantity of information arriving at its eyes, the bee's nervous system functions in the same sort of way as the AND gate in the demon-automaton of Figure 2.2. Having fewer possible outputs than inputs, it discards information and reduces entropy.

2.3   Alternative views of information

We have come across two approaches to the idea of entropy so far, deriving from classical thermodynamics and Shannon's communication theory respectively. From the 1960s onwards a third version has developed: that of computational complexity. Where classical concepts of entropy derived from mechanical engineering, and Shannon's concept from telecommunications engineering, the latest comes from computer science. The key concepts appear to have been independently developed by Chaitin (1999) in the US and Kolmogorov in Russia. Their presentation, while not contradicting what Shannon taught, gives new insights that are particularly helpful when we come to consider the role that information flows play in mass production industries.

2.3.1   The Chaitin–Kolmogorov concept of information

Chaitin's algorithmic information theory defines the information content of a number to be the length of the shortest computer program capable of generating it. This introduction of numbers is a slight shift of terrain. Shannon talked about the information content of *messages*. Whereas numbers as such are not messages, all coded messages are numbers. Consider an electronically transmitted message. It will typically be sent as a series of bits, ones and zeros, which can be considered as a binary number. An information theory defined in terms of numbers no longer needs the support of a priori probabilities. Whereas Shannon's theory depended upon the a priori probability of messages, Chaitin dispenses with this support.

As an example of the algorithmic approach consider the Mandelbrot set (Figure 2.3). This image is created by a very simple computer program, based on the iteration

$$z \leftarrow z^2 + c$$

where z and c are complex numbers (vectors with 2 elements). The Mandelbrot set became the emblem of Chaos Theory in the 1980s because it vividly illustrated the central idea of that theory, namely that a simple *nonlinear* generator can give

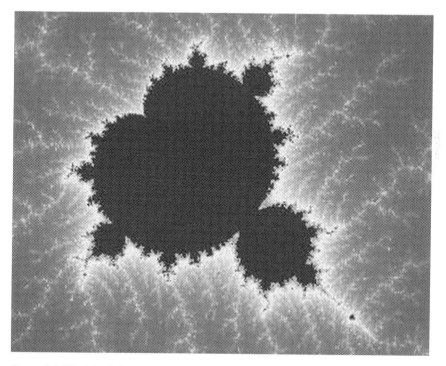

Figure 2.3 The Mandelbrot set, a complex image generated from a tiny amount of information.

rise to fantastically complicated behaviour. (The nonlinearity in the Mandelbrot generator lies in the squaring of z.)

Although the image file for the picture is large, about 6 million bits, a program to generate it can be written in a few thousand bits. If one wanted to send the picture to someone who had a computer, it would take far fewer bits to send the program than to send the picture itself. This only works if both sender and receiver have computers capable of understanding the same program. Chaitin's definition of information has the disadvantage of seeming to make it dependent upon particular brand of computer used. One could not assume that the length of a program to generate the picture would be the same on an Apple as on an IBM.

In principle one could chose any particular computer and fix on it as the standard of measure. Alternatively one could use an abstract computer, much as Watt used an abstract horse. Chaitin follows Watt, using a *gedankenapparat*, the Universal Turing Machine, as his canonical computer (see chapter 5 for more on this). Thus he defines the information content of a sequence S as the shortest Turing machine tape that would cause the machine to halt with the sequence S on its output tape.[3]

An unsettling result from information theory is that random sequences of digits contain more information than anything else. According to common sense, information is the very opposite of randomness. We feel that information should be associated with order, but Shannon's identification of information and entropy amounts to equating information with *dis*order. To illustrate this let's compare a long random number with π. We know from Shannon that 1 million tosses of a fair coin generates 1 million bits of information. On the other hand, from Chaitin we know that π to a precision of a million bits contains much less than 1 million bits, since the program to compute π can be encoded using much fewer bits. Thus π must contain less information than a random sequence of the same length.

But what do we mean by random? And how can we tell if a number is random? The answer now generally accepted was provided by Andrei Kolmogorov, who defined a random number as *a number for which there exists no formula shorter than itself*. By Chaitin's definition of information a random number is thus *incompressible*: a random number of n bits must contain n bits of real information.

A fully compressed data sequence is indistinguishable from a random sequence of 0s and 1s. This not only follows directly from Kolmogorov and Chaitin's results but also from Shannon, from whom we have the result that for each bit of the stream to have maximal information it must mimic the tossing of a fair coin (that is, be unpredictable, random).

We have a paradox: one million digits of π are more valuable and more useful than one million random digits. But they contain less information. The digits of

---

[3] There is, in principle, no algorithm for determining the shortest Turing Machine tape for an arbitrary sequence. $3 \div 7$ is a rule of arithmetic, an algorithm that generates the sequence 0.428571428571. So this sequence is presumably less random than 0.328571428771 (we changed two digits). But in practice we can never be sure.

π are more valuable because they are harder to come by. They are more useful because a host of other formulae use π. They contain less information because each and every digit of π was determined, before we started calculating it, by π's formula. Thus in a sense the entire expansion of π is redundant if we have its formula. Valuable objects are generally redundant. We thus have three concepts that we must distinguish with respect to sequences: their information content, their value, and their utility.

Concept	Meaning
Information	Length of program to compute the sequence.
Value	Cycles it takes to compute the sequence.
Utility	The uses to which the sequence can be put.

The *value* of a sequence is measured by how hard we must work to get it. π is valuable because it is so costly to calculate. We can measure the cost by the number of machine cycles a computer would have to go through to generate it.[4] As with information content, this definition is dependent upon what we take as our standard computer. A more advanced computer can perform a given calculation in fewer clock cycles than a more primitive one. For theoretical purposes any Universal computer will do. Information theorists typically use machine cycles of the Universal Turing Machine (UTM) for their standard of work. We will follow them in defining the information content of a sequence in terms of the length of the UTM program that generates it, and the value of a sequence in terms of the UTM cycles to compute it.

Now the UTM is an imaginary machine, a thought experiment, living in the platonic ideal world of the mathematician. Its toils are imaginary, consuming neither seconds nor ergs; its effort is measured in abstract cycles. But any physical computer existing in our material world runs in real time, and needs a power supply. Valuable numbers – tomorrow's temperature for example – whose computation requires large number of cycles on the Met Office super computers, take real time and energy to produce. The time depends on clock speed, and the energy depends on the computer's thermodynamic efficiency.[5] If we abstract from changes in computer technology, information value in UTM cycles is an indication of the thermodynamic cost of producing information. It measures how much the entropy of the rest of the universe must rise to produce the information.[6]

---

[4] We are identifying the value of a sequence with what Bennett (1988) calls its logical depth.

[5] The UTM plays, for computational complexity theory, the role of Marx's 'labour of average skill and intensity' in the economic theory of value. Improvements in computer technology are analogous to changes in the skill of the worker.

[6] This is what Norretranders (1998) calls *exformation*.

2.3.2   *Chaitin and Boltzmann*

Having traced the conceptual thread of entropy from Boltzmann through Shannon to Chaitin, it is worth taking stock and asking ourselves if Chaitin's definition of entropy still makes sense in terms of Boltzmann's definition. To do this we need to move from numbers to their physical representation. A material system can represent a range of numbers if it has sufficient well-defined states to encode the range. Will a physical system in a state whose number has, according to Chaitin, a low entropy, have a low entropy according to classical statistical mechanics?[7]

What we will give is not a proof, but at least a plausible argument that this will be true. As a *gedanken* experiment we will consider a picture of the Mandelbrot set rendered on digital paper. Digital paper is a proposed display medium made of thin films of white plastic. In the upper layer of the plastic there is a mass of small bubbles of oil, in the middle of each of which floats a tiny ball. One side of the ball is white and the other black. Embedded within the ball is a magnetized ferrite crystal with its North pole pointing towards the black end.[8] If the paper is embedded in an appropriate magnetic field all of the balls can be forced to rotate to have their white half uppermost, making the paper appear white. Applying a South magnetic pole to a spot on the paper will leave a black mark where the balls have rotated to expose their dark half. When it is passed through an appropriate magnetic printer, patterns can be drawn. A sheet of digital paper with a Mandelbrot set image on it nicely straddles the boundary between an industrial product and a number or information structure.

According to algorithmic information theory, the Mandelbrot set image represents a relatively low entropy state, since the length of the program to compute it contains fewer bits than the image. Does it also represent a low entropy state in statistical mechanics?

The second law of thermodynamics states that the entropy of a closed system is non-decreasing. So we would expect that a picture of the Mandelbrot state drawn on digital paper would tend to change into some other picture whose state would represent a higher entropy level. In fact there are good physical reasons why this will take place. If a local area is all white or all black, the magnetic poles are aligned as shown in the top of Figure 2.4. In this configuration the like poles tend to repel one another, and over time some of the poles will tend to flip to the configuration shown in the bottom half of the diagram.

The rate at which this occurs depends upon the temperature, the viscosity of the fluid in which the balls are suspended, and so on, but in the long run entropy will take hold. The image will gradually degrade to a higher entropy state, both in thermodynamic terms and in algorithmic terms. The program necessary to produce the degraded picture is bound to be longer than the program that produced

---

[7] We need this step if we are to apply Chaitin's theory to labour processes that produce real physical commodities. We need an epicurean not a platonist theory.

[8] We are giving a somewhat stylized account of digital paper for the purposes of this argument.

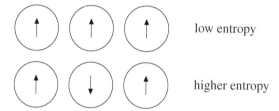

Figure 2.4 Configurations of parallel poles are unstable and tend to evolve towards the anti-parallel configuration.

the pristine one. Hence thermodynamic and algorithmic entropy measure the same scale.

The example we have given is stylized but the thermodynamic degradation of digital information is not hypothetical. Magnetic tape libraries have a finite life because of just this sort of flipping of the magnetized domains on which the information is stored.

2.3.3 *Paradoxes of randomness and compressibility*

The idea that information content and randomness are equivalent is, at first sight, far from intuitive. But this is what information theory teaches us, so it is worth confronting some of the apparent paradoxes that arise from the information theoretic approach.

Kolmogorov identifies the randomness of a number with its incompressibility (via the 'no shorter formula' proposition). There seems to be a contradiction – or a tension, at least – between this conception of randomness as a property *of a number* and the 'ordinary' conception of randomness as a property of a *mechanism for generating numbers*. (As in the statisticians' talk of a 'random variable' as a variable whose values are determined by the outcome of a 'random experiment'.)

To expose the tension, consider a random number generator (RNG). Suppose it's a true quantum RNG, set to produce a series of uniformly distributed ten-digit numbers. The standard definition of randomness would be that (a) each possible ten-digit number is produced with equal probability, and (b) the drawings are independent, so that previous drawings give no hint as to what's coming next. Given point (a), if we leave our RNG running for long enough it's bound to produce numbers such as 1111111111 and 0123456789. But these don't appear to be 'random numbers' on the Kolmogorov definition since they have simple formulae ('a sequence of ten 1s', 'the integers 0 to 9 in sequence'). The paradox is then that the output of a random number generator (i.e. a device that generates numbers at random) seems bound to output nonrandom numbers.

But this is not a valid objection to Kolmogorov. Yes, an RNG will produce some sub-sequences that in themselves conform to a simple formula, but how do we find them in the voluminous output of the device? We have to search for them. Strictly speaking, numbers such as 1111111111 are not produced by the random number generator itself, but rather by a further program that is a prefix to the RNG and that searches for such patterns in its output. The algorithmic information theoretic approach to this would be to add the information content of the RNG to the program which selects the 'nonrandom' sub-sequences.

To get at a second paradox we will report a little experiment. We have an ASCII file of the first eleven chapters of David Ricardo's *Principles of Political Economy and Taxation*: it's 262899 bytes. We ran the bzip2 compressor on it and the resulting file was 61193 bytes, a bit less than a quarter of the original size. Suppose for the sake of argument that bzip2 (an excellent open-source compression program, written by Julian Seward) is a perfect byte-stream compressor: in that case the 61193 bytes represent the incompressible content of the Ricardo chapters. They measure the true information content of the larger file. That seems fair enough, we're all familiar with the idea that written English contains a good deal of rdncy!

The second part of the experiment was to generate another file of 262899 bytes of printable ASCII characters (the same length as Ricardo), this time using a pseudo-random number generator, namely the rand() function in the GNU C library. Running bzip2 on the resulting file produced a compression to slightly over 80 per cent of the original size.

The first question is why we're able to get any compression at all on the 'random' ASCII file? Well, for comparability with Ricardo's text our random bytes were all printable characters. These are a subset of the possible byte values,[9] and so all the possible byte values do not occur with equal probability in our artificial file. Therefore the stream is in principle compressible.

The more interesting question concerns the information content of the files. We have already accepted the idea that the 61193 bytes of bzipped Ricardo represent the irreducible information content of the original Ricardo text. Then by the same token it seems the 218200 (or so) bytes of bzipped rubbish from the random number generator represent the true information content of the (pseudo-)random byte stream. The rubbish contains almost four times as much information as the Ricardo. This is what's hard to take.

The first point to be made here is that standard data compression programs use certain fixed algorithms to compress files. In the case of bzip2 the Burrows–Wheeler block-sorting algorithm is used (Burrows and Wheeler, 1994), along with Huffman coding (Huffman, 1952). Such algorithms do a good job in a wide range of cases, but they don't know how to obtain the maximum compression of the stream we're talking about here, which would be an encoding of the generator program.

OK, so the gibberish produced by rand() does not truly have an information content four times that of Ricardo's text, because it was in fact generated by a relatively short program. But suppose we arranged to have a similar text file produced by a true quantum RNG, and passed that to bzip2. Presumably, the

_____

[9] There are $256 = 2^8$ possible values for 8-bit bytes.

degree of compression would be similar to what we actually saw (that is, a little bit of compression would be available on account of the restriction to printable bytes). We can pose the question again on this assumption: Does 200 kilobytes of quantum gibberish really contain more information that 200 kilobytes of David Ricardo?

In the ordinary run of things we make the distinction between information as such and its utility, and in those terms it's clear that the Ricardo is of much greater utility than the gibberish. Even so, intuition rebels at the idea that the rubbish carries *any* information. We have a conception of 'useless information' alright, but it seems doubtful that a random byte stream satisfies the ordinary definition of useless information. In ordinary speech, information has to be *about* something; and it's useless if it's about something that is of no interest. If I never watch TV, the weekly guide to Cable TV programming may contain useless information: it's of no more interest to me than a random byte stream. Nonetheless, I recognize that the TV guide does contain (quite a lot of) information; it is certainly about something.

But the distinction that we're tempted to make here – useless information in the unwanted text versus no information at all in the random byte stream – just reflects our (naturally) human-centred perspective. If we're talking about a truly random byte stream, it contains a good deal of information 'about' the physical process that produced it (nuclear decay, for example).

The 'digital paper' example in section 2.3.2 above suggests a further angle on the issue. Let's go back to the ASCII Ricardo. Its incompressible length was (we said) 61193 bytes. Now suppose the hard drive is exposed to radiation that results in random bit-flipping, which changes some of the bytes in the Ricardo file. At some later point we try compressing the file again. We find that it won't compress as well as before. Its information content has increased due to the random mutation of bytes! Meanwhile, of course, its value as a representation of what Ricardo said is eroding. Can we make any sense of this? Yes. The degraded work does contain more information, since to reconstruct it one would need to know the trajectories of the cosmic rays which degraded the stored copy, as well the original text. We may not be interested in the paths of these cosmic rays, but it is additional information, provided to us courtesy of the Second Law. And in fact we sometimes *are* interested in the information inscribed by radiation damage, for example in archaeological dating.

Information exists even if it is not useful. Take the case of hieroglyphs. Prior to 1822 they were effectively meaningless to moderns. But once Young and Champollion worked out, with the help of the Rosetta stone,[10] that they represented a language, they became useful historical documents. Their information content was not created *ex nihilo* in 1822, but must have been there all along.

---

[10] The inscription on the Rosetta Stone is a decree of King Ptolemy V Epiphanes, dating from 196 BC. It is repeated in hieroglyphs, demotic and Greek. By using the Greek section as a 'key', Thomas Young and Jean-François Champollion worked out that hieroglyphs were not ideograms, as previously thought, but represented a language, the ancestor to Coptic.

In the end, whether or not information is useful to us is a matter of our selfish thermodynamic concerns. Does it enable us to change the world in a way that saves us work or produces us energy? This is an anthropospective projection. It is not a property of the information, but a property of the user of the information which is cast back onto the information itself. Information theory, in its epistemological break, had to divest itself of anthropospective views, just as astronomy and biology did with Galileo and Darwin.

3 Labour productivity

Those who possess rank in a manufacturing country, can scarcely be excused if they are entirely ignorant of principles, whose development has produced its greatness. The possessors of wealth can scarcely be indifferent to processes which, nearly or remotely have been the fertile source of their possessions. Those who enjoy leisure can scarcely find a more interesting and instructive pursuit than the examination of the workshops of their own country, which contain within them a rich mine of knowledge, too generally neglected by the wealthier classes.

(Babbage, 1832: Preface)

3.1 Raising production in general

In this chapter we examine the means by which labour productivity increases over time. The level of our analysis here is essentially technical. We are looking at productivity in physical terms rather than in value terms. We are not at this point interested in how many Euros' or dollars' worth of output each worker produces per hour. Instead we are looking at physical production – tons of steel, meters of rope, numbers of cars, and so on.

This concentration on physical productivity means that our focus must be one industry at a time. We cannot yet consider the economy as a whole since, without introducing prices or other means of valuation, we lack any scale by which we could measure the aggregate product. The total product of the economy comprises a heterogeneous mixture of goods, in technical terms a *vector* or list of numbers, such as

(x tons of steel, y cars, z barrels of oil, ...)

Vectors are a means of describing positions in multi-dimensional space. To get an unitary measure of change in production you need to render these specific quantities comparable, by mapping them onto a *scalar* quantity such as monetary value. For the moment we consider one product at a time, and the natural units of that product will provide us with our scale.

We are primarily interested in the flow of product per unit time – 17 million tons of steel per year, 15 meters of cloth per hour. We are also interested in product flow per unit time per worker since this is the dimension along which the wealth of society in general increases.[1]

There are three fundamental ways by which the flow through any production process can be increased, namely,

(1) accelerating the production cycle;
(2) eliminating wasted effort; and
(3) parallelizing production.

These basic methods apply whether the production process is human or animal, mechanical or biological, carried out by men, bees or robots.

3.1.1   Entropy analysis

Before going into the above-mentioned methods of increasing productivity, it will be useful first to extend our analysis of information and entropy to look at the changes in entropy that take place in during industrial production.

We have already considered the thought experiment of digital paper (section 2.3.2). We showed that if you wrote text on such paper, although this text represented information, it contained much less information than the paper could potentially hold. If we transfer what we have learned from this example to ordinary paper, and the process of producing a book, we see that the production process encompasses two opposite phases.

First, we have the production of the paper. This is an entropy-*reducing* process. The blank sheets of paper obviously have low information content with respect to human language, but they also constitute a low-entropy state with respect to the raw material. In a sheet of paper the cellulose fibres are constrained in both orientation and position. With regard to orientation, the fibres must lie in a plane rather than being free to take up any angle. This implies a reduction in the volume of state space that the fibres occupy, and thus, from Boltzmann, a corresponding reduction in entropy. The fibres are also constrained to exist within a small volume a few hundredths of a millimeter thick. This restriction in physical space obviously entails a smaller entropy, as shown in our discussions of Maxwell's demon.

Second, there is the inscription of the text – whether by hand, as in the distant past, or using a printing press. This is an entropy-*increasing* process. Imagine that the text to be printed exists as binary data in a file on disk, encoded using ASCII or Unicode.[2] Clearly the printed book contains this information, since by sending the book in the mail to someone we enable them to recreate the relevant binary

---

[1] Abstracting for now from the division of this wealth between the different classes in society, a matter which we take up in later chapters.

[2] ASCII is the American Standard Code for Information Interchange, a code which uses 7 bits to represent each letter or symbol. It is restricted to the characters appearing on US typewriters. Unicode is a newer 16-bit standard that can represent every letter or glyph used in any of the world's languages, including ideographic scripts like those of China and Japan.

file. Thus, by the equivalence of information and entropy, we have increased the entropy of the book relative to the blank sheets of paper. For another perspective, consider the fact that while all blank sheets are alike, printed sheets can be different. The number of possible different pages that can be printed is so huge as to dwarf the concept of astronomically large.[3] Since entropy is logarithmically related to the number of possible states, the increase in the number of possible states implies a rise in entropy.[4]

In the first phase a low-entropy material is created; in the second phase the entropy of this material is increased in a controlled way. Initially *natural* information is removed; subsequently *anthropic* or human-created information is added. The natural information removed in the first stage is of no interest to us, while that added in the second stage is dictated by our concerns.

The first process – pulping wood, bleaching it, forming it into sheets, drying it – has to use energy to produce the reduction in entropy. Thermodynamics gives any local reduction in entropy its energy price. The second process, increasing entropy, could in principle be done at no energy cost.[5] In practice our technologies are not that efficient. Still, the power consumption of a print-works is a lot lower than that of a paper mill.

Research is currently underway to develop nano-technologies that use self-assembly of microstructures. In this case the increase in entropy that occurs as the structures acquire form and information is achieved directly by thermodynamic means, albeit starting off from precisely controlled compositions and temperatures (Kim and Whitesides, 1995; Whitesides, 1995).

3.1.2   Replicated parts

Consider two books by two different authors, each 200 pages long, printed with the same size of letters. Each has roughly the same amount of information added to the paper in the printing process, but the information is different in each case. On the other hand two copies of a given book have the same information added. The added information is what on the one hand differentiates books, and on the other makes replication possible.

It is easy to see the relevance of information theory to the printing industry. Its product, after all, contains information in the everyday as well as the technical sense of that word. Does this approach provide insights into how other production processes function?

---

[3] If we allow 40 lines of 60 characters, with these characters drawn from a lexicon of all of the world's languages, we have of the order of some 10^{10000} possible printed pages. For comparison, the volume of the universe in terms of the Planck dimension – the quantum of space, 10^{-35} m – is of the order of 10^{210}.

[4] It may be objected that while there is a vast number of possible pages that could be printed, we are only interested in printing a particular page. This is true, but it is the particularity of the page that constitutes the added information and thus the added entropy.

[5] The controlled NOT gate proposed for quantum computing is in principle a mechanism by which a process analogous to the printing of information onto blank paper can take place in a reversible and thus non energy-consuming way DiVincenzo (1995).

For a rather different example, consider the process of producing cloth. The starting material is wool or cotton fibres in a random tangled state. This is first carded to bring the fibres into rough alignment, and then simultaneously twisted and drawn to spin the fibres into yarn. In the yarn both the volume and orientation of the fibres are sharply reduced. Energy is used to reduce the entropy of the cotton. The weaving of the cotton then increases the entropy by allowing two possible orientations of the fibres at right angles to one another (or more if we take into account the differences in possible weave). In the case of man-made fibres the extrusion and drawing processes that precede spinning are designed to align the polymer molecules with the axis of the fibres, again clearly an entropy-reducing process.

Other industries that use thin, initially flat materials clearly have a lot in common with printing. The manufacture of car body parts from sheet steel and the garment industry share the pattern of producing a low-entropy raw material and then adding information to it. In pressed steel construction, added information is encoded in the shape of the dies used to form the car doors, roof panels, etc. We can quantify this information using Chaitin's algorithmic theory, as proportional to the length of the numerically controlled machine tool tape that is used to direct the carving of the die. In the making up of garments from bolts of cloth, the added information comes in the form of the patterns used to cut the cloth.

All of these processes involve the replication of standard products, dependent on the existence of materialized information in the form of patterns and dies. If steam powered the industrial revolution, the technologies of replication were the key to mass production.

The classic example of the importance of accurate replication was in the production of the Colt revolver in the mid 19th century. Prior to Colt's establishing his factory the gun trade was dominated by handicraft manufacturing techniques. The different parts of a gun's mechanism were individually made by a gunsmith so that they fitted accurately together. While the components of an individual fowling piece might fit together beautifully, if the hammer were removed from one gun it would be unlikely to fit accurately into another. Mass production required the use of replicated interchangeable parts. For parts to be interchangeable they must be made to very precise tolerances. This improvement in the accuracy of production involves the parts having a lower entropy – occupying a smaller volume of phase space – than the old hand made parts. Again by the equivalence of information and entropy, this means that the standardized parts embody less information than the hand-made ones. This makes sense: for example, it may have been possible to identify the maker of a hand-made gun, while this would be impossible with a standardized Colt.

In the 19th century, prior to the introduction of numerically controlled machine tools, replicated parts had to be composed of circular and planar elements which could be produced on lathes or milling machines. Such products clearly have limited information content: in turning a smooth-bore gun barrel, for example, one only has to specify three parameters, namely the inner and outer radii and the length.

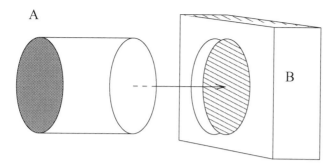

Figure 3.1 When inserting axle *A* into bearing *B* we want to minimize the conditional
information $H(B|A)$, between *B* and *A*.

If an axle and a bearing are being produced separately to fit together, then one
wants the uncertainty in the surface of the bearing, given the surface of the axle,
to be reduced below a certain limit.

Information theory analyses this in terms of *conditional entropy*, which Chaitin
formulates as follows: the conditional entropy of a character sequence *B* depen-
dent upon a sequence *A*, which we write as $H(B|A)$, is given by the length of
the shortest-prefix Turing machine program that when fed with the program for *A*
will generate *B*.

How can we apply this concept to our previous mechanical example? Let
A stand for an encoding of our axle and *B* an encoding of our bearing (see
Figure 3.1). We divide space up into cells of a fixed size, let us say a $\frac{1}{10}$th of
a millimeter on edge. If the space is occupied by metal we denote this with a 1
otherwise we denote it by a 0. We can then use arrays of characters to represent
slices through the axle, as in Figure 3.2.

According to the Chaitin view, the information content of the cross section
through the axle is given not by this array of 1s and 0s but by the shortest program
to generate it. Here is an example of a short program that will print out the pattern
in Figure 3.2:

```
program circ ;
const
    b: array [boolean] of char = ( '1', '0' );
    c = 20;
    r = 18;
var
    a: array [ -c ..c ,-c ..c ] of boolean ;
begin
```
$$a \leftarrow \sqrt{\iota_0^2 + \iota_1^2} < r;$$
```
    write(ba);
end .
```

Figure 3.2 A slice through the axle.

We cannot guarantee to have found the shortest such program.[6] Indeed Chaitin shows that in the general case one can never prove that a given program is the shortest to produce a particular output. But the program is considerably shorter than the pattern it produces, and by adjusting the definition of the variables c and r one could generate arbitrarily sized circular patterns of 1s in a field of 0s.

Clearly, if the bearing exactly fitted the axle then the expanded encoding for a slice through the bearing would be an array similar to Figure 3.2 but with the 1s and 0s interchanged. This can be produced by a trivial change to the program `circ`, the addition of a single statement. All that is required is that the line

write(b_{nota});

---

[6] The program is in Vector Pascal, a rather concise programming language; see Cockshott and Renfrew (2004).

```
0 0 0 0 0 0 1 1 1 1 1 1 1 1 1 1 1 1 1 1 1 1 1 1 1 1 1 1 1 1 1 1 1 1 1 1 1 0 0 0 0 0 0 0
0 0 0 0 0 0 1 1 1 1 1 1 1 1 1 1 1 1 1 1 1 1 1 1 1 1 1 1 1 1 1 1 1 1 1 1 0 0 0 0 0 0 0 0
0 0 0 0 0 0 0 1 1 1 1 1 1 1 1 1 1 1 1 1 1 1 1 1 1 1 1 1 1 1 1 1 1 1 1 0 0 0 0 0 0 0 0 0
0 0 0 0 0 0 0 0 1 1 1 1 1 1 1 1 1 1 1 1 1 1 1 1 1 1 1 1 1 1 1 1 1 1 0 0 0 0 0 0 0 0 0 0
0 0 0 0 0 0 0 0 0 1 1 1 1 1 1 1 1 1 1 1 1 1 1 1 1 1 1 1 1 1 1 1 1 0 0 0 0 0 0 0 0 0 0 0
0 0 0 0 0 0 0 0 0 0 0 1 1 1 1 1 1 1 1 1 1 1 1 1 1 1 1 1 1 1 1 0 0 0 0 0 0 0 0 0 0 0 0 0
0 0 0 0 0 0 0 0 0 0 0 0 1 1 1 1 1 1 1 1 1 1 1 1 1 1 1 1 1 1 1 0 0 0 0 0 0 0 0 0 0 0 0 0
0 0 0 0 0 0 0 0 0 0 0 0 0 0 0 1 1 1 0 1 1 1 1 1 0 0 0 0 0 0 0 0 0 0 0 0 0 0 0 0 0 0 0 0
0 0 0 0 0 0 0 0 0 0 0 0 0 0 0 0 0 0 1 1 0 0 0 0 0 0 0 0 0 0 0 0 0 0 0 0 0 0 0 0 0 0 0 0
0 0 0 0 0 0 0 0 0 0 0 0 0 0 0 0 0 0 1 0 0 0 0 0 0 0 0 0 0 0 0 0 0 0 0 0 0 0 0 0 0 0 0 0
0 0 0 0 0 0 0 0 0 0 0 0 0 0 0 0 0 0 0 0 0 0 0 0 0 0 0 0 0 0 0 0 0 0 0 0 0 0 0 0 0 0 0 0
```

Figure 3.3 Part of a pin with a fault on its circumference.

replaces the line

write(b_a);

This must come close to minimizing the conditional entropy of the two parts.

Suppose that the parts were less than perfectly made, so that there were rough spots on the surface of the axle. Figure 3.3 shows a cross section through a pin A' that is notionally circular but in fact has a step on it, as might be generated by improper turning.

If we still have our perfectly formed circular hole B, then the conditional entropy $H(B|A')$ of the hole and the imperfect pin is much greater than before. Working in the domain of generator programs we would need to add the following lines to the generator of A' to make the bitmap for B.

$a_{r,1}$ ← false;
$a_{r,2}$ ← false;
$a_{r+1,0}$ ← false;
$a_{r,0}$ ← false;
$a_{r-1,-1}$ ← true;
write(b_{nota});

This obviously contains extra information: the bitmap of A' must be adjusted to generate that of B. In pre-industrial production, the extras steps in the generator program would correspond to additional steps of filing and grinding to make the parts fit. The aim of standardized production is to arrive at a situation where independently made parts, derived from a common technical specification, fit together because the conditional information of the mating parts is minimal.

With these ideas in place, we are now ready to examine the three modes of increasing the productivity of labour mentioned above.

3.2   Accelerated production

The most obvious way in which production can be increased is by accelerating the production process itself, by making people and machines work longer and faster.

3.2.1   *Longer days*

If the working day is increased from 8 hours to 12 while the same tempo of work is maintained, then output per worker will rise by a half. The effect, over a 24-hour day, is analogous to increasing the average intensity of labour. Similarly if a machine is used for 12 hours a day rather than for 8, we have the same effect as if the machine ran 50 per cent faster.

From the standpoint of society as a whole, however, there are real differences. If machines are scarce, an economy can increase its output by using them on a 24-hour shift system. But if a system of three 8-hour shifts is used, then three times as many workers are required. Total production will rise threefold, but output per worker remains the same.[7] On the other hand, if the working day is extended to 12 hours and two shifts are worked, total output and output per worker both go up. This fact encourages employers to lengthen the working day whenever the labour supply is limited. Further, if daily wages fail to rise in proportion to hours, longer hours mean more profit.

But the scope for extending the working day is relatively limited. The maximum feasible working day is perhaps 16 to 18 hours under the most exploitative conditions, less than a doubling of the pre-industrial working day. Such gains are small compared to those available from technology. Furthermore, no free workers would willingly work such hours. The working day is ever the inverse reflection of workers' liberty: as workers gain political rights and influence, the working day is shortened and other ways have to be found to increase productivity.

3.2.2   *Studied movements, intensified labours*

Today we think of mass production in terms of the mechanized production line introduced by Henry Ford at the start of the 20th century. But mass production started much earlier. In the 18th century, before steam or water power were generally applied, mass production took place in manufactories.[8] In a manufactory, the work was done with hand tools, by groups of workers using a division of labour.[9]

It is a common observation that a person's speed at any particular task improves with practice. Through practice, sequences of muscle movements cease to be under conscious control and become reflexes. We no longer have to think about them: we do them automatically and we do them fast. Early manufacturing based itself upon this principle. Each worker had a simple repeated task, performed largely under reflex control. Production was accelerated both by the increased speed that came from practice, and by eliminating the 'lost time' which would otherwise be spent changing from one task to another. The combination of faster

---

[7] The labour required to produce one unit of output may fall slightly, since the depreciation of the machines may not rise proportionately with their intensity of use.

[8] *Manu*factory, from *manus*, the Latin for hand.

[9] 'A tool is usually more simple than a machine; it is generally used with the hand, while a machine is frequently moved by animal or steam power. The simpler machines are often merely one or more tools placed in a frame, and acted on by a moving power.' (Babbage, 1832: ch. 1)

movements and the elimination of wasted time could lead to remarkable improvements in productivity. This was, of course, the message of Adam Smith's famous discussion of the division of labour in pin-making in *The Wealth of Nations*.

But the drawbacks of this form of production are obvious. People are, for the duration of the working day, used as automatons, their minds and imaginations rendered redundant. We use the present tense advisedly: plenty of consumer goods in our shopping-malls today come from third world manufactures where children work as machines.

3.2.3 Mechanical sequencing and power

Nearly all human productive activity involves movements by the hands or limbs. The fingers must move in a precise sequence of motions to manipulate the tool and produce the desired effect on the product. The speed with which this can be done depends on both a flow of information and a flow of energy. The information is supplied by the brain in the form of nervous impulses, sent in the correct sequence to the hand. The energy is supplied by the muscles of the hand and arm, which accelerate the hands-plus-tools while overcoming mechanical resistance.

There is a limit to how fast even the most practiced hand can move, a limit to how fast a seamstress or tailor can sew. This is imposed both by the brain's inability to provide the nervous impulses faster than a certain rate, and by the speed with which the fingers can be moved. A whole class of industrial appliances accelerated production by first providing a self-acting mechanism to supply the information input, and then providing an external source of power to drive the process.

The classic example was the sewing machine. The first functional sewing machine was invented by the French tailor Barthelemy Thimonnier in 1830. He was almost killed by enraged French tailors who burnt down his sewing machine factory because they feared unemployment. Walter Hunt followed with America's first sewing machine in 1834, but he too failed to pursue his invention for fear of causing unemployment. Sewing machines did not go into mass production until the 1850s. The first commercially successful sewing machine was the one designed by Isaac Singer. The Singer machine used the lock-stitch mechanism patented earlier by Howe (Figure 3.4). It differed from a tailor in using two threads instead of one. The upper needle simply moved up and down while the cloth was dragged past it. Meanwhile a shuttle containing a second reel of thread was rotated through the loops created in the first thread. Singer's machine could be operated either by a treadle or by a crank. It was a huge success and Singer and Howe both became multi-millionaires.

The key to the sewing machine's success was the fact that it greatly increased productivity in sewing cloth together. The number of stitches a person could make per hour increased by an order of magnitude, owing to two effects. First, the much stronger muscles of the leg replaced those of the hand in moving the needle. Second, the sequence of needle movements was no longer generated by the human nervous system translated into finger movements. Dexterity gave way to rotary action as cams, cranks and levers sequenced the thread movements to generate

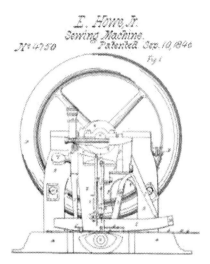

Figure 3.4 The lockstitch sewing machine of Elias Howe.

the lock stitch. The cams could operate far faster than the nimblest fingers, turning every tailor into a Rumpelstiltskin.

As we have said, training can accelerate manual skills immensely, as the control of our muscles is transferred from conscious to reflex action. But such acceleration meets its limits in the reflex speed of our nervous system and ability of our hand muscles to accelerate and decelerate our fingers. A machine with an external power source is freed from these limits. The required sequence of movements is now encoded in the mechanical linkages. Rotate the drive shaft faster and the sequence speeds up. The ultimate limit now becomes either friction or the strength of steel exposed to sudden acceleration and deceleration.

3.2.4   *Algorithmic and thermodynamic entropy*

The automatic control mechanism of the treadle sewing machine allows muscular effort of the foot to produce an embodied information structure in the twists and loops of the stitches. It is worth noting here, that when we deal with a repeated process such as stitching the algorithmic and thermodynamic conceptions of entropy diverge.

If an automaton is to produce a repeated pattern $P = c^n$, containing n repetitions of a basic 'cell' c, then we would expect the algorithmic information to be bounded by $H(c) + H(n)$. That is, it will be bounded by the information content of the basic cell plus the information content of the number n, But since an integral number can always be expressed in binary notation, the information content of n must be bounded by the number of binary digits in n. Thus on algorithmic grounds we would expect $H(P) \leq H(c) + \log_2 n$.

On the thermodynamic view, this formula does not necessarily hold; the thermodynamic analysis of production is more complex. Making one hundred stitches

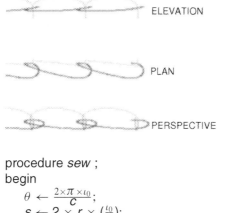

ELEVATION

PLAN

PERSPECTIVE

procedure *sew* ;
begin

$$\theta \leftarrow \frac{2 \times \pi \times \iota_0}{c};$$

$$s \leftarrow 2 \times r \times \left(\frac{\iota_0}{c}\right);$$

$$x1 \leftarrow \begin{cases} r + s & \text{if } \iota_0 \bmod c < h \\ s - r \times (\cos(\theta)) & \text{otherwise} \end{cases};$$

$$y1 \leftarrow 0.5 \times r \times \sin(\theta + \pi);$$

$$z1 \leftarrow 0.125 \times r \times \cos(\theta);$$

$$x2 \leftarrow x1 + r \times (-0.2 + 0.45 \times \sin(\theta));$$

$$y2 \leftarrow -2 + 0.1 \times r \times \sin\theta;$$

$$z2 \leftarrow r \times (-0.35 + 0.35 \times \cos\theta);$$

end ;

Figure 3.5 The Lock-stitch presented in plan, elevation and perspective views, along with a generating action program. All the steps of the action program depend on sine and cosine functions of θ, which represents the angular rotation of the sewing machine's drive wheel. The computer algorithm has to specify 6 degrees of freedom, 3 for each thread. This is to ensure that our modeled thread does not intersect itself. A practical sewing machine will work by controlling 4 degrees of freedom: the movement of the cloth, modeled in the algorithm by s; the vertical movement of the needle ($y1$); and the circular movement of the lower thread ($x2$ and $z2$).

clearly involves about one hundred times more physical work than doing one. Some of that work will be dissipated in frictional heat, a clear entropy increase. Another part goes into bending and twisting thread, both in the stitches and in the cloth being worked on. This increase in the entropy of the thread absorbs another portion of the work. Thus the thermodynamic entropy increase varies as $nh(s)$, where $h(s)$ is the increase in the entropy of the thread involved in doing a single stitch.[10]

---

[10] For macroscopic products the thermodynamic entropy changes are much larger than the algorithmic entropy changes. For sophisticated nanosystems which may be built in the future evolving along conservative lines, like Feynmann's proposed quantum simulator (Feynmann, 1999) the thermodynamic and algorithmic entropies of repeated patterns may be equivalent.

3.3   Parallelizing production

The sewing machine greatly increased the productivity of tailors, but it did not usher in a social revolution. Individual tailors could still afford to work on their own since the price of sewing machines was within their reach. The sewing machine in fact became a staple means of domestic production, allowing women to clothe their families more cheaply. It was compatible with the continued self-sufficiency of the farm household.

3.3.1   More people

Today, however, most work done by sewing machines is done in factories. Millions of women are employed in Asia sewing garments for western chain stores. In these factories productivity will be somewhat higher than in domestic production, owing to the mechanisms analysed by Adam Smith over 200 years ago: the division of labour and the repeated execution of the same task. But these gains are not huge. So what has happened to transform the sewing machine from a tool of family independence to an instrument of exploitation?

We can identify two factors. First, the big difference in wealth between the already industrialized nations of Europe, North America, Australia and Japan means that there is a huge demand in these countries for cheaply made clothes. Since the goods are being exported across the world, the trade inevitably falls into the hands of capitalist middlemen. These middlemen, through their contacts and wealth, are in a position to supply material to, and sell on the products made by, individual seamstresses. With the passage of time it becomes advantageous to them to bring the workers under one roof and turn the seamstresses into direct employees. In so doing they gain better control over the labour process, can impose stricter work discipline, and save the costs of distributing cloth to lots of home-workers.

A second cause is the dominance of distribution in the developed capitalist world by big chain stores selling branded goods. Such companies can place contracts for large numbers of identical garments with local manufacturers. They require cheap standardized garments produced either in sweatshops or by home-workers subject to the control of subcontractors.

The employers can exploit the machinists because the employers are rich and well connected, whereas the machinists are poor. The employers don't exert their control due to any particularly superior technology, but due to their social position. They have this position on account of their role in an international capitalist trade network, and this network in turn depends upon the prior industrial development of the richer nations, going back two centuries.

3.3.2   More spindles

It was not sewing machines that drove the birth of the industrial revolution, but spindles.

spinn'ing *n.* ~-*jenny*, spinning-machine with several spindles; ~-*wheel*, simple spinning-apparatus in which spindle is driven by wheel worked by hand or foot.

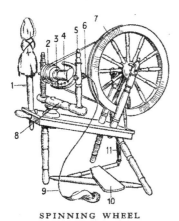

SPINNING WHEEL

1. Distaff. 2. Flier or spindle whorl. 3. Hackle. 4. Bobbin. 5. Maiden. 6. Spindle. 7. Wheel. 8. Mother-of-all. 9. Yarn. 10. Treadle. 11. Footman

Figure 3.6 Treadle spinning wheel.

Immediately prior to industrialization, yarn in Europe was produced by domestic treadle spinning wheels. The wooden spinning wheel looks a much more primitive machine than Singer's sewing machine, but in many ways they were very similar devices. They were both driven by foot power and both were, in a sense, *single-threaded*. The spinning wheel allows the twisting and drawing out of a single strand of thread. Both involve a modicum of hand control – guiding the cloth in one case, drawing out the yarn in the other. Like the early sewing machines the spinning wheel was essentially a domestic instrument of production; no factory system based on spinning wheels ever established itself.

The mechanization of spinning took what was essentially a more adventurous course than Singer and Howe's mechanization of sewing. Compton's Mule (see Figure 3.7) replaced the hand actions of the spinner with a sequence of mechanical movements, while multiplying the number of spindles and mounting these on a moving carriage. The sequence of actions is as follows.

(1) The carriage moves out, drawing the as yet unspun yarn through rollers that impede its progress. In the process, the spindles impart a twist onto the yarn. This emulates the first action of the hand spinner as she moves her hand away from the spindle, stretching the yarn.

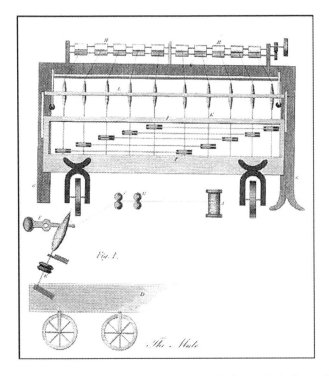

Figure 3.7 Compton's Mule. Note the multiplicity of spindles and the moving frame
which substituted for the stretching movement of the human spinner's
arms.

(2)   The carriage stops and the spindles start winding the thread onto bobbins.
Simultaneously the carriage moves back to the starting position as the thread
is drawn in.
(3)   The cycle repeats.

The mule was, in the terminology of the day, *self-acting* – we would now say
automated. It carried out its basic sequence of operations so long as power was
supplied. Human intervention was restricted to loading and unloading bobbins
and connecting broken threads.

The fact that the mule was water- or steam-powered meant that it could spin
each individual thread faster, but this was not critical: the really important thing
was the parallelism. Combined with self-action, this allowed the number of
threads spun by each worker to grow enormously. The system shown in Figure 3.7
exhibits an 10-fold multiplication of productivity; later mules increased the level
of parallelism to the order of 100-fold.

3.3.3 From Samian ware to UV lithography: the development of printing-like technologies

We will now look at a quite different method of raising productivity, one which has a long history and is transforming society even now. We're talking of 'printing-like' technologies – casting, moulding and printing proper – in which a relatively large investment is made in a 'master' of some kind, and then multiple copies are produced relatively cheaply, in many cases exploiting parallelism to the maximum.

One of the earliest mass production industries was the Roman Samian ware industry, which flourished from the first to the third century AD. It produced ochre coloured pottery kitchenware vessels with raised designs as shown in Figure 3.8. These were unlike earlier pottery styles in that large numbers of identical pieces were produced. The key to this was the use of casting.

Pottery vessels went through two earlier stages of development. In the first phase pots were made by hand-shaping the clay prior to firing. Next came the invention of the potter's wheel. Perhaps the earliest rotary production tool, this accelerated the production of circular vessels. The rotation of the wheel meant that the potter had only to specify two parameters for each vertical position on the pot: the inner and outer radii. The 'specification' was achieved via the placement of the potter's thumb and forefinger relative to the axis of the wheel. The wheel enabled production of pots with a reduced algorithmic information content. The pots were more even and their production was easier. The potter's wheel was the progenitor of a whole class of rotary tools such as lathes and drills.

The next development dispensed with the wheel and introduced moulds. Clay was pressed into a pre-shaped mould and took on its entire shape in a single operation. With the wheel, shaping was still a sequential process. A one dimensional path, a spiral, was traced out in the frame of reference of the pot by the potter's grip. With casting, the shaping became a parallel, two dimensional

Figure 3.8 Samian ware was an advance in pottery, since moulding allowed mass production. Photo by Andreas Franzkowiak.

process. The mould is a two dimensional surface with information encoded as raised and lowered details. Consider what this implies.

(1) The shape is impressed onto the whole surface simultaneously. Of course this is only approximately true with the mould for a curved vessel, but we can idealize this as a process in which an approximately flat die comes into contact with a roughly flat sheet of clay, imposing detail right across the surface. (This idealization becomes more realistic in subsequent developments of this sort of production, as we shall see below.)

(2) Whereas the wheel accelerated production by reducing the algorithmic information of the product, moulding did not have this disadvantage. It allowed arbitrarily detailed patterns to be embossed on the piece. The product of the wheel must be a solid of revolution (and arguably much of the beauty of hand-turned pottery stems from this constraint). Moulding allowed decoration to run riot. Samian ware shows an almost Victorian love of fancy detail.

(3) No two pots turned on the wheel are the same, but the Samian ware industry was able to churn out masses of identical bowls. Moulding allowed standardized mass production. This was helped along by the fact that moulding can be *recursive*. A pottery mould is a negative image of the final pot, with raised areas on the pot corresponding to depressions in the mould. But if the mould itself were ceramic, it could be made by pushing a positive pattern piece into an unformed mould, and then baking the mould. Suppose that a mould could be used 100 times before it wore out. Suppose further that the 'master' used to make the mould could be used for that purpose 100 times. In that case this two-step process could turn out 10,000 copies of the original pattern piece.

It is worth returning at this point to the paradox relating algorithmic to thermodynamic entropy in production, first mentioned in section 3.2.4. There we said that the algorithmic information in repeated production grows by a law of the form $H(P) \leq H(c) + \log n$ where P is the total product made up of n repetitions of a 'cell' c. In the process of reproduction as a whole there are two terms, the first given by the complexity of the original and a second (logarithmic) term given by the number of repetitions.

In the case of Samian ware there was the original work of producing the master or pattern piece which corresponds to $H(c)$, but then the number of copies that could be made grows exponentially with the number of successive steps of copying. If the master is used directly to produce the pots then L pots can be made, where L is the lifetime of the master. If the master produces moulds, which in turn produce the pots, then L^2 pots can be made, and so on. If we invert this relationship, we find that the number of successive steps of copying will be related to the number of pots produced, n, as $\log_L(n)$, a relationship suggested by the predictions of information theory.

The application of mass production to *iron-working* required a similar path. The crucial step here was the ability to cast iron. Prior to the development of the blast furnace, the production of iron objects required repeated hammering to forge a shape out of the bloom. The resulting wrought iron was tough but costly; its use was limited to tools and weapons. As Douglas Fisher points out, the transition from the medieval *stackofen* to the blast furnace was gradual. As higher temperatures were achieved, the side effect of molten iron trickling out of the bottom of the furnace was a nuisance to the iron workers.

> This iron, having absorbed enough carbon to transform it into cast iron, which is brittle and unworkable in the forge, was an annoyance to the smelter whose object was to produce low carbon wrought iron. As yet he had no use for cast iron and returned it to the furnace to be remelted.
>
> (Fisher, 1963: 27)

However, the smelters eventually realized that cast iron was not without its merits. Fisher suggests that its earliest use may have been in the production of church bells, previously cast in bronze, followed by cannon and cannon balls. Over time, the development of iron-casting permitted the mass production of a wide range of iron utensils for applications where high tensile strength was not essential. Iron stoves, pipes and cookware became available for domestic use. Cast iron pillars could be used to support the large working areas of mills. Cast iron members operating in compressive mode could be used for bridges. These products could be mass produced from a single wooden pattern, from which sand-moulds were taken. As with Samian ware, exuberant decorative detail was made possible by the new technology.

The subsequent development of the Bessemer process allowed the same sand-mould technology to be applied to steel production so that even parts used in tension could be cast. The mass production of car engines, for example, would have been impossible without castings.

Again we have a technology that utilizes the parallel formation of a product, hence enabling a huge extension of production.

In the 20th century one saw a recapitulation of history as *plastic moulding* became possible. As with cast iron, this enabled the mass production of domestic utensils. The significant differences were that plastics were lighter, and they could be formed to higher dimensional accuracy than cast iron. In products from vacuum cleaners to buckles we see a progressive replacement of cast or pressed metal parts by moulded plastic ones. Aside from the reduction in weight, manufacturing costs are reduced by replacing a sequence of metal-forming steps by the parallel formation of the product in a mould.

Although we began our discussion of printing-like technologies with Samian ware, the casting of pottery vessels was not the first use of impressions. The use of seals as a certificate of authenticity in correspondence certainly came earlier. Sumerian cultures used cylindrical seals that could be rolled onto wet clay tablets. Roman administrative authorities used circular stamps, looking much like modern postmarks, to mark government property. The stamping of coins is another example. The purpose in these cases was to have a mark that was uniquely identifying, yet easy to apply. The master stamp or seal was difficult to replicate (and deliberately so), but the stamping was straightforward. A particular information structure then authenticates an object, or a claim on an object.

These uses of printing are, however, specialized activities, not involving mass production. Everything changes with the development of the printing press and moveable type. Printing replaces the serial production of the scribe with parallel processing. An entire folio of several pages is formed with a single impression. Here we have the clearest, the archetypal, example of this class of production process. Information, encoded in the physical structure of the array of type is simultaneously transferred across an entire plane surface onto a receiving medium, the paper. It is clear that what we have transferred is information: we can read it. The transfer is done by a physical movement of the press at right angles to the paper.

But in printing, actually making marks on paper is the final step in the process of information copying. What made the printing press revolutionary in Europe was the moveable type. As Babbage noted, printing by means of moveable type

> possesses a singular peculiarity, in the immense subdivision of the parts that form the pattern. After that pattern has furnished thousands of copies, the same individual elements may be arranged again and again in other forms, and thus supply multitudes of originals, from each of which thousands of their copied impressions may flow.
>
> (Babbage, 1832: ch. 11)

One could, in principle, carve an entire page of a book as a single block, using etching or engraving as in old Chinese wood-block printing. But this approach is highly labour-intensive. The use of pre-cast type drastically reduces the labour required to make the master.

The information in a page of type comes at two conceptual levels. The semantic level, of primary interest to the reader, is given by the sequence of words. But this can be decomposed, in European languages, into a sequence of letters from a small, fixed alphabet. The shape of these letters forms a second level of information. In hand-written text each letter 'A', 'B' or 'W' will be different. In printed text they are all more or less identical, 'BBBB...B'. The type used in each B is cast from the same mould. This means that the information in a page of printed text is much less than that in a page written by hand.

In summary, the cheapness of printing stemmed from the following considerations.

(1)   Each folio off the press was practically identical to the preceding one.[11] In algorithmic terms, this means that we are exploiting the logarithmic term of the repeated production cost. In terms of labour time, it makes use of the fact

---

[11]   But not truly identical. There is a residual element of randomness in hot metal typography: the physical instances of a particular letter in a given font are not identical, and neither are the physical copies of a book in a given printing. This slight irregularity – very much less than with hand-copied text, of course – is pleasing to bibliophiles. The output of modern high-resolution printers, using digital fonts, seems boringly uniform by comparison.

that repeated copies cost only the labour required to load a sheet of paper and operate the press through one cycle.

(2) The fact that individual letters do not have to be carved (other than once, in making the original mould) reduces typesetting to the choice of appropriate letters.

Taken together, these factors generated a huge increase in the productivity of information copying, which in turn was the material precondition for generalized literacy and the eventual development of industrial civilization.

The process of parallel transfer of information to the product, initiated with ceramic casting, creates an independent existence for the information source. In the case of seals this independent existence was harnessed to certify the validity of documents: only the holder of a particular seal could validate a document. But the invention of moveable type transformed this relationship. The particular configuration of type used in an edition of a book became incidental as the pieces of type themselves were re-usable. The printers' plates are of little value in themselves. The information that is impressed on the page is only secondarily the particular shapes of the letters used. A different choice of typeface alters all of these shapes, yet leaves the book substantially unaltered. It becomes clear that what is being transferred is an information structure that has multiple possible representations. The book, defined as a sequence of characters, is an abstract identity surviving its impressions.

We have, then, a three-stage evolution of the relationship between labour and information in the product.

(1) In handicraft work, the information is impressed on the product by the bodily movement of the artisan and has no independent existence.

(2) In pattern- or mould-based production, the handicraft work is captured once in a pattern or mould from which multiple copies are made. The pattern piece is then an independently existing encoding of the information, whose possession implies social power. This is either overt in the case of the holder of a seal of office, or implicit in the iron-master's ownership of a store-room of pattern pieces for standard products. These pieces embody much more labour than the individual products they inform, and their monopolization gives market power to their owner.

(3) In printing, the information structure becomes abstracted from the impressing apparatus and potentially mobile. A printer with the text of a book can have it typeset and turn off an impression at will. All that is required is the labour of typesetting, which is typically less than the labour of authorship. Printing breaks the link between material possession and ability to reproduce.

If the labour of writing is to be recompensed in a society of independent commodity producers, the sequence of words itself has to be made an item of property. Hence the printing press, in combination with bourgeois social relations, gives rise to the law of copyright. Information becomes property independent of its material embodiment.

It is noteworthy that whereas in the case of literary authorship, the direct producer of the information usually ends up owning it, this has not been the case for pattern-making. The author owned his copyright, but the iron-master owned the patterns, not the pattern maker. Why the difference?

Several factors seem to have contributed. The ponderous nature of the patterns made them analogous to other products of direct labour which, in bourgeois right, always belong to the employer. A pattern used in sand casting was apparently no different from any other piece of exact carpentry. The pattern-maker might be a more skilled worker, and paid better than a moulder, but he was still an employee working at his master's direction. In addition, in the casting of machine parts the pattern would often be an embodiment of information already recorded in the form of technical drawings by an engineer.

Backing up a step, one has to ask why the pattern-maker ends up as a wage labourer, surrendering his right to the information he produces, while the author typically remains an independent agent. The decisive factor has to be the extent to which the process of producing information structures can be carried out independently. An author can write 'on his own account', since there is little need for collective input to his production. The work of the pattern-maker, on the other hand, forms part of an industrial division of labour.

The ultimate function of any system of property law is to ensure the reproduction of the agencies of production, be they individuals, firms or the state. In a commodity-producing society, non-state agents of production can survive only by the sale of their product. If that product is an information structure, the agency that bears the cost of making it will tend to own it. They can then survive by selling either the information itself, or the use of the information.

Printing technology gave us the mass production of images. Picture prints could be cheaply turned out, provided that a human artist had made the master copy. This might be an etching or a lithograph, but in any case the information on the page came via the human eye, brain and hand. This meant that making the master was an inherently serial process. The camera changes this.

Photography literally means 'drawing with light', but this is an understatement – in fact, it is printing with photons.[12] Instead of a metal plate coming down on the paper at centimetres per second, wavefronts of light traveling at 300,000 kilometers a second impose their image on the film. As in printing, they work on the whole frame simultaneously.

The photographic image is a work of nature. The human photographer, where he is present, has the role of selecting the vital instant at which nature can do its work. With photography Landauer's aphorism that 'information is physical' is literally made manifest. Photography was our first technology to encounter the limits that nature places on the handling and transmission of information. Let's consider some of these constraints.

---

[12] True photo*graphy* had to await the laser printer, whose hair-thin beam, like the engraver's stylus, forms its image one stroke at a time.

Although the light waves that impinge on the film approach at the ultimate speed, Einstein's *c*, this does not produce the acceleration in process that one might expect. To form an image we need photons to interact with tiny crystals of silver iodide, seeding their photo-decomposition. Where struck by photons the crystals break down to leave black colloidal silver. Each individual crystal makes a binary 'choice': either it is hit by a photon and decomposes, or not. If struck, it evolves to a black dot; if not, it will be dissolved away in the developing process. But we don't want our picture to be just black and white, we want shades of grey. Suppose we want to have 100 shades of grey available. Then we need 100 crystals in each small area that we can resolve. If we have crystals that are, say, $\frac{1}{10}$mm across then 100 crystals will fit onto each square millimeter of film.

When we take a picture we exploit the probabilistic nature of the photo-decomposition process. If an exposure caused all crystals to absorb photons, we would get a totally black surface. If it was so short that no photons hit any crystals, the film would be left white. To get an acceptable grey to black range, we need an exposure such that, given the ambient light levels, about 50 per cent of the crystals on a randomly chosen part of the film will decompose. The longer we hold the shutter open, the more likely it is that enough photons arrive at the surface. Because the arrival of photons is a random process the actual number of crystals triggered will vary. An area with 100 crystals 'should' have half its crystals black, but sometimes it has 40, sometimes 60. This gives the film a grainy, noisy look. The error induced by photon quantization is referred to as 'shot noise', and its degree is proportional to the square root of the number of photons arriving on a sensor.

We can remove the graininess by using smaller crystals. By courtesy of the Law of Large Numbers, as you increase the number of crystals in each small area, the percentage that will turn black at any given light level becomes more predictable; as shown below, the error in our estimates of the light level falls.

Number of crystals	Expected brightness error
10	16%
100	4.6%
1000	1.5%

This effect is visually apparent as a smoother, less grainy image. Having smaller crystals enables us to capture more information about the light falling on each small area of film, but this gain in information about light levels comes at a cost: it makes the film slower. Smaller crystals have a lower probability of absorbing a photon, so we have to open the shutter for longer to capture our picture. If we wish to gain maximal information about intensity, we're restricted to photographing static scenes.

We are up against the fact that information is not only physical, it is physically quantized. The information available about a scene is encoded in the trajectories of photons arriving from it. There are only a finite number of these available. The number of photons arriving sets a limit on how much we can know about the scene. A fast film allows us to image rapidly moving objects, but the cost is a coarse and grainy image. An alternative is to supplement the supply of photons. In film studios where they want to capture motion and still have high quality images, they have to use intense artificial lighting.

The letter λ is conventionally used to represent the wavelength of light or other electromagnetic radiation. Visible light has a $\lambda \approx 0.5\mu = \frac{1}{2,000,000}$th of a meter. λ determines the smallest details that we can in principle represent by photography. You cannot use photography to form a pattern of light and dark whose smallest features are smaller than light waves. This is mainly of relevance in microscopy or the manufacture of microscopic components. But as micromanufacture has become the governing technology of our age, this constraint weighs more and more heavily upon us.

Sound recording involves copying in two senses. In the first sense a musician plays a piece, this is recorded, and subsequently people can listen to a 'copy' of that performance. These copies are separated from the original in time. The second sense involves making distinct copies of the recording itself. These copies can then be separated in space, allowing people to listen to the performance in many different places simultaneously.

Copying in the first sense is inherently sequential (as is the act of listening). The piece has to be performed from beginning to end and recorded as it takes place. Copying in the second sense can be either parallel or sequential. The production of records – whether the old analog ones or modern CDs – is a special example of a casting process. A master disk, on which a negative image of the tracks has been cut, is used to press out the disks from hot soft plastic. As such it is a parallel process: the entire recording is transferred to the disk in a single step. When music is recorded onto tapes, on the other hand, the copying process is inherently sequential. A degree of parallelism can be achieved only by having large numbers of tape recorders operating at the same time.

The transition from Edison's original cylindrical phonograph to disc recording was driven by the need to economize on copying. A cylinder could not be pressed out but had to be cut sequentially. The cheapness of disc-pressing is what created a mass market for sound recordings. At first sight, the recording industry appears simply to present an instance of the mass production of a material object – much like Samian ware – and in this context the efficiency of the productive process was vital. But the Internet has revealed what should always have been clear: tangible records were just one means to the copying of performances. People had to buy the material object – the disc – to get the information it contained. All products contain information, added during production, but for some products – initially books, then records and now software – their real use value resides in their information content. Nowadays, of course, one can buy (or otherwise acquire) copies of performances in the form of 'pure information', for example as WAV or MP3 files.

Radio and television take the technologies of sound recording and photography and add the principle of broadcasting. Here the product, namely radio waves, is a direct physical, though 'immaterial' embodiment of information. Once released, broadcast information is available to anyone within reach of the transmitter. The number of copies of a broadcast musical performance that are heard is limited only by the number of receivers within range. The marginal labour embodied in each heard performance tends to zero as the number of listeners goes up. To produce, say, a live musical broadcast there is a certain fixed cost: the time of the musician, the time of the technicians operating the broadcasting equipment, the depreciation on the equipment. These costs are essentially unrelated to the number of listeners. The only component of the cost of broadcasting that relates to the number of listeners is the power used by the transmitter, which tends to be a relatively small part of the total cost.

From its inception therefore, broadcasting was an implicitly 'communist' medium, where performances are given away free to listeners. This free distribution meant that the labour required to run the broadcasting system had to be in a sense directly social labour. The BBC provides a model of this where what is essentially a special tax, the Radio License, was levied to provide the service. The private-sector equivalent, broadcasting funded by advertising, essentially taxes the sellers of mass produced goods to meet broadcasting costs. Once radio and TV advertising is introduced, manufacturers of consumer goods are forced to finance TV, or lose out to competitors who do.

Arguably, the free nature of broadcasting prefigures a general transition of the mode of material production to one favourable to communism. As production becomes more and more dominated by the principle of copying information – a principle that has been in development ever since Roman pottery-casting – the underlying rationale for commodity production and market mechanisms is increasingly undermined. Commodity forms of production can only be sustained by increasingly elaborate and 'unnatural' legal constructs that enforce property rights over information.

Printed circuits and integrated circuits: The dominant technology of the first decade of the 21st century is digital electronics. This technology has seen sustained rates of growth of productivity that outstrip anything seen in past generations. At the heart of this growth has been the progressive refinement of copying technologies.

The key component of contemporary digital technology is the NMOS transistor. This is the basic element which, repeated millions of times over, builds our computers, cell phones, etc. A transistor comprises three electrical contacts: the source, the gate and the drain (Figure 3.9 shows a stylized cross section). It is basically an electrically controlled switch – an 'atom' of circuitry which changes its state (Can current flow from the source to the drain?) depending on

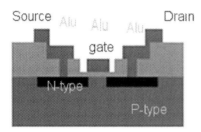

Figure 3.9 NMOS Transistor.

a modulating influence (Is a charge applied to the gate?). When the switch is off, current cannot flow: it cannot pass from the N-type silicon around the source to the surrounding P-type semi-conductor. To turn the switch on, a positive charge is applied to the gate. This repels positive charge carriers from beneath the gate, creating a temporary N-type channel linking the source to the drain.

The components of the transistor occupy a thin layer in the surface of a silicon chip. The key to the manufacture of digital electronic devices is to lay out and interconnect large numbers of these transistors on a chip. In the spirit of the quotation from Babbage with which we opened this chapter, and in view of the fact that so much that we take for granted in the early 21st century is based on the transistor, it may be worth spelling out in some detail how the process works.

Figure 3.10 shows the fabrication steps involved in making NMOS semiconductor chips (with the focus on a single transistor). Reading from left to right and top to bottom the steps are:

(1) Start with a polished wafer of P-doped silicon.
(2) Oxidize the wafer to form an SiO_2 layer about half a micron thick by heating the wafer to around 1000°C in an oxygen atmosphere.
(3) Apply a layer of photoresist on the wafer. This is done by rapidly spinning the wafer so that drops of photoresist spread out to form a uniform layer before drying.
(4) Use photolithography to define the source and drain areas of the transistors. This involves shining UV light through a shadow mask, ensuring that only some areas of the photoresist are exposed to the light. The exposed area undergoes chemical changes allowing it to be washed away by a developing fluid. After this step the information structure on the mask has been mapped onto a pattern of holes and lands in the photoresist. The photoresist is then baked so that it can resist acid, which will be used to etch holes in the oxide layer.
(5) Expose the wafer to hydrofluoric acid to dissolve the the oxide wherever there are holes in the resist. The acid does not dissolve pure silicon, so the etching stops once it is through the oxide layer.

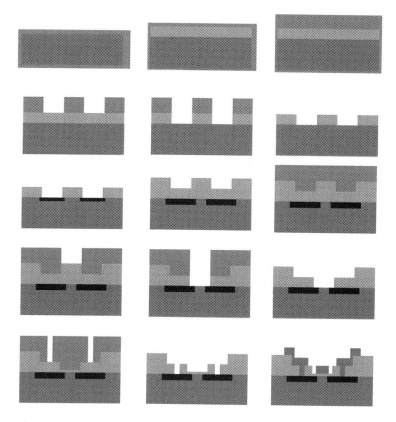

Figure 3.10 NMOS fabrication steps.

(6) The photoresist is dissolved by an organic solvent, leaving a pattern of holes and lands in the oxide layer that matches the pattern on the original mask. (We are now at the right end of the second row in Figure 3.10.)

(7) The silicon under the holes is now doped to N-type (black in the diagram) by diffusing phosphorous into it. This step forms the source and drain of the transistors.

(8) Repeat the oxidation of step 3 to grow a fresh layer of SiO_2.

(9) Apply a new layer of photoresist. We are now at the end of the third row of the diagram.

(10) Expose the photoresist under a new mask and etch a hole through the oxide to expose the area of the silicon that will become the gate of the transistor. We are now at the end of the fourth row of the diagram.

(11) A further oxidation step places a very thin insulating layer (a few hundred angstrom) across the top of the gate area. This has to be thin to allow sufficiently strong electric fields through from the gate to switch the transistor.

We don't show this step in the diagram, but the resulting oxide layer can be seen in subsequent images.

(12) Another sequence of photoresist coating, UV exposure and etching is used to cut contacts through the oxide down to the source and drain. We are now at the middle of row five.

(13) The wafer is coated with aluminium. This forms the wires on the surface of the chip. The wafer is subjected to yet another round of photoresist coating, exposure and etching to cut the uniform aluminium layer into a network of wires joining the chips. This yields the final circuit.

The crucial repeated step in this manufacturing process is photolithography, which is used to transfer patterns from a mask to the chip. The ability to project a clear image of a very small feature onto the wafer is limited by the wavelength of the light that is used, and the ability of the reduction-lens system to capture enough diffraction orders off the illuminated mask. Current state-of-the-art photolithography tools use Deep Ultraviolet (DUV) light with wavelengths of 248 and 193 nm, which allow minimum feature sizes on the order of 130–190 nm. Tools are under development which will use 157 nm wavelength DUV in a manner similar to current exposure systems. In addition, Extreme Ultraviolet (EUV) radiation systems are currently under development which will use 13 nm wavelengths, approaching the regime of x-rays, and should allow feature sizes below 45 nm.

The number of transistors that can be produced per square centimeter of silicon obvious varies inversely as the square of the feature size. If you half the feature size you can produce, then the number of transistors you can make goes up four times. Productivity gains have also come through increasing the sizes of the wafers used, allowing more transistors to be printed with each processing cycle.

The production of Integrated Circuits (ICs) shows very clearly how manufacturing moves towards being a process of copying information. In making a new processor chip, there are two main costs.

(1) The work of creating the original design for the chip. This design typically takes the form of a CAD (Computer Aided Design) file, or set of files, which is transferred to the master masks used in chip production. Each generation of chips uses smaller transistors. The number of transistors used in this year's model is likely to be twice as many as in the model released two years ago. So the labour of design grows over time, even as the cost of producing the individual components falls.

(2) The capital cost of setting up the IC fabrication line. This tends to rise from generation to generation since the equipment used must be increasingly precise, the standards of cleanliness in the production facilities become more stringent, and the imaging equipment becomes more and more esoteric.

The combined effects of these factors means that while there has been a rapid exponential growth in the number of transistors produced, with a doubling-time of the order of two years, the number of firms able to bear the development costs of new products falls. This has led to an increasingly monopolized system of manufacture. One company, Intel, has ended up dominating the world production of CPU chips, with only marginal competition from a few smaller firms such as AMD.

PCR and genomics: The 1950s saw both the birth of the electronic computer industry and the discovery of the structure of DNA. It became clear that living organisms could be seen as self-replicating information structures. The reproduction of cells had as a precondition the copying of genetic information. The biotechnology industry rests fundamentally upon these insights. But since the invention of the Polymerase Chain Reaction (PCR), a copying technology has become a key part of the industrial process for biotechnology.

PCR is a technique for copying DNA. A polymerase enzyme from a thermophilic bacterium is placed in a solution of DNA bases and an initial starter quantity of DNA. The temperature of the solution is then cycled up and down. Each time the solution is warmed up, the double strands of DNA disassociate. As it is cooled, the polymerase enzyme builds up a complementary strand of bases on each single strand. This regenerates a complete double stranded molecule of DNA. Thus each cycle doubles the number of molecules, each of which is a copy of the original starter molecule. Here in the PCR process we seen the full industrial application of the principle discussed in sections 3.2.4 and 3.3.3 whereby the algorithmic information in repeated production grows by a law of the form $H(P) \leq H(c) + \log n$ where P is the total product made up of n repetitions of c. If one wants to make n copies of a DNA molecule containing c bases by automated DNA synthesis followed by the PCR, then there will be two phases. In the first phase a small number, in principle as few as 1, copies are made of the DNA using an automated synthesis machine. The number of steps to be followed here will be of the order c. Next the PCR is used to repeatedly double the number of DNA molecules we have. This phase will have to be repeated of the order of $\log_2 n$ times.

With the Polymerase Chain Reaction we see that the regulation of the productivity of an industrial process follows directly from the laws of algorithmic information theory.

4 Babbage and the birth of digital technology

4.1 Copy and calculating

We have emphasized the role of copying as a key factor in the growth of labour productivity over the centuries. The importance of this was first recognized by Charles Babbage, who described copying, 'in its most extensive sense', as 'a principle which pervades a very large portion of all manufactures and... one upon which the cheapness of the articles produced seems greatly to depend.' He remarked on the fact that when many copies are to be made of an original piece, the manufacturer can afford to lavish great 'care and pains' on the original.

> It may thus happen, that the instrument or tool actually producing the work, shall cost five or even ten thousand times the price of each individual specimen of its power.
>
> (Babbage, 1832: ch. 11)

Surveying the industries of his age, Babbage saw that 'operations of copying' were to be found, notably, in printing, casting and moulding.

Babbage was driven to write his *Economy of Machinery and Manufactures* because of the efforts he had put in to develop his pioneering computing machines. For these he required the reliable production of highly accurate gears and other parts. Given the technologies available at the time, this was a real struggle. He had to visit and become familiar with a multitude of manufacturing activities, and then he 'was insensibly led to apply to them those principles of generalization to which my other pursuits had naturally given rise'. The modes of thought that he had acquired as a mathematician and the first computer designer allowed him to see the key underlying principles at work in manufacturing production.

His analysis of industrial production was immensely influential economically and politically. The two leading economists of the mid-nineteenth century, Karl Marx and J. S. Mill, drew heavily on Babbage for their analysis of industry. Marx's distinction between manufacture and machine industry derives essentially from Babbage. Babbage's emphasis on the technologies of copying was not, however, fully appreciated by his followers and tended to be filtered out of their accounts. One of the themes of this book, as should be clear by now, is that

concepts deriving from computing and information technology are key to understanding industrial production. We will now go on to look at the development
of the modern computer, starting with the work of Babbage. The next chapter
follows up with an account of Alan Turing's contribution.

4.2   Tables

The way in which we do calculations is culturally and historically determined. At
school we learnt arithmetic, but a particular kind of arithmetic, using a decimal
number system derived from India via Arabia. Some of us also learned an alternative way of writing numbers, Roman notation. We may have wondered how on
earth the Romans did arithmetic with their numbers, since they seem so ill adapted
to the kind of arithmetic we learned at school. The answer is that the Romans used
pocket calculators.

Figure 4.1 shows a schematic diagram of a Roman pocket abacus, a number of
which have been retrieved in archaeological digs. Looking at them one realizes
that Roman numerals were a notation perfectly suited to recording the results
of calculations using their abaci. They did not have to use their numerals to do
computations, since these could all be done on the abacus. In fact, it was not until
the middle ages that the idea of doing calculations using nothing but pen and ink
was introduced to Europe. Up until then the term *arithmetic* referred to doing
calculations with an abacus or a reckoning table. Reckoning tables were inscribed
with lines upon which coins of different denominations were placed and moved
about in a similar way to the beads of an abacus.

To work with such a device you need to be able to count, and also to understand
the rules for shifting beads and carrying. To add IIII to the DXXVI shown in
Figure 4.1 you would move beads in the top row across.

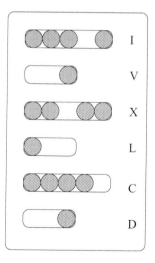

Figure 4.1 A Roman abacus showing the number DXXVI, or 526 in decimal notation.

abacus	my head
DXXVI	IIII
DXXVII	III
DXXVIII	II
DXXVIIII	I

You have now moved all the I beads across to the right and still have I to add. To do this you have to carry: you shift the I beads back to the left and attempt to move the V bead to the right. But it is already to the right, so you carry again, shifting the V to the left and moving one of the X beads to the right. This gives the answer DXXX = 530.

Compare this to the way you were taught to do arithmetic at school. We want:

$$\begin{array}{r} 526 \\ +\quad 4 \\ \hline 530 \end{array}$$

You add 4 + 6 and get 10, so you write down 0 in the rightmost place of the bottom line and carry the 1. Then you add the carried 1 to 2 to get 3, and finally add 0 to 5 to get 5. To accomplish this you must have memorized your addition tables for all the digits from 0 to 9:

0	1	2	3	4	5	6	7	8	9
1	2	3	4	5	6	7	8	9	10
2	3	4	5	6	7	8	9	10	11
3	4	5	6	7	8	9	10	11	12
4	5	6	7	8	9	10	11	12	13
5	6	7	8	9	10	11	12	13	14
6	7	8	9	10	11	12	13	14	15
7	8	9	10	11	12	13	14	15	16
8	9	10	11	12	13	14	15	16	17
9	10	11	12	13	14	15	16	17	18

Note that each entry in that table could be computed using your fingers, or using an abacus, but by memorizing the table you may speed up the process.[1] If you learnt this table – and similar subtraction, multiplication and division tables – then using the rules of long addition, long multiplication and so on, you were equipped to do calculations on numbers of arbitrary length. When it was introduced, this system was called not arithmetic but *algorithmics*, from the name of the Arabian author of a popular maths book of the period. To be useful, algorithmics depended on the memorization of tables, which in turn implies a certain amount of time as a child learning the tables by rote. Algorithmic calculation, in other words, presupposed a certain social investment in education.

For the normal tasks of commercial calculation, adding, subtracting and multiplying were enough. But with the development of oceanic navigation more sophisticated maths was called for. The masters of ships had to know where

---

[1] Only *may*, since a skilled abacist may be able to do it faster.

they were. Latitude (distance from the equator) was relatively straightforward, since the equator – the great circle perpendicular to the earth's axis of rotation – is an imaginary but non-arbitrary line. Longitude was much trickier, being a matter of separation from an arbitrary zero meridian. (Any great circle through the poles has an equal claim on representing 0° of longitude.) Given an accurate reckoning of the current time at a location of known longitude (say Greenwich, which you take to be at 0°) and an observation of the elevation of the sun at your current location, you could determine your longitude. But chronometers were not up to the job (think of pendulum clocks at sea). Sobel (1996) describes the long struggle to develop the accurate naval chronometers needed for keeping track of the current Greenwich time. One John Harrison finally came up with a good enough clock, but meanwhile – the problem being of desperate urgency – several fancier methods were explored, including Galileo's suggestion of using the observed behaviour of the moons of Jupiter as a longitude-finder. And these methods demanded sophisticated tables of ephemera.

As Dionysius Lardner, Babbage's not altogether reliable popularizer, put it:

> These tables are connected with the various sciences, with almost every department of the useful arts, with commerce in all its relations; but above all, with Astronomy and Navigation. So important have they been considered, that in many instances large sums have been appropriated by the most enlightened nations in the production of them; and yet so numerous and insurmountable have been the difficulties in attending the attainment of this end, that after all, even navigators, putting aside every other department of art and science, have, until very recently, been scantily and imperfectly supplied with the tables indespensibly necessary to determine their position at sea.
>
> (Lardner, 1834)

Such tables stored up the results of long and complex calculations, in a similar way to the times-tables we learnt at school. But the preparation of trigonometric tables was an altogether more difficult task.

4.3 Prony, Babbage and the division of mental labour

In the wake of the introduction of the metric system in France towards the end of the 18th century, Gaspard de Prony, director general of the French Ordnance Survey, was given the task of producing a set of decimalized logarithmic and trigonometric tables. Given how proud the French were of their new metric system, Prony's charge was 'not only to compile tables which left nothing to be desired about their accuracy, but also to make of them "a monument to calculation the greatest and the most impressive that had ever been executed or even conceived".' Prony quickly realized that, using existing methods, he would not live to see the project completed. What could he do? He took inspiration from Adam Smith.

Having one day noticed, in the shop of a seller of old books a copy of the
first English edition 1776, of Smith's 'Treatise on the Wealth of Nations',
I decided to acquire it, and on opening the book at random, I came across
the chapter where the author had written about the division of labour; citing,
as an example of the great advantages of this method, the manufacture of
pins. I conceived all of a sudden the idea of applying the same method to the
immense job with which I had been burdened, to manufacture my logarithms
as one manufactures pins.

(de Prony, 1824)

Babbage, with his eye for interesting technological advances, took note of de
Prony's work and discussed it at length in his *Economy of Machinery and Manufactures*. Prony's workforce was divided into three sections. The first section,
composed of 'five or six of the most eminent mathematicians in France', had
the task of investigating, 'amongst the various analytical expressions which could
be found for the same function, that which was most readily adapted to simple
numerical calculation by many individuals employed at the same time'. This then
they passed on to the second section, consisting of 'seven or eight persons of
considerable acquaintance with mathematics', whose job was 'to convert into
numbers the formulae put into their hands by the first section'. The numerical
versions of the formulae were then delivered to the third section, the engine room
of the business:

The members of this section, whose number varied from sixty to eighty, received certain numbers from the second section, and, using nothing more than
simple addition and subtraction, they returned to that section the tables in a
finished state. It is remarkable that nine-tenths of this class had no knowledge
of arithmetic beyond the two first rules which they were thus called upon
to exercise, and that these persons were usually found more correct in their
calculations, than those who possessed a more extensive knowledge of the
subject.

(Babbage, 1832: sec. 244)

The bulk of the work, therefore, was done by people who had no knowledge
of mathematics other than the 'first two rules of arithmetic', addition and subtraction.[2] How was it possible to reduce the calculation of complicated trigonometric
functions to simple steps of addition or subtraction? The key lies in the recognition
of two points.

---

[2] Prony preferred to use people with the minimum possible level of skill to do the bulk of the work.
Such people were obviously cheaper to employ, but also had the advantage that their lack of
knowledge made it easier to reduce them to the role of automata. Employers in the UK today
are beginning to take a similar attitude towards the computing graduates they employ, saying that
their technical training in mathematics and computing should be drastically reduced, to about a
third of their university education. The rest of their time should be spent on business studies!

(1) A trigonometric function can be approximated to an arbitrary degree of accuracy over a short portion of its range by an appropriate polynomial. That is to say if we have some trigonometric function of x we can approximate it by an expression of the form:

$$a_0 + a_1 x + a_2 x^2 + a_3 x^3 + \cdots + a_n x^n$$

where the a_i terms are constants and n is the maximum degree of the polynomial approximation.

(2) It so happens that tables of such functions can be computed using repeated additions using what was termed 'the method of differences'.

Trigonometric functions require quite long polynomials to give a reasonable approximation, so to illustrate how the method of differences works we will use a simpler example invented by Babbage himself: calculating the number of cannon balls in a pile.

In some old castles in Britain you still see rows of cannon ranged on the battlements with pyramidal piles of cannon balls by their side. Consider the relationship between the length of the pile edge at its base (or, equivalently, the number of layers in the pile) and the number of balls in such piles. This is given by the first two columns of Table 4.1. Suppose that this sequence can be represented by a polynomial: since the cannon balls fill a volume in space we can safely assume that the polynomial will be a cubic.[3] But the interesting thing comes if we analyse the table itself in the way shown in the rightmost three columns of Table 4.1, which hold the 1st, 2nd and 3rd difference terms.

The first difference is computed by subtracting the current entry in the table from its successor, giving the sequence $3, 6, 10, \ldots$ If we think about it, the 1st differences are in fact the numbers of balls in each successive triangular layer of the pyramid of cannon balls as we work down from the top.

The second difference is obtained by subtracting successive terms of the 1st difference from one another, giving the sequence $3, 4, 5, \ldots$ This is the number of balls on the edges of successive horizontal layers of the pile.

The third difference is always 1. This corresponds to the fact that as we go down the pile, each layer has edges that are one ball longer than the last. (And since the 3rd difference is a constant, the 4th and higher differences are all zero.)

Along with the knowledge that the third difference is constant, the bold-faced sequence in Table 4.1 (that is, 1, 3, 3, 1) contains sufficient information for us to reconstruct the whole table up to an arbitrary number of layers of balls. The trick is to perform the inverse operation of differencing, namely integration, and to do it in simple stages. Let us follow the method of M. de Prony and employ a division of labour.

---

[3] It is. Write the cubic as $f(x) = ax + bx^2 + cx^3$. Since we know the values of $f(x)$ for $x = 1, 2, 3$, we can write down a set of three simultaneous equations and solve for the unknown parameters, getting $a = 1/3$, $b = 1/2$ and $c = 1/6$.

Table 4.1 The number of balls in pyramidal piles

Layers	Balls	1st difference	2nd difference	3rd difference
1	1			
2	4	3		
3	10	6	3	
4	20	10	4	1
5	35	15	5	1
⋮	⋮	⋮	⋮	⋮

1

4

10

20

Imagine a long desk at which are seated three clerks, Alphonse, Bartholomew and Christian. Alphonse is given the task of producing a table of 100 rows, to be formed by starting with the initial 2nd difference and successively adding the constant 3rd difference. He therefore produces:

3
4
5
⋮

When he finishes, he hands this table to Bartholomew and starts work on his next table of 100 numbers.

Bartholomew has the task of forming a new table of 100 numbers by adding the numbers produced by Alphonse to a running total that starts with the initial 1st difference. His table looks like this:

$$3$$
$$3 + 3 = 6$$
$$4 + 6 = 10$$
$$5 + 10 = 15$$
$$\vdots$$

Finally, Christian takes the table from Bartholomew and adds the 1st differences to the starting value of the entire table. He produces a column looking like

$$1$$
$$3 + 1 = 4$$
$$6 + 4 = 10$$
$$10 + 10 = 20$$
$$15 + 20 = 35$$
$$\vdots$$

After a delay equal to the time for the first two clerks to complete their first tables, the third is working at full speed doing simple additions to turn out the final table. Each page of the table represents the accumulated work of three clerks who work in parallel on the arithmetic, forming a sort of pipeline of numbers.

Presumably the clerks will become very quick at their simple, repetitive jobs. And by employing a longer desk – a longer pipeline – the method of differences could be applied to higher order polynomials. For instance one might use the polynomial

$$1 - \frac{x^2}{2} + \frac{x^4}{24} - \frac{x^6}{720}$$

to approximate $\cos(x)$ when preparing a table. This would require six clerks per desk. Multiple desks in a room would have clerks working on different ranges of the cosine table.

4.4 Babbage's machines

Naturally, there is a significant possibility of error with this sort of manual calculation. If a small error is made in one of the higher-order differences it will propagate down that table and contaminate all of the downstream calculations. The consequences will be more serious, the higher the order of the difference in which the error occurs. If one could afford to have all of the calculations done twice this would significantly reduce the likelihood of error. But it is quite possible that certain operations are more likely to generate mistakes than others. In that case two clerks working independently might make the same mistake, and the resulting error would go undetected.

In his later years, Babbage recalled that while labouring with Herschel to correct such mistakes in tables of logarithms, he had exclaimed 'I wish that these tables could be computed by steam!' – and had then set his mind to solving just that problem. The ground had already been prepared by Adam Smith and de Prony – Smith through his explication of the principle of the division of labour, and de Prony by his application of this principle to the preparation of tables. The division of labour is a prelude to mechanization, because it reduces the basic operations of production to their simplest, most elementary form.

> The division of labour suggests the contrivance of tools and machinery to execute its processes. When each processes, by which any article is produced, is the sole occupation of one individual, his whole attention being devoted to a very limited and simple operation, improvements in the form of his tools, or in the mode of using them, are much more likely to occur to his mind, than if it were distracted by a greater variety of circumstances. Such an improvement in the tool is generally the first step towards a machine.
>
> (Babbage, 1832: sec. 225)

To this end Babbage developed his Difference Engine. The first prototype could handle third-order differences, and operates as a proof of concept. Having established the principle, he then set about raising money for a much larger machine suitable for the industrial production of tables. This machine was to to be able to compute 7th order differences to a very high precision, over 30 digits. This compares favourably with our electronic computers, whose default accuracy is currently about 15 digits in 'double precision' arithmetic. Babbage's engine was to be equipped with a printer to ensure that results of calculations were transferred to paper without the possibility of human error intervening.

The project to build the second difference engine eventually foundered due to a combination of factors: Babbage's poor relations with his chief engineer, his insistence on continually improving the design, and above all, the great difficulty he had in obtaining precisely and repeatably engineered components. The basic soundness of the design was, however, demonstrated in the 1990s when the Science Museum in London used Babbage's original drawings to have the machine constructed. It was found to work just as designed.

The principle of the machine's operation can be explained by reference to Figure 4.2. This shows the small prototype machine that Babbage constructed between 1828 and 1833. Suppose we were to set the machine to calculate the number of cannon balls in piles as described previously. Each of the difference terms shown at the top of Table 4.1 would be entered into one of the columns of the machine by rotating the digit wheels. Then the handle would be turned. With each rotation of the handle, the 1st difference would be added to the total. The 2nd difference is then added to the first difference and then the 3rd difference to the 2nd. It thus emulated in machinery the division of labour developed by de Prony.

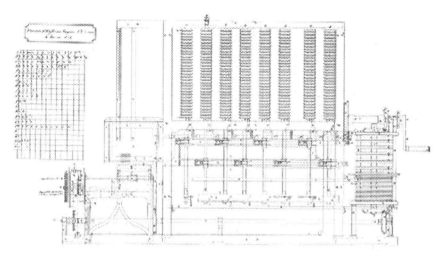

Figure 4.2 Babbage's prototype difference engine, from his engineering drawings.

The difference engine was the first machine capable of calculating and tabulating mathematical functions. But it was restricted to a small class of functions, those that could be approximated by polynomials. To do this it used two basic principles: storage of numbers, and addition. It turns out that subtraction could be performed by a subtle trick. Suppose I have a decimal adding machine that can handle two digits. That is, it can represent numbers from 0 to 99. Now I want to subtract 3 from 25 using this machine. How can I do it? By adding 97. $25 + 97 = 122$, but since the machine can only represent two digits it will show the answer as 22. This is the same result we get by doing $25 - 3 = 22$.

But there are four basic arithmetic operations: addition, subtraction. multiplication and division. Babbage, having seen that he could mechanize repeated addition and subtraction, sought to produce a machine that could handle a much wider range of calculations. This led him to his 'analytical engine', which prefigured the modern computer. Its key components were

(1) A set of number registers to store decimal numbers. These were similar to those of the difference engine. Babbage referred to these registers as $V_1, V_2, \ldots$ indicating that they were used to hold variables.
(2) A component which Babbage, in the industrial terminology of his day, called the *mill*. This was capable of performing the four basic operations of arithmetic on two numbers.
(3) An instruction store made up of punched cards. Each card specified three variable registers and an arithmetic operation. For instance it might specify a calculation such as $V_4 = V_1 + V3$.
(4) A set of data cards which held numbers to be loaded into the registers.
(5) A printer to produce the results.

Babbage realized that were such a machine to be constructed, it would be capable of mechanizing any calculation that a human mathematician might attempt. Technical and financial difficulties prevented it from being built, but already at the dawn of the industrial age the essential principles of the modern computer had been laid down. Implementation had to await the work of another great mathematician, Alan Turing. That story is taken up in the next chapter.

5 From machines to the universal machine

5.1 Processing information

In earlier chapters, we have seen how we may use physical concepts of energy and power to characterize the effort involved in producing artifacts. There, we noted that Watt used an abstract measure of horsepower, without reference to any particular or standard horse. We also introduced the cybernetic concept of information to characterize the information-bearing content and effectiveness of representations in messages. Just like Watt, Shannon used an idealized measure of the size of messages as numbers of abstract bits, without reference to any particular representations of ones and zeros. We will now turn our attention to how we might characterize the effort involved in processing the information that messages carry. As with work and information content, we will seek an abstract measure that does not depend on any concrete apparatus for manipulating messages.

It is important to clarify that there are a number of practically essential stages in processing information which are formally irrelevant to measuring the effort involved. For example, supposing we are sending messages consisting of simple arithmetic formulae for evaluation and we have encoded the characters making up the written formulae as binary codes for ASCII. Suppose we've just received a message consisting of the bit sequence:

```
001100010011001000101011001100100011001100101010001100110011
010000111111
```

We know each character is represented as 8-bit ASCII so we separate out the individual codes:

```
00110001 00110010 00101011 00110010 00110011 00101010
00110011 00110100 00111111
```

Next we turn to a table of ASCII codes and their textual equivalences, as shown in Table 5.1. we look up each code in turn giving the character sequence:

```
1 2 + 2 3 * 3 4 ?
```

Suddenly, we recognize a familiar kind of expression: 'what is twelve plus twenty-three times thirty-four?'

Table 5.1 ASCII codes

Code	Character
...	...
00101010	*
00101011	+
...	...
00110001	1
00110010	2
00110011	3
00110100	4
...	...
00111111	?
...	...

However, in order to *recognize a familiar expression*, our brains actually have to do analogous work to that involved in turning the original bit sequence into textual characters. That is, we have to identify the separate symbols (words)

```
<integer 12> <operator +> <integer 23> <operator *>
<integer 34> <terminator ?>
```

by grouping related characters together (lexical analysis). We then make sure that the sequence of symbols is grammatical (syntactical analysis), unlike, say

```
2 + * 4 ?
```

This involves recognizing not just that we have a sequence of *integers* separated by *operators* and ending with a *terminator* but also that we do multiplication before addition, so the structure is more like:

```
<integer 12> <operator +>
( <integer 23> <operator *> <integer 34> )
<terminator ?>
```

where we use (...) to group the strongly connected sub-sequence.

Now, what we've done so far has been to change from one representation to another. In a literal sense we have already *processed information*, but the purpose of the message was to require us to evaluate the formula 12+23*34. We can view this formula as a set of instructions:

Multiply twenty three by thirty four and then add twelve.

When we talk about information processing we mean the application of rules to *values* to produce new values. The entities *integer* and *operator* are syntactic constructs with no necessary meanings. We *interpret* the syntactic integers as denoting semantic value and the operators as denoting semantic rules. Hereinafter, when we talk about *measuring information processing*, we will mean the deployment of some yet to be identified metric for expressing the effort involved in applying rules to values. For the present, we won't worry unduly about the effort involved in transforming messages from one representation to another. Nonetheless, this does involve real effort and we will return to its characterization later on.

5.1.1 Characterizing information processing

Let us stay with the example $12+23*34$ and explore in more detail what is involved in evaluating it. To begin with, consider carrying out this sum using pencil and paper. First of all, we need to multiply 23 by 34:

```
 23  *
 34
 - - -
690  +
 92
 - - -
782
```

We:

- multiplied 23 by 30 giving 690. To do this we:
    - wrote down a 0
    - multiplied 3 by 3 giving 9, which we wrote down;
    - multiplied 2 by 3 giving 6, which we wrote down;
- next we multiplied 23 by 4 giving 92. To do this we:
    - multiplied 3 by 4 giving 12, wrote down 2 and carried 1;
    - multiplied 4 by 2 giving 8, and added in the carried 1 giving 9, which we wrote down;
- finally, we added 690 and 92 giving 782. To do this we:
    - added 0 and 2 giving 2, which we wrote down;
    - added 9 and 9 giving 18, wrote down 8 and carried 1;
    - added 6 to the carried 1 giving 7, which we wrote down.

It looks as if we carried out four multiplication steps and four addition steps but that is misleading. Each of these steps involved our brains in elementary mental arithmetic, probably unconsciously accessing long-familiar tables of addition and multiplication. But we have no idea how those tables are held in our brains or what is involved at the neural level in making use of them.

Suppose instead we had used a pocket calculator. For the first stage, we might have:

- entered 34 for which we:
    - pushed the 3 key;
    - pushed the 4 key;
- pushed the * key;
- entered 23 for which we:
    - pushed the 2 key;
    - pushed the 3 key;
- pushed the = key.

Now it looks as if we carried out six keystrokes, but again we have no idea how the rules of pocket calculator use are stored in our brains or what's involved in deploying them.

Furthermore, in moving the effort of arithmetical processing from our brains to the digital circuits inside the calculator, we have involved myriads of transistors which are interacting dynamically with each other. In principle we could locate the calculator design and use a logic state analyser to trace which transistors switch as the arithmetic takes place, far more easily than we can measure the equivalent neural activity in brains.[1] Nonetheless, it is not clear that trying to measure either neural or digital activity is necessarily a useful way of characterizing information processing effort, for much the same reason that James Watt did not invoke a real horse to characterize power. Every brain is different and there are thousands of different designs for digital arithmetic circuits, so choosing any one as a standard may not tell us anything very useful about information processing either in general or in other brains and circuits.

As it turns out, our first approach of counting operations is highly fruitful for measuring information processing, once we have decided on an appropriate abstraction away from concrete brains and circuits.

It is important to note that there are three components to performing the calculations: the specification of the required sum, the rules for performing arithmetic, and a mechanism for putting those rules into effect, that is for *interpreting* the rules. In measuring the information content and entropy of carrying out rules we need to take all three components into account. As we shall see in the next section, by a cunning choice of representations, we can still use information theoretic measures to characterize rules as well as the information to which the rules are applied, because rules and their interpreting mechanisms themselves may also be given encodings. Thus, we can get a handle on the effort involved in processing information by considering how the entropy of concrete representations of information changes as its processing progresses.

---

[1] This will slowly change as real-time brain imaging becomes both cheaper and more precise.

5.2   Turing machines

We now introduce the *Turing Machine* (TM) as a *universal* basis for characterizing information processing. TMs are named for their progenitor Alan Turing (see Hodges, 1983), who made outstanding foundational contributions to Computer Science a good 10 years before the construction of the first modern digital computer. We will further discuss the context in which TMs were elaborated in a later section but note here that Turing developed them in the 1930s in exploring the mathematical limitations to *effective calculation* or *computation*.

TMs (Turing, 1937) are based on Turing's abstractions from a human being performing arithmetic using pencil and paper, much as we have described arithmetic above. He observed that, in principle, a person might use paper divided up into squares with just one symbol in each square. He also observed that when the current piece of paper is full a person will use a new blank sheet. Finally, he noted that a person will move backwards and forwards from sheet to sheet, changing what's written already as well as writing new symbols.

Thus, the process could be simplified by using a linear *tape* composed of individual *cells* each of which may contain one symbol. There must be some means of inspecting and changing the symbols in the cells, and of considering different cells in turn. These might be achieved by a *head* which can read or write a current cell, and by a mechanism to move the head one cell to the left or right over the tape (or to move the tape by one cell). See Figure 5.1.

Finally the whole process must be driven by rules that indicate, for a given symbol on the current cell, how, if at all, the symbol is to be changed and which cell should be inspected next, that is whether the tape should be moved one place to the left or the right under the head. Note that, in performing arithmetic, a person will successively carry out the distinct activities of addition, subtraction, multiplication and division, with their own specific sets of rules. In general, rules may be grouped to correspond to distinct *states* in which specific activities may be carried out.

Thus, a TM rule is usually characterized as specifying:

- in some (old) state;
- with some (old) symbol on the current cell under the head;
- change the old symbol to some new symbol;
- change to some new state, which may just involve staying in the old state;
- move the tape under the head one cell to the left or right.

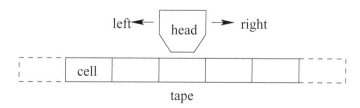

Figure 5.1 Turing machine.

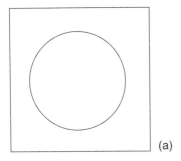 (a)   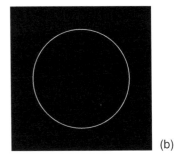 (b)

Figure 5.2 (a) Circle. (b) Inverse circle.

Such rules are usually written as:

$$(State_{old}, Symbol_{old}) \rightarrow (State_{new}, Symbol_{new}, Direction)$$

where $State_{exp}$ is usually a number, though a word will do just as well, *Symbol* is usually a single character, and *Direction* is either *L(eft)* or *R(ight)*.

5.2.1   Example: bitmap inversion

For example, consider inverting a black and white image, where every black pixel becomes white and every white pixel becomes black – see Figure 5.2.

Suppose we use a bitmap representation where a white pixel is held as a 0 and a black pixel is held as a 1. Figure 5.3 shows a considerably smaller version of Figure 5.2 in this new form.

We can linearize a matrix of bits by putting each row after the previous one, for example for circle (a):

```
0 0 0 0 0 0 0 0 0 0 0 1 1 0 0 0 0 0 1 0 0 1 0 0 0
1 0 0 0 0 1 0...
```

Clearly, we can put this onto a TM tape, with one bit in each cell, and with ∗s at either end to delimit the image.

```
0 0 0 0 0 0 0 0        1 1 1 1 1 1 1 1
0 0 0 1 1 0 0 0        1 1 1 0 0 1 1 1
0 0 1 0 0 1 0 0        1 1 0 1 1 0 1 1
0 1 0 0 0 0 1 0        1 0 1 1 1 1 0 1
0 1 0 0 0 0 1 0        1 0 1 1 1 1 0 1
0 0 1 0 0 1 0 0        1 1 0 1 1 0 1 1
0 0 0 1 1 0 0 0        1 1 1 0 0 1 1 1
0 0 0 0 0 0 0 0 (a)    1 1 1 1 1 1 1 1 (b)
```

Figure 5.3 (a) Circle as bitmap. (b) Inverse circle as bitmap.

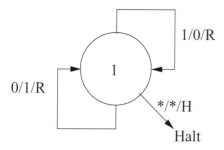

Figure 5.4 Inverting bitmap TM.

We can now define a set of TM rules to invert such an image. Assuming we start over the leftmost 0 or 1, if we find a 0 we change it to a 1 and move the TM right, and if we find a 1 we change it to a 0 and again move the TM right. Only one state is needed:

```
1. (1,0)  ->  (1,1,R)
2. (1,1)  ->  (1,0,R)
3. (1,*)  ->  (1,*,H)
```

Note rule 3, which, on encountering the rightmost *, enters a terminating *Halt* state denoted by direction H. Figure 5.4 shows a diagrammatic representation of this TM. States are numbered circles and transitions are arcs between states, labeled *old symbol/new symbol/direction*. Figure 5.5 shows a sequence of stages of running this TM.

5.2.2   *Example: copying*

Let us now consider a TM to make a copy of a sequence of 1s and 0s between *s:

$$* \ 1 \ 0 \ 1 \ 1 \ * \ \rightarrow \ * \ 1 \ 0 \ 1 \ 1 \ * \ 1 \ 0 \ 1 \ 1 \ *$$

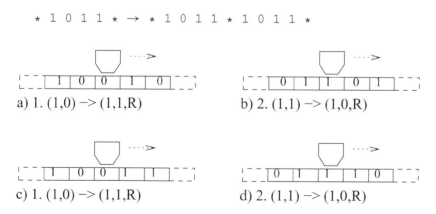

a) 1. (1,0) -> (1,1,R)   b) 2. (1,1) -> (1,0,R)

c) 1. (1,0) -> (1,1,R)   d) 2. (1,1) -> (1,0,R)

Figure 5.5 Inverting bitmap execution.

The machine will proceed as follows:

- Starting at the leftmost *, it moves right;
- If it finds a 0 then it:
    - replaces it with a X;
    - moves right to a blank space;
    - writes a 0;
    - moves left to the X;
    - writes a 0;
    - moves right.
- If it finds a 1 then it:
    - replaces it with a Y;
    - moves right to a blank space;
    - writes a 1
    - moves left to the Y;
    - writes a 1;
    - moves right.
- And if it finds a * then it:
    - moves right to a blank space;
    - writes a *;
    - halts.

See Figure 5.6.

Figure 5.7 shows a diagrammatic representation of this TM, and Figure 5.8 shows successive stages in processing the tape * 1 0 *, with the head position marked by (...).

This TM has two features of note. The first is the use of additional symbols as way of remembering how the computation is proceeding. Here we used X or Y to mark the last symbol found and hence how it is to be restored. In general, a TM may use arbitrary amounts of tape and arbitrary symbol sequences as 'rough working' or a 'scratch pad' during a computation.

The second is the use of potentially arbitrary additional amounts of space on either side of the initial sequence of tape symbols. Here, we can easily establish how much extra tape is needed for copying a symbol sequence but, in general, there is no mechanical way of determining how much space a computation will require. We will return to this in a later section.

It is also important to note that this copying TM is a step beyond printing presses that make copies of fixed-size chunks of text. The TM makes copies of arbitrarily sized symbolic encodings of information: there is no size limit on what it may copy provided the beginning and end are clearly delimited.

5.2.3 Example: searching

We will now consider a TM that locates a target sequence of binary symbols in another sequence, like searching for a word in a piece of text. We assume that, on

State 0	Start	State 4	Move left to find next to copy
1.	`(0,*) -> (1,*,R)`	13.	`(4,1) -> (4,1,L)`
		14.	`(4,0) -> (4,0,L)`
State 1	Found next to copy	15.	`(4,*) -> (4,*,L)`
2.	`(1,0) -> (2,X,R)`	16.	`(4,X) -> (1,0,R)`
3.	`(1,1) -> (3,Y,R)`	17.	`(4,Y) -> (1,1,R)`
4.	`(1,*) -> (5,*,R)`		
		State 5	Move right to copy * and halt
State 2	Move right to copy 0	18.	`(5,1) -> (5,1,R)`
5.	`(2,1) -> (2,1,R)`	19.	`(5,0) -> (5,0,R)`
6.	`(2,0) -> (2,0,R)`	20.	`(5,*) -> (5,*,R)`
7.	`(2,*) -> (2,*,R)`	21.	`(5,B) -> (5,B,H)`
8.	`(2,B) -> (4,0,L)`		

State 3	Move right to copy 1
9.	`(3,1) -> (3,1,R)`
10.	`(3,0) -> (3,0,R)`
11.	`(3,*) -> (3,*,R)`
12.	`(3,B) -> (4,1,L)`

Figure 5.6 States of the Copying TM.

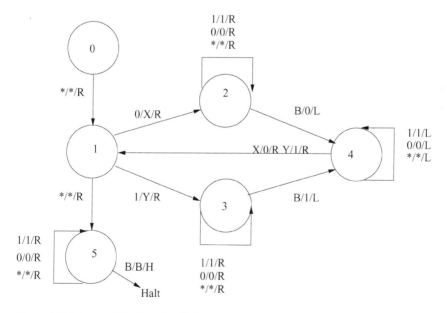

Figure 5.7 Schema of the Copying TM.

```
(*) 1 0 *          →    * (1) 0 *          →    * Y (0) *          →
* Y 0 (*)          →    * Y 0 * ()         →    * Y 0 (*) 1        →
* Y (0) * 1        →    * (Y) 0 * 1        →    * 1 (0) * 1        →
* 1 X (*) 1        →    * 1 X * (1)        →    * 1 X * 1 ()       →
* 1 X * (1) 0      →    * 1 X (*) 1 0      →    * 1 (X) * 1 0      →
* 1 0 (*) 1 0      →    * 1 0 * (1) 0      →    * 1 0 * 1 (0)      →
* 1 0 * 1 0 ()     →    * 1 0 * 1 0 (*)
```

Figure 5.8 Copying TM executing.

the tape, the required sequence is on the left, and that the sequences are separated and terminated by *s. For example, to find 101 in 1001011010, the initial tape is:

```
*101*1001011010*
```

The TM looks for each symbol in the first sequence in turn. In order to keep track of which symbols it has already found, it marks 0s as A and 1s as B. For example, suppose the TM has located the first 10:

```
*BA1*BA01011010*
```

When the TM fails to match the next symbol in the required sequence it restores all the symbols it has found in the second sequence, apart from the first symbol which it marks to make sure it doesn't look at it again, using a X for a 0 and a Y for a 1. It also restores the required sequence ready for the next attempt.

In our example, the TM next fails to match the final 1 so it restores the 0 and marks the initial 1 with Y. It then restores the sequence it's looking for before trying again:

```
*101*Y001011010*
```

When the TM finds the required sequence, both it and the found sequence have been marked with As and Bs, and the failed matches have been marked with Xs and Ys. For example:

```
*BAB*YXXBAB1010*
```

The TM then restores the failed matches:

```
*BAB*100BAB1010*
```

State 0   Start
1.   (0,*) -> (1,*,R)

State 1   Pick up next required symb
2.   (1,*) -> (11,*,R)
3.   (1,0) -> (2,A,R)
4.   (1,1) -> (6,B,R)

State 2   Looking for 0, right to *
5.   (2,0) -> (2,0,R)
6.   (2,1) -> (2,1,R)
7.   (2,*) -> (3,*,R)

State 3   Found *, looking for 0
8.   (3,X) -> (3,X,R)
9.   (3,Y) -> (3,Y,R)
10.   (3,A) -> (3,A,R)
11.   (3,B) -> (3,B,R)
12.   (3,*) -> (3,*,H)
13.   (3,0) -> (4,A,L)
14.   (3,1) -> (8,1,L)

State 4   Match, left to *
15.   (4,X) -> (4,X,L)
16.   (4,Y) -> (4,Y,L)
17.   (4,A) -> (4,A,L)
18.   (4,B) -> (4,B,L)
19.   (4,*) -> (5,*,L)

State 5   Found *, get next required symb
20.   (5,0) -> (5,0,L)
21.   (5,1) -> (5,1,L)
22.   (5,A) -> (1,A,R)
23.   (5,B) -> (1,B,R)

State 6   Looking for 1, right to *
24.   (6,0) -> (6,0,R)
25.   (6,1) -> (6,1,R)
25.   (6,*) -> (7,*,R)

State 7   Found *, looking for 1
27.   (7,X) -> (7,X,R)
28.   (7,Y) -> (7,Y,R)
29.   (7,A) -> (7,A,R)
30.   (7,B) -> (7,B,R)
31.   (7,*) -> (7,*,H)
32.   (7,0) -> (8,0,L)
33.   (7,1) -> (4,B,L)

State 8   Match fail, restore partial match
34.   (8,A) -> (8,0,L)
35.   (8,B) -> (8,1,L)
36.   (8,*) -> (9,*,R)
37.   (8,X) -> (9,X,R)
38.   (8,Y) -> (9,Y,R)

State 9   Mark 1st in partial match
39.   (9,0) -> (9,X,L)
40.   (9,1) -> (9,Y,L)
41.   (9,X) -> (9,X,L)
42.   (9,Y) -> (9,Y,L)
43.   (9,*) -> (10,*,L)

State 10   Restore required and retry
44.   (10,0) -> (10,0,L)
45.   (10,1) -> (10,1,L)
46.   (10,A) -> (10,0,L)
47.   (10,B) -> (10,1,L)
48.   (10,*) -> (1,*,R)

State 11   Success, restore before match
49.   (11,X) -> (11,0,R)
50.   (11,Y) -> (11,1,R)
51.   (11,A) -> (11,A,H)
52.   (11,B) -> (11,B,H)

Figure 5.9 States of the Searching TM.

If the TM hits the rightmost * then it has failed to find the required sequence. The TM rules are shown in Figure 5.9. Figure 5.10 provides a graphical representation.

This TM is considerably larger than the copying TM. More states are required because searching requires more actions than copying. And additional symbols

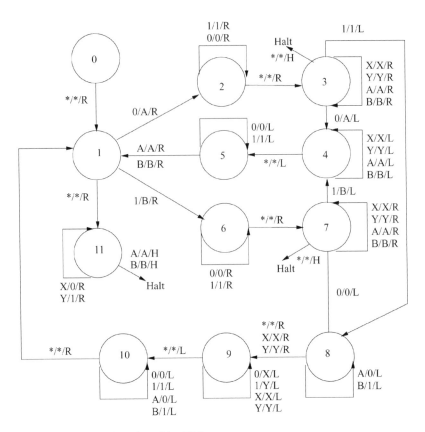

Figure 5.10 Schema of the Searching TM.

are needed to keep track of different intermediate information during the search. In general, the number of rules for a TM increases as the product of the number of states and the number of symbols. In principle, a tape may have arbitrary symbols in arbitrary positions so each state must account exhaustively for each symbol to ensure that all possible error configurations are detected.

In practice, however, a TM will not have exhaustive symbol coverage because, assuming the tape is always correctly prepared, it is often possible to rule out encountering some symbols in some states. For example, in the search TM, we know that if we're going rightward in state 1, having selected the next 0 or 1 to look for, then we know we won't find an A or B before the next * unless the tape is corrupted.

While this is a somewhat inefficient strategy for locating one symbol sequence in another, it is nonetheless eminently viable. For example, a human who can't read Japanese trying to identify a station on a Tokyo metro map might do worse than to systematically compare station sign characters with map characters, and keep track of which station names on the map they've already checked.

5.3   The universal Turing machine

A central argument in this book is that value derives from human labour because it is universal as a means of transforming reality, in the sense that, in principle, any human can perform any task any other human can perform, allowing for normal variations in strength, skill and learning capability. Thus, we may view human beings as *universal labour machines*.

Turing's deep insight was that it is possible to elaborate a *universal Turing machine* (UTM) which is capable of performing any computation. That is, a UTM can solve any problem which can be characterized by an individual problem-specific TM processing a problem-specific tape. In this section we will consider the UTM in more detail. In a subsequent section we will see that there are also fundamental limitations to what even a UTM can achieve. And in the final section we will consider the implications of the UTM and its limitations for both human and mechanical labour.

We have seen that during the execution of an arbitrary TM on an arbitrary tape, in some state with some symbol under the tape head, there is a corresponding instruction that specifies how the symbol is to change, the direction in which the tape is to be moved and the new state. We start to elaborate a UTM by first choosing an encoding – that is, a representation – of the arbitrary TM's instructions and tape themselves as sequences of symbols on the UTM's tape. We have also seen that during execution of a TM, some cognizance is required of the current state and symbol in finding the next instruction, and of the tape head position in knowing where to write the new symbol and move the head. Thus, the UTM must also explicitly record all these on its tape.

We show below a possible UTM tape organization.

$$-state\ symb!inst_1 - inst_2 - \ldots - inst_M!symb_1 \ldots head \ldots symb_N$$

From left to right, we see:

- an initial '-';
- the current state (*state*) and symbol (*symb*);
- a separating '!';
- the instructions (*inst_i*) separated by '-'s;
- a separating '!';
- the tape symbols (*symb_i*) with the tape head position symbol (*head*) which temporarily replaces that current symbol.

Given this tape organization, a UTM could execute the encoded TM and tape by repeatedly:

- searching the instruction encoding for an instruction that starts with the current state and symbol;
- copying the new state from that instruction to replace the current state;

- finding the head symbol in the tape encoding and replacing it with the new symbol from the instruction;
- moving either to the left or right of the new symbol, remembering the symbol there, replacing it with the head, and moving left to replace the current symbol with the remembered symbol.

We will not present the full UTM here, or consider the technical details of representing a bi-directional tape as a uni-directional tape. Nonetheless, note that the above summary is couched in terms of searching and copying, operations that we have already described in detail in previous sections. There is a rather dense account of the UTM in Turing (1937), and a more lucid presentation in Minsky (1967).

As a very simple example, again consider the TM to negate a sequence of 1s and 0s:

```
1. (1,0)  ->  (1,1,R)
2. (1,1)  ->  (1,0,R)
3. (1,*)  ->  (1,*,H)
```

Figure 5.11 shows successive stages of the tape for a UTM running this TM (1011R-1110R-1*1*H) with initial tape 01100. Note that the head position symbol is ˆ and the state is always 1.

At the initial stage 1, with the head over the leftmost tape symbol, the current state/symbol is 10, indicating that the state is 1 and the symbol under the head is 0. At stage 2, a 1 (for an inverted 0) has been written at the head position, the head has moved right, and the symbol under the head is 1. At stage 3, a 0 (for an inverted 1) has been written at the head position, the head has moved right, and the symbol under the head is again 1. And so on.

5.3.1   *Turing machine variants*

A TM consists of a single control unit inspecting and modifying a single tape, and in the control unit there is always just one instruction corresponding to the current state and tape head symbol. It might appear that further generalizing these characteristics would enhance the power of a TM, for example providing it with

```
1.   -10!1011R-1110R-1*1*H!ˆ1100
2.   -11!1011R-1110R-1*1*H!1ˆ100
3.   -11!1011R-1110R-1*1*H!10ˆ00
4.   -10!1011R-1110R-1*1*H!100ˆ0
5.   -10!1011R-1110R-1*1*H!1001ˆ
```

Figure 5.11 UTM with inverting bitmap TM.

multiple control units or multiple tapes or, rather than a unique instruction for each state and symbol, a set of alternative instructions. In fact, it is straightforward to show that all of these apparent improvements have direct equivalents in the original TM formulation.

First consider a TM with a head that can simultaneously inspect and modify multiple tapes, so each instruction specifies several old symbols and several new symbols. This is analogous to a contemporary computer simultaneously inspecting and modifying several, usually 8, bits in one RAM location. Suppose we number the cells on the first tape as $T1_1, T1_2, \ldots$, the cells on the second tape as $T2_1, T2_2, \ldots$, the cells on the third tape as $T3_1, T3_2, \ldots$; and so on. Then we may map these tapes onto a single tape by interleaving the cells: $T1_1, T2_1, T3_1, \ldots, T1_2, T2_2, T3_2, \ldots, T1_3, T2_3, T3_3, \ldots$. Each TM instruction that previously simultaneously affected N tape cells is now replaced by N instructions that sequentially inspect and modify successive positions on one tape.

Next consider a TM with multiple control units, running distinct instruction sets but all able to simultaneously inspect and modify different positions on a single tape. This is like several TMs sharing a common tape, and is analogous to contemporary computers whose CPUs have multiple cores running distinct programs but sharing a common cache. This may be realized by a modified UTM whose tape includes an encoding of each distinct TM and its current state and symbol, and where the simulated tape has distinct tape head markers. This UTM then runs each TM by turns.

Finally consider a TM with multiple instructions which may have the same current state and symbol but different new states and symbols, and directions. At each execution step, where several instructions satisfy the current state and symbol, one is chosen at random. This is known as a *non-deterministic* TM, in contrast to the familiar deterministic TM, where there always a unique instruction for a given state and symbol. A non-deterministic TM may be converted to a (possibly large) set of deterministic TMs where each has a different combination of single instructions chosen from the overlapping sub-sets. These TMs are then run on a modified UTM for multiple control units inspecting multiple copies of the same tape.

5.4 Decidability and the Church–Turing thesis

There is compelling evidence that Turing's formulation of computability is universal in a different but equally vital sense, namely, that *any possible computation* can be expressed as a Turing machine. To explore this further, we must first quickly recap the modern history of the foundations of mathematics.

At the start of the twentieth century, the British logicians Whitehead and Russell (1910–13) published a monumental work, *Principia Mathematica* (PM), in which they sought to show that all of discrete mathematics could be elaborated as theorems proved from a surprisingly small base set of axioms and rules of inference. Subsequently, the German logician Hilbert proposed a programme of exploring the PM approach to determine whether or not it was:

- *consistent*, that is, it was not possible to prove true both a mathematical theory and its direct negation;
- *complete*, that is, every true mathematical theory could be proved true;
- *decidable*, that is, there should be an algorithm for determining the truth or falsity of any mathematical statement.

Alas, Gödel (1962) showed that the system of PM could not be both complete and consistent. He did this by constructing a statement within the formalism of PM which asserts its own unprovability. If this statement were in fact provable within the system we would have a contradiction; the system would be inconsistent. Alternatively, the statement is true (that is, it is not provable), in which case the system is incomplete: it contains statements which, while true, are not provable.

The remaining requirement of decidability is based on the idea of an *algorithm* as a mechanical procedure for applying rules to manipulate sequences of symbols into some canonical form where no further rules apply. Thus, establishing the decidability of mathematics requires the ability to repeatedly apply rules to an arbitrary mathematical statement until the process terminates leaving a simple assertion of the statement's truth or falsehood.

Turing elaborated his machines in exploring how algorithms as mechanical procedures might best be characterized. At around the same time, Church (1936) presented the *lambda calculus* and Kleene (1935) *recursive function theory*. In short order, it was demonstrated that all three approaches were equivalent in that any statement in one system had an equivalent statement in the other two. This led to the assertion of what is now known as the Church–Turing thesis, that all possible formulations of algorithm, or effective computation, would have equivalent expressive powers.

Note that the term here is 'thesis', not the stronger 'theorem', as we have no way of capturing, let alone proving the equivalence, all possible formulations of algorithm. Nonetheless, this thesis has been strongly borne out, and despite numerous attempts no one has yet come up with a characterization of algorithm that is not equivalent to Turing machines. In particular, modern digital computers and their strongly related programming languages have been shown to satisfy the Church–Turing Thesis, which in turn implies that our computers have the same universal properties as TMs.

5.4.1   *The halting problem and undecidability*

Just as Gödel had shown, by constructing counter examples, that it was impossible find a consistent or complete formulation of mathematics, Turing demonstrated that mathematics embodied undecidable problems, by constructing a mathematical statement whose truth or falsehood could not be established by an algorithm.

A requirement of an algorithm, or effective calculation, is that the application of rules to symbols should eventually halt or terminate. It then seems reasonable to ask whether or not there is a way to modify a UTM to check whether or not an arbitrary TM halts on an arbitrary tape.

This is not as odd as it sounds: the use of computer programs to explore the properties of other programs is fundamental to software development. For example, people write computer programs in programming languages using text editors. A text editor is itself a program which has been written in a programming language using a text editor. Given the program text for a text editor it would be natural to use that editor to edit its own text.

More germane, when someone has written a program in a 'high-level' language like Java or HTML, it must then be *compiled* into the very low level machine code instructions that are executed automatically by a computer's central processing unit (CPU). Now, a compiler is itself a program, and the first compilers for high level languages were necessarily written using low level instructions. However, once there is just one compiler for a high-level language, it becomes possible to write many other programs in that language, including other compilers, including compilers for that language itself!

Just as a word processor checks the spelling and grammar of natural language texts, so a compiler first checks the spelling and grammar of programming language texts. So maybe a compiler could be written that would check whether or not the algorithm described by a program's text would halt.

Determining whether or not a TM terminates is known as the *Halting Problem*. In the same paper in which he introduced TMs, Turing also showed that the Halting Problem is undecidable. That is, there are TMs for which it is impossible to determine whether or not they halt on an arbitrary tape. Turing used a variety of Cantor's diagonalization to demonstrate the undecidability of the Halting Problem. Here, we will use a simple demonstration by contradiction: we will assume that we can build a halting checker from a UTM and then use it to sketch the construction of a TM whose halting behaviour is indeterminate.

Figure 5.12 shows the stages in the construction of a TM whose termination cannot be determined:

- Stage 1 shows the assumed halting-checker TM taking a TM and tape as input, and halting in either the 'Halts' or 'Doesn't halt' state depending on whether or not the test TM halts on the test tape;
- Stage 2 shows the 'Halts' state replaced with a state that loops endlessly, so if the test TM does halt on the test tape then the modified halting checker doesn't halt;
- Stage 3 shows the text for the modified halting checker from stage 2 given as input to itself. Now:
  - if the modified halting checker in stage 2 decides that the test TM does halt then it enters the endless loop so it doesn't halt, so when it is applied to itself it must halt in the 'Doesn't halt' state;
  - if the modified halting checker in stage 2 decides that the test TM doesn't halt then it enters the 'Halts' state and halts, so when it is applied to itself it must enter the endless loop and so doesn't halt.

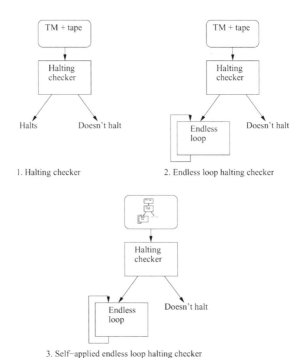

1. Halting checker

2. Endless loop halting checker

3. Self–applied endless loop halting checker

Figure 5.12 Undecidability of Halting Problem.

We have a contradiction, from which we conclude that we cannot construct the halting checker. That is, the Halting Problem for TMs is undecidable.

The Church–Turing Thesis also implies that any fundamental limitation to any one formulation of the notion of algorithm also applies to all the other equivalent formulations or embodiments, including digital computers and programming languages. A direct result of the undecidability of the Halting Problem is that there is no effective procedure for telling if an arbitrary computer programs halts. Thus, it is impossible to tell how much memory or time an arbitrary program requires, and hence how much power will be consumed by its execution.

A corollary of the Halting Problem shows that it is impossible to tell if two arbitrary TMs always compute the same outputs from the same inputs, that is, the equivalence of TMs is undecidable. Quite apart from making formal challenges to claims of software plagiarism deeply problematic, this strongly affects our ability to determine the information-theoretic properties of algorithms, as we shall consider later.

Nonetheless, it is important not to read too much into undecidability results. These are statements of the impossibility of establishing a general mechanical procedure to determine some property of a computation. However, they do not rule out the possibility of deciding properties for specific individual TMs.

Thus, there are well known *heuristics* used by mathematicians, and increasingly embodied in automatic theorem provers, which can be used to check, say, whether or not a TM halts, or whether two TMs are equivalent. The limitation is that it is impossible, in general, to tell in advance whether or not the use of such a heuristic will be successful.

5.5   The TM computability of markets

It has been alleged that market economies are somehow too rich or complicated or dynamic to be modelled by effective computational techniques. Noting that Cockshott et al (Michaelson and Cockshott, 2006; Cockshott and Michaelson, 2007; Cockshott *et al.*, 2008) dispute both the conceptual and physical possibility of non-effective computation in general, here we will next demonstrate how an idealized market system might be realized as a TM.

Consider the following summary of how a firm behaves:

(1) It writes to all its suppliers asking them their current prices.
(2) It replies to all price requests that it gets, quoting its current price p_i.
(3) It opens and reads all price quotes from its suppliers.
(4) It estimates its current per-unit cost of production.
(5) It calculates the anticipated profitability of production.
(6) If this is above the current rate of interest, r, it increases its target production rate u_i by some fraction. If profitability is below r a proportionate reduction is made.
(7) It now calculates how much of each input, j, is required to sustain that production.
(8) It sends off to each of its suppliers, j, an order for amount U_{ij} of their product.
(9) It opens all orders that it has received and totals them up.

    (a) If the total is greater than the available product it scales down each order proportionately to ensure that what it can supply is fairly distributed among its customers.

    (b) It dispatches the (partially) filled orders to its customers.

    (c) If it has no remaining stocks it increases its selling price by some increasing function of the level of excess orders, while if it has stocks left over it reduces its price by some increasing function of the remaining stock.

(10) It receives all deliveries of inputs and determines at what scale it can actually proceed with production.
(11) It commences production for the next period.

A full discussion may be found in chapter 15.

Note that there are two implied forms of information. First of all, all suppliers provide current price information on demand to all firms. While each firm will only use a tiny fraction of all possible commodities in its own production process, in principle any firm may obtain information about the prices of all commodities. This is equivalent to all firms sharing a common information server where they regularly update their own commodity price details. Thus, price information is essentially *public*.

Secondly, each firm makes some, presumably rational, calculation about what commodities to purchase, how production should proceed and the implications of pricing decisions. To inform this decision making, they will probably also keep records of their own production activities, prices and sales, along with what they deem relevant histories of supplier and competitor prices. This internal information is essentially *private*.

Let us make the eminently reasonable assumption that an individual firm's pricing strategy is itself effectively computable: prices take a finite time to determine and human beings are organic machines – see below. In that case each firm may be modelled as a multi-tape TM, accessing a private tape for its local calculations and a shared public tape of every other firm's prices.

Hence, a market may be conceived of as a hybrid multi-tape, multi-head TM which we may map onto a single-tape TM as follows. First of all, we interleave all the cells for the private tapes and the public tape, as described above for the multi-tape, single head TM, modifying each individual TM appropriately to find both its private and the public information from the shared tape. We now have a multi-head single tape TM so we next modify the UTM, again as described above, to take it in turns to simulate each TM on the common tape.

We seem to have linearized what was a parallel activity so we might appear to give advantage to those TMs that have earliest access to the public information. In fact, each TM always has most up to date information about its immediate predecessors so random placing of very large numbers of TMs should smooth away any inequities of ordering. Alternatively, the UTM may be further modified so that all TMs read from the public tape, calculate using their private tapes, and write to the public tape, in what is effectively lock step, so they all have consistent access to the same information.

5.5.1   *Information and complexity in Turing machines*

The fundamental difference between TMs and almost all other formulations of effective calculation is that a set of TM quintuplets is actually a specification for how to build a physical machine to perform the computation they describe. In contrast, other formal theories of computation – such as recursive function theory and lambda calculus, and their modern realizations as programming languages – all presuppose the presence of a separate interpreting mechanism for performing computations specified in the corresponding notations. That mechanism might be a mathematician or logician who understands the semantics of the notation, or it might be an embodiment of the notation's semantics in another machine, for example a digital computer running an interpreter written in some programming language. Thus there is an intuition that the TM notation, being so self-contained, is somehow a particularly succinct encoding of a computation.

The work of the information theorists Kolmogorov and Chaitin adds strong credence to this suggestion. They have shown that, in principle, for any computation there is a smallest TM capable of realizing it, where 'smallest' has the strict information-theoretic sense we discussed earlier. They have also shown that a TM encoding of a computation is more succinct than any other known encoding.

Note the careful use of 'suggestion', 'in principle', 'known'. First of all, we cannot know all possible formulations of computability so there may yet be one more succinct than TMs. In any case, finding a smallest TM for some computation is another recursively undecidable problem. While it is possible to enumerate all TMs as sets of quintuples expressed using a specific number of symbols, the equivalence of TMs is undecidable and so there is no way to tell if some TM smaller than an original performs the same computation. No matter: it may still be possible to determine heuristically, for some specific computations, whether or not there is an equivalent concrete minimal TM.

In any case, given a TM encoding we can establish the informational cost of replicating and distributing programs as well as data. This is a key component of any activity driven by computers, enabling both standardization of base operating environment and maintenance of consistency across systems. For example, these are fundamental considerations for a manufacturing plant of a dozen automatic machine tools, for a firm with hundreds of networked office systems, for an internet information provider deploying tens of thousands of indistinguishable search engines or servers, for hundreds of millions of households receiving unnoticed overnight software upgrades to their personal computers or digital TV systems, and for hundreds of millions of mobile phone users downloading service and game software from different suppliers on different mobile networks.

Perhaps of even greater significance, TMs are used as a standard for measuring the *complexity* of programs, that is how many operations they perform for a given amount of data. This enables us to at worst characterize and at best give precise estimates of how long a program will take to run. In turn, we can then explore, for example, the program's resource needs in terms of computer provision and energy consumption, its likely impact on the scheduling and resourcing of other activities, and ultimately whether or not the its use is practicable.

Once again note that as the halting problem is undecidable we have no effective procedure for determining how long an arbitrary TM takes. Nonetheless, there are well established analytic techniques for determining the complexities of individual TMs.

Complexity is denoted using *big O* notation (Sedgewick and Flajolet (1996)), where 'O' denotes 'order'. For example, consider going through a stack of N unordered letters to separate out those for each distinct recipient. Each item of post is inspected once. Assuming it takes the same amount of time for each letter, T_l, the total time $T_l \times N$ grows uniformly with the number of items. The process is said to take *linear* time of *order* $O(N)$. Now consider going through a stack of parcels. Handling each parcel takes longer than handling a letter but, again assuming each parcel takes the same time, T_p, the total time $T_p N$ still grows uniformly with the number of parcels and is still characterized as $O(N)$.

Next consider searching for a name in a telephone directory. Here the information is ordered so a good strategy is to start in the middle. If the name isn't on the centre pages, then if it's in the front half of the directory start again in the middle of the front half; otherwise start again in the middle of the back half; and so on. Thus, the number of names to be searched is repeatedly halved until either it is found or it is determined not to be in the directory. At worst, a directory of N pages will have to be halved $\log_2(N)$ times,[2] so the process is said to be $O(\log_2 N)$ or of logarithmic complexity. Note that for different sizes of directory pages, the time to search each pair of pages will differ but the maximum number of pages to be explored is still $\log_2(N)$.

Now consider constructing an input–output table showing the quantities of commodity category i required as input to produce a unit of output of commodity category j, for N distinct commodity types. If we suppose that every commodity category contributes to every other commodity category, then we need to acquire $N \times N = N^2$ values. Here the data grows with $O(N^2)$.

Next consider trying to crack a combination lock by trying all possible combinations. If there are N digits and each digit is between 0 and 9 then there are $10 \times 10 \times 10 \times \ldots \times 10 = 10^N$ possible combinations, so this process is of order $O(10^N)$ or exponential complexity.

Finally, consider trying to deliver copies of this book to every Institute of Econophysics in the UK but by the shortest route possible. Say there are N institutes and we know the distances between all pairs of institutes. Then we need to explore routes from N possible first destinations to $N-1$ second destinations to $N-2$ third destinations and so on, giving $N \times (N-1) \times (N-2) \times \cdots \times 2 \times 1 = N!$ possible routes. This is of order $O(N!)$ or factorial complexity.

In general, an algorithm whose order is a polynomial function of the number of inputs, N, is termed *polynomial* (P), and an algorithm whose order is greater than polynomial is termed *non-polynomial* (NP). Note that x^N grows far faster than N^x as N changes.[3] NP computations quickly become intractable – even though they are in computable in principle, in practice they require infeasible computing power and time.

5.5.2 The complexity of planning

The planning of production has long been derided as unworkable for an entire economy – despite its patent efficacy for global multi-commodity organizations with turnovers considerably larger than many national economies. At one extreme, it has even been suggested that planning is 'hypercomputational' or uncomputable, for example by Murphy (2006) and Marciszewski (2002). Noting Cottrell *et al.* (2008)'s detailed rejoinder to Murphy, we reiterate that all economic

---

[2] If $N = 2^x$ then $x = \log_2(N)$. E.g., $16 = 2 \times 2 \times 2 \times 2 = 2^4$ so $4 = \log_2(16)$.

[3] E.g., let $x = 2$: $10^2 = 100$; $2^{10} = 1024$; $20^2 = 400$; $2^{20} = 1048576$; $30^2 = 900$; $2^{30} \approx 10^9$.

activity depends on finite cycles of decision making based on rational calculation. If planning is hypercomputational then so must be market economies.

More reasonably, it has been argued, for example by Nove (1983), that the sheer scale of a modern economy makes planning infeasible in terms both of data gathering and the tractability of computation. Cottrell and Cockshott (1993) offer a detailed critique of Nove based on improved algorithmic techniques. Here, we explore how we may derive a complexity bound for planning, showing that classical planning is formally tractable, and with current technology, feasible.

The simplest Sraffian input–output system (Sraffa (1960)) requires the solution of a system of equations of the form:

$$A_a p_a + B_a p_b + \cdots + K_a p_k = A p_a$$
$$A_b p_a + B_b p_b + \cdots + K_b p_k = B p_b$$
$$\vdots$$
$$A_k p_a + B_k p_b + \cdots + K_k p_k = K p_k$$

where X is the quantity produced annually of commodity x, X_y is the quantity of y used to produce X and p_x is the unknown unit value of commodity x. Given known Xs and X_ys, we wish to solve the system for the p_xs.

These equations may be expressed as:

$$MP = QP$$

where M is an input–output matrix of the quantities X_y, P is a vector of unknown unit prices p_x and Q is a diagonal matrix of annual commodity quantities X. A little rearrangement and factoring gives:

$$MP = QP \longrightarrow MP - QP = 0 \longrightarrow (M - Q)P = 0 \longrightarrow BQ = 0$$

where $B \equiv M - Q$.

This homogeneous system has a non-trivial solution if B is singular, that is if it has a zero determinant. Then the system might be solved by a traditional method like Gaussian elimination on B, which here involves repeatedly removing terms for unit prices from successive equations. Thus, after cycle k, equation k has non-zero terms only for prices k to N, and at the end of N cycles the Nth equation just has a simple equivalence for price N.

In general, removing one term across two equations of T terms involves $O(T)$ calculations. At first we have N equations of N terms, requiring $O(N^2)$ calculations, then $N - 1$ equations of $N - 1$ terms, again requiring $O(N^2)$ calculations, and so on, giving $N \times O(N^2)$, which is $O(N^3)$ overall.

In the next phase, the value for price N is substituted in equation $N - 1$ to find a value for price $N - 1$. Prices $N - 1$ and N are then substituted in equation $N - 2$

to find a value for price $N - 2$, and so on, so that after a further N cycles all prices are known. This phase is $O(N^2)$, a factor of N less than the order of the first.

$O(N^3)$ is formally polynomial, and tractable. In reality, though, Gaussian elimination and related methods are only just technically feasible at present for manipulating matrices for real-world economies involving several million commodities. This would require the coordination of tens of thousands of current generation processors each with many gigabytes of memory. Nonetheless, internet companies like Google, offering fast information retrieval over very large data sets, are now starting to deploy this scale of compute resource.

Furthermore, each output commodity only requires a relatively small number of other commodities as direct inputs and so most elements of the input–output matrix are 0s: the matrix is said to be *sparse*. Sparse matrix algorithms offer considerable improvements on worst-case Gaussian elimination as only a small fraction of the total number of elements are manipulated on each cycle.

In the meantime, excellent results may be obtained from iterative approximations with the substantially smaller orders. For example, Cottrell *et al.* (2008) describe the following approach. The input–output matrix specifies the input quantity of every commodity required to produce unit outputs. We start with an assumed quota of final outputs and calculate the requisite number of inputs to produce them. The number of inputs will now exceed the original number of outputs so the latter are incremented accordingly. The additional outputs must also be produced so the process is repeated to find their input requirements, which again increment the outputs. The number of outputs will increase on every cycle but by smaller and smaller amounts: it is clearly not feasible to produce an output which requires even more of itself as an input. The process converges in a number of cycles, say C, determined by the precision of the underlying numeric representation, typically tens of cycles. Thus C is many orders of magnitude smaller than N.

In the worst case, if every output requires every input then on each cycle there will be N additional input requirements for each of N commodities and so the overall order would be $O(CN^2)$. However, as noted above, each commodity requires only a very small number of other commodities as inputs.

5.6   RUR or Robots R Us

The English usage of the word 'robot' dates from the 1920s and the play *Rossum's Universal Robots* (Capek, 1999). The play was originally in Czech, and the name Robot is an abbreviation of the Czech *robota* meaning labour or work. The Universal Robots are thus universal labourers. Rossum,[4] a businessman, introduces his universal mechanical workers, able to do anything that a human worker could do. The play focuses on the threat to human workers posed by these robots.

---

[4] A pun on the Czech word for reason.

Figure 5.13 The Unimate Robot, introduced in 1961 (reproduced from computer animation).

The domination of the worker by the machine was a common theme of art from the 1920s onwards – Fritz Lang's *Metropolis* (1927), Charlie Chaplin's *Modern Times* (1936) and Kurt Vonnegut's *Player Piano* (1952) being obvious examples – but there was something special about Capek's robots. The machines in *Modern Times* are recognizable as machines, and specific in their purpose. Capek conjured the nightmare prospect of a single machine that is universal, that can do anything that a worker can do, a machine from which no job is safe. The robot or android went on to be a staple of science fiction in the 1950s and 60s in the work of writers like Asimov (1950) and Dick (1968). Their robots were machines in human form, such perfect simulacra that they could pass unnoticed in a crowd.

When industrial robots were first built, in the 1960s, they were very crude in comparison. The Unimate series that came to be widely used in car factories had a single arm and a 'hand' to grip with, but were fixed to the floor and immobile. They were able to replace assembly-line workers putting parts onto, or spray-painting, cars, but would not have been able to drive the car away at the end. Unimates were an advance on the automatic production line equipment of the '30s in which each machine on the line was different and had a specialized purpose, but they were far from the Universal Robots envisaged by Capek.

Babbage's exclamation 'I wish that these tables could be computed by steam!' was made against the background of the first industrial revolution. The Fordist production lines of the second industrial revolution were the social stimulus to the dystopian art of Chaplin, Lange and Capek. They also provided in 1937 the intellectual climate in which Turing could make his conceptual leap from the Decision Problem to the Universal Computer. The next year, Capek's play was broadcast on BBC Television, the first TV science fiction production. In Capek, we see the notion of Universal Robots machines that can do any task; from Turing, we have the idea of a machine that can do any mathematical task.

Turing (1950) argues that it should be possible to build machines that could think and interact with us in a way that was indistinguishable from interacting with a human. For this interaction to be fair to the machine it is to take place remotely, over a data-link. Turing does not demand that his intelligent machine look and feel like a human. He does predict that human intellectual capacities will eventually be equaled by machinery. According to his view, the obstacles to machine intelligence were matters of engineering rather than principle.

Computing power has obviously advanced a lot since the early 1950s. Certain problems, for example chess playing, which featured prominently in early discussions of Artificial Intelligence, have now been solved. There are now many programs for the PC that can defeat most master players under tournament conditions. Even world champions have been defeated by chess computers. In 1997, a version of IBM's Deep Blue computer defeated world champion Gary Kasparov 3.5–2.5. But technically we are still miles away from developing the sort of Universal thinking Robots foreseen by Capek. Tasks which did not initially seem so hard – such as computer vision – have proven to be very difficult to solve.[5]

The key conceptual and technical requirement is to enable interaction with machines based on a shared general model of reality. This is not simply a matter of overcoming communication problems in image and speech recognition, and in speech synthesis, but more profoundly of giving machines *real-world semantics*, that is models of the world as rich as those that have made us humans the dominant species.

While the cognitive abilities of robots are a central problem, their mechanical engineering has proven almost as problematic. How do you get a machine to walk about with an independent internal power supply? How do you devise a mechanical power source which, for moderate loading, is as fast and responsive as muscle?

Until these problems are solved, we humans will remain the only Universal Robots. Until then human labour remains the ultimate resource in our economies.

5.6.1   *Robots of the world unite*

In chapter 1.1 we asked why given that mechanical power had replaced horse power, human labour power had not become equally redundant. Why is it that labour continues to be the dominant source of value? The basic answer is that labour continues to be essential to all production processes and this in turn stems from the inability of current technology to replace all aspects of human work.

Nonetheless, let us now assume that continuing development in computer science and artificial intelligence result ultimately in devices which can perform universal labour, and explore the implications. First of all, as disussed in chapter

---

[5] For a recent review of the issues see Saygin *et al.* (2000) and Feigenbaum (2003).

6, classical economics assumes that human labour is the source of new value, and that machines, as means of production, only transmit the value they embody from the human labour expended in their construction. Suppose humans may now be replaced arbitrarily by robots able to perform universal labour. Robots are machines, are means of production, so it appears that they can only transmit the value they embody from their original human progenitors. Thus, the use of robots is really no different to any substitution of technology for labour.

However, it seems unsatisfactory for the ability to produce value to necessarily be a property of protoplasmic but not mechanical beings. If robots really do perform universal labour, then they must produce value, just like humans.

To be able to perform universal labour, universal robots must be endowed with attributes equivalent (in the relevant respects) to those of the humans they replace. Thus, they must have the capacities to:

- form rich internal models of the reality they engage with;
- communicate with each other using shared linguistic notations and interpretations;
- associate with each other to perform collective tasks within a division of labour;
- analyse, plan and organize collective tasks.

Most crucially, they must be able to interact directly with humans as equivalents, if not as equals.

Above we discussed the undecidability results for TMs and saw that they also hold for all equivalent *Turing computable* (TC) formalisms and realizations, including digital computers. Universal robots will almost certainly contain digital computers as their central information processing components and so will be subject to the same limitations. In the wake of Gödel's incompleteness theorem it was argued by Nagel and Newman (1959) (among others) that humans cannot be subject such constraints. Since humans have formulated undecidability results by going beyond mathematical formalism, this shows that 'the resources of the human intellect have not been, and cannot be, fully formalized...' (Nagel and Newman, 1959: 101). However, 34 years later Ammon (1993) reported a computer-generated proof of Gödel's theorem. This suggests that it is possible for a machine to establish undecidability results with appropriate heuristics, and a heuristic is nothing more than a rule-governed procedure. Thus, it is no longer tenable to claim that Gödel's theorem shows that human reasoning transcends formalism.

Furthermore, human beings are finite machines with finite memories and finite lives, albeit fabricated from self-assembling biochemical components. Thus, it seems far more likely that the human brain has at best the same computational properties as any other finite realization of a TC system.

If universal robots are truly our equivalents and have all the hallmarks of sentience, then what might be their social status? Robots are built by humans so perhaps they are human property. But if robots are truly sentient then, as property, they are not in essence distinguishable from human slaves. Asimov (1950) explores this in engaging detail.

Incidentally, Asimov also formulated the famous 'Three Laws of Robotics', namely:

(1)   A robot may not injure a human being, or, through inaction, allow a human being to come to harm.
(2)   A robot must obey the orders given it by human beings except where such orders would conflict with the First Law.
(3)   A robot must protect its own existence as long as such protection does not conflict with the First or Second Law.

These are more stringent requirements than we typically place on our fellow humans. Any machine capable of understanding and applying them would indeed be a sentient, moral being.

To return to the status of universal robots: if, like us, they are endowed with universal social entitlements,[6] then presumably in a capitalist economy they may choose to alienate their labour and enter the labour market in direct competition with humans.

Of course, as with all technologies, universal robots will not be deployed until they are cheaper to build and use, and hence produce a greater surplus, than the humans they replace. However, perhaps their agendas will not coincide with those of humans; perhaps universal robots will not be enslaved as readily as we enslave each other, with pay-cheques or with chains.

---

[6]   Variously: 'Life, Liberty and the Pursuit of Happiness'; 'Liberty, Equality, Fraternity'; 'From each according to their ability, to each according to their need'.

6 Political economy: value and labour

This chapter plays a bridging role. In the previous chapters of this Part we have presented what one might call a philosophical history of technology. We have discussed technologies from the steam engine to the electronic digital computer, but not from a purely technical point of view: we sought to bring out the connections between the technologies themselves and their scientific underpinnings and consequences, as well as their social motivations and effects. And in particular we sought to show that a wide range of seemingly disparate socio-economic and technical phenomena can be unified by taking the perspective of the science of information. In the next Part we focus on theoretical analysis of the economy. The present chapter lays the groundwork for understanding the economic debates to which the following chapters contribute. It follows the historical approach, devoting particular attention to the classical political economists (hence cashing out part of the meaning of the 'Classical' of our title). One thrust of our argument will be that the ideas of the classicals are much more helpful then one might think, from opening a modern economics textbook.

6.1 Smith and Watt

Chapter 1 discussed the development of the physical concept of work by James Watt. It is probably no coincidence that Watt's colleague at the University of Glasgow, Adam Smith, was in the same period developing what would later be called the labour theory of value. We say 'probably' no coincidence because although we gather that Smith and Watt were friends and discussed intellectual matters together,[1] we don't know if there was any direct connection between Watt's development of the concept of work and Smith's conception of labour as the basis of value; this remains an intriguing speculation. Certainly Watt's work and Smith's labour are not the same thing – we have pointed this out above – yet the abstraction is similar. As Smith remarks, 'The greater part of people ... understand better what is meant by a quantity of a particular commodity than by a quantity

---

[1] 'Watt's workshop was a favourite resort of Smith's during his residence at Glasgow College, for Watt's conversation, young though he was, was fresh and original, and had great attractions for the stronger spirits about him' (Rae, 1965: 74).

of labour. The one is a plain palpable object; the other an abstract notion, which, though it can be made sufficiently intelligible, is not altogether so natural and obvious' (Smith, 1974: 134–5).

The 'abstract notion' of labour employed by Smith is not entirely new with him. His friend David Hume had written that 'every thing in the world is purchased by labour' in his *Political Discourses* of 1752 and John Locke had hinted at a labour theory of value in the chapter on property in his *Of Civil Government*. But these earlier statements were undeveloped and Smith was in a sense striking out on his own, since he was writing against the background of a 'natural law' tradition in which value was analysed in terms of 'utility and scarcity' (Hutchinson, 1988) and not, as Smith would have it, in terms of labour.[2]

Smith began his career as a moral philosopher, particularly concerned with the analysis of human sympathy, but he later turned his attention to political economy and of course his magnum opus was *An Enquiry into the Nature and Causes of the Wealth of Nations* (1776). The opening sentence of this work announces a perspective in which labour plays a central role:

> The annual labour of every nation is the fund which originally supplies it with all the necessaries and conveniences of life which it annually consumes, and which consist always either in the immediate produce of that labour, or in what is purchased with that produce from other nations.
>
> (Smith, 1974: 104)

Smith is interested in the proportion this 'produce' bears to 'the number of those who are to consume it' (or real Gross Domestic Product per capita, as we might say today), and he remarks that

> this proportion must in every nation be regulated by two different circumstances; first, by the skill, dexterity, and judgment with which its labour is generally applied; and, secondly, by the proportion between the number of those who are employed in useful labour, and that of those who are not so employed.
>
> (Smith, 1974: 104)

We can think of this as the identity

$$\frac{\text{output}}{\text{population}} \equiv \frac{\text{output}}{\text{worker}} \times \frac{\text{workers}}{\text{population}}$$

where output per worker, or labour productivity, is governed by Smith's 'skill, dexterity, and judgment'.

---

[2] The natural law approach stemmed from the work of the German jurist Samuel Pufendorf. Gershom Carmichael, also a Professor at Glasgow, produced an edition of Pufendorf's *De officio hominis et civis* which was very influential in Scottish intellectual circles.

The first three chapters of *The Wealth of Nations* are given over to a discussion of the division of labour, which Smith sees as the key to increasing labour productivity. We have already alluded to this in chapters 3 and 5. In a society where the division of labour has taken hold, individual producers do not produce their own subsistence; they produce a surplus, over their own requirements, of their own product, and rely upon others for articles they require but do not themselves produce. Smith takes for granted that the developed form of this interdependency is *commodity production* (the term is actually Marx's). That is, individual producers confront each other as independent property owners, and produce their respective goods as commodities, products destined for exchange via a market. In this respect Smith's argument is lacking in generality (as Marx would point out): commodity exchange via the market is one way – historically a very important way, to be sure – of organizing an economy based on a complex division of labour, but it is not the only way. The alternative is that the division of labour is planned, and that the goods produced by the specialized workers are *transferred* to their consumers rather than purchased by the consumers. This is the model followed in the division of labour within a peasant household or, on a larger scale, in the planned industrial economy that existed in the Soviet Union from the late 1920s till the late 1980s.

At any rate, talk of commodity exchange as a concomitant of the division of labour leads Smith to money in chapter IV of *The Wealth of Nations*, and thence to value. The term 'value', as applied to goods and services, has various meanings or shades of meaning. When we talk of a commodity's being 'good value' or 'value for money' we mean that it has a favourable ratio of useful or desirable qualities to price. This corresponds to the first pole of the opposition Smith established, between 'value in use' (or use value) and 'value in exchange' (or exchange value).

> The word value, it is to be observed, has two different meanings, and some-times expresses the utility of some particular object, and sometimes the power of purchasing other goods which the possession of that object conveys. The one may be called 'value in use'; the other, 'value in exchange'. The things which have the greatest value in use have frequently little or no value in exchange; and, on the contrary, those which have the greatest value in exchange have frequently little or no value in use. Nothing is more useful than water: but it will purchase scarce anything; scarce anything can be had in exchange for it. A diamond, on the contrary, has scarce any value in use; but a very great quantity of other goods may frequently be had in exchange for it.
>
> (Smith, 1974: 131–2)

In light of subsequent developments in modern economics, it is worth noting that for Smith (and for the classical political economists in general) 'value in use' seems to be understood as an objective category. Smith is perfectly confident in saying that water is highly useful and diamonds have little value in use; there is no suggestion that this could be a matter of 'individual tastes and preferences'. Even when objective, in the sense of being independent of individual tastes, value in use can depend on the situation. Which has the greater value in use, a hammer or a screwdriver? It's not a matter of opinion, but it depends on the task in hand. By contrast, modern economics has replaced the term 'value in use' by 'utility', and has cast utility not as a matter of the objective usefulness of goods but as a matter of the subjective 'psychic satisfaction' an individual derives from consumption of the good. This rather strange analysis would seem to apply best (if at all) to the highly refined luxury products of an advanced culture. Which has the greater utility, a novel by Charles Dickens or one by Jane Austen? A bottle of California Chardonnay or a Chablis? Here the satisfaction obtained by the individual is all we have to go on.

Although classical 'value in use' is not a subjective matter, it is clearly relative to the state of technology. We can infer from Smith's dismissal of diamonds as having 'scarce any value in use', if we didn't know it already, that diamond-tipped drills were not in use for oil exploration in Smith's day.

Anyway, having made the distinction between use value and exchange value, Smith proceeds to concentrate on the latter. He sets himself three problems.

> In order to investigate the principles which regulate the exchangeable value of commodities, I shall endeavour to show:
>
> First, what is the real measure of this exchangeable value; or, wherein consists the real price of all commodities.
>
> Secondly, what are the different parts of which this real price is composed or made up.
>
> And, lastly, what are the different circumstances which sometimes raise some or all of these different parts of price above, and sometimes sink them below their natural or ordinary rate; or, what are the causes which sometimes hinder the market price, that is, the actual price of commodities, from coinciding exactly with what may be called their natural price.
>
> (Smith, 1974: 132)

In understanding these questions it is important to be clear on terminology. Smith's first question concerns the 'measure' of exchangeable value: he wants to know how exchange value is best measured or expressed. This is quite distinct from the question of the *determination* of exchange value. Well, actually 'determination' can mean two things. It *can* mean measurement, as in 'How would you determine the height of that tree?' (By triangulation, perhaps.) Or it can mean causation: in this sense the height of the tree is determined by its genetic material (Is is a dogwood or a redwood?) and its environment (How much sunlight and water were available to it?). When we use the phrase 'determination of value' below we take it strictly in the second sense, to refer to the causal processes governing the exchange value of commodities.

Smith's second question (What are the different parts of which real price is made up?) relates to the determination of value, but note that he seems to prejudge the issue, taking for granted that exchange value is determined by an adding up of component parts. His third question introduces the important concept of 'natural price': this is the price that is just sufficient to call forth a supply of the product that meets the demand for it. In Smith's view natural price constitutes the 'centre of gravitation' of actual, day-to-day market prices. To update Smith's Newtonian metaphor using the language of modern dynamics we might talk of natural price as an *attractor* for market price. We shall have more to say about this below.

6.2 Labour commanded as a measure of value

The title of Smith's Chapter V – 'Of the Real and Nominal Price of Commodities, or their Price in Labour, and their Price in Money' – tells us where he's headed on his first question. He is emphatic that the 'real' price of commodities must be measured by 'labour commanded'.

> Labour was the first price, the original purchase-money that was paid for all things. It was not by gold or by silver, but by labour, that all the wealth of the world was originally purchased; and its value, to those who possess it, and who want to exchange it for some new productions, is precisely equal to the quantity of labour which it can enable them to purchase or command.
>
> (Smith, 1974: 133)

In the day-to-day operations of a market economy it is 'natural' to express the exchange value of goods in terms of money: the money one would have to hand over to acquire the good, or that one could realize by selling it. But Smith argues this measure is superficial and potentially misleading. Superficial, because it does not take into account the point that the 'real price of everything, what everything really costs to the man who wants to acquire it, is the toil and trouble of acquiring it.' Potentially misleading, because money is not constant in its own value over time. A better measure of the exchangeable value of a commodity is the quantity of labour which it enables its possessor to 'purchase or command'. Smith's particular formulation of labour commanded is appropriate to an age when people (of a certain class, of course) were accustomed to hiring servants. Thus if I own a commodity with a market value of one guinea (twenty-one shillings), and if the labour of a servant can be had for one shilling per day, then with the money obtained by selling the commodity I can command the labour of a servant for three weeks. For the modern reader an alternative version of Smith's calculation may seem more natural: the 'labour commanded' by a commodity represents the time you would have to work (say, at the average wage) in order to buy the commodity. In both cases – Smith's version and the modern one – the calculation of labour commanded is the price of the item divided by some measure of the wage, usually an average.

This is a good comparative measure of the cost of goods to a working consumer at widely separated points in time, or across nations at a point in time if the exchange rates of national currencies are a questionable guide to the respective purchasing power of the currencies in their home economies. Thus for instance a new Ford Model A car (4-door model) cost $570 in 1928, while a new Ford Escort 4-door cost about $11,000 in 2000. Is the Escort in 2000 really almost 20 times as costly as the 1928 model? Not in any meaningful sense. The average hourly wage for manufacturing workers was $0.56 in 1928, and $14.50 in 2000. If we take a working month to be 160 hours, this means that the labour commanded by the Model A in 1928 was 6.3 months, while the labour commanded by the Escort in 2000 was 4.7 months: in real terms, the Escort is cheaper than the Model A.[3]

Notice that the labour time required to produce a good and the labour it commands in exchange are not the same thing. Say a basic car in the USA today commands five months' labour at the average wage. What can we say about the labour time required to *produce* a car? Well, suppose that were also five months; in that case the average worker could work five months to obtain a commodity that embodies five months' labour. That is, his wage over the period would equal the value of the output he produces over the same period. But this means that the workers' wages would exhaust the value of the product – there would be nothing left over for profit. If the profit margin on car production is positive, it must be that wages per month are less than the exchange-value produced per month, or in other words the labour-time required to make the car is less than the labour-time it commands. If the car commands five months' labour, it might take, say, three worker-months to produce. Further, the factors making for changes in the labour required to produce a commodity, and those making for change in the labour it commands, are not the same. A change in the wage rate will alter the amount of labour commanded by any commodity of given price, while it is changes in technology, not wages, that produce changes in the labour time required to produce things.

We have explicated Smith's idea that 'labour commanded' is the best measure of value, but was he right? His successor in the line of classical political economy, David Ricardo, disagreed. Ricardo accepted Smith's point that plain money-price is not a good measure since money is variable in its own value, but he turned that argument against Smith: wages are variable too.

Writing in the early nineteenth century, Ricardo took it for granted that the wage was basically a subsistence wage, and as such was primarily governed by the price of food, 'corn' in particular. So suppose something happens that lowers the price of corn relative to other commodities; the wage will be pushed down too. If the prices of other commodities remain relatively stable, then on Smith's measure 'real prices' (in terms of labour commanded) have risen. According to Ricardo this is specious: it's wages (and corn) that have fallen, not prices that have risen.

This objection on Ricardo's part is bound up with a quest that absorbed a great deal of his intellectual energy, namely the search for an 'invariable standard of value': when A rises relative to B, how can we tell whether it is 'really' A that has risen or B that has fallen? Many later economists have suspected that this is

---

[3] The data in this paragraph were collected from The Bureau of Labor Statistics and *Collectibles Corner* for August 27, 1999, at www.krause.com.

a will-o'-the-wisp. At any rate, it seems that Smith would probably have stuck to his guns: if I have to work more hours to purchase a unit of commodity X than before, then X has become more expensive in real terms, regardless of how the change came about.

One's sympathies may be pulled either way in this debate. But it's worth noting that subsequent writers who have taken seriously the problem of measurement have tended to gravitate to Smith's solution.[4] Keynes, in his *General Theory of Employment, Interest and Money* (1936) grappled with the measurement issue and concluded that the only measures he could be confident in were sums of money and hours of labour time; he worked in terms of the 'wage-unit', deflating money-prices by the average wage. Farjoun and Machover, in their *Laws of Chaos* (1983), similarly operationalize their concept of 'specific price' (that is, price per hour of labour-time embodied in the product) by using the ratio of money-price to the average wage in the numerator.

Ricardo's objection has some force, but its force is reduced by the changes in the economy since his day. Wages are no longer strictly subsistence wages, and they are no longer so dependent on the price of any particular commodity: the 'corn'-based counter-example to Smith's idea is no longer plausible.

6.3   Labour time and the determination of value

Having argued that labour commanded is the best measure of value, Smith turns in Chapter VI of *The Wealth of Nations* to 'the Component Parts of the Price of Commodities'.

> In that early and rude state of society which precedes both the accumulation of stock and the appropriation of land, the proportion between the quantities of labour necessary for acquiring different objects seems to be the only circumstance which can afford any rule for exchanging them for one another. If among a nation of hunters, for example, it usually costs twice the labour to kill a beaver which it does to kill a deer, one beaver should naturally exchange for or be worth two deer. It is natural that what is usually the produce of two days' or two hours' labour, should be worth double of what is usually the produce of one day's or one hour's labour.
>
> (Smith, 1974: 150)

Here we have it – the idea that the labour time required to produce a given product governs or determines the exchange value of the product. There is, Smith says, a 'natural' proportionality between required labour time and exchange value. He proceeds to qualify this idea, saying that labour which is harder, or requires more skill, will count for more than simple labour. More importantly, he implicitly qualifies the idea with his opening clause, confining it to an 'early and rude state of society'. We'll turn to Smith's qualifications shortly but first, at the risk of belabouring the obvious, we'll ask why he put forward the basic idea in the first place.

---

[4] Many economists are happy to take the numbers as given, and gaily go ahead with crunching them.

One possibility is the notion that 'fair's fair' – the goods on one side of a barter transaction 'ought to' embody the same number of hours of labour-time as the goods on the other side. But it's unlikely that this is what Smith had in mind.[5] More likely, he was thinking in terms of self-interested calculation. If I'm in possession of a beaver which 'usually' costs $2h$ hours to kill and I'm contemplating exchanging this for deer that 'usually' cost h hours apiece, then I'm not interested in exchange unless the ratio is at least one beaver per two deer; otherwise I could do better by hunting deer myself. The possessor of the deer is thinking symmetrically, and is willing to part with the deer only if two deer will fetch at least one beaver. In each case the question is: How am I doing in exchange versus proceeding on my own account? And the upshot is that exchange will take place only if both parties are willing, which requires that, as Smith says, one beaver should exchange for two deer.

The presupposition here – implied in Smith's 'usually' – is twofold: the individual hunters are of roughly equal productivity, and they're aware of that fact. An interesting question arises if the hunters are somewhat specialized (one can kill beaver more effectively and one is better at hunting deer). Then, it seems, a wedge may open up: there's an overlap between (a) the exchange ratio below which hunter A reckons he's better off going it alone and (b) the exchange ratio above which hunter B favours autarky. In other words, there's a range of exchange ratios at which they'd both find trade advantageous, so where does the ratio settle? This sort of analysis was beyond Smith, but it was the basis of Ricardo's theory of comparative advantage. Ricardo concluded that such a wedge could indeed appear in international trade, due to the limited mobility of both labour and capital across national boundaries, in which case exchange ratios were not fully determined by labour-time embodied, and could vary over a certain range.

Holding Ricardo off for a moment, let's return to Smith. He had said that the labour time required to produce a commodity affords the only plausible rule that might govern the ratio in which it commonly exchanges against other commodities. But he had restricted this proposition to the 'early and rude' state of society. Why?

Reading further, it seems that, for Smith, the distribution of the product of labour is the key factor. In the early and rude state, 'the whole produce of labour belongs to the labourer; and the quantity of labour commonly employed in acquiring or producing any commodity is the only circumstance which can regulate' its exchange value. By contrast, in a developed market economy, where 'stock [i.e. capital] has accumulated in the hands of particular persons', we have a state where

> the whole produce of labour does not always belong to the labourer. He must in most cases share it with the owner of the stock which employs him. Neither is the quantity of labour commonly employed in acquiring or producing any commodity, the only circumstance which can regulate the quantity which

---

[5] Unlikely, because elsewhere in *The Wealth of Nations* Smith is quite explicit in saying that considerations of fairness have little purchase in economic affairs.

it ought commonly to purchase, command, or exchange for. An additional quantity, it is evident, must be due for the profits of the stock which advanced the wages and furnished the materials of that labour.

(Smith, 1974: 152)

The profits of stock, says Smith, constitute a second 'component part' of price, over and above the wages of labour. He then goes on to say that the rent due to the landlord constitutes a third component part of price. Exchange value can no longer be based on labour alone.

Smith has got into a muddle here. He seems to have persuaded himself that if the prices of commodities remained proportional to the labour time required to produce them then profit would be ruled out. But this doesn't follow at all. In a capitalist economy the exchange values of commodities cannot, in general, equal the *wages paid* in their production, else there would be no profit. But the propositions (a) that prices are proportional to the labour time required to produce things, and (b) that prices are equal to the wages paid in the production of things, are quite distinct: neither one implies the other.

Smith seems closer to getting it right when he writes, 'The value which the workmen add to the materials ... resolves itself ... into two parts, of which the one pays their wages, the other the profits of their employer' (Smith, 1974: 151). That is, one can think of the value of a commodity as being determined by the labour time required to produce it, and then, as a distinct question, consider the 'resolution' or decomposition of this value into wages and profit. This was the position taken by David Ricardo, the first writer after Smith to make real progress in political economy.

6.4 Ricardo: clarity achieved

The labour theory of value (LTV) – that is, the idea that, to a first approximation, the value in exchange of commodities is in proportion to the labour time required for their production – is first clearly and unequivocally expressed by Ricardo. As we have said, he cut through Adam Smith's confusion on this point, rescuing the LTV from its confinement to a prehistoric world of independent hunters. The LTV is given pride of place in Ricardo's *Principles of Political Economy and Taxation*; the opening words of Chapter 1 are

The value of a commodity, or the quantity of any other commodity for which it will exchange, depends on the relative quantity of labour which is necessary for its production, and not on the greater or less compensation which is paid for that labour.

(Ricardo, 1951: 11)

We will examine three questions in relation to Ricardo's LTV: What is the proper domain of this theory? How does Ricardo justify it? How does the theory handle profit and rent?

On the first question, Ricardo clearly demarcates the commodities whose value is governed by the LTV, namely those that are *reproducible via the application of labour*. If we're talking about bottles of Chateau Latour Pauillac 1996[6] or paintings by Matisse the LTV is of no help. The prices of such items are unrelated to the labour-time that went into making them, and depend jointly on their scarcity and how badly rich people want to own them. But such commodities are the exception.

> These commodities, however, form a very small part of the mass of com-modities daily exchanged in the market. By far the greatest part of those goods which are the objects of desire, are procured by labour; and they may be multiplied, not in one country alone, but in many, almost without any assignable limit, if we are disposed to bestow the labour necessary to obtain them.
>
> (Ricardo, 1951: 12)

This statement in itself takes us onto the second issue, Ricardo's justification of the theory. He talks of commodities which 'may be multiplied... almost without any assignable limit, if we are disposed to bestow the labour necessary to obtain them'. This must be taken to the letter: ultimately, *only* labour is required to produce such things. Of course, tools and materials may be (usually are) needed, but these in turn can be resolved into the labour time required to produce them. Ricardo takes the example of cotton stockings.

> First, there is the labour necessary to cultivate the land on which the raw cotton is grown; secondly, the labour of conveying the cotton to the country where the stockings are to be manufactured, which includes a portion of the labour bestowed in building the ship in which it is conveyed, and which is charged in the freight of the goods; thirdly, the labour of the spinner and weaver; fourthly, a portion of the labour of the engineer, smith, and carpenter, who erected the buildings and machinery, by the help of which they are made; fifthly, the labour of the retail dealer, and of many others, whom it is unnecessary further to particularize.
>
> (Ricardo, 1951: 25)

In this light Ricardo seems to be thinking: what else other than labour *could* account for the value of commodities?

Let's pause on this for a moment. One possible objection would be, what about the natural resources involved? Surely human labour doesn't produce stockings from nothing. Parallel to Ricardo's catalogue of the particular sorts of labour required to produce the stockings, one might think of the soil in which the cotton grows, the sunlight and rain that sustain its growth, the wind that powers the ship, and so on. Yes, of course, but Ricardo's thinking is that these resources come free, and so don't contribute to the economic cost of the stockings. (But if the cotton

---

[6] Bargain price on the Internet as of this writing: $1799.99 apiece.

needs artificial irrigation, then the labour time required to arrange that has to be reckoned in.)

A second and deeper question is, how is Ricardo able simply to add up the various sorts of labour he mentions? Clearly he is following Smith in thinking of 'labour in the abstract', such that one can add the labour of the farmer, the seaman, the shipwright, the spinner and so on without any conceptual difficulty. But what licenses this? If we were like the bees, wolves or horses of chapter 1 this wouldn't work. Imagine a humanity composed of sub-species, some of whom were only capable of spinning, some only of seafaring, and so on. Then adding up hours of 'human labour' would be no more meaningful that adding up hours of operation of the Large Hadron Collider and of an electric toaster. But in fact we are the 'Universal Robots' of section 5.6. A normal human being is capable of performing a huge variety of tasks. In many cases this involves training, but we can treat this in the spirit of Ricardo's analysis by resolving the cost of training into the labour time it takes (work on the part of the student or apprentice and the teacher).

In sum Ricardo is saying, not only is labour required for the production of every commodity but in a real sense human labour is the only true cost. The amount we can have of any given commodity is ultimately governed by the amount of labour time we're willing to put into making it, directly and indirectly. And he's confident that this basic information will come through in exchange ratios. Why does an iPod cost 30 times as much as a pizza? According to Ricardo, the only rational explanation is that the iPod takes about 30 times as much labour to produce. Of course, like Smith before him and Marx after him, Ricardo was well aware that a host of contingent, 'accidental' factors can drive the prices of commodities up or down relative to their 'centres of gravitation'. What he's claiming to theorize is that 'centre', or 'natural price'.

6.4.1 Ricardo on profit and rent

We noted earlier that Ricardo objected to Smith's 'component parts' or 'adding up' theory of value. The motivation for Smith's theory was the observation that the price of any given commodity has to afford not just wages for the workers but also profit for the capitalist and rent for the landlord. Ricardo recognizes this, but he conceptualizes it differently. In brief,

(1) price (accidental factors aside) is determined by the labour time required to produce the commodity, as we've said.

(2) The wage is determined by forces of supply and demand in the labour market. Along with the hours of direct labour performed, this fixes the share of price going to wages.

(3) The share of price going as rent is determined by a specific mechanism which we'll describe below; and

(4) profit is a 'residual', whatever is left over. All being well, from the capitalist's point of view, this will be positive but there's nothing to stop it being zero or negative (costs exceed price and the capitalist makes a loss).

So Ricardo has a 'breaking down theory' not an 'adding up theory'. We'll deal with two additional issues here: first, the promised explanation of how rent is determined; and second, a significant – but, according to Ricardo, quantitatively minor – qualification to the LTV that is demanded by the careful analysis of profitability.

Ricardo's theory of rent is couched in terms of the economy of his day (corn growing figures largely) but is in fact very general. Let's start out with an economy that is supporting a relatively small population. The corn required to feed that population can be grown on the best, most fertile land, and is therefore quite cheap. Now the population grows. To produce more corn we must bring less fertile land into cultivation.[7] Then, Ricardo says, we'll run into 'diminishing returns': the labour required to produce the last bushel of corn will increase, and the price will have to rise. But what if I'm still farming the best land, and therefore producing corn at a cost substantially below the new price? Then I get a sort of bonus: there's only one price for corn – the new, higher price – and I get to sell my cheap corn at that price. This bonus Ricardo calls 'rent'. If I'm a tenant farmer, my landlord can cream it off by raising my rent, in the ordinary contractual sense of the word. If I'm farming my own land the rent is no less real, it just flows to me.

The most striking example of Ricardian rent on a world scale today is the revenue enjoyed by the Middle Eastern oil producers. The world oil price (gyrations apart) has to cover the cost of production in the less productive oil-fields (e.g. in the USA). The cost of production in Saudi Arabia, for example, is very much less than that and the Saudis (or some of them) reap the benefit in massive oil-rents.[8]

In relation to Ricardo's theory of value, the key point is that rent, in the economic sense, is not a magnitude 'determined in advance' that governs the prices of commodities, it's a consequence of differential production costs (see also Digression 6.1).

Now to profits once more. We said that Ricardo conceives of profit as a residual. Nonetheless, he has the idea that 'in equilibrium' (not a term he used, but it captures his thought) the rate of profit in different industries or trades should be the same (after adjusting for differential riskiness and other possible complications). Smith and Marx had the same thought. If the rate of profit were not the same across industries then capitalists have an incentive to get out of low-profit industry X and into high-profit industry Y, which would shift the prices of X and Y, meaning that we're not in equilibrium.

The question then is this: is a single rate of profit across all industries compatible with the labour theory of value as stated above? And the answer is, in general,

---

[7] Or we could farm the best land more intensively (applying more fertilizer and so on). Ricardo's theory handles this case just fine but the exposition is simpler if we imagine less good land being used.

[8] It is easy to find statistics on the market price of oil, not so easy to find figures for its cost of production. But studies by the International Energy Agency cited on the Internet put the cost of production in Saudi Arabia at about 2 or 3 dollars per barrel.

Digression 6.1 Rent and Nature's Bounty

Adam Smith had said that in agriculture 'nature labours along with man', and that rent 'may be considered as the produce of those powers of nature, the use of which the landlord lends to the farmer.' It represents 'the work of nature which remains, after deducting or compensating every thing which can be regarded as the work of man.' Ricardo turned this on its head. Rent does not reflect nature's bounty but rather her stinginess: 'In proportion as she becomes niggardly in her gifts, she exacts a greater price for her work.' (Ricardo, 1951: 76)

If there were a limitless supply of top quality corn-growing land, corn land would command no rent. If all the world's oil-fields were as productive as the Saudi ones, there would be no oil rent.

---

no, for a relatively subtle reason. Ricardo expressed it in terms of the 'durability of the instruments of production'. Suppose, he said, that industry X requires a bigger investment in long-lasting means of production (e.g. fixed capital) than industry Y. To keep things simple, let's assume that the products of both X and Y require 100 hours of labour time per unit (total, direct plus indirect), so that the simple LTV would predict they'd have same value. The trouble is that if prices conformed to the strict LTV, X wouldn't be as profitable as Y. Since X employs more durable capital, the time-phasing of the 100 hours of labour that go into its product must differ from that of Y. Specifically, more of the labour must be carried out 'earlier', relative to the time when the product is finally sold. So the capitalists in X are out of pocket earlier. If they're to get the same rate of return (per cent per annum) on their outlay as the Y capitalists, the return on their earlier investment must be compounded, or in other words their price must be higher than the LTV predicts.

Ricardo had no access to statistics on the degree to which fixed capital is used in different industries, but he could observe the economy around him. His judgment was that this 'modification' to the LTV was far from being fatal to the theory. As we'll see below, some of his followers took a different view.

6.5 Marx's contribution

We have commented on various aspects of Marx's theories in several other chapters. Here we are concerned specifically with his contribution to the development of the labour theory of value that he 'inherited' from Ricardo.

One aspect is worthy of mention here, but will be taken up in chapter 11. That is, Marx argued that although Ricardo had given a largely correct account of the theory as it applied in a capitalist economy, he hadn't stopped to ask why the products of labour take the form of commodities in the first place, and why the labour time required to produce them manifests itself in the form of exchange value. This is the issue of the 'form of value'.

In this chapter we confine ourselves to two points: Marx's distinction between labour and labour-power, and his development of Ricardo's 'modification' of the labour theory of value due to the differential 'durability of the instruments of production' in different industries.

6.5.1   *Labour and labour-power*

Let us start with Ricardo on wages:

> Labour, like all other things which are purchased and sold, and which may be increased or diminished in quantity, has its natural and its market price. The natural price of labour is that price which is necessary to enable the labourers, one with another, to subsist and to perpetuate their race, without either increase or diminution.
>
> (Ricardo, 1951: 93)

This looks reasonable enough, but wait: the labour theory of value said that the natural price of each commodity depends on the labour time it embodies. Here the commodity we're talking about is labour itself. It seems as if we *ought* to say that the wage is governed by the labour time embodied in labour – but what is that supposed to mean? We could say it's identically 1, or it's not defined, neither of which seem helpful. So how is Ricardo able to give a sensible answer – is he somehow being inconsistent?

In explicating Marx's answer, it will be helpful first to make a terminological point. We have spoken of exchange value and use value: what shall we mean by the term *value*, without any qualifier? In Marx's *Capital* this is used as a term of art, denoting the sum of the direct and indirect labour time required to produce a commodity. (The question of the labour theory of value is then: to what extent or under what conditions do prices reflect or correspond to values?) We will use this terminology below, although we'll sometimes write *labour-values* for Marx's values if there's any ambiguity.

That said, Marx's claim is that the expression 'the value of labour' is not meaningful. What Ricardo is really talking about above is, in Marx's terms, the value of *labour-power* – that is, the worker's *capacity to work*. Labour is not a commodity that could be bought and sold at a point in time, it's an *activity*. The wage is not the 'price of labour' but the rental-price of labour-power. In the wage transaction the worker binds over to the capitalist his capacity to work for some definite period. The capitalist then sets the worker to work, but how much labour he actually gets depends on how hard his overseer presses, how fast the line runs, how rebellious the worker is. Unlike 'the value of labour', the value of labour-power is a valid concept and it comes down, pretty much, to what Ricardo said: it's the labour time that is required to maintain and reproduce the worker's capacity for working, in other words the labour time embodied in the goods the workers need to maintain themselves and their families.

Marx's distinction was a useful clarification of previous classical usage, which in effect amounted to a play on the word 'labour'. At the same time it opened the door for his concept of exploitation. Marx asked, where does profit come from? This can seem very puzzling if we think in terms of exchange of commodities, ruled by the LTV. In any given transaction, goods that contain x amount of labour exchange against other goods that also contain x amount (in general via the mediation of money, of course), so how can a capitalist come out ahead? Even if the reciprocity of the LTV is broken, that doesn't seem to help. If in a given trade goods embodying $x + h$ hours exchange against goods containing $x - h$ hours then one party has gained at the other's expense, but what needs explaining is the existence of net profit on a macroeconomic scale.

The answer, Marx said, lies in the special commodity labour-power. The worker sells to the capitalist labour-power which embodies (let's say) 5 hours; that is, the value of the worker's means of subsistence amounts to 5 hours per day. But once he gets through the factory gates or the office door, he finds that the working day is 8 hours. The worker therefore performs 3 hours of 'surplus labour' per day and this is manifest in 3 hours' worth of surplus value accruing to the capitalist. Marx calls the labour time workers spend in reproducing the value of their wages the 'necessary labour time', and he calls the ratio of surplus labour time to necessary labour time the *rate of surplus value*. In the example just given the rate of surplus value is $^3/_5 = 0.6$.

Marx's theoretical accomplishment here was to explain how profit could arise, while maintaining in strong form the assumption that all commodities exchange in line with the labour time they embody. It was also, of course, an ideological accomplishment, providing intellectual ammunition to the workers' movement. Prior to Marx the 'Ricardian socialists' had arrived at something like Marx's notion of exploitation – it was, after all, implicit in Ricardo – but Marx gave it coherent and forceful expression.

6.5.2   The transformation problem

Recall Ricardo's point that if the 'durability of the instruments of production' differs across industries, the strict LTV is incompatible with all industries' earning the same rate of profit. Marx took up this point in somewhat different terms; we need to introduce a few more items of Marx's terminology at this point.

Smith and Ricardo had talked of fixed and circulating capital ('fixed' referring, for example, to buildings and machinery, and 'circulating' to raw materials and work in progress). Marx retained this distinction but added a second, between *variable* and *constant* capital. Variable capital is what the capitalist lays out in wages. It is called 'variable' not because wages are variable (though they may be) but because there is a systematic variation (increment) between the value of wages and the value produced by the workers who receive those wages – this flows from the analysis of exploitation mentioned above. All the rest of capital, fixed or circulating, is constant capital – constant because there's no systematic increment. All the capitalist can hope for, on average, is that the elements of his

Table 6.1 Differing organic composition generates differing profit rates

Industry	Capital: Total $C + V$	Constant C	Variable V	S/V	S	$S/(C + V) = r$	Value of output $C + V + S$
X	1000	500	500	0.6	300	$\dfrac{300}{1000} = 30\%$	1300
Y	1000	750	250	0.6	150	$\dfrac{150}{1000} = 15\%$	1150
Aggregate	2000	1250	750	0.6	450	$\dfrac{450}{2000} = 22.5\%$	2450

constant capital will *retain* their value over time. However, these 'elements of constant capital' will change their shape: materials that stood in stockpiles leave the factory worked up into the final product, machinery and buildings gradually depreciate. Depreciation is conceived not as a *destruction* of value, but rather a passing-on. If you will, the labour time previously stored up in the machine gradually 'leaches out' into the product. When the machine is worn out its value has passed fully into the product.

One more term: the capital in any given industry divides into constant and variable, and the ratio of the two will differ across industries. Marx calls the ratio of constant capital to variable capital the *organic composition of capital*. Thus a high organic-composition industry is one in which a relatively small workforce uses a lot of valuable machinery, or processes a lot of valuable materials.

We are now ready to express Ricardo's problem in Marx's terms. Consider two industries, X and Y, the organic compositions of whose capitals are 1:1 and 3:1 respectively. Suppose that the rate of surplus value is the same in both industries, say 0.6 as in the example above.[9] And suppose the total capital advanced in each industry is 1000 per year. Then we get the situation shown in Table 6.1 (never mind the 'Aggregate' row, we'll come back to that later). In industry X, the total capital breaks down into 500 constant and 500 variable; in industry Y, 750 and 250. S denotes surplus value and V denotes variable capital, so S/V is the (common) rate of surplus value, which we apply to each industry's variable capital to give the figure in the S column. The rate of profit, r, is measured as the ratio of the surplus to the total capital advanced. Industry X shows a rate of profit twice as high as Y.

The rate of profit we have calculated for each industry in Table 6.1 is what we may call the 'value rate of profit': all magnitudes are assumed to be denominated in hours of labour time. The rate of profit observed by any real firm is, however,

[9] Marx thought there would be forces tending to equalize the rate of surplus value across industries. Recall that this rate is the ratio of (value of wages) to (value added by the workers). If wages are equal and the intensity of labour is equal in two industries, then those industries will have the same rate of surplus value – even though the value of gross output per worker might be quite different due to different employment of constant capital.

the money- or price-rate. To calculate it, we'd have to replace the figures in the table with the corresponding figures in price terms: for C the aggregate price of the non-labour inputs, for V the monetary wage-bill and for S the monetary surplus of sales revenue over costs. However, according to the LTV this should not make much difference, since prices $\approx$ values.

So there's a fork: either we maintain the LTV and conclude that industries with substantially differing organic composition of capital realize substantially different rates of profit, or we maintain the proposition than ('in equilibrium') all industries earn the same rate of profit and conclude that the LTV is incorrect.

A little background: this issue, which came to be known as the transformation problem, is addressed by Marx in Volume III of *Capital*. In Volume I, in which Marx presents his basic analysis of capitalist production, the LTV had been taken for granted. Nonetheless, Marx is willing to accept that the LTV is not strictly correct, and, like Ricardo, he believes that the rate of profit should be equalized across industries. But he insists that his analysis of exploitation is correct, which he takes to mean that (a) the aggregate price of output equals the aggregate value of output and (b) the aggregate profit equals the aggregate surplus value.

It was clearly incumbent upon Marx to explain how this could be worked out, and he took a first step in this direction. Consider the 'Aggregate' row of Table 6.1, where we have added up the figures for the two industries. The aggregate rate of profit (in value terms) is 22.5 per cent. If we were to apply this to the outlays of 1000 for each industry, we'd conclude that the aggregate price of each industry's output should be $1000 \times 1.225 = 1225$, as opposed to the labour-value figures of 1300 for X and 1150 for Y. So far, so good: each industry earns 22.5 per cent and Marx's two conditions hold: aggregate value = aggregate price = 2450, and aggregate surplus value = aggregate profit = 450. One can take this perspective: surplus value is *produced* industry by industry, but when it comes to share-out time, each participates on a *pro rata* basis (once again, 'in equilibrium'). Each industry gets a share of the total surplus value proportional to capital advanced.

We want a term for the prices that will do the job that Marx indicates, and he coined one: *prices of production*. These are the prices that give each industry or sector an equal rate of profit on capital advanced. They are hypothetical, because everyone knows that every industry does not earn the same rate of profit in any finite chunk of historical time, but they are in a sense 'nearer to reality' than labour-values if we assume with Marx and Ricardo that there exists a strong *tendency* for the rate of profit to become equalized.

We said above that Marx had taken 'a first step' in the direction of computing prices of production. What more did he have to do? The difficulty is that the calculations based on the 'Aggregate' row of Table 6.1 still assume that the value figures for the *inputs* to production are usable 'as is': each industry advances 1000. Consider the C figures: as given, these represent the aggregate *value* of the non-labour inputs for each industry. But since Marx's first 'transformation' step has shifted prices away from what the LTV would predict, it seems that we should go back and re-visit the inputs: it may be that if we re-evaluate the elements of constant capital in price terms the resulting figures do not agree with the 500 and 750 given for C in industry X and Y respectively.

To do this properly we would need not just a toy table with two industries but a tableau of the economy as a whole. Then we could take the 'transformed' prices of the outputs and feed them back into the system as the prices of inputs. In computational terms, what is called for is an iterative algorithm:

(1) $i = 0$; compute the first approximation to prices of production just as Marx did, but on an economy-wide scale.
(2)   Take the round-i prices of production and use them to re-evaluate the inputs to production, and so re-evaluate the capital advanced by each industry.
(3)   Re-evaluate the output prices as per Marx, but on the basis of the new numbers for capital advanced; $i \leftarrow i + 1$.
(4)   Have the computed prices changed appreciably from the last round to this one? If so, go to step 2; if not, stop.

Savvy readers will notice that what we have given above appears to be a somewhat cumbersome way of describing a result that could be presented more compactly using the notation of linear algebra. Even savvier readers will appreciate that the iterative procedure we have outlined is in fact how one would best go about the calculation for a large input–output table using a computer.

The trouble for Marx's project is that if you carry out the calculation specified above – that is, iterate until you have essentially the same prices on the input and the output side – you will find that, in the general case, both of Marx's invariance conditions (total price = total value and total profit = total surplus value) are *not* preserved. This was shown by Ladislaus von Bortkiewicz in an article published in 1907 that went unnoticed at first but won him posthumous fame. The system has a degree of freedom which allows one to impose one of Marx's invariance conditions as a normalization, but not, in general, both of them.

Marx must be credited with giving a clearer and more explicit statement of the transformation problem than Ricardo. He should also be credited with intellectual honesty since the problem was clearly inconvenient to him. Nonetheless, in a sense, Marx was hoist by his own petard on this issue. Nothing forced him to insist on his two invariance conditions, but having done so he was then open to the charge of inconsistency (but see digression 6.2). One could easily get the impression that the validity of the LTV hinged on whether Marx had got his transformation calculations right, which is far from the truth.

6.6   Two challenges to the labour theory of value

In this chapter we have taken the labour theory of value seriously. But you won't find this theory discussed in current textbooks of economics. What happened? Over the century and a half since Marx's *Capital* was published the LTV has been subject to two major attacks. In the last quarter of the nineteenth century it was challenged by economists of what came to be known as the neoclassical

---

Digression 6.2 Interpreting Marx

Few readers will be surprised to learn that the view we present of Marx's 'transformation problem' is not accepted by all Marx scholars. The Temporal Single-System (TSS) school, in particular, would reject both our account and that of von Bortkiewicz as distortions of Marx. The key point is how one interprets Marx's conception of value. We have claimed that for Marx, value means the sum total of the labour time directly and indirectly required to produce a given commodity. We take this to be essentially the same as what Ricardo had in mind, and we take it be a quantity which is determined by technological factors (taking technology in a broad sense to include the social organization of labour). On the TSS view, Marx meant by 'value' the sum of (a) the *direct* labour time required to produce the commodity and (b) the labour-time equivalent of the monetary value of the non-labour inputs. Component (b) is calculated by multiplying the price of the non-labour inputs by a conversion factor that is the reciprocal of the so-called MELT (Monetary Equivalent of Labour Time), which in turn is calculated using the economy-wide ratio of monetary value-added to hours worked over some given period. On this interpretation of value one can argue that Marx's one-step 'transformation' was OK in itself, and doesn't need the sort of iterative completion we indicated.

We recognize that the writings of any theorist as original and fecund as Marx must be open to multiple interpretations, but in our view the TSS interpretation of Marx's *value* is forced and untenable. For the other side of the argument see, e.g., Kliman (2007).

---

school, who claimed that the correct approach to value was via the concepts of utility and scarcity,[10] not labour time. The success of this school in side-lining the LTV was partly due to the political acceptability of their theory. After Marx (if not already before), the LTV was linked with concepts such as exploitation, class struggle and communism. The neoclassicals calmed things down: value was all about individuals making choices, trade-offs, in face of (inevitably) limited resources. In the second half of the twentieth century another attack was mounted, this time by economists who saw themselves as building on Ricardo's approach, yet argued that labour time was otiose – a useless detour – in a neo-Ricardian theory of value. We'll consider these challenges in turn.

6.6.1 *Utility and the marginalist theory of value*

The anti-classical, marginalist theory of value is particularly associated with the names of W. S. Jevons, Carl Menger and Léon Walras, who mounted their

---

[10] Thus reverting to the 'natural law' tradition which Adam Smith had quietly but firmly rejected in *The Wealth of Nations* (see section 6.1 above).

attack in the early 1870s.[11] But the spirit of their objection to Ricardo had been expressed pithily by Richard Whately in 1832: 'It is not that pearls fetch a high price *because* men have dived for them; but on the contrary, men dive for them because they fetch a high price.' (And they fetch a high price because people find them very desirable, a matter of subjective preference or 'utility'.) This, in a nutshell, is the subjective argument against the LTV. At first glance it seems to have some force. It's true that simply spending a lot of time in producing something does not make it valuable – not if nobody wants it. And it's also true that when people expend time and energy and put themselves in danger pearl-diving, it's because they know that pearls will bring a good price. But think about it a little more. What if pearls washed up on the beach and could be gathered as easily as sea-shells? They would not command anything like their current price, regardless of how 'highly valued' they are as ornaments. (In fact, of course, while pearls would remain just as pretty they would lose their social cachet: duchesses and their emulators want to be seen wearing something *expensive* – something that other people had to spend a lot of time making – not just something pretty.)

Ricardo put it very clearly: the *precondition* for a commodity's having value is that it is an object of demand, but given that it's demanded, the magnitude of its value depends on the labour required to produce it. The quantity that people want of (reproducible) commodity X doesn't matter, provided they want it at all. Quantity supplied will adjust to match demand, and once the adjustment is complete prices will be (approximately) proportional to labour times. Neither does it matter what people are *willing to pay* for X. The market will be in equilibrium when demand equals supply at a price in line with labour content. If you're not willing to pay that much, you don't get any. If you'd be willing to pay a lot more you are in luck, you don't have to. In the limiting case where nobody is willing to pay a price for X that corresponds to its labour content, X doesn't get produced.[12]

On the Ricardian view consumer demand may be important in its own right but it plays little role in the theory of value. Shifts in demand cause market prices to diverge from their 'centres of gravitation' for a while but those 'centres' are unaffected. The factors that drive prices up or down on a long-term basis are those that produce a change in the required labour time, most likely either changes in technology or depletion of natural resources.

The crude version of the subjective theory of value – in which value seems to depend entirely on consumers' tastes and preferences – played an important polemical role, but it's not what you find in today's textbooks. The textbooks contain the theory devised by Alfred Marshall, the great English compromiser, who found a way to 'reconcile' Ricardo and his critics.[13]

---

[11] 'Anti-classical' and 'attack' are the right words. Jevons, for example, spoke of the 'mazy and preposterous assumptions of the Ricardian School' (Jevons, 1871).

[12] For example, as of this writing, star-gazing vacations on the moon. But that may come.

[13] Marshall's *Principles of Economics* (1890) was hugely influential and went through eight editions in his lifetime, the last published in 1920. Marshall was also responsible for establishing economics as an academic discipline, founding the Economics Tripos at Cambridge in 1903.

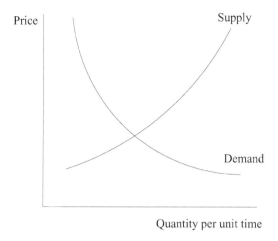

Price

Supply

Demand

Quantity per unit time

Figure 6.1 The celebrated Marshallian supply–demand cross.

As anyone who has taken a course in economics knows, this is the apparatus of the supply curve and the demand curve (Figure 6.1). The demand curve represents the quantity of commodity X that consumers are willing to buy, per unit time, at various possible prices. It slopes downward due to 'diminishing marginal utility': the nth unit of good X consumed per week (say) is subjectively less valuable than unit $n - 1$. The supply curve represents the quantity firms are willing to supply, again at each possible price. It slopes upward due to increasing marginal cost: to produce more, firms have to take on more labour and work their production facilities more intensively, giving rise to an increase in the cost of each extra unit produced; for this to be worthwhile, the price must be higher. Market equilibrium requires that the quantity consumers are interested in buying coincides with the quantity firms are interested in supplying: price is determined where supply and demand cross.

Marshall's supply–demand cross obviously has its uses but from a theoretical point of view it is unsatisfying. The question has been switched. Ricardo (and Smith, and Marx) wanted to know what determines the 'natural price' of commodities, the attractor for market prices. Their focus was both long-run and *systemic*: the virtue of the LTV was that it gave an explanation of exchange-value based on a cause outside of, and underlying, the circle of mutually-determining money prices and costs. Marshall shifted the focus to the short run, and to a *microeconomic* approach. To explain the price of commodity X you need to know the supply curves of the firms producing X. And to construct those supply curves you need to know the prices of the inputs used by the firms. Prices determine prices. Well, yes, in a sense they do, but something important in the way of scientific insight has been lost.

Ricardo's labour time gets a look-in, in the Marshallian apparatus, via the supply curve. If a commodity embodies a great deal of labour time then the wage-bill for producing that commodity is high, and the supply curve will sit relatively high on the price axis, hence intersecting the demand curve at a high level. But the wage-bill appears as just one money cost among others; the idea all costs can be resolved into labour time is submerged. In addition, with the Marshallian cross it appears that you can't determine price without knowing demand. That is because the supply curve slopes upward. And that was due to increasing marginal cost. But this, Ricardo would say, is a short-run phenomenon. Diminishing returns to the application of labour (the basis of increasing marginal cost) is something that Ricardo expected to see in *agriculture*, due to the limited supply of the most fertile land (see the discussion of rent in section 6.4.1 above), but not in manufacturing. If we want more of commodity X, in the long run, we not only apply more direct labour but also scale up the production facilities accordingly (hence, more indirect labour). Once we're done there's no reason to expect that the labour time *per unit* of the product will be higher than before. So here's what you can do to get the Ricardian theory back out of Marshall's cross:

- Draw the (long-run) supply curve as horizontal. Then demand determines the quantity consumed but not price.
- Argue that the vertical location of the horizontal supply curve depends on the sum of the direct and indirect labour time required.

To be 'fair' to neoclassical economics, we should point out that while the Marshallian cross is the staple of undergraduate textbooks, it's not what is taught in graduate school. There, in the theory of general equilibrium, transitive preference orderings confront convex production sets (Debreu, 1959). The critique that prices are explained by prices does not apply. But the critique that we're lacking a key level of explanation does apply. Why does a laptop computer cost 50 times as much as a pizza? Here are three answers:

(1)   The laptop requires 50 times as much labour to produce (Ricardo).
(2)   The configuration of supply and demand is such that the curves intersect at the observed respective prices (Marshall).
(3)   These are the prices that appear in the solution vector to the equations of general equilibrium, assuming that a solution exists – and also that the solution is unique, unless you'd prefer an explanation of why a pizza costs 50 times as much as a laptop (Debreu).

If the first answer is even approximately true, it gives an important insight that is totally missing from the others.

6.6.2   *Sraffa and the redundancy of labour values*

Both Ricardo and Marx started out from the labour theory of value. The LTV appears in pride of place at the start of their respective expositions and is taken for granted in their discussions of a wide range of economic phenomena. Nonetheless, they both recognized that this theory is incompatible with an equal rate of profit across industries that have (in Marx's terminology) unequal organic compositions of capital. Both spoke of a necessary 'modification'. Marx conceived of a set of 'prices of production' that would yield a uniform rate of profit, and referred to these as modified values.

Briefly, the 'redundancy' critique of the labour theory of value goes like this: if your basic idea is that 'natural prices' ought to be such as to give a uniform rate of profit, there's no need to take labour-values as a starting point. The LTV just gets in the way of the correct solution. Paul Samuelson expressed this in his 'erase-and-replace' critique of Marx. What's the correct way of carrying out the 'transformation' from values to prices of production? It's easy, you erase values and replace them with prices of production (Samuelson, 1972: ch. 153).

In the background to Samuelson's article (which was one shot in a debate that raged in the economics journals in the 1970s) was Piero Sraffa's brilliant mathematical reconstruction of Ricardian theory (Sraffa, 1960), the founding document of the neo-Ricardian school. Sraffa showed that you could write down a set of equations that defined prices of production for each industry provided you had the following information.

- The matrix of 'technical coefficients' indicating how much of each industry's product is needed as input for each other industry.
- The vector of direct labour coefficients indicating how much direct or current labour is needed per unit of the product in each industry.
- Either a given real wage-rate or a given rate of profit. (Whichever of these variables is not given will be part of the solution.)

Labour-values are the sum of the direct and indirect labour required to produce each commodity. To calculate labour-values you need the first two sorts of information mentioned above but not the third. Given the way the calculations work out – specifically, the compounding effect due to a positive rate of profit – there is in general no mathematical function that takes you from labour values to prices of production. In other words, there exists a basic information set from which we can calculate *either* labour-values or prices of production, but if we want prices of production there's no sense in going *via* labour values; in fact, in general it can't be done.

One further point demands attention. In general, prices of production differ from values – but how much do they differ? The divergence comes from the theoretical postulate of a uniform rate of profit on capitals of differing organic composition. This divergence will be greater (a) the greater is the overall rate of profit and (b) the more uneven is the distribution of organic composition. To put it the other way round, if the overall rate of profit were zero and/or if every industry had the same organic composition, prices of production would be the same as values.

This suggests that if the rate of profit is 'moderate' and the organic composition of capital is not too widely scattered around its average, labour-values will be approximately 'right'. In a practical sense that sounds positive for the LTV. In a strictly theoretical sense, however, the LTV is downgraded. It's a 'special case'. The 'correct' theory is that of prices of production and the LTV may give an acceptable approximation under certain conditions. Under other conditions the LTV may give wildly 'wrong' results. Or so it seems.

6.7   The probabilistic response

There's nothing wrong with Sraffa's or Samuelson's mathematics, yet we do not accept the 'redundancy' critique of the labour theory of value. Our reasons flow from two sorts of investigations that have been carried out since the early 1980s: on the one hand, the theoretical account of the capitalist economy as a disorderly system with very large degrees of freedom, initiated by Farjoun and Machover (1983); and on the other, empirical work on labour-values and prices of production stemming from Shaikh (1984).

   These issues are taken up in chapters 7 and 10; here we anticipate, enumerating some of the most relevant points without argument.

(1)   Not only is the rate of profit not uniform – everyone knows that – but neither is it uniform 'in equilibrium'. For a random variable such as the rate of profit the appropriate equilibrium concept is that of *statistical equilibrium* (chapter 7). The dispersion of profit rates around their average is roughly stable over time (while individual firms and industries bump around, changing their places in the distribution).

(2)   Many studies show a close correlation between market price of output and labour-value across industries. Ricardo's intuition that the LTV gives a good approximation was correct.

(3)   Further, several studies show a negative or inverse correlation between profit rates and organic composition of capital across industries – precisely the result that Ricardo and Marx thought they had to avoid, leading to their 'modifications' to the basic LTV.

(4)   As an empirical matter, labour-values and prices of production seem to be roughly equally good as predictors of market prices. It's not the case that prices of production are 'right' and labour-values the poor cousin.

   This is all very exciting from a scientific point of view. We posed above the simple-minded but revealing question for any theory of value: why does a laptop cost 50 times as much as a pizza? (Or vary the example to taste.) We expressed our dissatisfaction with the neoclassical answer, but the Sraffian answer is really no better – it has to be some generalized verbiage along the lines of, 'This price ratio is such as to give pizza bakers and laptop makers the social average rate of profit, given the input–output matrix and the vector of direct labour requirements.' The answer given by the labour theory of value, however, is, as economists like to say, a 'testable hypothesis'. Not only that, but the theory is an engine capable of giving rise to a series of further testable hypotheses – and that (in large measure) is how science advances.

Part II

Exchange, money and capital

7 The probabilistic approach to economic variables

In this chapter we discuss the differences between statistical and mechanical concepts of equilibrium in systems with huge numbers of degrees of freedom.

7.1 Probabilistic models

Once we know the possible outcomes of a situation it is natural to consider how *probable* each of those outcomes are. The probability of an event is a number in the interval 0 to 1, where 0 represents an impossible event and 1 a certain event.

For example, if we perform a large number of coin tosses we soon discover that about half the outcomes are heads, and half are tails. So although we cannot predict the outcome of a particular flip, we can say that the outcome is equally likely to be heads or tails, or more precisely the probability of heads or tails is one half, $P(X = \text{heads}) = P(X = \text{tails}) = 1/2$, where X is the outcome of the coin toss.

Knowing that $P(X = \text{heads}) = 1/2$ means that about half the time a coin will land heads. In fact, this is a probabilistic prediction of the frequency of a particular outcome. It does not predict what will actually occur, but what will probably occur, given knowledge of the possible outcomes. Although weaker than a deterministic prediction a probabilistic prediction is still very useful for acting in the world. For example, knowing that an area has a high probability of earthquake activity tells us to build robust homes, even though we do not precisely know when an earthquake will strike.

The theory of probability is an appropriate tool for situations where we simply do not know the full range of causal mechanisms that determine the outcome of a situation, or cases in which we think we know what determines the outcome but in practice it is difficult to use our theories to make robust predictions. In such cases we give up on the idea of predicting actual outcomes but instead predict what will probably occur given the known possible outcomes. Instead of using a deterministic model to predict the *value* of a *variable* x, such as predicting whether $x = \text{heads}$ or $x = \text{tails}$, we use a probabilistic model to predict the *distribution* of a *random variable* X, such as predicting that $P(X = \text{heads}) = 1/2$ and $P(X = \text{tails}) = 1/2$, which is equivalent to stating that the distribution of X is uniform, that is all outcomes have an equal probability of occurring.

Consider the purchasing decisions of all individuals in the USA during one month. There is an enormous range of reasons why certain goods are sold in certain amounts for certain prices. Some goods are bought regularly in stable amounts, such as basic utilities like gas and water, other goods are ephemeral and their sales are contingent on transient fashions, such as the market for children's toys. The weather can affect sales. People are very different and have different goals and tastes. Some goods wear out periodically and may need to replaced. In sum, there are almost as many reasons for exchange events as there are events themselves.

The variability and contingency that necessarily occurs when complex and intelligent human beings competitively interact with each other implies that it is impractical to try to model market exchanges in detail. Although it is possible to model and predict human behaviour in controlled experimental settings that constrain the space of possible actions, or in situations where conventions or rules play an important part, it is not possible to model the everyday creativity of market participants aiming to satisfy their goals in open-ended and mutually constructed economic environments. It is evident that, ignoring special cases, predicting the actual price of a good on a particular day, or predicting the demand for a newly invented commodity type, is a lost cause. Prices and goods are always changing. A market economy is therefore an ideal candidate for probabilistic modelling.

7.1.1   A simple exchange economy

Recently physicists have turned their attention to economic phenomena, creating a new field called econophysics. Econophysics approaches to traditional economic problems are essentially probabilistic in nature. We can illustrate this approach by examining a very simple model of a market economy developed by the physicists Dragulescu and Yakovenko (2000).

Imagine a simple economy consisting of N people, which we shall call actors. Each actor has an amount of money m, which for the sake of concreteness let's assume is denominated in dollars. The total amount of money in the economy, which is simply the sum of all the individual money amounts held by each actor, is a fixed constant M.

In a market economy people exchange goods and services for amounts of money. But we'll completely abstract from the nature of those goods and services, the time they take to produce or complete, and who does what and when. We won't consider institutions either, so firms, banks and the economic operations of the state are out of the picture. Instead, we will focus on an essential characteristic of a dynamic monetary economy – the fact that money is continually exchanged between actors in different amounts but is almost always conserved.[1] We will not attempt to deterministically model all the local reasons why particular actors exchange particular amounts of money at particular instants of time, but instead

---

[1] In 1994 Scottish avant-garde artists Bill Drummond and Jimmy Cauty burnt one million pounds, earned from the sales of their pop records. But such events have low probability.

assume that all this contingency can be modelled as random noise. Given these mighty abstractions a single procedure can drive the dynamics of the simple model:

(1)   Randomly pick two actors a buyer and seller so that each actor has the same chance of being selected.
(2)   Randomly pick a price p for the transaction within the range from 0 to the the amount of money held by the buyer.
(3)   Reduce the money held by the buyer by p and give it to the seller.

Economic change is simulated by repeatedly applying this rule to the population actors. The rule transfers random amounts of money between randomly selected individuals. And that's all there is to it. Call this model the *simple economy* model. As mentioned, it is a very simple model. It is so simple it is perhaps difficult to believe that it can contribute much to our understanding. But in fact it is able to replicate one of the enduring and characteristic empirical regularities of market economies.

The number of actors with \$0, \$1,..., \$M in their pockets can be counted. Each dollar amount can be considered a 'bin', and any particular actor at any particular time is 'in' one of these bins depending on how many dollars they hold. For example, if we initialize the model so that each actor has the same amount of money (M/N dollars), and then measure the size of each of the dollar bins, we find that the money distribution is *degenerate*. Every bin is empty, except for M/N, which is of size N. The distribution is called degenerate because there is only one possibility.

But if our exchange procedure is applied repeatedly the distribution will begin to diverge from its degenerate state as money is exchanged in unequal amounts between the actors. Some actors will be lucky and enjoy a sequence of advantageous trades and obtain great wealth, while others may repeatedly spend money and get very little in return. If this process is continued the economy settles to a Boltzmann–Gibbs distribution, $P(m) \propto \lambda e^{-\lambda m}$. The money distribution is highly unequal. The majority of actors have very little money, whereas exponentially few have a great deal. In fact, a very small number of individuals have relatively enormous amounts of money.[2]

Remarkably the exponential distribution of wealth is found in real data from real economies. There is some divergence from an exponential distribution in the top 5 to 10 per cent of wealthy individuals, but an exponential distribution accurately describes the vast majority of the population (Dragulescu, 2002; Dragulescu and Yakovenko, 2002), whichever advanced capitalist country is considered.[3] The distribution is also stable over long periods of time. Although mean wealth

---

[2]   You can watch this process in real-time on the web; see Wright (2008a).
[3]   Some of the empirical studies use income over a time period as a proxy for instantaneous wealth, but the details do not matter here.

Digression 7.1   The Boltzmann–Gibbs distribution

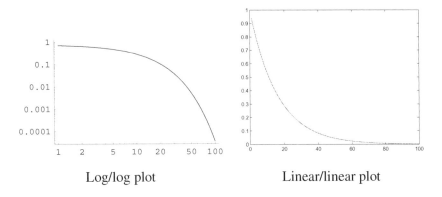

Log/log plot   Linear/linear plot

The Boltzmann–Gibbs distribution characterizes the energies of particles in a thermodynamic system. It has the general form $P(\epsilon) = Ce^{-\frac{\epsilon}{T}}$, where ϵ denotes the energy of a particle. The graph above shows the shape of this distribution on a log–log plot and a linear plot. It is a particular example of an *exponential* distribution.

This distribution arises as a consequence of the fact that in a closed system of particles the total energy must be conserved but random energy exchanges between these particles cause the energy to be spread through the population in a particular pattern. The probability of an individual particle successively gaining additional energy from a sequence of exchanges is quite low. So we would expect to see most particles having low energy (the most likely case), but a small number with a disproportionately large amount of energy. The plot shows that the probability of a particle's having the highest energy (100) is very low.

Dragulescu and Yakovenko (2002) have argued that since money is conserved in the exchange of commodities the distribution of money should follow a similar functional form. We will see in chapter 11 that the assumption of conservation of money can only be held to a limited extent in a capitalist economy with modern banks.

---

may change from one year to the next, the overall functional form of the wealth distribution remains exponential. In conclusion, the simple probabilistic model in spite of (or due to?) its high level of abstraction and simplicity has replicated an important feature of modern capitalist economies.

One might think that differences in wealth arose in part from accident of birth combined and in part from personal virtues. We may accept that our choice of parents is fortuitous, but surely effort, diligence and intelligence explain the rest?

Well in some societies that might be true. But Yakovenko and Dragulescu seem to be telling us that in a monetary society, one dominated by the sale of goods and services for money, one need look no further than the workings of blind chance to account for the distribution of wealth. The same statistical laws which govern the random jostling of tiny atoms, the ineluctable progression towards maximum entropy, ensure that money will be distributed very unevenly. A small minority will have a lot of money and a large number of people will have very little.

Why does this distribution arise? It's essence is easy to grasp: in each transaction there can be a winner and a loser. By chance a few people will have a long winning streak and end up with much more than the rest.

7.1.2   The concept of statistical equilibrium

The simple economy model illustrates the concept of a statistical equilibrium. Over time the distribution of wealth in the economy converges to an exponential distribution, and stays there. Even though the individual economic actors continue to exchange money, and ascend or descend the wealth scale, the overall distribution of wealth in the economy remains constant. Some poor people may get rich, some rich people get poorer, but the overall situation remains the same. A small number of people end up with a lot of money.

Contrast this kind of equilibrium with the better known concept of a mechanical equilibrium. For example, consider a set of weighing scales, 1kg on the left plate, and 1kg on the right: the scales balance, all forces equalize, and the arms are still. The system is is in mechanical equilibrium and will remain so until some external force is applied. A statistical equilibrium is a different kind of equilibrium. Unlike a mechanical equilibrium, in which the system configuration remains static, a system can be in statistical equilibrium even when its configuration is continually changing. It is the probability distribution over possible system configurations that remains constant over time. For example, if we sample the distribution of money in the simple economy over a period of time, and then repeat this experiment at a later time, the two distributions will be nearly identical with high probability, despite money continually changing hands. Therefore, unlike a mechanical equilibrium, there is always the possibility that a system in statistical equilibrium will spontaneously deviate from equilibrium. But the probability it will do so is small. For example, the probability that the simple economy will spontaneously return to its initial egalitarian wealth distribution is so vanishingly small it may as well be considered impossible.

The standard economic theories we have inherited from the twentieth century are deterministic models, following the path laid down by theorists in the nineteenth century who copied the tools and methods of the prevailing mechanical theories in the physical sciences (Mirowski, 1989). The first definitive formulation of this approach is Debreu's short book *The Theory of Value* (Debreu, 1959), in which a market economy is pictured as a huge deterministic calculator that computes a set of market exchanges between economic actors, agreeable to all, given initial endowments of goods. In this model the concept of a mechanical equilibrium is employed to understand the meaning of economic phenomena. But unlike mechanical configurations of matter, which do sometimes come to rest, a market economy never does: it is inherently a dynamic system, with economic actors whose agency continually upsets any possibility of the attainment of a mechanical equilibrium. A market economy is more like a bag of marbles vigorously shaken than a set of weighing scales at rest.

The simplest case of a statistical equilibrium analysed in the physical sciences is that of an ideal gas. An ideal gas consists of millions of identical particles enclosed in a container that is perfectly insulated. The volume and temperature of the gas are assumed to be constant. Every gas particle continually moves within the container, bouncing off the walls and other particles, changing direction, and gaining or losing speed depending on the local contingencies that determine collision outcomes. At the micro-level there is seeming chaos. Despite all the uncoordinated chaos, however, all the particles are connected to each other via the principle of the conservation of energy. Each collision conserves energy, therefore the total energy of the system is constant. Hence, if one particle is travelling unusually fast, and has a large kinetic energy, then this necessarily implies that some other particles must move at a slower speed. It is a physical impossibility that all particles have the highest kinetic energy at the same instant of time. In other words, there is a shared pool of available energy that is distributed amongst the gas particles. This total energy is a macro-level constraint on the micro-level disorder. All possible system configurations, that is possible distributions of kinetic energy amongst the gas particles, cannot violate this global constraint.

The fundamental law of equilibrium in statistical mechanics is the Boltzmann–Gibbs law, which states that the probability distribution of energy ϵ is

$$P(\epsilon) \propto \frac{1}{T} e^{-\epsilon/T}$$

where T is the temperature of the gas, or the average energy per particle.[4] This is the exponential distribution once again. This is not too surprising when we consider that the simple economy model and the ideal gas are formally equivalent.

Simple economy	Ideal gas
Large number of identical actors	Large number of identical particles
Each actor has money m_i	Each particle has energy ϵ_i
Total money M is constant	Total energy E is constant
Exchange is money conserving	Collisions are energy conserving
Economy enters statistical equilibrium	Gas enters statistical equilibrium
Boltzmann–Gibbs money distribution	Boltzmann–Gibbs energy distribution
$P(m) \propto \lambda e^{-\lambda m}$	$P(\epsilon) \propto \lambda e^{-\lambda \epsilon}$
$1/\lambda$ is average wealth	$1/\lambda$ is average temperature

[4] This can be rewritten as $P(\epsilon) \propto \lambda e^{\lambda \epsilon}$ where $\lambda = \frac{1}{T}$.

7.1.3 The maximum entropy distribution

In section 1.4 the second law of thermodynamics was introduced. The law states that the total entropy in a closed system tends to increase. The simple economy and ideal gas are closed systems. The second law implies that the equilibrium distribution, which we have seen is the exponential distribution, must be the distribution that has maximum entropy given the overall constraint on the total money in the economy (or the total energy of the gas). Let's check this. Consider the following entropy measure for the simple economy:

$$-\sum_{m=0}^{M} P(m) \ln P(m) \tag{7.1}$$

where $P(m)$ is the probability that a randomly picked actor has money m. There are N actors in the economy and M dollars, both of which are conserved. Let n_m be the number of actors that hold m dollars. It is necessarily the case that:

$$\sum_{m=0}^{M} n_m = N$$

and

$$\sum_{m=0}^{M} n_m m = M$$

The probability that a randomly picked actor will have money m is $P(m) = n_m/N$. If we substitute $n_m = P(m)N$ into the above two equations we get two constraints on the probabilities:

$$\sum_{m=0}^{M} P(m) = 1$$

which is the simple constraint that all probabilities must sum to one, and

$$\sum_{m=0}^{M} P(m)m = \frac{M}{N}$$

which is the constraint that the probabilities must conform to the total wealth constraint.

The mathematical problem is to determine a formula for $P(m)$ that meets the constraints and maximizes the value of the entropy equation. This problem can be solved in a variety of ways, the details of which are unimportant.[5] But it turns out that the solution is indeed the Boltzmann–Gibbs (exponential) distribution $P(m) \propto \lambda e^{-\lambda m}$. The exponential distribution of wealth is therefore the most *disorderly* distribution under the assumption that the only constraint on the system is conservation of money. Clearly, if the economic system were composed of more sophisticated agents such as 'economic demons', who, for example, formed coalitions or initiated joint plans in order to consciously change the wealth distribution, then new constraints on the probabilities would need to be considered, and the mathematical argument would change. But the fact that the majority of the empirical wealth distribution in capitalist economies is exponential suggests that such factors are not significant between individuals in the exponential regime of the wealth distribution.

In reality, unlike in the simple economy model, there are many schemes for money reallocation, for example limited redistribution of income via state taxes. But it is a surprising fact that such mechanisms do not affect the overall functional form of the wealth distribution. Markets appear to have a very robust tendency to maximize entropy, and generate highly unequal, predominantly exponential wealth distributions.

We'll revisit the topic of inequality in Chapter 13, where we'll discover that the full wealth and income distributions have lower entropy than the exponential distribution. So new causal factors, missing from this simple economy model, are at work, which place further constraints on the probabilities $P(m)$. This implies that some kind of entropy-reducing demonic work is being performed to 'sort' money amongst different economic classes.

7.1.4 Random agents versus rational agents

It may be objected at this point that economic actors are clearly purposive and it is therefore essential to model individual rationality, even when considering macro-level phenomena, such as emergent wealth and income distributions. For instance, people do not exchange money according to random rules, and, depending on the amounts involved, often think very carefully about what they spend. But this objection confuses epistemology with ontology, a picture with reality. A random model need not imply that the causality it represents is random, only that it it is intrinsically difficult to model all the causality in perfect detail. The randomness is intended to represent *all* the many and varied rational (or otherwise) decisions of the economic actors.

The underlying assumption of the rational actor approach to economics is that macro phenomena are reducible to and determined by the mechanisms of individual rationality. Farjoun and Machover (1983) noted some time ago that the successful physical theory of statistical mechanics is in direct contradiction to this assumption. For example, classical statistical mechanics models the molecules of a gas as idealized, perfectly elastic billiard balls. This is of course a gross

---

[5] The interested reader should consult Kapur (1989) and Kapur and Kesavan (1992).

oversimplification of a molecule's structure and how it interacts with other molecules. Yet statistical mechanics can deduce empirically valid macro-phenomena. Aleksandr Khinchin, who helped to make classical statistical mechanics into a mathematically rigorous subject, put it this way:

> Those general laws of mechanics which are used in statistical mechanics are necessary for any motions of material particles, no matter what are the forces causing such motions. It is a complete abstraction from the nature of these forces, that gives to statistical mechanics its specific features and contributes to its deductions all the necessary flexibility.... [T]he specific character of the systems studied in statistical mechanics consists mainly in the enormous number of degrees of freedom which these systems possess. Methodologically this means that the standpoint of statistical mechanics is determined not by the mechanical nature, but by the particle structure of matter. It almost seems as if the purpose of statistical mechanics is to observe how far reaching are the deductions made on the basis of the atomic structure of matter, irrespective of the nature of these atoms and the laws of their interaction.
>
> (Khinchin, 1949: 8–9)

The method of abstracting from the mechanics of individual rationality, and instead emphasizing the particle nature of individuals, is valid because the number of degrees of freedom of economic reality is very large. We can picture individual decision making as a highly simplified random selection from possibilities constrained by overall macro-level principles, such as the conservation of money. At this level of abstraction, individual psychology can be modelled as extraneous noise.

In the next chapter we will examine the simple economy, and its relation to the physical equations of statistical mechanics, in more detail.

8 The statistical mechanics of money

In a closed economic system, money is conserved. Thus, by analogy with energy, the equilibrium probability distribution of money must follow the exponential Boltzmann–Gibbs law characterized by an effective temperature equal to the average amount of money per economic agent. We demonstrate how the Boltzmann–Gibbs distribution emerges in computer simulations of economic models. Then we consider a thermal machine, in which the difference of temperatures allows one to extract a monetary profit. We also discuss the role of debt, and models with broken time-reversal symmetry for which the Boltzmann–Gibbs law does not hold.

8.1 Introduction

The application of statistical physics methods to economics promises fresh insights into problems traditionally not associated with physics (see, for example, Farmer *et al.* (2005)). Both statistical mechanics and economics study big ensembles: collections of atoms or economic agents, respectively. The fundamental law of equilibrium statistical mechanics is the Boltzmann–Gibbs law, which states that the probability distribution of energy ε is $P(\varepsilon) = Ce^{-\varepsilon/T}$, where T is the temperature, and C is a normalizing constant (Wannier, 1966). The main ingredient that is essential for the textbook derivation of the Boltzmann–Gibbs law is the conservation of energy. Thus, one may generalize that any conserved quantity in a big statistical system should have an exponential probability distribution in equilibrium.

An example of such an unconventional Boltzmann–Gibbs law is the probability distribution of forces experienced by the beads in a cylinder pressed with an external force (Mueth *et al.*, 1998). Because the system is at rest, the total force along the cylinder axis experienced by each layer of granules is constant and is randomly distributed among the individual beads. Thus the conditions are satisfied for the applicability of the Boltzmann–Gibbs law to the force, rather than energy, and it was indeed found experimentally (Mueth *et al.*, 1998).

We claim that, in a closed economic system, the total amount of money is conserved. Thus the equilibrium probability distribution of money $P(m)$ should follow the Boltzmann–Gibbs law $P(m) = Ce^{-m/T}$. Here m is money, and T

is an effective temperature equal to the average amount of money per economic agent. The conservation law of money (Shubik, 1997) reflects their fundamental property that, unlike material wealth, money (more precisely the fiat, 'paper' money) is not allowed to be manufactured by regular economic agents, but can only be transferred between agents.[1]

It is tempting to identify the money distribution $P(m)$ with the distribution of wealth (Ispolatov *et al.*, 1998). However, money is only one part of wealth, the other part being material wealth. Material products have no conservation law: They can be manufactured, destroyed, consumed, etc. Moreover, the monetary value of a material product (the price) is not constant. The same applies to stocks, which economics textbooks explicitly exclude from the definition of money (McConnell and Brue, 1996). So, in general, we do not expect the Boltzmann–Gibbs law for the distribution of wealth. Some authors believe that wealth is distributed according to a power law (Pareto-Zipf), which originates from a multiplicative random process (Montrell and Shlesinger, 1982). Such a process may reflect, among other things, the fluctuations of prices needed to evaluate the monetary value of material wealth.

8.2   Boltzmann–Gibbs distribution

Let us consider a system of many economic agents $N \gg 1$, which may be individuals or corporations. We only consider the case where their number is constant. Each agent i has some money m_i and may exchange it with other agents. It is implied that money is used for some economic activity, such as buying or selling material products; however, we are not interested in that aspect. Similarly to Ispolatov *et al.* (1998), for us the only result of interaction between agents i and j is that some money Δm changes hands: $[m_i, m_j] \rightarrow [m'_i, m'_j] = [m_i - \Delta m, m_j + \Delta m]$. Notice that the total amount of money is conserved in each transaction: $m_i + m_j = m'_i + m'_j$. This local conservation law of money (Shubik, 1997) is analogous to the conservation of energy in collisions between atoms. We assume that the economic system is closed, i. e. there is no external flux of money, thus the total amount of money M in the system is conserved. Also, initially, we do not permit any debt, so each agent's money must be non-negative: $m_i \geq 0$. A similar condition applies to the kinetic energy of atoms: $\varepsilon_i \geq 0$.

Let us introduce the probability distribution function of money $P(m)$, which is defined so that the number of agents with money between m and $m + dm$ is equal to $NP(m)\,dm$. We are interested in the stationary distribution $P(m)$ corresponding to the state of thermodynamic equilibrium. In this state, an individual agent's money m_i strongly fluctuates, but the overall probability distribution $P(m)$ does not change.

---

[1] Our approach here is very similar to that of Ispolatov *et al.* (1998). However, they considered only models with broken time-reversal symmetry, for which the Boltzmann–Gibbs law typically does not hold. The role of time-reversal symmetry and deviations from the Boltzmann–Gibbs law are discussed in detail in Section 8.7.

The equilibrium distribution function $P(m)$ can be derived in the same manner as the equilibrium distribution function of energy $P(\varepsilon)$ in physics (Wannier, 1966). Let us divide the system into two subsystems 1 and 2. Taking into account that money is conserved and additive: $m = m_1 + m_2$, whereas the probability is multiplicative: $P = P_1 P_2$, we conclude that $P(m_1 + m_2) = P(m_1)P(m_2)$. The solution of this equation is $P(m) = Ce^{-m/T}$; thus the equilibrium probability distribution of money has the Boltzmann–Gibbs form. From the normalization conditions $\int_0^\infty P(m)\,dm = 1$ and $\int_0^\infty m\,P(m)\,dm = M/N$, we find that $C = 1/T$ and $T = M/N$. Thus, the effective temperature T is the average amount of money per agent.

The Boltzmann–Gibbs distribution can be also obtained by maximizing the entropy of money distribution $S = -\int_0^\infty dm\,P(m)\ln P(m)$ under the constraint of money conservation (Wannier, 1966). Following original Boltzmann's argument, let us divide the money axis $0 \leq m \leq \infty$ into small bins of size dm and number the bins consecutively with the index $b = 1, 2, \ldots$ Let us denote the number of agents in a bin b as N_b, the total number being $N = \sum_{b=1}^\infty N_b$. The agents in the bin b have money m_b, and the total money is $M = \sum_{b=1}^\infty m_b N_b$. The probability of realization of a certain set of occupation numbers $\{N_b\}$ is proportional to the number of ways N agents can be distributed among the bins preserving the set $\{N_b\}$. This number is $N!/N_1!N_2!\ldots$ The logarithm of probability is entropy $\ln N! - \sum_{b=1}^\infty \ln N_b!$. When the numbers N_b are big and Stirling's formula $\ln N! \approx N \ln N$ applies, the entropy per agent is $S = (N \ln N - \sum_{b=1}^\infty N_b \ln N_b)/N = -\sum_{b=1}^\infty P_b \ln P_b$, where $P_b = N_b/N$ is the probability that an agent has money m_b. Using the method of Lagrange multipliers to maximize the entropy S with respect to the occupation numbers $\{N_b\}$ with the constraints on the total money M and the total number of agents N generates the Boltzmann–Gibbs distribution for $P(m)$ (Wannier, 1966).

8.3 Computer simulations

To check that these general arguments indeed work, we performed several computer simulations. Initially, all agents are given the same amount of money: $P(m) = \delta(m - M/N)$, which is shown in Fig. 8.1 as the double vertical line. One pair of agents at a time is chosen randomly, then one of the agents is randomly picked to be the 'winner' (the other agent becomes the 'loser'), and the amount $\Delta m \geq 0$ is transferred from the loser to the winner. If the loser does not have enough money to pay ($m_i < \Delta m$), then the transaction does not take place, and we proceed to another pair of agents. Thus, the agents are not permitted to have negative money. This boundary condition is crucial in establishing the stationary distribution. As the agents exchange money, the initial delta-function distribution first spread symmetrically. Then, the probability density starts to pile up at the impenetrable boundary $m = 0$. The distribution becomes asymmetric (skewed) and ultimately reaches the stationary exponential shape shown in Fig. 8.1. We used several trading rules in the simulations: the exchange of a small constant amount $\Delta m = 1$, the exchange of a random fraction $0 \leq \nu \leq 1$ of the average

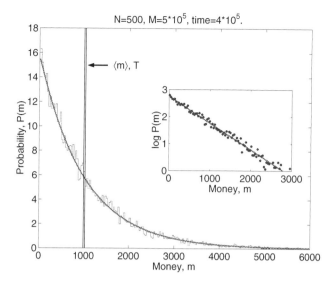

Figure 8.1 Histogram and points: stationary probability distribution of money $P(m)$. Solid curves: fits to the Boltzmann–Gibbs law $P(m) \propto \exp(-m/T)$. Vertical lines: the initial distribution of money.

money of the pair: $\Delta m = v(m_i + m_j)/2$, and the exchange of a random fraction v of the average money in the system: $\Delta m = v\,M/N$. Figures in the paper mostly show simulations for the third rule; however, the final stationary distribution was found to be the same for all rules.

In the process of evolution, the entropy S increases in time and saturates at the maximal value for the Boltzmann–Gibbs distribution. This is illustrated by the top curve in Fig. 8.2 computed for the third rule of exchange. The bottom curve in Fig. 8.2 shows the time evolution of entropy for the first rule of exchange. The time scale for this curve is 500 times greater than for the top curve, so the bottom curve actually ends at the time 10^6. The plot shows that, for the first rule of exchange, mixing is much slower than for the third one. Nevertheless, even for the first rule, the system also eventually reaches the Boltzmann–Gibbs state of maximal entropy, albeit over a time much longer than shown in Fig. 8.2.

One might argue that the pairwise exchange of money may correspond to a medieval market, but not to a modern economy. In order to make the model somewhat more realistic, we introduce firms. One agent at a time becomes a 'firm'. The firm borrows capital K from another agent and returns it with an interest rK, hires L agents and pays them wages W, manufactures Q items of a product and sell it to Q agents at a price R. All of these agents are randomly selected. The firm receives the profit $F = RQ - LW - rK$. The net result is a many-body exchange of money that still satisfies the conservation law.

Parameters of the model are selected following the procedure described in economics textbooks. The aggregate demand-supply curve for the product is taken

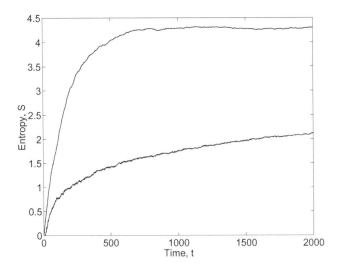

Figure 8.2 Time evolution of entropy. Top curve: for the exchange of a random fraction ν of the average money in the system: $\Delta m = \nu M/N$. Bottom curve: for the exchange of a small constant amount $\Delta m = 1$. The time scale for the bottom curve is 500 times greater than indicated, so it actually ends at the time 10^6.

to be $R(Q) = V/Q^\eta$, where Q is the quantity people would buy at a price R, and $\eta = 0.5$ and $V = 100$ are constants. The production function of the firm has the conventional Cobb-Douglas form: $Q(L, K) = L^\beta K^{1-\beta}$, where $\beta = 0.8$ is a constant. In our simulation, we set $W = 10$. By maximizing firm's profit F with respect to K and L, we find the values of the other parameters: $L = 20$, $Q = 10$, $R = 32$, and $F = 68$.

However, the actual values of the parameters do not matter. Our computer simulations show that the stationary probability distribution of money in this model always has the universal Boltzmann–Gibbs form independent of the model parameters.

8.4   Thermal machine

The money distribution $P(m)$ should not be confused with the distribution of wealth. We believe that $P(m)$ should be interpreted as the instantaneous distribution of purchasing power in the system. Indeed, to make a purchase, one needs money. Material wealth normally is not used directly for a purchase. It needs to be sold first to be converted into money.

Let us consider an outside monopolistic vendor selling a product (say, cars) to the system of agents at a price p. Suppose that a certain small fraction f of the agents needs to buy the product at a given time, and each agent who has enough money to afford the price will buy one item. The fraction f is assumed to be sufficiently small, so that the purchase does not perturb the whole system significantly. At the same time, the absolute number of agents in this group is assumed to be big enough to make the group statistically representative and characterized by the Boltzmann–Gibbs distribution of money. The agents in this group continue to exchange money with the rest of the system, which acts as a thermal bath. The demand for the product is constantly renewed, because products purchased in the past expire after a certain time. In this situation, the vendor can sell the product persistently, thus creating a small steady leakage of money from the system to the vendor.

What price p would maximize the vendor's income? To answer this question, it is convenient to introduce the cumulative distribution of purchasing power $\mathcal{N}(m) = N \int_m^\infty P(m')\,dm' = Ne^{-m/T}$, which gives the number of agents whose money is greater than m. The vendor's income is $fp\mathcal{N}(p)$. It is maximal when $p = T$, i. e. the optimal price is equal to the temperature of the system. This conclusion also follows from the simple dimensional argument that temperature is the only money scale in the problem. At the price $p = T$ that maximizes the vendor's income, only the fraction $\mathcal{N}(T)/N = e^{-1} = 0.37$ of the agents can afford to buy the product.

Now let us consider two disconnected economic systems, one with the temperature T_1 and another with T_2: $T_1 > T_2$. A vendor can buy a product in the latter system at its equilibrium price T_2 and sell it in the former system at the price T_1, thus extracting the speculative profit $T_1 - T_2$, as in a thermal machine. This example suggests that speculative profit is possible only when the system as a whole is out of equilibrium. As money is transferred from the high- to the low-temperature system, their temperatures become closer and eventually equal. After that, no speculative profit is possible, which would correspond to the 'thermal death' of the economy. This example brings to mind economic relations between developed and developing countries, with manufacturing in the poor (low-temperature) countries for export to the rich (high-temperature) ones.

8.5 Models with debt

Now let us discuss what happens if the agents are permitted to go into debt. Debt can be viewed as negative money. Now when a loser does not have enough money to pay, he can borrow the required amount from a reservoir, and his balance becomes negative. The conservation law is not violated: The sum of the winner's positive money and loser's negative money remains constant. When an agent with a negative balance receives money as a winner, it uses this money to repay the debt until the balance becomes positive. We assume for simplicity that the reservoir charges no interest for the lent money. However, because it is not sensible to permit unlimited debt, we put a limit m_d on the maximal debt of an agent: $m_i > -m_d$. This new boundary condition $P(m < -m_d) = 0$ replaces the old boundary condition $P(m < 0) = 0$. The result of a computer simulation with $m_d = 800$ is shown in Fig. 8.3 together with the curve for $m_d = 0$. $P(m)$ is again given by the Boltzmann–Gibbs law, but now with the higher temperature $T = M/N + m_d$, because the normalization conditions need to

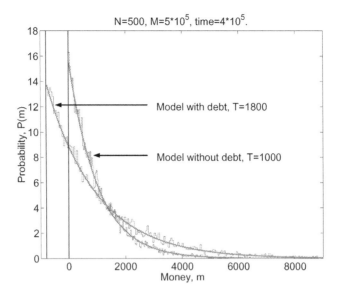

Figure 8.3 Histograms: stationary distributions of money with and without debt. Solid curves: fits to the Boltzmann–Gibbs laws with temperatures $T = 1800$ and $T = 1000$.

be maintained including the population with negative money: $\int_{-m_d}^{\infty} P(m)\,dm = 1$ and $\int_{-m_d}^{\infty} m\,P(m)\,dm = M/N$. The higher temperature makes the money distribution broader, which means that debt increases inequality between agents.[2]

Imposing a sharp cutoff at m_d may be not quite realistic. In practice, the cutoff may be extended over some range depending on the exact bankruptcy rules. Over this range, the Boltzmann–Gibbs distribution would be smeared out. So we expect to see the Boltzmann–Gibbs law only sufficiently far from the cutoff region. Similarly, in an experiment by Mueth *et al.* (1998), some deviations from the exponential law were observed near the lower boundary of the distribution. Also, at the high end of the distributions, the number of events becomes small and

---

[2] In general, temperature is completely determined by the average money per agent, $\langle m \rangle = M/N$, and the boundary conditions. Suppose the agents are required to have no less money than m_1 and no more than m_2: $m_1 \leq m \leq m_2$. In this case, the normalization conditions $\int_{m_1}^{m_2} P(m)\,dm = 1$ and $\int_{m_1}^{m_2} m\,P(m)\,dm = \langle m \rangle$ with $P(m) = C\,e^{-m/T}$ give the following equation for T:

$$\coth\left(\frac{\Delta m}{T}\right) - \frac{T}{\Delta m} = \frac{\overline{m} - \langle m \rangle}{\Delta m}, \tag{8.1}$$

where $\overline{m} = (m_1 + m_2)/2$ and $\Delta m = (m_2 - m_1)/2$. It follows from Eq. (8.1) that the temperature is positive when $\overline{m} > \langle m \rangle$, negative when $\overline{m} < \langle m \rangle$, and infinite ($P(m) = \text{const}$) when $\overline{m} = \langle m \rangle$. In particular, if agents' money are bounded from above, but not from below: $-\infty \leq m \leq m_2$, the temperature is negative. That means inverted Boltzmann–Gibbs distribution with more reach agents than poor.

statistics poor, so the Boltzmann–Gibbs law loses applicability. Thus, we expect the Boltzmann–Gibbs law to hold only for the intermediate range of money not too close either to the lower boundary or to the very high end. However, this range is the most relevant, because it covers the great majority of population.

Lending creates equal amounts of positive (asset) and negative (liability) money (Shubik, 1997; McConnell and Brue, 1996). When economics textbooks describe how 'banks create money' or 'debt creates money' (McConnell and Brue, 1996), they do not count the negative liabilities as money, and thus their money is not conserved. In our operational definition of money, we include all financial instruments with fixed denomination, such as currency, IOUs, and bonds, but not material wealth or stocks, and we count both assets and liabilities. With this definition, money is conserved, and we expect to see the Boltzmann–Gibbs distribution in equilibrium. Unfortunately, because this definition differs from economists' definitions of money (M1, M2, M3, etc. (McConnell and Brue, 1996)), it is not easy to find the appropriate statistics. Of course, money can be also emitted by a central bank or government. This is analogous to an external influx of energy into a physical system. However, if this process is sufficiently slow, the economic system may be able to maintain quasi-equilibrium, characterized by a slowly changing temperature.

We performed a simulation of a model with one bank and many agents. The agents keep their money in accounts on which the bank pays interest. The agents may borrow money from the bank, for which they must pay interest in monthly installments. If they cannot make the required payments, they may be declared bankrupt, which relieves them from the debt, but the liability is transferred to the bank. In this way, the conservation of money is maintained. The model is too elaborate to describe it in full detail here. We found that, depending on the parameters of the model, either the agents constantly lose money to the bank, which steadily reduces the agents' temperature, or the bank constantly loses money, which drives down its own negative balance and steadily increases the agents' temperature.

8.6   Boltzmann equation

The Boltzmann–Gibbs distribution can be also derived from the Boltzmann equation (Lifshitz and Pitaevskiĭ, 1993), which describes the time evolution of the distribution function $P(m)$ due to pairwise interactions:

$$\frac{dP(m)}{dt} = \int \int \{-w_{[m,m']\rightarrow[m-\Delta,m'+\Delta]}P(m)P(m') \tag{8.2}$$
$$+ w_{[m-\Delta,m'+\Delta]\rightarrow[m,m']}P(m-\Delta)P(m'+\Delta)\} \, dm' \, d\Delta.$$

Here $w_{[m,m']\rightarrow[m-\Delta,m'+\Delta]}$ is the rate of transferring money Δ from an agent with money m to an agent with money m'. If a model has time-reversal symmetry, then the transition rate of a direct process is the same as the transition rate of the reversed process, thus the w-factors in the first and second lines of Eq. (8.2) are equal. In this case, the Boltzmann–Gibbs distribution $P(m) = C \exp(-m/T)$ nullifies the right-hand side of Eq. (8.2); thus this distribution is stationary: $dP(m)/dt = 0$ (Lifshitz and Pitaevskiĭ, 1993).

8.7   Non-Boltzmann–Gibbs distributions

However, if time-reversal symmetry is broken, the two transition rates w in Eq. (8.2) may be different, and the system may have a non-Boltzmann–Gibbs stationary distribution or no stationary distribution at all. Examples of such kind were studied by Ispolatov *et al.* (1998). One model was called the multiplicative random exchange. In this model, a randomly selected loser i loses a fixed fraction α of his money m_i to a randomly selected winner j: $[m_i, m_j] \rightarrow [(1-\alpha)m_i, m_j+\alpha m_i]$. If we try to reverse this process and appoint the winner j to become a loser, the system does not return to the original configuration $[m_i, m_j]$: $[(1-\alpha)m_i, m_j+\alpha m_i] \rightarrow [(1-\alpha)m_i+\alpha(m_j+\alpha m_i), (1-\alpha)(m_j+\alpha m_i)]$. Except for $\alpha = 1/2$, the exponential distribution function is not a stationary solution of the Boltzmann equation derived for this model. Instead, the stationary distribution has the shape shown in Fig. 8.4 for $\alpha = 1/3$, which we reproduced in our numerical simulations. It still has an exponential tail end at the high end, but drops to zero at the low end for $\alpha < 1/2$. Another example of similar kind was studied by Chakraborti and Chakrabarti (2000). In that model, the agents save a fraction λ of their money and exchange a random fraction ϵ of their total remaining money: $[m_i, m_j] \rightarrow [\lambda m_i + \epsilon(1-\lambda)(m_i+m_j), \lambda m_j + (1-\epsilon)(1-\lambda)(m_i+m_j)]$. This

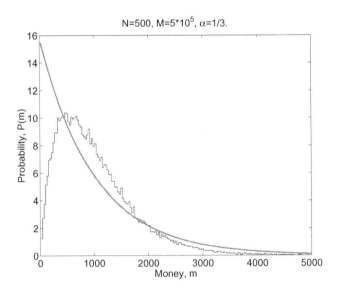

Figure 8.4 Histogram: stationary probability distribution of money in the multiplicative random exchange model studied by Ispolatov *et al.* (1998). Solid curve: the Boltzmann–Gibbs law.

exchange also does not return to the original configuration after being reversed. The stationary probability distribution was found by Chakraborti and Chakrabarti (2000) to be nonexponential for $\lambda \neq 0$ with a shape qualitatively similar to the one shown in Fig. 8.4.

Another interesting example of a non-Boltzmann–Gibbs distribution occurs in a model with taxes and subsidies. Suppose a special agent ('government') collects a fraction ('tax') of every transaction in the system. The collected money is then equally divided between all agents of the system, so that each agent receives the subsidy δm with the frequency $1/\tau_s$. Assuming that δm is small and approximating the collision integral with a relaxation time τ_r (Lifshitz and Pitaevskiĭ, 1993), we obtain the following Boltzmann equation

$$\frac{\partial P(m)}{\partial t} + \frac{\delta m}{\tau_s}\frac{\partial P(m)}{\partial m} = -\frac{P(m) - \tilde{P}(m)}{\tau_r}, \tag{8.3}$$

where $\tilde{P}(m)$ is the equilibrium Boltzmann–Gibbs function. The second term in the left-hand side of Eq. (8.3) is analogous to the force applied to electrons in a metal by an external electric field (Lifshitz and Pitaevskiĭ, 1993). The approximate stationary solution of Eq. (8.3) is the displaced Boltzmann–Gibbs one: $P(m) = \tilde{P}(m - (\tau_r/\tau_s)\delta m)$. The displacement of the equilibrium distribution $\tilde{P}(m)$ by $(\tau_r/\tau_s)\delta m$ would leave an empty gap near $m = 0$. This gap is filled by interpolating between zero population at $m = 0$ and the displaced distribution. The curve obtained in a computer simulation of this model (Fig. 8.5) qualitatively agrees with this expectation. The low-money population is

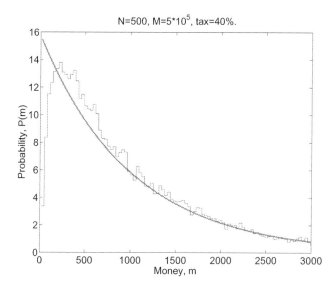

Figure 8.5 Histogram: stationary probability distribution of money in the model with taxes and subsidies. Solid curve: the Boltzmann–Gibbs law.

suppressed, because the government, acting as an external force, 'pumps out' that population and pushes the system out of thermodynamic equilibrium. We found that the entropy of the stationary state in the model with taxes and subsidies is few per cent lower than without.

These examples show that the Boltzmann–Gibbs distribution is not fully universal, meaning that it does not hold for just any model of exchange that conserves money. Nevertheless, it is universal in a limited sense: For a broad class of models that have time-reversal symmetry, the stationary distribution is exponential and does not depend on the details of a model. Conversely, when time-reversal symmetry is broken, the distribution may depend on model details. The difference between these two classes of models may be rather subtle. For example, let us change the multiplicative random exchange from a fixed fraction of loser's money to a fixed fraction of the total money of winner and loser. This modification retains the multiplicative idea that the amount exchanged is proportional to the amount involved, but restores time-reversal symmetry and the Boltzmann–Gibbs distribution. In the model with $\Delta m = 1$ discussed in the next Section, the difference between time-reversible and time-irreversible formulations amounts to the difference between impenetrable and absorbing boundary conditions at $m = 0$. Unlike in physics, in economy there is no fundamental requirement that interactions have time-reversal symmetry. However, in the absence of detailed knowledge of real microscopic dynamics of economic exchange, the semiuniversal Boltzmann–Gibbs distribution appears to be a natural starting point.

Moreover, deviations from the Boltzmann–Gibbs law may occur only if the transition rates w in Eq. (8.2) explicitly depend on the agents money m or m' in an asymmetric manner. In another simulation, we randomly preselected winners and losers for every pair of agents (i, j). In this case, money flows along directed links between the agents: $i \rightarrow j \rightarrow k$, and time-reversal symmetry is strongly broken. This model is closer to the real economy, in which, for example, one typically receives money from an employer and pays it to a grocer, but rarely the reverse. Nevertheless, we still found the Boltzmann–Gibbs distribution of money in this model, because the transition rates w do not explicitly depend on m and m'.

8.8   Nonlinear Boltzmann equation vs. linear master equation

For the model where agents randomly exchange the constant amount $\Delta m = 1$, the Boltzmann equation is:

$$\frac{dP_m}{dt} = P_{m+1} \sum_{n=0}^{\infty} P_n + P_{m-1} \sum_{n=1}^{\infty} P_n$$

$$- P_m \sum_{n=0}^{\infty} P_n - P_m \sum_{n=1}^{\infty} P_n \tag{8.4}$$

$$= (P_{m+1} + P_{m-1} - 2P_m) + P_0(P_m - P_{m-1}), \tag{8.5}$$

where $P_m \equiv P(m)$ and we have used $\sum_{m=0}^{\infty} P_m = 1$. The first, diffusion term in Eq. (8.5) is responsible for broadening of the initial delta-function distribution. The second term, proportional to P_0, is essential for the Boltzmann–Gibbs distribution $P_m = e^{-m/T}(1 - e^{-1/T})$ to be a stationary solution of Eq. (8.5). In a similar model studied by Ispolatov *et al.* (1998), the second term was omitted on the assumption that agents who lost all money are eliminated: $P_0 = 0$. In that case, the total number of agents is not conserved, and the system never reaches any stationary distribution. Time-reversal symmetry is violated, since transitions into the state $m = 0$ are permitted, but not out of this state.

If we treat P_0 as a constant, Eq. (8.5) looks like a linear Fokker-Planck equation (Lifshitz and Pitaevskiĭ, 1993) for P_m, with the first term describing diffusion and the second term an external force proportional to P_0. Similar equations were studied by Montrell and Shlesinger (1982). Eq. (8.5) can be also rewritten as

$$\frac{dP_m}{dt} = P_{m+1} - (2 - P_0)P_m + (1 - P_0)P_{m-1}. \tag{8.6}$$

The coefficient $(1 - P_0)$ in front of P_{m-1} represents the rate of increasing money by $\Delta m = 1$, and the coefficient 1 in front of P_{m+1} represents the rate of decreasing money by $\Delta m = -1$. Since $P_0 > 0$, the former is smaller than the latter, which results in the stationary Boltzmann–Gibbs distributions $P_m = (1 - P_0)^m$. An equation similar to Eq. (8.6) describes a Markov chain studied for strategic market games by Shubik (1999). Naturally, the stationary probability distribution of wealth in that model was found to be exponential.

Even though Eqs. (8.5) and (8.6) look like linear equations, nevertheless the Boltzmann equation (8.2) and (8.4) is a profoundly nonlinear equation. It contains the product of two probability distribution functions P in the right-hand side, because two agents are involved in money exchange. Most studies of wealth distribution (Montrell and Shlesinger, 1982) have the fundamental flaw that they use a single-particle approach. They assume that the wealth of an agent may change just by itself and write a linear master equation for the probability distribution. Because only one particle is considered, this approach cannot adequately incorporate conservation of money. In reality, an agent can change money only by interacting with another agent, thus the problem requires a two-particle probability distribution function. Using Boltzmann's molecular chaos hypothesis, the two-particle function is factorized into a product of two single-particle distributions functions, which results in the nonlinear Boltzmann equation. Conservation of money is adequately incorporated in this two-particle approach, and the universality of the exponential Boltzmann–Gibbs distribution is transparent.

8.9   Conclusions

Throughout we assumed some randomness in the exchange of money. The results of our paper would apply the best to the probability distribution of money in a closed community of gamblers. In more traditional economic studies, the agents exchange money not randomly, but following deterministic strategies, such as maximization of utility functions (Shubik, 1997; Bak *et al.*, 1999). The concept of equilibrium in these studies is similar to mechanical equilibrium in physics, which is achieved by minimizing energy or maximizing utility. However, for big ensembles, statistical equilibrium is a more relevant concept. When many heterogeneous agents deterministically interact and spend various amounts of money from very little to very big, the money exchange is effectively random. In the future, we would like to uncover the Boltzmann–Gibbs distribution of money in a simulation of a big ensemble of economic agents following realistic deterministic strategies with money conservation taken into account. That would be the economics analog of molecular dynamics simulations in physics. While atoms collide following fully deterministic equations of motion, their energy exchange is effectively random due to complexity of the system and results in the Boltzmann–Gibbs law.

We do not claim that the real economy is in equilibrium. (Most of the physical world around us is not in true equilibrium either.) Nevertheless, the concept of statistical equilibrium is a very useful reference point for studying nonequilibrium phenomena.

9   A probabilistic approach to the law of value

In this chapter we take a probabilistic approach to what was the foundational question of political economy: what is the relationship, if any, between the time it takes people to produce things and the prices these things exchange for? We have explored this question in relation to the writings of Smith, Ricardo and Marx in chapter 6; in this chapter we take a closer look at Marx's version of the theory and then develop the argument by means of a simulation model.

9.1   The law of value

Marx, following Ricardo, held a labour theory of the economic value of reproducible commodities. According to Marx the value of a commodity is determined by the prevailing technical conditions of production and measured by the socially necessary labour-time required to produce it (Marx, 1976). The value of a commodity is to be distinguished from its price, which is the amount of money it fetches in the marketplace. Although economic actors may differ in their subjective evaluations of the worth or 'value' of commodities there are emergent regularities in commodity economies that ensure that prices tend to 'gravitate' around labour values.

An important feature of Marx's theory of value is the strong distinction between value and price. Prices are what we see everyday in a market economy, but we never see values. In Marx's view the unknown and hidden real values of commodities constrain and shape the formation of commodity prices, whether we are aware of it or not, and despite the subjective evaluations we may form of the relative importance of the available goods and services. Prices are noisy and at any precise time are subject to multiple causes, not least the scarcity or abundance of goods, or the shifting tastes of the consuming public. Marx's theory of value is not intended as a direct explanation or prediction of particular prices on particular days, but abstracts from temporary or accidental conditions, and instead investigates a necessary determinant of price.

There is nothing unusual about this approach. In fact, the logical separation of different mechanisms that in practice mutually interact to cause an event to occur is a necessary part of scientific inquiry. For example, the law of gravity is a common and permanent factor that partially controls the movement of objects on earth. But the fact that books stay on shelves or planes fly does not invalidate the law; rather, the law explains the need and function of bookshelves and wings. And although the law of gravity cannot always be used to predict the trajectory of objects, it is nonetheless a real causal factor. Similarly, the law of value is a theory of a common and permanent factor that partially controls the movement of prices in commodity economies. The fact that a monopolistic firm may permanently over-charge for its services, or the price of non-reproducible goods, such as great works of art, appear to have no relationship to labour-time, does not invalidate the law of value.

It is important to develop theories of single mechanisms hypothetically considered to be working in isolation. Only then can we hope to predict actual events. Newton famously asserted, contrary to all appearances, that all bodies move at constant velocity unless an external force is applied. This is not an empirical statement, because apart from the odd special case, most bodies do not move at constant velocity. Simplification and abstraction is necessary in order to identify underlying, hidden causal mechanisms, particularly if the events that need to be explained, whether movement of bodies or movement of prices, are multiply determined by lots of different mechanisms working together.

In a theoretical simplification of capitalism often referred to as the 'simple commodity economy', Marx claims that prices will tend to 'correspond' to labour values. Only a few simple conditions need be met for this to occur:

> For prices at which commodities are exchanged to approximately correspond to their values, nothing more is necessary than 1) for the exchange of the various commodities to cease being purely accidental or only occasional; 2) so far as direct exchange of commodities is concerned, for these commodities to be produced on both sides in approximately sufficient quantities to meet mutual requirements, something learned from mutual experience in trading and therefore a natural outgrowth of continued trading; and 3) so far as selling is concerned, for no natural or artificial monopoly to enable either of the contracting sides to sell commodities above their value or to compel them to undersell. By accidental monopoly we mean a monopoly which a buyer or seller acquires through an accidental state of supply or demand.
>
> The assumption that the commodities of the various spheres of production are sold at their value merely implies, of course, that their value is the centre of gravity around which their prices fluctuate, and their continual rises and drops tend to equalise.
>
> (Marx, 1971: 178)

The theory of the law of value motivates such statements. It is a fundamental building block of Marx's economics.

The law of value is intended to explain how the total labour of a society of commodity producers, who freely exchange their products in a marketplace, is divided and allocated to different branches of production via the market mechanism. The exchange of commodities at prices that deviate from values is the mechanism by which social labour-time is transferred from one sector of production to another. When prices equal values the division of labour has reached an equilibrium that satisfies social demand: 'the law of value is the law of equilibrium of the commodity economy'.

> [I]t is only through the 'value' of commodities that the working activity of separate independent producers leads to the productive unity which is called a social economy, to the interconnections and mutual conditioning of the labour of individual members of society. Value is the transmission belt which transfers the movement of working processes from one part of society to another, making that society a functioning whole.
>
> (Rubin, 1973: 81)

In brief, the law of value is the process by which a simple commodity economy (i) reaches an equilibrium, in which (ii) prices correspond to labour values, and (iii) social labour is allocated to different branches of production according to social demand (where 'social demand' is understood to mean consumption requirements constrained by income).

We will investigate Marx's claim in some detail. The main result is that Marx's law of value does emerge as an unintended consequence of uncoordinated market activity. We will see how the law of value naturally emerges from 'behind the backs' of economic actors solely via money flows that place budget constraints on their local evaluations of commodity prices, which are otherwise subjective and unconstrained. The probabilistic model reveals particularly simple and satisfying dynamic relationships between values, prices, social labour-time and money.

It must be emphasized, however, that Marx did not think that prices correspond to labour values in capitalism. Instead, he thought there was a systematic deviation between labour values and profit-equalizing 'prices of production'. But here we wish to exclude this complication and instead concentrate on a hypothetical case of the law of value operating in isolation.

9.2   The model

We will now outline a computer model that shows how the law of value emerges. The model consists of N workers (numbered $1, \ldots, N$) who produce, consume and exchange L types of commodities (numbered $1, \ldots, L$), a fixed amount of paper money M, which is distributed amongst the workers, a market mechanism that mediates commodity exchange.

For simplicity, we will assume that every worker specializes in the production of a single commodity at any one time. All commodities are simple, and do not require other commodities for their manufacture. Each commodity requires the work of a single worker for its production. Constant returns to scale prevail and consequently there is no rationale for the existence of firms. Workers never cease production.

We assume that all workers have the same skill and the amount of labour that each requires to produce a given good is known. For example, a worker who specializes in commodity type j produces at a rate of $1/l_j$ units per time step. This implies that l_j is the labour value of commodity j. Labour in is homogeneous and productive techniques are assumed not to change. Once a commodity is produced it remains the property of the worker until they consume it or sell it. The model keeps track of how much of each commodity is currently owned by each worker.

Workers produce according to the following rule:

> *Production update rule P_1*: (Deterministic). At the start of the simulation initialize the endowment vector for actor i to zero: $\mathbf{e}_i = \mathbf{0}$.
>
> Actor i subsequently generates one unit of commodity $A(i)$ every $l_{A(i)}$ time steps, and the appropriate element of the endowment vector, $\mathbf{e}_i[A(i)]$, is incremented by one.

Although no producer is more efficient than another a distinction between socially necessary labour-time and actual labour-time expended can be maintained. Over-production of a commodity relative to the social demand implies that some of the labour-time expended was socially unnecessary.

9.2.1 Actor consumption

Every actor desires to consume all commodity types. This behaviour can be interpreted as subsistence or aspirational. A consumption column vector, $\mathbf{c} = (1/c_1, \ldots, 1/c_L)$, where $c_j \geq 0$, defines the desired rate of consumption events for all actors. For example, every actor desires to consume commodity j at a rate of $1/c_j$ units per time step. The consumption vector is identical and fixed for all actors and represents an economy with homogeneous tastes that do not change. Note the asymmetry between production rates and consumption rates: an actor always meets its single production rate, but only conditionally meets its consumption rates. Actual consumption rates depend on the availability of commodities produced by other actors.

Actors consume according to the following rule:

> *Consumption update rule C_1*: (Deterministic). At the start of the simulation initialize the consumption deficit vector for actor i to zero: $\mathbf{d}_i = \mathbf{0}$.
>
> Actor i subsequently generates one unit of consumption deficit for each commodity $j = 1, \ldots, L$ every c_j time steps, and the appropriate element of the deficit vector, $\mathbf{d}_i[j]$, is incremented by one.
>
> Each time step actor i consumes $\mathbf{o}_i = \min(\mathbf{e}_i, \mathbf{d}_i)$ commodities from its endowment to satisfy its current consumption deficit. A new endowment vector, $\mathbf{e}_i' = \mathbf{e}_i - \mathbf{o}_i$, and a new deficit vector, $\mathbf{d}_i' = \mathbf{d}_i - \mathbf{o}_i$ are formed.

Note that in each time step more than one commodity may be consumed, although only one commodity may be worked on. The assumption of universal and constant production and consumption vectors could be relaxed by introducing supply and demand noise due to heterogeneity of consumption tastes and production efficiency, but we won't pursue this extension.

9.2.2   The reproduction coefficient

The reproduction coefficient, $\eta = \sum_{j=1}^{L} l_j / c_j$, measures whether, given the 'social facts' of the production and consumption vectors, the economy may realize an overall social surplus, deficit or balance. A value of $\eta = 1$ implies the economy can achieve a state of simple reproduction (where total production equals total consumption), $\eta > 1$ implies an economy permanently in overall deficit (unrealized consumption capacity) and $\eta < 1$ implies an economy permanently in overall surplus (redundant production capacity). We will restrict our attention to economies with $\eta = 1$ that can theoretically achieve a balance between supply and demand but may over-and under-produce commodities due to a sub-optimal division of labour.

9.2.3   Money

Each actor i owns a sum of symbolic money, $m_i \geq 0$, which is used to purchase commodities for consumption. The total amount of money in the economy, $M = \sum_{i=1}^{N} m_i$, is conserved. The unit of measure of money is the 'coin', although it is an arbitrarily divisible unit. Coins are neither produced nor consumed by actors. Actors exchange money for commodities, and therefore gain money when they sell, and lose money when they buy. Complications due to changes in the money supply are ignored.

9.2.4   Subjective prices

Actors form subjective evaluations of commodity prices during bi-lateral exchange. Two requirements are placed on the evaluations: (i) a purchaser cannot offer more coins than they possess, and (ii) offer prices must not be fixed *a priori*. The second requirement is important because the law of value trivially does not hold in an economy of homogeneous, *a priori* evaluators. For example, if every actor evaluated commodity j at 0 coins for all time then prices cannot converge to labour values. The law of value operates 'behind the backs' of economic actors because they adapt to changing local circumstances that are not of their own choosing but the result of global properties of the economic system.

   To simulate adaptation we could select a machine learning algorithm, which has some psychological plausibility, that minimizes the consumption error. But this is an unnecessary level of detail at present. Instead, actors form selling and buying prices for each commodity according to:

> *Price offer rule O_1*: (Stochastic). The price of commodity j according to actor i is $p_j^{(i)}$, and is randomly selected from the discrete interval $[0, m_i]$ according to a uniform distribution. The price is random but bound by the number of coins currently held.

The actors are adaptive in a weak sense: if they have less (resp. more) coins they probably will offer less (resp. more). Their changing circumstances are defined solely by how many coins they hold. The law of value, if it is to function, must therefore do so only via money flows, not by directly influencing or changing individual cost evaluations. O_1 is one of many possible adaptive rules, but it is the simplest, and represents minimal theoretical commitment to the decision processes employed by actors in real economies. In addition, Gode and Sunder (1993) have shown that random traders with a budget constraint realize the same allocative efficiency as human actors under the same market discipline, so there is reason to believe that market structure plays a more important causal role than the individual rationality. Our aim is to concentrate on the structural determinations of the conditions under which evaluations take place, rather than the process of evaluation itself. Rule O_1 assumes that, absent a decision theory, a range of possible decision outcomes are equally likely.

9.2.5   The market

Periodically actors meet in the marketplace. Trading behaviour continues until the market is cleared when for every commodity type there are either no buyers or no sellers. Commodities are bought and sold in single units. A cleared market does not imply that all needs are satisfied or all commod- ities sold.

> *Market clearing rule M_1*: (Stochastic). Initialize the set of uncleared commodities to $C = \{j : 1 \leq j \leq L\}$.

(1)   Randomly select an uncleared commodity j from the set C according to a uniform distribution.

(2)   Form the set of candidate sellers S, which contains all actors with a desire to sell commodity j (i.e., $S = \{x : e_x[j] > d_x[j], 1 \leq x \leq N\}$). Select the seller s from S according to a uniform distribution.

(3)   Form the set of candidate buyers B, which contains all actors with a desire to buy commodity j (i.e., $B = \{x : d_x[j] > e_x[j], 1 \leq x \leq N\}$). Select the buyer b from B according to a uniform distribution.

(4)   If no seller or no buyer (i.e., $S = \emptyset \lor B = \emptyset$) then remove commodity j from C; otherwise, invoke market exchange rule E_1 (see below).

(5)   Repeat until there are no remaining uncleared commodities (i.e., $C = \emptyset$).

Rule $\mathbf{M_1}$ matches buyers with sellers who then conditionally exchange coins for commodities according to:

> *Market exchange rule $\mathbf{E_1}$*: (Stochastic). Given a buyer b and seller s of commodity j with offer prices $p_j^{(b)}$ and $p_j^{(s)}$ respectively, determined by price offer rule $\mathbf{O_1}$, select the exchange price, x, from the discrete interval $[p_j^{(b)}, p_j^{(s)}]$ according to a uniform distribution. The exchange price is randomly selected to lie between the two offer prices.
>
> If the buyer has sufficient funds ($m_b \geq x$) then the transaction takes place. Actor b loses x coins and gains one unit of commodity j, and the appropriate element of its endowment vector, $\mathbf{e}_b[j]$, is incremented by one. Actor c gains x coins and loses one unit of commodity j, and the appropriate element of its endowment vector, $\mathbf{e}_s[j]$, is decremented by one.

Rules $\mathbf{M_1}$ and $\mathbf{E_1}$ do not represent a typical Walrasian market in which transactions take place at equilibrium after a process of extended price signalling or 'tatonnement'. Instead, transactions occur at disequilibrium prices, commodities may go unsold, and the same commodity type may exchange for many different prices in the same market period. Further, commodities in oversupply may initially fail to sell only to find willing buyers at a later time, and commodities in under-supply may not necessarily realize a higher price. In sum, although the rules do implement short-term price signalling due to disequilibrium between supply and demand the detailed dynamics of this process are not straightforward, and can only be approximated by mathematical models that assume continuous price adjustment.

9.2.6 Division of labour

The set $A_j = \{i : 1 \leq i \leq N, A(i) = j\}$ contains those actors that specialize in the production of j. The set $D = \{A_j : j = 1, \ldots, L\}$ partitions the actors into production sectors and represents the total division of labour of the economy. The division of labour is dynamic because actors can change what they produce. Actors attempt to meet their consumption requirements but do not explicitly maximize wealth. They switch from one production sector to another according to the following rule:

> *Sector-switching rule $\mathbf{S_1}$*: (Stochastic). For actor i at the end of every nth period of length T time steps form the consumption error, defined as the Euclidean norm of the consumption deficit vector, $\|\mathbf{d}_i^{(n)}\|$. $\|\mathbf{d}_i^{(n)}\|$ is compared to the consumption error of the previous period $\|\mathbf{d}_i^{(n-1)}\|$. If $\|\mathbf{d}_i^{(n)}\| > \|\mathbf{d}_i^{(n-1)}\|$ then randomly select a new production sector from the available L according to a uniform distribution. In other words, if the consumption error has increased from the previous period then swap to a new sector.

T is a constant multiple of the maximum consumption period, $\max(c_i)$, such that actors produce and have the opportunity to sell at least one commodity before sampling the consumption error and deciding whether to switch.

There are no switching costs. The result of all actors following rule S_1 is to perform a parallel search over possible social divisions of labour. Dissatisfied actors randomly switch to new sectors in search of sufficient income to meet their consumption requirements.

9.2.7   Simulation rule

The cycle of production, consumption, exchange and reallocation of social labour proceeds according to the following rule:

Simulation rule R_1: Randomly construct production (**l**) and consumption vectors (**c**) for the economy, such that the reproduction coefficient $\eta = 1$. Allocate M/N coins to each of the N actors (the initial distribution does not affect the final outcome).

(1)   Increment the global time step.
(2)   For each actor invoke production rule P_1.
(3)   For each actor invoke consumption rule C_1.
(4)   Invoke market clearing rule M_1.
(5)   For each actor invoke sector-switching rule S_1.
(6)   Repeat.

The ruleset for the simple commodity economy

$$SCE = \{R_1, P_1, C_1, O_1, \{M_1, E_1\}, S_1, \}$$

defines the computational model. The implementation has five parameters: (i) the number of actors N, (ii) the number of commodities L, (iii) the amount of coins in the economy M, (iv) an upper bound, R, on the maximum possible consumption period, which is used to constrain the random construction of production and consumption vectors during initialization, and (iv) a switching parameter C that is the constant multiple of the maximum consumption period required by sector-switching rule S_1.

9.3   Simulation results

Computational models are suited to the detailed analysis of causal processes that are not amenable to straightforward mathematical treatment. The detailed supply and demand dynamics in this model are an example. But unlike mathematical proofs, which normally quantify over the whole parameter-space, the execution of a computational model is only a single sample of the parameter-space. It isn't practical to explore the entire parameter-space so the sampling process is biased toward subspaces that may be feasibly computed (for example, the time cost of the simulation rapidly increases with N), are realistic (for example, economies with a single coin are not considered) and conform to the requirements for the law of value to operate (for example, if the consumption period of a commodity j greatly exceeds the number of actors, i.e., if $R \gg N$, then the probability that a seller of j will find a buyer in the marketplace is low; hence exchange becomes occasional, failing a requirement for the law of value to operate). All simulation runs follow a similar pattern of initial non-equilibrium activity prior to settling down to stable averages and stationary distributions (appendix B contains further experimental details). We will measure the stationary distributions of the division of labour and market prices. But many other variables of interest could be tracked.

9.3.1 Division of labour

The distribution of actors in each sector of the economy settles to a normal distribution centred on a mean sector size. Figure 9.1 shows the stationary distributions of a typical sample. The equilibrium mean size of sector j is always approximately $N(l_j/c_j)$. Figure 9.2 reveals this relationship sampled over many runs.

Definition 1. A division of labour is *efficient* if for every commodity type the number of commodities produced equals the social demand.

Proposition 1. Let $a_j = |A_j|/N$ be the proportion of actors producing commodity j. Then $a_j = \frac{l_j}{c_j}$ ($j = 1, \ldots, L$) is an efficient division of labour.

Proof. The social demand for commodity j is $\frac{N}{c_j}$ units per unit time. When $a_j = \frac{l_j}{c_j}$ the number of units produced is $N\frac{a_j}{l_j} = \frac{N}{c_j}$ units per unit time, which equals the social demand. □

On average the division of labour is approximately efficient, but due to stochastic fluctuations perfect efficiency is not achieved. An efficient division of labour implies that the global consumption error is minimized and all actors meet their consumption requirements. Actual simulation runs only approximate maximum consumption, and unsold commodities and unsatisfied demands either stabilize or slowly accumulate over time. The results show that the **SCE** attains a (dynamic) equilibrium of the division of labour, and that the labour equilibrium is approximately efficient.

9.3.2 Objective prices

The stationary distributions of commodity prices can be approximately fitted by exponentials. Figure 9.3 shows the evolution of mean prices during a typical

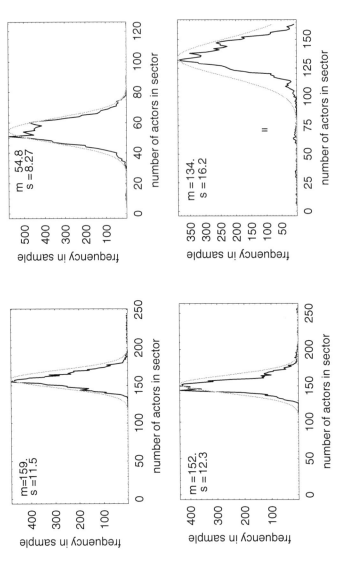

Figure 9.1 Stationary distributions of sector sizes with fitted normal distributions collected from a random sample of a 4-commodity economy with parameter settings N:500, L:4, M:2.5 × 10⁵, R:25, C:2. The mean division of labour, (159, 54.8, 152, 134), is close to the theoretical efficient division of labour, $N(\frac{L_i}{C_i}) = (152, 56, 146, 146)$.

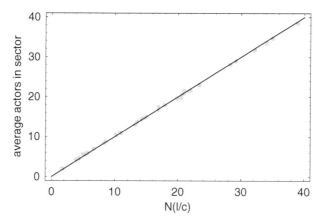

Figure 9.2 Relationship between mean sector size and $N \frac{l_i}{c_i}$ from 20 random samples of 3-commodity economies with parameter settings N:50, L:3, M:2500, R:25, C:2. The straight line represents the identity relationship $y = x$.

run and the associated stationary distributions. The price distributions have an exponential tail at the high end, but drop to zero at the low end, but the exponential distribution accurately models the price distributions over most of the price range. In equilibrium a single commodity type does not have a single price, but has a range of prices that occur with differing but fixed probabilities.

The law of value states that, in equilibrium, market prices 'correspond' to labour values. The Pearson correlation coefficient, r, between two vectors, $\mathbf{x}$ and $\mathbf{y}$ measures the linear relationship between them ($-1 \leq r \leq 1$). A value of -1.0 is a perfect negative (inverse) correlation, 0.0 is no correlation, and 1.0 is a perfect positive correlation. $r = 1.0$ implies that there is a single scalar constant, λ, such that $\mathbf{x} = \lambda \mathbf{y}$. We will check the correspondence between market prices and labour values by measuring their correlation.

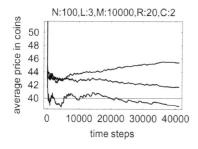
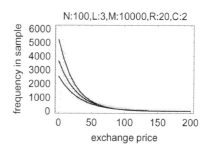

Figure 9.3 Evolution of mean commodity prices in a 3-commodity economy (left figure) and stationary distribution of commodity prices with fitted exponential distributions (right figure).

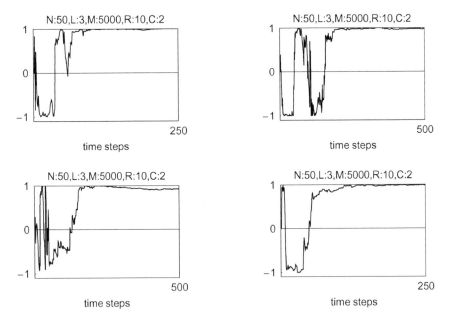

Figure 9.4 Evolution of vector correlation of mean prices and labour values over four samples of 3-commodity economies.

Denote the average price of commodity j by $\langle p_j \rangle$. Figure 9.4 graphs representative time series of the correlation between the market price column vector $\mathbf{p} = (\langle p_1 \rangle, \ldots, \langle p_L \rangle)$ and the labour values column vector $\mathbf{v} = (l_1, \ldots, l_L)$ (recall that l_j is the time period required to produce commodity j). We can now state the main simulation result of this chapter: the correlation between mean market prices and labour values approaches unity in equilibrium. Appendix B contains further experimental results that demonstrate the robustness of this result.

The results show that the **SCE** attains a (dynamic) equilibrium in which the mean equilibrium price of a commodity, measured over a sampling period, is proportional to the labour-time required to make it. Prices 'gravitate' around labour values and this equilibrium coexists with local and subjective pricing decisions constrained only by money endowments.

The equilibrium constant of proportionality, λ, between mean prices and labour values, such that $\mathbf{p} \approx \lambda \mathbf{v}$, must have dimensions *coins per unit labour-time*. λ summarizes the causal relationship between expenditure of labour-time in production and the representation of that time in the market price of commodities. It measures how much labour-time money represents. Duménil (1983) and Foley (1982) emphasize the importance of this constant in Marxist economic theory. They define it in the context of a capitalist economy.

Definition 2. The *Monetary Expression of Labour-time* (MELT) is the ratio of the net product at current prices relative to the productive labour expended in an economy over a given period of time.

In a simple commodity economy there is no distinction between gross and net product and hence the MELT is the ratio of the product at current prices relative to the labour expended, which can be directly measured as:

$$\lambda = \frac{\gamma M}{\sum_{i=1}^{L} l_i v_i} \tag{9.1}$$

where γ is the proportion of the total money in the economy that on average exchanges per unit time (so γM is the average velocity of money), and v_j is the average exchange velocity of commodity j. The numerator in the definition is the rate of money exchange, the denominator is the rate of labour-time exchanged in the form of commodities, and the MELT is the ratio of the two, measured in coins per unit of labour-time. This definition translates into a computational rule to sample λ that executes per application of rule $\mathbf{R_1}$. The mean velocities of commodities and coins are calculated as historical averages. Figure 9.5 plots equilibrium mean prices, $\langle p_j \rangle$, against labour values multiplied by the MELT, λl_j, for a typical run of a 10-commodity economy. It demonstrates that the MELT is the constant of proportionality implied by the correlation results. The role of money as a representation of labour-time is particularly clear in this relationship.

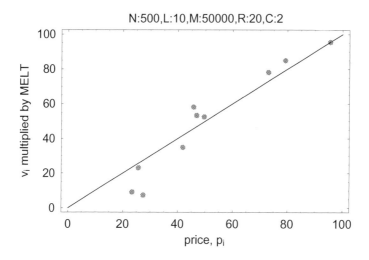

Figure 9.5 Stationary market prices and MELT transformed labour values in a 10-commodity economy with $r = 0.96$. The straight line represents the identity relationship $y = x$.

The definition of the MELT is not a causal theory of how the MELT is determined. The value of MELT will vary under different 'institutional' arrangements, such as how the market operates in detail, what kind of money and commodity throughput obtains, and so forth. Unlike the venerable quantity theory of money $MV = PT$ (where M is money, V is money velocity, P is the price level, and T the level of transactions), which is an accounting identity between market phenomena, the MELT abstracts a non-obvious causal relationship between non-market phenomena (production times) and market phenomena (prices).

9.4   Analysis

The results of the simulation experiment demonstrate that (i) a (dynamic) equilibrium is reached, in which (ii) mean prices are linearly related to labour values by a constant of proportionality called the monetary expression of labour-time (MELT), and (iii) social labour is allocated approximately efficiently. The computational model generates these regularities, but it does not provide an adequate explanation of them. The law of value *emerges* from dynamic interactions of the constituent parts of the **SCE**, but a theory is required to explain this emergence.

The qualitative theory of the law of value was most fully developed by Isaak Rubin in his 1928 book, *Essays on Marx's Theory of Value*. In what follows, the **SCE** is modelled by a system of ordinary differential equations that refer to the means of the variables of interest, thereby extending Rubin's theory.

The mathematical analysis aims to provide an intuitive explanation of the gross causal features of the computational model rather than provide definitive proofs of its properties or develop an accurate stochastic theory of the steady distributions. The mathematical model is a derivative and highly simplified analysis of the causal properties of the computational model. For example, discrete change is approximated by continuous change under the assumption that the size of discrete variables in the computational model is large compared to their change in magnitude per time step.

9.4.1   The labour equation

Let's think about what is happening when we run the simulation. We know that the rate money enters and leaves the market, or money velocity, is a proportion of the total money in the economy, which we will denote as γM ($0 \leq \gamma \leq 1$). Assume that γ is fixed constant (an approximation). A money allocation column vector, $\mathbf{b}(t) = (b_1, \ldots, b_L)$, where $\sum_{j=1}^{L} b_j = 1$ and $0 \leq b_j \leq 1$, represents the instantaneous proportion of the total money flow received by each sector at time t. The sectoral income rate is therefore given by $b_j \gamma M$.

The labour allocation column vector, $\mathbf{a}(t) = (a_1, \ldots, a_L)$, where $a_j = |A_j|/N$ (see section 9.2.6), $\sum_{j=1}^{L} a_j = 1$ and $0 \leq a_j \leq 1$, represents the proportions of actors 'employed' in each sector at time t.

Use the mean price of a commodity to approximate its price distribution. Recall that the average price of commodity j is $\langle p_j \rangle$. The average cost of the universal commodity bundle, given current prices, is then $\sum_{j=1}^{L} \langle p_j \rangle / c_j$.

Actors switch sectors based on the consumption error, which is a function of the quantities of commodities received. To simplify the analysis we will use price signals, in the form of the mismatch between income and the average cost of the commodity bundle, as a proxy for the consumption error. This simplifying assumption holds for the remainder of the analysis.

Each sector has an ideal expenditure rate that represents the money that would need to be spent in order for the constituent actors to meet their desired consumption rates. The rate is a function of the number of actors in the sector and current prices, and is given by: $a_j N \sum_{k=1}^{L} \langle p_k \rangle / c_k$.

The sectoral income error, denoted ϕ_j, measured in coins per unit time, is the difference between the actual income rate and the ideal expenditure rate:

$$\phi_j(t) = b_j \gamma M - a_j N \sum_{k=1}^{L} \frac{\langle p_k \rangle}{c_k}$$

A value of $\phi_j > 0$ implies a sectoral 'profit' (the sector receives more income than its constituent actors require to purchase the commodity bundle), $\phi_j < 0$ implies a sectoral deficit (there is insufficient income for the actors employed in the sector to purchase the commodity bundle), and $\phi_j = 0$ implies sectoral income equals ideal expenditure.

Approximate the switching behaviour of actors by assuming that the rate of change of labour allocation (or sector size) is proportional to the sectoral income error:

$$\frac{d}{dt} a_j = \psi \phi_j(t) = \psi \left(b_j \gamma M - a_j N \sum_{k=1}^{L} \frac{\langle p_k \rangle}{c_k} \right) \tag{9.2}$$

where $\psi > 0$ is a reaction coefficient. It follows from the definition that $\phi_j < 0$ implies a net decrease in the sectoral population, and $\phi_j > 0$ a net increase, subject to the constraint $\sum_{j=1}^{L} a_j = 1$. Call 9.2 the *labour equation* because it defines how the allocation of labour to different sectors of production changes according to the money income received from the sale of commodities. The labour equation for the whole economy in vector notation is:

$$\dot{\mathbf{a}} = \psi (\gamma M \mathbf{b} - N (\mathbf{p} \cdot \mathbf{c}) \mathbf{a}) \tag{9.3}$$

where $\mathbf{p} \cdot \mathbf{c}$ is the dot product of the average price vector and the consumption vector.

The production rate for commodity j is given by $a_j N / l_j$. Define the average price of a commodity to be the current sectoral income rate divided by the sectoral production rate:

$$\langle p_j \rangle = \frac{\gamma M}{N} \frac{b_j}{a_j} l_j \tag{9.4}$$

Hence, each $\langle p_j \rangle$ is a function of a_j and b_j.

9.4.2   The money equation

The labour equation describes how the division of labour changes depending on current incomes. But we do not yet have a model of how changes in incomes depend on the current division of labour.

A sector's income depends on the number of commodities produced. The maximum possible social consumption rate or 'social demand' for commodity j is N/c_j. The sectoral 'production error', denoted ξ_j, measured in units of commodity j per unit time, is the difference between supply and demand:

$$\xi_j(t) = \frac{a_j N}{l_j} - \frac{N}{c_j}$$

A value of $\xi_j > 0$ implies over-production, $\xi_j < 0$ implies under-production, and $\xi_j = 0$ implies supply equals social demand. It is assumed that market rule $\mathbf{M_1}$ operates such that it can be approximated by the expected relationship between supply, demand and price: commodities in over-supply have lower average prices than those in under-supply. This implies that the rate of change of sector income is negatively proportional to the production error:

$$\frac{d}{dt} b_j = -\omega \xi_j(t) = -\omega N \left(\frac{a_j}{l_j} - \frac{1}{c_j} \right) \tag{9.5}$$

where $\omega > 0$ is a reaction coefficient. It follows from the definition that $\xi_j < 0$ implies an increase in sectoral income, and $\xi_j > 0$ a net decrease, subject to the constraint $\sum_{j=1}^{L} b_j = 1$. Call 9.5 the *money equation* because it defines how the allocation of money to different sectors of production changes according to the over or under-production of commodities. The money equation for the whole economy in vector notation is:

$$\dot{\mathbf{b}} = -N\omega(\mathbf{Al} - \mathbf{c}) \tag{9.6}$$

where $\mathbf{A}$ is the L by L diagonal matrix with element (i, i) equal to a_i and element (i, j) $(i \neq j)$ zero.

9.4.3 Equilibrium

The $2L$ labour 9.3 and money 9.6 equations mutually interact and describe the evolution of the division of labour via the mechanism of market price changes. The causal schema is as follows: (i) an existing division of labour results in (ii) over and under-production of commodities that causes (iii) error-correcting price changes on the market due to supply and demand, which (iv) generate changes in sectoral incomes that (v) cause actors that cannot meet their consumption requirements to swap sectors, resulting in (vi) a new division of labour. Some mathematical results are now derived that show that the mutual interaction results in an equilibrium point at which prices equal labour values.

Definition 3. A *simple commodity system* is described by the following system of $2L$ coupled differential equations:

$$\dot{\mathbf{a}} = \psi(\gamma M \mathbf{b} - N(\mathbf{p} \cdot \mathbf{c})\mathbf{a}) \tag{9.7}$$
$$\dot{\mathbf{b}} = -\omega N(\mathbf{Al} - \mathbf{c}) \tag{9.8}$$

and

$$\langle p_j \rangle = \frac{\gamma M}{N} \frac{b_j}{a_j} l_j$$

subject to the constraints

$$\sum_{j=1}^{L} a_j = 1, \qquad 0 \leq a_j \leq 1$$

$$\sum_{j=1}^{L} b_j = 1, \qquad 0 \leq b_j \leq 1$$

$$\sum_{j=1}^{L} \frac{l_j}{c_j} = 1 = \eta \qquad l_j, c_j > 0$$

$$M, N > 0 \qquad \omega, \psi > 0$$

$$0 \leq \gamma \leq 1$$

Lemma 1 (Equilibrium point). The simple commodity system has the unique equilibrium point

$$\mathbf{a}^* = \left(\frac{l_1}{c_1}, \frac{l_2}{c_2}, \ldots, \frac{l_L}{c_L} \right) = \mathbf{b}^* \tag{9.9}$$

(The proof is in appendix A.)

This lemma states that $\dot{\mathbf{a}}_j = \dot{\mathbf{b}}_j = 0$ (i.e., the system is at rest) when the proportion of actors employed in a sector equals the proportion of money received by the sector, and that proportion is l_j/c_j. This makes intuitive sense: every actor consumes the same consumption bundle, therefore, on average, they require the same income (otherwise actors move to different sectors and the system is not at rest). The lemma does not imply that every actor receives the same income in equilibrium, only that sectoral averages are equal. (In fact, the stationary income distribution in the **SCE** is highly unequal and approximately exponential).

Lemma 2 (Global stability). The equilibrium point is globally asymptotically stable. (The proof is in appendix A.)

This lemma states that the system, regardless of its initial conditions, always approaches the equilibrium point. The simple commodity system is a feedback system that functions to minimize both income and production 'errors'. This formalizes Rubin's assertion that

> [a] given level of market prices, regulated by the law of value, presupposes a given distribution of social labour among the individual branches of produc- tion. . . . Marx speaks of the 'barometrical fluctuations of the market prices'. This phenomenon must be supplemented. The fluctuations of market prices are in reality a barometer, an indicator of the process of distribution of social labour which takes place in the depths of the social economy. But it is a very unusual baro- meter; a barometer which not only indicates the weather, but also corrects it.
>
> (Rubin, 1973: 78)

Lemma 2 explains why simulation runs tend to equilibrium.

Corollary 3 (Efficient division of labour). The division of labour is efficient in equilibrium.

Proof.   By lemma 1 the proportion of actors in sector j at equilibrium is $a_j = l_j/c_j$, which by proposition 1 is efficient.   □

Corollary 3 is an explanation of why the simulation tends to an approximately efficient division of labour. The experimental results do not exhibit perfect effi- ciency because the **SCE** is non-deterministic and undergoes stochastic fluctua- tions in equilibrium.

Theorem 4 (The law of value). Labour values are global attractors for average market prices.

$$\lim_{t\to\infty} \mathbf{p}(t) = \lambda \mathbf{v} \tag{9.10}$$

Proof. Substituting the equilibrium point, $a_j = l_j/c_j = b_j$, into 9.4 yields $\langle p_j \rangle = \lambda l_j$, which by lemma 2 is the globally asymptotically stable market price.

$\square$

At equilibrium the average price of a commodity is proportional to the labour-time required to make it. The constant of proportionality, $\lambda = \gamma M/N$, represents the monetary value of one unit of labour-time. Theorem 4 accounts for the observed correlations between prices and labour values.

In equilibrium actors receive equal mean incomes but are engaged in productive activity of unequal periods. Hence, commodities that take longer to produce sell for higher mean market prices. This is the fundamental reason why prices correspond to labour values at the equilibrium of the simple commodity economy.

9.4.4 *Disequilibrium deviation of price from value*

A key insight of Marx's theory of the law of value is that prices refer to amounts of labour time and deviations of prices from values are social error signals that function to redistribute labour. Only in the hypothetical situation of balanced supply and demand in which labour is efficiently distributed are prices proportional to labour values. We can analyse the deviation of price from value out of equilibrium by introducing the concept of labour commanded.

Definition 4. A commodity commands an amount of labour in exchange. The *labour commanded* by a commodity is its money price divided by the MELT, measured in units of labour-time. The mean labour commanded

$$\langle \epsilon_j \rangle = \frac{\langle p_j \rangle}{\lambda} \tag{9.11}$$

represents how much social labour-time a commodity on average fetches in the marketplace.

If a commodity type commands an amount of social labour $\epsilon_j < l_j$ then it is *undervalued*, if it commands amount $\epsilon_j > l_i$ it is *overvalued*. The labour commanded is an objective property of the exchange, and is distinct from any subjective valuations of the utility of the transaction from the perspective of a particular actor. At equilibrium $\langle \epsilon_j \rangle = l_j$ for all $j = 1, \ldots, L$ but otherwise commodities sell below value or above value, in accordance with the laws of supply and demand.

An act of exchange involves more than swapping of a commodity for an amount of money. It is also an exchange of a representation of an amount of social labour-time, measured by the labour commanded, for an amount of private labour-time actually expended in the production of the commodity. Normally this is not an exchange of equivalents.

If the global division of labour mismatches the social demand then labour associated with scarce commodities is rewarded with access to additional social

labour-time, whereas labour associated with unwanted commodities is punished
by a reduction of access. Out of equilibrium not all private labours are mutually
equalized and not all private labours are socially necessary. But if the reallocation
of labour resources is based on these monetary reward signals then the feedback
loop completes and a division of labour emerges in which unnecessary private
production is minimized and prices approach labour values. The dynamic relationship between labour embodied and labour commanded as regulator of the
division of labour is apparent in the following relationship

$$\dot{\mathbf{a}}_j = a_j \left(\frac{\langle \epsilon_j \rangle}{l_j} - 1 \right) \psi \gamma M \tag{9.12}$$

which is derived in appendix A. The term in brackets is positive if the commodity
type is overvalued (implying an increase in the sector size) and negative if the
commodity type is undervalued (implying a decrease in the sector size). Equation
9.12 reveals the causal connection between labour allocation and prices that
occurs under the surface of the simple commodity economy. It is a precise formulation of Rubin's observation that 'value is the transmission belt that transfers
the movement of working processes from one part of society to another, making
that society a functioning whole' (Rubin, 1973: 81) that summarizes how the
interaction of private commodity producers, using a monetary representation of
the total social labour-time, spontaneously allocates labour to different branches
of production according to social demand.

The precise price distribution will be sensitive to the particular price offer
rule (or rules) employed by the actors. The more important point, therefore,
is that in statistical equilibrium the same commodity type realizes a range of
different market prices, $p_k^{(1)}$, $p_k^{(2)}$, ..., each of which represents different transfers
of social labour-time between buyer and seller. The role of the mismatch between
labour embodied and labour commanded in regulating the division of labour is
apparent 'on average' and is a property of the price distributions, not a property
of individual transactions. Hence, a commodity type may be correctly valued
in equilibrium while, at the same time, particular transactions may represent
under or over-valuations of the commodity instance. The law of value states that,
whatever the precise distribution of exchange prices, mean equilibrium prices are
proportional to labour values.

9.5   Discussion

The choice of modelling symbolic money (e.g. paper or coins), which has nominal
but no intrinsic value, rather than money in the form of a commodity such as gold,
which has intrinsic value in virtue of the labour required for its production, differs
from Marx's presentation but has the advantage of separating two definitions that
may be easily conflated in his analysis of money (for a discussion, see Foley
(1983)): (i) the 'value of money', which is the inverse of the MELT and is the
labour-time represented by the monetary unit (e.g. 1 hour of social labour-time

is represented by 1 coin), and (ii) the 'value of the money commodity', which is the amount of social labour-time required for the production of a unit of the money commodity (e.g. 1 ounce of gold requires 1 hour of social labour-time for its production).

(Roemer, 1982: 27–31) argues that in a simple commodity economy the only prices capable of reproducing the system are those proportional to embodied labour times. The derived prices satisfy the constraints of the economic situation represented as a linear programming problem. The deduction abstracts from market interactions that occur in historical time and disequilibrium supply and demand dynamics; hence, the mechanism by which such prices are reached is absent. The model is constraint-based rather than causal. The idea that labour values are *attractors* for prices in the simple commodity economy does not contradict this static result. A dynamic analysis, however, is a more stringent test of the conceptual integrity of the Marx–Rubin law of value, which is essentially concerned with how markets function to allocate social labour-time via error-correcting price signals. In static models, such as Roemer's, prices are nominal and lack a causal connection with the reallocation of labour. The mechanism of the law of value should not be reduced to its attractor.

Krause (1982) understands the importance of the dynamic coordination of concrete labours in market economies via the price mechanism. He contends that most modern formulations of the labour theory of value assume that concrete labours of different types are equivalently valued, an assumption he labels 'the dogma of homogeneous labour' (Krause, 1982: 160–161). According to Krause, the 'supposition of homogeneous labour supplants any analysis of the specific coordination of concrete labours' (Krause, 1982: 101). The static methods employed by Krause, which represent the economic situation in terms of linear algebra, are sophisticated, and can quantify over complex production structures, in particular the production of commodities by means of others. In contrast, the dynamic approach taken here is relatively immature and models a simple production structure. Unlike static approaches, however, the dynamic approach can model the coordination of concrete labours, and this reveals a new dynamic relationship between homogeneous and heterogeneous labour.

Following Krause let α_{ij} be the reduction coefficient of concrete labour type i to j ($i \neq j$), such that 1 hour of labour of type i is equivalent to α_{ij} hours of labour type j, where the equivalence relation is induced by market exchanges. The assumption of homogeneous labour is that $\alpha_{ij} = 1$ for all i and j. The reduction coefficients in the simple commodity system are:

$$\alpha_{ij} = \frac{\langle p_i \rangle / l_i}{\langle p_j \rangle / l_j} = \frac{b_i / a_i}{b_j / a_j}$$

Note that the assumption of homogeneous labour is not made. Theorem 4 can be reformulated as

$$\lim_{t \to \infty} \frac{b_i}{a_i} = 1$$

and by the quotient rule for limits it follows that for all $i = 1 \ldots L$ and $j = 1 \ldots L$

$$\lim_{t \to \infty} \alpha_{ij} = 1 \qquad (9.13)$$

The statement that labour values are attractors for prices is equivalent to the statement that homogeneous reduction coefficients are attractors for heterogeneous reduction coefficients. Krause writes: 'It is conceivable that certain assumptions about the mechanism of coordination could *produce* equal reduction coefficients. But the classical/contemporary labour theory of value does not formulate such assumptions, so the homogeneity is mere dogma' (Krause, 1982: 101). But it is inaccurate to state that the Marx–Rubin formulation of the law of value assumed homogeneous labour without justification. The law of value is a dynamic theory of labour allocation based on the tendency of heterogeneous labour to be homogenized via commodity exchange, and in this sense is very different from modern static formulations of it. The reduction coefficients are continuously calculated by a distributed computation that is implemented through the actions of the economic actors. Homogeneity emerges in the simple commodity economy under the assumption that economic actors have equal productive powers as members of the same species, strive for equal renumeration for their labour time, that is they consider themselves equal, and are free to realize their equality through unconstrained economic activity. Rubin states that the '*equalization of exchanged commodities* reflects the basic social characteristic of the commodity economy: *the equality of commodity producers*'. The **SCE** models this ideal situation by allowing identical actors to freely move between sectors of production in order to meet identical consumption requirements. In reality, things are not so simple, and in the context of tendencies to narrow the wage dispersion, Rubin (1973, ch. 15) discusses factors that prevent homogenization.

9.5.1   *Labour values as attractors for prices*

The law of value is a phenomenon that emerges from the dynamic interactions of private commodity producers. In the model presented (i) labour values are global attractors for market prices, (ii) market prices are error signals that function to allocate the available social labour between sectors of production, and (iii) the tendency of prices to approach labour values is the monetary expression of the tendency to efficiently allocate social labour. The constant of proportionality of the linear relationship between labour values and market prices is the monetary expression of labour-time (MELT), which measures how many units of money represent one unit of social labour-time. The MELT summarizes a non-obvious causal relationship between non-market phenomena (production times) and market phenomena (prices), and links the total available social labour-time to its monetary representation. The concept of labour commanded, which measures how much social labour-time a commodity fetches in the marketplace, is important for theorizing how deviations of price from value are labour re-allocation 'signals'.

The labour commanded by a commodity normally mismatches the private labour-time expended in its construction, indirectly signalling whether the labour was socially necessary or not.

The law of value operates 'behind the backs' of actors via money flows that place income constraints on their local evaluations of commodity prices. The equilibrium of the simple commodity economy is a statistical equilibrium, in which a single commodity type may realize many different prices. In consequence, the regulating role of exchange value is a property of price distributions, not individual transactions. Further, the law of value can only emerge in broad models of economic systems that complete the feedback loop between production, consumption, exchange *and* reallocation of labour resources.

An actor engaged in free exchange derives personal benefit from transactions and the immediate apprehension of this fact motivates subjective theories of value. But an exchange has causal consequences beyond the immediate moment and the satisfactions of mutual commerce that derive from its embodiment within a system of generalized commodity production. Actors do not normally think money into existence although they do decide to spend more or less of what they have. Their income is a local representation of a global resource constraint not under their subjective control. Although money *exchanges* according to demands for use-values, and is normally accompanied by the satisfaction of desires, it *refers* to amounts of social labour-time. Local flows are easier to apprehend than global reference, which partially accounts for the relative neglect of objective theories of value.

10 Value in the capitalist economy

We are now in a position to take up the issues that we raised at the end of chapter 6. At that point we had examined the labour theory of value (LTV) as put forward Smith, Ricardo and Marx. We had noted that this theory appeared to run into a problem with regard to the presumed equalization of the rate of profit across industries. Specifically, the LTV in its simplest form predicted that the rate of profit would vary inversely with the 'organic composition of capital' (Marx's term) or capital-intensity of the various industries. Both Ricardo and Marx saw this as problematic, and Marx devoted considerable intellectual effort to solving the resulting 'transformation problem'. And we had put on the table the neo-Ricardian contentions (a) that Marx failed to solve the transformation problem, and (b) that anyway it wasn't really a 'problem', since all one had to do was get rid of the LTV and shift over to a Sraffian theory of prices of production – 'erase and replace' in Samuelson's phrase. In response to these points we claimed that recent developments, both theoretical and empirical, gave support to the LTV and cast doubt on the neo-Ricardian critique. It is time to make good on those claims.

The intervening chapters have laid some of the groundwork for a response. Chapter 7 has set out the probabilistic approach to economic variables, and chapter 9 has validated the labour theory of value for a 'simple' commodity-producing economy (without the requirement of a uniform rate of profit on capital). The latter argument does not, of course, address the neo-Ricardian critique directly (since that critique centres on the supposedly uniform rate of profit) but it nonetheless advances the argument by an important step, showing how approximate proportionality between labour-content and price can emerge via a process that operates (in Marx's phrase) 'behind the backs of' the human participants in the economy.

We have claimed that advances both theoretical and empirical have called for a re-evaluation of the LTV. In this chapter we begin by outlining the theoretical developments, then turn to the empirical evidence. On the theoretical side, the most significant development in the last several decades is the book by Emmanuel Farjoun and Moshe Machover, *Laws of Chaos* (1983). This remarkable book appeared before the term 'econophysics' came into use, but it adumbrated the econophysics approach, applying the methodology of Statistical Mechanics to economic phenomena – while at the same time being informed by a clear understanding of the problems and approaches characteristic of classical political economy.

Farjoun and Machover supply a definite mechanism supporting a stochastic version of the LTV. This mechanism is 'statistically emergent'. It is not the result of agents' paying conscious attention to the labour-content of commodities in the mode of Smith's hunters of deer and beaver, and it would seem to be invisible to methodological individualism. Yet the probability law in question clearly must be realized via the interactions of a multitude of capitalists and workers. The situation is analogous to statistical mechanics. The ideal gas laws, for instance, are statistically emergent from the interaction of millions of individual molecules. We start by giving a brief account of their theory of price.

10.1   Farjoun and Machover's approach to price

Farjoun and Machover pointed out that since Boltzmann physicists have been able to make useful predictions about the aggregate behaviour of systems which, at a small scale, appear random and chaotic.

At a small scale the movements of molecules in a gas or a liquid are random, and this random movement is visible, as Einstein pointed out in 1905, in the form of Brownian motion – the jiggling about of small particles such as pollen grains in water observed under the microscope. But at a large scale these random motions even out, allowing useful generalizations – the gas laws, the laws of thermodynamics. Farjoun and Machover argued that economists were stuck with an early-nineteenth century model of causality. If this was dropped then quite different modes of reasoning about the economy would become possible. Dispensing almost completely with orthodox economic theory, they derived a series of interesting predictions about capitalist economies. One of these was that market prices would be closely correlated with labour values.

In science, predictions always seem more convincing than 'postdictions' (explanations after the fact). The fact that Farjoun and Machover's theoretical results were rapidly confirmed by empirical research lends their results weight, the more so when one considers that their predictions ran counter to received opinion in economics. We cannot give a full account of their theory here – the reader should consult their book. Rather, we offer a simplified account which, we hope, may convey some intuitive understanding of the mechanism they proposed for the operation of the law of value.

Consider all of the commodities sold by firms in a given country over the course of a week. These will constitute a vast array of different goods and services, some expensive and some cheap. Some will require a lot of labour to make, some a little. Suppose that the law of value holds and prices of commodities are closely proportional to their labour content. How should we measure this?

Farjoun and Machover introduce a random variable – 'specific price', denoted by ψ – which represents the price commanded by an hour's worth of embodied labour. The idea is that we express all of the national production of different goods – A380 airbuses, chocolate digestive biscuits, disposable nappies, etc. – in

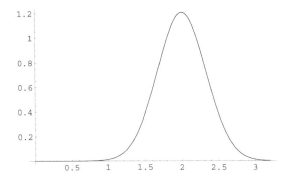

Figure 10.1 Farjoun and Machover's predicted form of ψ, the ratio of price to labour-content.

terms of their labour content. We divide this up into units of one hour each, and imagine that we randomly select an hour's worth from this huge aggregate. We then look at how much that hour's worth sells for.

They predicted that if one were to graph the frequency of occurrence of different values of ψ, over a sufficiently large sample of hours of embodied labour, the distribution would look like Figure 10.1: the familiar bell curve of the normal or Gaussian distribution.

The normal distribution, as its name implies, is one of the most common sorts of distribution; lots of observations take this form. For example if you were to plot the heights of 10-year old boys in the city of London, you would get a normal distribution. If you plot the weights of a sufficiently large sample of one-pound coins you will get a normal distribution. If you plot the number of photons arriving per second in a telescope from some distant star you will get a normal distribution. In fact, whenever the feature you are measuring represents the summation of a large number of random, independently operating causal processes, its distribution will tend to the normal.

This distribution, written as $N(\mu, \sigma)$, is characterized by two numbers: its mean (μ) or average, which corresponds to the peak of the curve, and its standard deviation (σ) which describes how wide the bell is. Farjoun and Machover predicted that the plot of prices to labour values would have a mean of 2 and a standard deviation of less than $1/3$. How did they arrive at this conclusion?

First, why did they expect the mean to be 2? In other words, why would one expect the average price of a commodity to be twice its labour-value? This is partly a matter of the unit of measurement they chose. As soon as you try to construct a theory of prices you are confronted with the question of the unit of measure. When we want to measure distance we can do it in meters, which are defined in terms of a constant of nature, the wavelength of a particular type of light. This gives us a standard that is unvarying across space and time. But when it comes to measuring price, what do we use? If we use money, should it be dollars, euros or yen? If we stick to a single national currency, how do we account for inflation?

To get around this problem Farjoun and Machover use the method favoured by Adam Smith and Maynard Keynes: they express price in terms of 'labour commanded' (see section 6.2). Specifically, they express it in units of the average hourly wage. Thus if a commodity – let's say, a 4-kilo cod – has a market price of £20 and the average wage is £8 per hour, the 'real price' of the cod is

$$\frac{£20}{£8/\text{hour}} = 2.5 \,\text{hours}$$

The 'hours' in the resulting expression have this interpretation: that's how long you would have to work to buy the cod.

Farjoun and Machover's 'specific price', ψ, is then the ratio of price, as calculated above, to labour-content. If our cod took one hour of direct plus indirect labour to bring to market, then its specific price is

$$\frac{2.5 \,\text{hours}}{1 \,\text{hour}} = 2.5$$

Note that this magnitude is dimensionless, since the hours have cancelled.

We would expect ψ to be greater than 1 since the selling price of any commodity can, as Smith showed, be decomposed into a part that pays wages and a part that pays profit. The selling price goes to pay wages, profit and the cost of materials. But the material costs likewise decompose into wages, profits and a residuum of raw material costs. As you push the process back more and more stages you find that the residual fraction of raw material costs tends to zero, so one can, to a good approximation, say the entire selling price goes ultimately to pay wages and profits.[1] Since Farjoun and Machover believed that in most capitalist countries value-added was split 50/50 between wages and profits, it follows that the average price of the product of an hour's labour will be twice the average wage for an hour's labour.

That explains why they expect the mean of $\psi =$ (price/labour content) to be 2. But why do they settle on a standard deviation of $1/3$? The argument here is very simple. They say that it is very rare for commodities to be sold so cheaply that the selling price would be insufficient to pay the direct and indirect wages needed to make it. The cutoff point here is a value of $\psi = 1$. Below this, the production of

---

[1] Marx objected to this, saying that the residual element of raw materials costs never quite reached zero. As a mathematical objection this is not very serious: the residual raw material cost exponentially approaches zero as a limit. As a sociological objection it has some weight since capitalist production presupposes the existence of capitalists who own raw materials and means of production and hire labour. If the raw materials and means of production were not in the hands of capital, then the workers would simply produce on their own account and there would be no division into wages and profits. Accepting this sociological point, Smith's mathematical approximation was reasonable.

the commodity would not be viable, as not even wage costs would be met. For the sake of argument they assume that there is only one chance in a thousand of a commodity selling this cheaply relative to its cost of production. Consulting a table of the normal distribution, one finds that the likelihood of values 3 standard deviations away from the mean is about $^1/_{1000}$, hence they derive that $\sigma = (\mu - 1)/3$; if $\mu = 2$, σ must equal $^1/_3$.

How do these predictions stack up against real data? Using data for the United Kingdom in 1984, the year after their book was published, we calculate that ψ can be pretty well approximated by a distribution with $\mu = 1.46$ and $\sigma = 0.151$.[2] At first sight this appears significantly different from the prediction they gave. But the difference is almost entirely due to the fact that in the UK in 1984 value-added was split between profits and wages in the ratio 1:2 instead of the equal split assumed by Farjoun and Machover. The full form of their prediction was that if e is the ratio of aggregate profit to aggregate wages, then ψ should follow the normal distribution with $\mu = 1 + e$ and $\sigma \leq e/3$. If we substitute the observed value of e for the UK in 1984 into the equations we find an almost exact agreement.

An interesting consequence of their theory is that it predicts that the correspondence between prices and labour values will be closer when the share of profit in national income declines. If the share of profit in the national income declines, then relative market prices can be expected to approximate more closely to relative labour values. Taking labour time as the 'signal' in prices, high profits allow room for prices to have a lower signal to noise ratio.

10.2   Information content of prices

The distribution of ψ is random, or entropic. One can calculate the entropy of a normally distributed random variable using an amended form of Shannon's formula. Shannon gave the entropy of a signal as

$$\sum_i -p_i \log_2(p_i)$$

where i takes on a set of discrete values corresponding to recognizably different quantizations of the signal. The height of the normal bell curve at any point x is given by the normal probability density function (pdf), $\phi(\mu, \sigma; x)$. This is a function over the reals such that

$$P(a < x < b) = \int_a^b \phi(\mu, \sigma; x)\, dx$$

That is, the probability that x will fall in the interval between a and b is given by the integral of the pdf from a to b. If we substitute this into the Shannon formula

---

[2] This result is derived from Cockshott and Cottrell (1998), with slight adjustment to bring the definition of ψ used in that paper in line with the definition used by Farjoun and Machover.

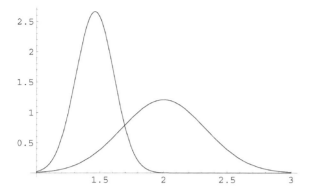

Figure 10.2 Farjoun and Machover's predicted ψ (right) compared with measured ψ for the UK in 1984 (left).

and integrate numerically, we can compute the entropy of a normal distribution with a given standard deviation.

What we find is that normal distributions with a small standard deviation have a low entropy and ones with a large standard deviation have a large entropy. Figure 10.2 shows the distribution of ψ predicted by Farjoun and Machover, compared with a normal distribution with the mean and standard deviation observed for the UK in 1984. The wider bell curve on the right has an entropy of 7.1 bits, the distribution on the left about 5.9 bits.

From the standpoint of the thermodynamic approach to the economy, the entropy of ψ, namely $H(\psi)$, measures the disorder of price with respect to value. From the standpoint of information theory, $H(\psi)$ measures how much information there is in the deviation of prices from values. Our computed values for $H(\psi)$ tell us that the market price of a commodity gives around 6 bits of information *distinct* from the information provided by its labour content. This raises the question, what about the rest? How much of the information in prices comes from labour values?

Given two random variables A and B, we can talk of a *conditional* entropy, $H(A \mid B)$. This means the entropy of A given B, or the disorder of A with respect to B. (Recall section 3.1.2 where we looked at the conditional entropy of an axle relative to a bearing.) The random variable ψ is, as we have said, the ratio of price to labour content. Writing π for price and λ for labour content, the entropy of the ψ bell curve can be expressed as $H(\psi) = H(\pi \mid \lambda)$. It represents the disorder of prices given labour content.

The information *shared* by the two random variables A and B, on the other hand, is called *mutual* information. This is calculated as $H(A) - H(A \mid B)$. We would like to know the mutual information of price and labour content, $H(\pi) - H(\psi)$, or in other words how much information is common to both price and value. To work it out we need some estimate of $H(\pi)$, the information content of prices as such. To do this accurately we would have to apply Shannon's entropy formula to all prices, giving

$$H(\pi) = \sum_{i=1}^{n} -p_i(\pi_i) \log_2 p_i(\pi_i))$$

where the p_is are the probabilities of the n possible prices. This would involve knowing the probability distribution of prices. How frequent are prices of £1.00? How frequent are prices of £2.00? We would need the answers for all possible prices, from the lowest at which a commodity can be bought – say 1 penny – up to the largest observed price, perhaps something like £1,000,000,000 for a large warship.[3] Although in principle this could be worked out, we don't have access to the data on real commodity prices required to get an answer, so we will use an alternative approach, based on coding theory, which will give us a rough estimate of the information content of prices.

Although prices can range from pennies to billions, a price in the billions will not be quoted down to the last penny. A shipyard that sells an aircraft carrier to the Navy need only quote to the nearest £ million. If you are buying a cooker in the price range £100 to £500, you look at the pounds and ignore the pennies. In general, prices need not be quoted to more than 3 significant figures, the rest is just noise – or a convention, like the last 99 on a £34.99 pair of shoes. Of course we also need to know the order of magnitude of the price: are the units, pennies, pounds, thousands of pounds? This implies that for most purposes prices can be written in scientific notation – for example, 1.47E3, or 1.47×10^3, to represent £1,470.00.

In a number with the format x.xxEy four decimal digits carry all the information. But four decimal digits can be encoded in just over 13 bits of information, so we can give a rough bound on the information content of a price as $H(\pi) < 14$. This implies that the mutual information shared between the price and value of a randomly selected commodity is likely to be less than $14 - H(\psi)$, or roughly 6 to 7 bits. We can plausibly assume that the shared bits of information will tend to be the leading bits of the price.[4]

10.3   Prices and the rate of profit

We are now ready to tackle head-on the issue of the relationship between the labour theory of value and the theory of prices of production based on an equalized rate of profit (i.e. the 'transformation problem').

---

[3] To match the definition of ψ we would have to weight the probability of each price by the amount of labour embodied in that price, but we need not be overly concerned with this technicality.

[4] This assumption is based on the empirical evidence outlined in section 10.4 below, specifically that the correlation between the log of price and the log of labour content is of the order of 0.95. This means that the error in log space between the two numbers – price and value – will be of the order of 5 per cent. If we write these numbers as binary-coded logarithms, it is therefore likely that at least the first 4 bits, and probably the first 5 bits, will be the same.

It will be useful first to inquire more closely into the status of the assumption of an equalized profit rate. Nobody believes that the rate of profit is *actually* uniform across industries or sectors of the economy. The claim made on behalf of the theory of prices of production has to be that there is a strong *tendency* for the rate of profit to become equalized and that it is legitimate, for theoretical purposes, to assume that this tendency is fully realized. Here we may distinguish two concepts of tendency: *historical* tendency, and what we might call *immanent* tendency. If the equalization of the rate of profit were a historical tendency, this would mean that if we took measurements of a given economy at two points in time (say, separated by a decade) we would expect to find, with high probability, that the rate of profit was more nearly uniform at the later observation. It's doubtful if this is what the theorists of prices of production have meant, but if they did mean this it is not correct. The data show a roughly constant degree of dispersion of profit rates around the social average. Industries and firms change their places in the distribution over time, but the distribution shows no trend towards collapsing to a single value.

That leaves the notion of an immanent tendency: this is the weaker claim that the forces making for equalization of the rate of profit are internal to, or inherent in, the market economy, while the 'disturbances' that counteract equalization and maintain dispersion are accidental, contingent. So even if there's no historical trend towards a more uniform rate of profit, it's still theoretically legitimate to ignore the random 'noise' and focus on the outcome that would emerge if the system were unperturbed – the supposed 'mechanical equilibrium' of the system, in the sense discussed in chapter 7.

Farjoun and Machover provide a powerful critique of this line of thinking (and also see Farjoun (1984)). They reject the claim that the forces making for dispersion of profit rates can be conceived as 'external' disturbances. Some such factors may be external (e.g. changes in the weather affecting the profitability of agriculture), but in the main the dispersing forces are inherent in inter-capitalist competition. The force making for equalization is the tendency of capitalists to invest preferentially in industries or sectors showing above-average profits, and this is indeed 'inherent'. But equally inherent is the search for profit by means of innovation in new products and processes, new markets, new sources of materials, and so on. And innovation of this sort opens up opportunities for above-average profits while at the same time pushing some industries into a low-profit state. Farjoun and Machover therefore argue that the concept of mechanical equilibrium (where opposed forces are in perfect balance and nothing changes) is totally inappropriate for the analysis of profit rates in a capitalist economy. We need to use the concept of statistical equilibrium, in which the system is not at all 'at rest', and the outcome of the opposed forces is a relatively stable *distribution* of profit rates, within which there is ceaseless motion of the 'particles'.

The greater the equilibrium dispersion of profit rates, the worse are neo-Ricardian prices of production as approximations to actual prices – or even to their 'centers of gravity', discounting the effects of short-run supply-demand disequilibrium. On the other hand, on the maintained hypothesis of an equalized rate of profit, the greater the dispersion of the capital to labour ratio (or organic composition), the worse are labour-values as approximations to actual prices. Since both of these distributions (profit rates and organic composition) are non-degenerate, the question of whether neo-Ricardian prices or labour-values offer the better systematic approximation to actual market prices is an empirical one. The evidence to date shows, with remarkable consistency across data-sets drawn from different capitalist economies and different time periods, that the labour theory of value is at least as good a predictor of actual prices as the neo-Ricardian theory. This claim is backed up in the following section.

10.4   Empirical evidence for labour theory of value

We have discussed above the theoretical challenges to the labour theory of value. The view of orthodox economics in the West is that the labour theory of value is 'discredited'. But it is noteworthy that the LTV has *not* been discredited by the the the discovery of empirical evidence that was inconsistent with the theory. In science, competing theories are supposed to be evaluated on the basis of their ability to explain observed data. Economics, it seems, does not proceed in this way. The practical political implications of different economic theories are so great that it is very difficult for scientific objectivity to take hold. While people build political parties on the basis of different economic theories, they don't fight in the same way over alternative theories of galactic evolution.

It was not until the 1980s that a serious scientific effort was made to test whether or not the labour theory of value actually held in practice. The pioneering work was done by Anwar Shaikh (1984) and his collaborators (Petrovic, 1987; Ochoa, 1989) at the New School in New York. Following this, there is now a considerable body of econometric evidence supporting the proposition that relative prices and relative labour values are highly correlated, or in other words, in favour of the LTV.

10.4.1   Calculating labour-values

The key to testing the labour theory of value has been the use of input–output tables. An input–output table is a way of showing the structural interaction of different industries. Such tables are constructed periodically by government statistical agencies for the leading economies. The idea behind them can be grasped by looking at the example in Table 10.1. This shows in a highly aggregated fashion the structure of an economy with four main industries, labeled A, B, C and D. The column corresponding to each industry shows how much of the output of each other industry is used as input by the given industry. Thus industry A uses 100 units of output from B and 10 from D. In an aggregated table, these quantities are denominated in monetary terms; we may think of them as being in billions of dollars. At the foot of the table we have rows showing the total wages and profits earned in each industry and the total final sales of the industry. The final sales row is the sum of the wages, profits, and indirect inputs above.

Table 10.1 Example input–output table

Industry	A	B	C	D	Final consumption
A		100	100	10	100
B	100				100
C		20			280
D	10		20		10
Wages	100	45	85	14	
Profits	100	35	95	16	
Sales	310	200	300	40	

We can use an input–output table to work out how many hours of labour go into producing the total output of each industry. We start up by simply adding up the number of units of labour that are directly employed in each industry. Dividing the directly utilized labour by the dollar value of the industry's output, we get an initial figure for the amount of labour in each dollar of output. For industry A, measuring the labour input by the wage bill, we see that $100/310 = 0.323$ units of labour go directly into each dollar of output. Since the table tells us the dollar amount of A's output used by every other industry, we can use this to work out the amount of indirect labour used in each industry when it spends a dollar on the output of industry A.

This gives a second estimate for the labour used in each industry, which in turn gives us a better estimate for the number of units of labour per dollar output of all industries. We can repeat this process many times, and as we do so our estimates will converge on the true value.

The description given can be presented more formally as an algorithm:

(1) Iteration 0: Calculate the labour-value per dollar for each industry, V_i, as the direct labour time expended in industry i ($i = 1, 2, \ldots, n$) divided by the monetary value of its output. Let $k = 1$ and go to step 2.

(2) Iteration k: Calculate the labour-value per dollar for each industry as the sum of (a) the direct labour time expended in that industry and (b) the indirect labour time embodied, all divided by the monetary value of its output. The indirect labour for industry i is calculated as $\sum_{j=1}^{n} A_{ji} \times V_j^-$, where A_{ji} is the input–output entry stating how much of input j is used in industry i, and V_j^- is the labour per dollar figure calculated for industry j at iteration $k - 1$.

(3) Do the V_js at iteration k differ appreciably from those calculated at iteration $k - 1$? If so, let $k = k + 1$ and go to step 2, otherwise stop and report the results.

How many iterations are needed? We find that for input–output tables of the size commonly produced by national statistical agencies, with about 50 to 100 industry categories, convergence is produced within 10 to 20 iterations. Computations of this sort are not particularly burdensome for a PC, though they were certainly more difficult to carry out in the pre-PC era, which may in part explain why empirical testing of the labour theory of value was not done before Shaikh's work in the 1980s.

If the labour theory of value is empirically correct, then we would expect to find that the figures for labour-time embodied per dollar do not vary greatly from industry to industry. (If the theory held *exactly*, which of course we would not expect, then the figure would be the same for all industries.)

10.4.2   The relationship of prices to values

The general procedure in studies of the relationship between price and value has been to use data from national input–output tables, as discussed above, to calculate the total labour content of the output of each industrial sector, and then to see how closely the aggregate money value of sales from each industry matches their total labour content. Various ways have been devised to measure the correspondence between prices and labour-values. Shaikh (1984) explains the details of the process, and also offers a theoretical argument in favour of a logarithmic specification of the price–value relationship, i.e.

$$\log(\text{price})_i = \beta_0 + \beta_1 \log(\text{value})_i + u_i$$

where β_0 and β_1 are parameters to be estimated and u_i is a multiplicative error or disturbance (multiplicative because the equation is in logs). The labour theory of value would predict $\beta_0 = 0$ and $\beta_1 = 1$.

Table 10.2 shows some results from Shaikh and his collaborators. As you can see, the average error when predicting prices in the USA using the labour theory of value is about 9 per cent. This has proven to be the case across many industries and several decades.

An alternative way of measuring the 'closeness' of prices to labour values is to draw a scatter plot relating the two and then try to fit a straight line to the data. If the labour theory of value is true, then the observations will tend to fall close to

Table 10.2 Average percentage deviations between market prices and labour values for the USA for selected years (Shaikh, 1998).

Year	Deviation
1947	10.5%
1958	9.0%
1962	9.2%
1967	10.2%
1972	7.1%
Average	9.2%

Table 10.3 Comparing the correlation of prices to labour values in different countries (Zachariah, 2006)

Country	Year	Number of industries	Price/labour correlation
Japan	1995	85	98.6%
Sweden	2000	48	96.0%
USA	1987	47	97.1%
Greece	1970	35	94.2%
UK	1984	101	95.5%
Germany	1995	33	96.5%
France	1995	37	97.6%

this line, and the line will pass through the origin. How close the observations are to the line is measured by the coefficient of determination or R^2 value of the data. If $R^2 = 1$ then all points fall on the line, which perfectly predicts the results. If the $R^2 = 0$ then the line is of no use at all in predicting the observations.

Studies utilizing data from the United States, Sweden, Greece, Italy, Yugoslavia, Mexico and the UK have produced remarkably consistent results, with strong correlations observed: R^2 values of well over 0.90. The literature also seems to show that the larger the population of the country, the closer is the fit between observed prices and labour values (Table 10.3). This may be an example of the way in which statistical regularities become more apparent the larger the population from which the observations are drawn.

In our presentation of the method of calculation of labour values from input–output tables (section 10.4.1) we said that you use the wages row of the table to estimate each industry's labour input. It could be argued that because this row is denominated in money, rather than in hours of labour, it is not really measuring labour inputs. It is possible to compensate for this by using data on hourly wage rates in the different industries. If we know the average hourly wage in an industry, we can translate that industry's wage bill into actual hours worked.

The effects of doing this for the United Kingdom are shown in Table 10.4.[5] In the published input–output tables, the labour input is expressed in £. Column (1) uses labour-value figures calculated on the assumption of a dummy wage-rate of £1 per hour for all industries. This is equivalent to assuming that any wage differentials across industries reflect differential rates of value-creation per clock hour. Column (2) is the same as (1) except for the exclusion of the oil industry, which is an outlier in the price–value regressions, presumably due to the high rent component (in the Ricardian sense) in oil extraction. Column (3) (which again excludes the oil industry) uses labour-value figures calculated using wages data from the *New Earnings Survey* to convert backwards from wages to hours for each industry – a correction relative to column (1) if (and only if) inter-industry wage

---

[5] For further details regarding these estimates, see Cockshott *et al.* (1995).

Table 10.4 Price regressions for the UK in 1984

	(1)	(2)	(3)
constant	−0.055	−0.034	−0.046
	(−2.04)	(−1.79)	(−2.00)
labour value	1.024	1.014	1.024
	(46.55)	(63.38)	(51.20)
N	101	100	100
R^2	.955	.976	.964

t-ratios in parentheses; all variables in logarithmic form.

differentials are the product of extraneous factors, and do not reflect differential rates of value-creation.

As can be seen from the column (2) figures, 'simple' labour values produce an R^2 of nearly 98 per cent when the oil sector is excluded and the dummy uniform wage is adopted. The effect of adjusting for differentials in wage rates and using raw labour hours in calculating the values gives a lower R^2 of just over 96 per cent. This is consistent with the hypotheses that:

(1) Labour of higher skills produces more value per hour.
(2) Inter-industry wage differentials at least partly reflect such skill differentials.

This suggests that the use of an industry's money wage bill as a proxy for its labour input is a valid procedure.

10.4.3 Sectoral profit rates

We mentioned above that Sraffian equalized-profit prices (prices of production) provide reasonably good predictions of actual prices, but they are not significantly better than the classical labour theory of value in this respect (Shaikh, 1998; Zachariah, 2006).

This ought to be surprising to proponents of the theory of prices of production. The last line of attack on the 'naive' labour theory of value is this: although the rate of profit might be a non-degenerate random variable (even 'in equilibrium'), it nonetheless ought to be *statistically independent* of the organic composition of capital. (This is a suitably weakened form of the 'equalized profit' proposition, maintaining the essential objection to the LTV, namely that it implies a negative relationship between profitability and organic composition.) But it turns out that this is not so.

Using capital stock data from the Bureau of Economic Analysis (BEA) along with the US input–output table for 1987, Cockshott and Cottrell (2003) examined the relationship between organic composition of capital and profit rate across US industries. In computing the organic composition of capital by industry it was necessary to aggregate some of the industrial categories in the input–output table,

Table 10.5 Profit rates and organic composition, BEA fixed capital plus one month's circulating constant capital as estimate of capital stock (c). Summary statistics weighted by denominator in each case.

	s/c	c/v	s/v
Mean	0.292	1.948	0.569
Standard deviation	0.221	3.042	0.500
Coefficient of variation	0.756	1.562	0.878
	s/c and c/v (weighted by c)	s/c and v/c (weighted by c)	
Correlation coefficient	−0.454	0.780	

since the BEA capital stock figures were not so finely broken down. This left 47 industrial categories. The BEA figures are for fixed capital alone; we assumed that in addition industries held stocks of work in progress valued at one month's prime costs (excluding wages). The capital stock figures used were then taken as the sum of work in progress plus plant and machinery.[6]

The results indicate that the tendency toward profit rate equalization is weak: organic composition was negatively correlated with profit rates for the US, as shown in Table 10.5. This table displays the correlation coefficient between the rate of profit and organic composition, and also between the profit rate and the inverse of organic composition, across 47 sectors of the US economy. The former coefficient, at −0.454, is statistically significant at the 1 per cent level. If, however, prices corresponded to the simple labour theory of value we would expect to find a positive linear relationship between profit rate and the inverse of organic composition (in other words, the relationship between profit rate and organic composition would be inverse, rather than negative linear), so the second coefficient is perhaps more telling: at 0.780 it has a p-value or marginal significance level of less than 0.0001.

Figure 10.3 offers another prespective on this analysis. It shows three sets of points:

(1) the observed rate of profit, measured as s/c where s denotes profit and c denotes capital stock;
(2) the rate of profit that would be predicted on the basis of the simple labour theory of value, i.e. $s'v/c$ where s' is the mean rate of exploitation in the economy as a whole and v is the per-industry variable capital or wage bill; and
(3) the uniform rate of profit that would be predicted on the basis of prices of production (mean s/c).

---

[6] We replicated the analysis under the alternative assumption that industry capital stocks were composed of BEA fixed capital plus 2 months' worth of wages plus 3 months' worth of circulating constant capital. The results were not materially different.

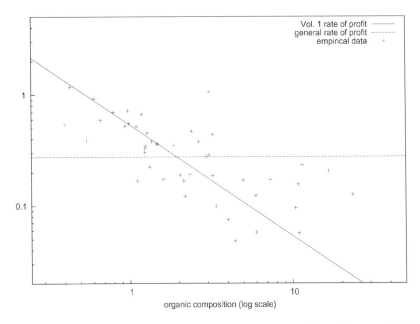

Figure 10.3 Relation between profit rates and organic composition, 47 sectors of the US economy, 1987.

The second set of points is labelled as the 'Vol. 1 rate of profit' in the graph, since it it what is implied by the labour theory of value as set out in volume 1 of *Capital* (and also in Ricardo).

It can be seen that the observed rates of profit fall close to the rates that would be predicted by the labour theory of value. The exception is for a few industries with unusually high organic compositions (c/v greater than 10). But what are these industries?

At an organic composition of 23.15, we have the electricity supply utilities with a rate of profit half way between that predicted by the simple labour theory of value and that predicted by the price of production theory. Then, at an organic composition of 16.4, we find the crude petroleum and natural gas industry, with a rate of profit substantially in excess of that predicted by the labour theory of value, and approximating much more closely to that predicted by an equalization of the rate of profit. But this industry would be expected, on the basis of the Ricardian theory of differential rent, to sell its product at a price well above its value and hence report above-average profits. In a similar position we find the oil refining industry with an organic composition of 9.4. Both oil production and oil refining have similar rates of profit, at 31 per cent and 32 per cent. Since the industry is vertically integrated, this would indicate that the oil monopolies chose to report their super-profits as earned *pro rata* on the capital employed in primary and secondary production. In both cases, however, the super-profit can be explained by differential rent.

Next one comes to the gas utilities, with a rate of profit of 20 per cent on an organic composition of 10.4. The labour theory of value would have predicted 7 per cent, and the theory of prices of production 32 per cent. But, like the electricity utilities, these industries are regulated, and one of the assumptions built into the regulatory system is that utilities should earn an average rate of profit.

10.4.4 Alternative value bases

A further issue demands attention here. The labour theory of value is in a sense a particular case of an 'x-content theory of value' or XTV. The LTV asserts that the prices of commodities will be roughly proportional to total embodied labour content; an XTV, in general, says that prices will be roughly proportional to the quantity of some input x embodied in commodities. The question arises: What is so special about labour? Couldn't some other x (oil, say) do the job just as well?

On theoretical grounds, any candidate for the place of x in an XTV has to satisfy three criteria:

- It must be a 'basic' commodity in Sraffa's sense, that is, one which enters either directly or indirectly into the production of all others. Labour certainly satisfies this criterion; oil probably does.
- It must not be producible via the application of labour along with an input of such natural resources as are effectively (over a relevant time-horizon) inexhaustible.
- It must be possible to conceive x as homogeneous, at least as a tolerable first approximation. (Otherwise it cannot figure as a scalar quantity, as does labour time.)

Several researchers have now considered this issue, and have concluded that although 'in principle' some alternative value-basis (or x) might be relevant under some economic circumstances, in fact labour-time is pre-eminent.[7] Consider Table 10.6. For the purposes of these regressions we used the Leontief inverse of the UK input–output tables (Central Statistical Office, 1988, Table 5) to calculate the total (direct plus indirect) electricity content, oil content and iron and steel content of the output of each industrial sector. Using the same methodology as in Table 10.4 (based on Shaikh, 1984), we then regressed aggregate price on these various 'values', both singly and in combination with labour values, in logarithmic form. The sample size is 100 for each of these regressions, the electricity industry being excluded from the equations including electricity-content, and similarly for oil and iron and steel.

From columns B, D and F it can readily be seen than none of the alternatives, taken alone, performs anything like as well as labour in accounting for market prices. The highest R^2, at 0.682, is obtained for electricity content, as against 0.955 for labour in column (1) of Table 10.4. Columns A, C and E show how the

---

[7] The argument that follows was originally published in Cockshott and Cottrell (1997).

Table 10.6 Regressions of price on labour values and some alternative 'value-bases' for the UK

	A	B	C	D	E	F
constant	−.056 (−2.06)	−0.169 (−2.425)	0.066 (3.15)	0.307 (3.16)	−0.067 −2.38	−0.263 (−2.47)
labour	1.030 (23.76)		0.904 (46.07)		1.048 (36.53)	
electricity	−0.009 (−0.19)	0.903 (14.60)				
oil			0.109 (7.43)	0.615 (13.29)		
iron and steel					−0.027 (−1.31)	0.445 (7.09)
Adjusted R^2	0.953	0.682	0.984	0.639	0.954	0.332

t-ratios in parentheses; all variables in logarithmic form.

alternatives perform when entered alongside labour values, enabling us to address the question of whether the alternatives contain any independent information, or in other words offer any marginal predictive power over prices when labour content is given. Only oil content passes this test. From the *t*-ratios (in parentheses below the coefficient estimates) it can be seen that while labour content retains its statistical significance in all cases, electricity content and iron and steel content become statistically insignificant in the presence of labour content. The fact that oil content contains some independent information regarding prices is presumably linked to the element of rent in the price of oil. The North Sea fields are not marginal, which means that the labour time taken to extract North Sea oil is less than the socially necessary amount (on a world scale). The price of oil being determined on the world market, UK oil will then sell at a price above that which corresponds to its particular labour content. Table 10.7 shows similar results are obtained when analysing the Greek economy.

Table 10.8 offers another perspective on this issue. It reports the coefficients of variation (standard deviation divided by the mean), across the sectors of the UK input–output tables, for *x*-content per £'s worth of output, where *x* equals

Table 10.7 Regression of alternative value bases for Greece (Tsoulfidis and Maniatis, 2002)

Value Basis	R^2
Agriculture	0.174
Electricity	0.668
Oil	0.674
Chemicals	0.702
Labour	0.942

Table 10.8 Coefficients of variation for x-content per £ of output

x	Coefficient of variation	C.V. relative to labour
labour	0.189	1.00
electricity	0.698	3.69
oil	2.156	11.41
iron and steel	1.477	7.81

Calculated from Central Statistical Office (1988, Table 5). Labour figures calculated recursively by authors.

labour, electricity, oil, and iron and steel respectively. This is the basic information supplied by the input–output tables: in Tables 10.6 and 10.4 it is worked up into regression format,[8] but it is worth considering 'raw'. Clearly, to the extent that x is conserved in exchange, one will find a relatively small coefficient of variation for x-content per £ of sales. From the second column of Table 10.8 we see that the coefficient of variation is almost four times as large for electricity as for labour, with those for oil and iron and steel being greater still.

10.4.5 Are the results real?

Some critics have claimed that the observed correlations between market prices and labour values arise as a statistical artifact (Kliman, 2002). What we are comparing is the aggregate selling price of, for example, all the iron and steel produced in the USA with the total labour that went into it, and similarly for all the other industries. What we see is that the value of an industry's sales is roughly proportional to the direct and indirect labour it uses. It has been argued that this is simply because a large industry has both large sales and a large workforce, while a small industry will have relatively low sales and a relatively small workforce. The correlation we see is spurious, arising as a mere consequence of differences in industry size.

However, the comparisons set out above – between labour-values and alternatives such as oil-values, electricity-values, and so on – tell us that the correlations between labour-values and prices represent something real. If 'industry size' generated spurious correlations for labour it would do the same for other inputs, and oil or electricity values would be strongly correlated with selling prices – but they are not. There *is* something special about labour.

The danger of spurious correlation is real enough in some contexts. Take for example a study of the association between alcohol consumption and violent crime. Suppose an investigator runs a regression with the number of violent crimes as the dependent variable and the amount of alcohol consumed as the independent variable, for a sample of cities of widely varying populations. We'd expect to

---

[8] That is, x-content per £'s worth of output is multiplied by the total monetary value of output to yield total x-content, on which the total monetary value of output is then regressed, in log form.

find a significant positive coefficient on alcohol consumption, but this would be of no scientific interest: simply, larger cities would be expected to show both more crimes and more alcohol consumed. The obvious correction here is to scale both variables of interest by expressing them in per capita terms, dividing by city population. If there is a still a significant positive association then this might be of sociological interest.

Correlations in which the units of observation are of different 'sizes' are not necessarily spurious, however. Consider a variant on the city-size example. Suppose a researcher has the hypothesis that population is the principal factor governing the size of cities as measured by their land area, or in other words that variations in population density are second-order. One way of assessing this claim would be to regress city land area on population and see if the relationship between these variables is close to proportional. In this case one is well aware that both land area and population are measures of city 'size', and the object of the exercise is to see how closely they are related. Now suppose someone were to object to this hypothetical study as follows: 'This is a case of spurious correlation. Of course, bigger cities will in general both occupy more land area and have larger populations. To overcome this problem you will have to deflate land area and population by a suitable measure of city size, say the number of residential units.' The objection is misplaced. In the first case above, city size (that is, population) was an independent 'third factor' that might plausibly induce an apparent correlation between crimes and alcohol consumption, while in the second case there is no such independent third factor in play.

The correlation of prices and values across industries is of the second sort. It forms part of an investigation into the closeness of two variables that are in themselves reasonable measures of the 'size' of industries, namely the aggregate market price of their output and the labour time embodied in that output. There is no independent third factor that could plausibly induce a spurious correlation here. The notion of the 'size' of an industry is rather vague, but in everyday terms it may well be taken to mean the number of people employed in the industry. A 'large' industry is one that employs lots of people. But the classical labour theory of value predicts that if an industry is large in this sense, then the value of its output will also be big. Which is just what we see.

11 Money, credit and the form of value

This chapter presents an analysis of money and credit; the following chapter extends the analysis to consider the role of banking and financial institutions in a capitalist economy. Our approach is informed by the information-theoretic concerns that lie at the core of this book. Our emphasis is therefore on money as an information structure and on the supporting technologies that permit this information structure to operate. We relate this to the historical process whereby labour came to be represented as money issued by the state. Our discussion starts out from Marx's conception of the form of value but the conclusions we reach regarding money differ somewhat from those of Marx, being influenced by the modern chartalist theorists (see section 11.2).[1]

11.1 Money and the form of value

Money exists within what Marx called the 'form of value', or the 'value-form'. This phrase has a double significance. First, it signifies that the exchange of commodities via money is the particular form under which a more general social function is realized, under particular historical conditions. We briefly discussed Marx's conception of commodity production as a specific historical form in section 6.1 but the idea demands greater elaboration at this point. In a letter to Ludwig Kugelmann of 1868, Marx wrote:

> Every child knows that any nation that stopped working, not for a year, but let us say, just for a few weeks, would perish. And every child knows, too, that the amounts of products corresponding to the differing amounts of needs demand differing and quantitatively determined amounts of society's aggregate labour. It is self-evident that this necessity of the distribution of social labour in specific proportions is certainly not abolished by the specific form of social production; it can only change its form of manifestation.... And the form in which this proportional distribution of labour asserts itself in a

---

[1] Readers interested in a modern presentation of Marx's theory of money should consult Itoh and Lapavitsas (1999) or Foley (1983).

state of society in which the interconnection of social labour expresses itself as the private exchange of the individual products of labour, is precisely the exchange value of these products.

(Marx, 1988: 67)

Here we have (a) the idea that the 'distribution of social labour in specific proportions' is a general requirement of social reproduction, coupled with (b) the idea that the 'form of manifestation' of this requirement may vary. Marx's chief criticism of Ricardo was that while he had correctly identified labour as the source of value, he had not given an explanation of why and under what historical conditions social labour should be made manifest in exchange value. We take up this point below.

The second meaning of 'the form of value' is that the exchange of commodities via money has an important *formal* aspect, in the sense in which we speak of formal logic: the manipulation of symbols according to definite rules. In chapter 1 of *Capital* Marx spent a lot of time developing a formal account of commodity exchange and value. Under the general heading of 'the value-form' he investigates the 'simple or accidental form', the 'total or expanded form' and the 'general form' (with numerous subdivisions of these categories) before finally arriving at 'the money form'. This is a difficult chapter to read, but is considered by some writers to be essential to understanding Marx's whole conceptualization of capitalism (Rubin, 1973).

Since the mid-nineteenth century the study of formal systems has advanced tremendously in its scope, and the tools available for constructing formalisms have multiplied. In this chapter we want to construct an analysis of the value-form using modern conceptual tools. The possibility of doing this is predicated on the fact that value and money are in the strict sense formal systems. They are systems of symbols whose time-evolution is governed by formal rules analogous to the term-rewrite rules used in certain branches of computing or logic. These are programmatic rules that tell you how to validly transform one algebraic formula into another. The ensemble of technical and accountancy practices of modern society can be thought of as rules operating on a vast 'formula' – society's commercial/monetary records. We attempt to identify these rules and explain their necessity.

First, however, we develop our account of the 'form of value' in the first sense noted above, asking why it is that commodity exchange occurs at all.

11.1.1 *Legally independent owners: economic subjects*

Commodity exchange presupposes the existence of *economic subjects*. An economic subject is an abstract category that encompasses both people and social organizations that engage in trade. The reason why economic subjects exist is twofold:

(1)   The units of production in a society are not self-sufficient.
(2)   There exists no overall system of social direction of labour.

In a capitalist economy, production and distribution are organized by firms or *enterprises*. An enterprise is a technical unit of production[2] and at the same time an economic subject. It can own things and it can buy and sell things. Economic subjects are ultimately the result of technology and a form of social division of labour. Capitalist production is social. The whole of society is involved in the division of labour. Enterprises don't produce for their own needs, they produce for society. This contrasts with the 'natural economy' of the peasant household, where the units of production and consumption coincide.

Technology forces each enterprise to produce just a few types of goods, while consuming many. Enterprises consume goods produced by others, which necessitates a circulation of products among the enterprises. But, given that they are all subjects owning property, how can circulation take place without a loss of property? The only possible way is the exchange mechanism. If products are exchanged as equivalents, then there is no loss of property. An enterprise exchanges something of no use to it for something that it needs. It is not interested in what its products are used for, but in the equivalents that it can get by selling them.

The category of economic subject is reflected juridically in the form of abstract legal personalities (Pashukanis, 1989). It may seem at first that when a firm is constituted as a 'legal personality' we are seeing the attributes of persons projected onto firms. But it may be better to view the matter the other way round. The properties of humans as legal personalities, able to own property, derive from the needs of the enterprise system. Historically most enterprises were sole proprietorships, and the rights of the sole proprietor shaped the concepts of capitalist law. But these sole proprietors were 'faces' for units of production. It was the reproduction of these units of production via trade that posed the requirement that their representatives could own and dispose of property. As Marx puts it,

> The guardians [of commodities] must . . . recognize each other as owners of private property. This juridical relation, whose form is the contract, whether as part of a developed legal system or not, is a relation between two wills which mirrors the economic relation. The content of this juridical relation (or relation between two wills) is itself determined by the economic relation. Here the persons exist for one another merely as representatives and hence owners, of commodities. As we proceed to develop our investigation, we shall find, in general, that the characters who appear on the economic stage are merely personifications of economic relations; it is as the bearers of these economic relations that they come into contact with each other.
>
> (Marx, 1976: 178–9)

The requirements flowing from the system of commodity exchange inform our whole contemporary outlook on what are 'natural' or 'human' rights. People have not always been legal personalities, bearers of inherent rights. To the framers of the US constitution certain rights may have appeared self-evident, but they were

---

[2] Or it may comprise several such technical units, e.g. factories.

self-evident only as the rights of white property owners. Black slaves and white indentured labourers were equally 'self-evidently' not the bearers of such rights. Going back further, members of a hunter-gatherer tribe or subsistence farming family were not economic subjects in the modern sense. The constitution of people as economic subjects is associated with the onset of commodity production and the establishment of money.

Today, capitalist enterprises are forced by their technology to be interdependent, but this is not the aboriginal condition. The aboriginal condition is virtual self-sufficiency, the self-sufficient household economy or village community. The existence of commodities and money did not originally spring from the demands of social reproduction alone.

The foregoing explains what we mean by the first aspect of 'the form of value'. To develop the second aspect – money as a formal system – we need first to give some historical background.

11.2   Two theories of money

The standard story of the development of money (which can be found in Adam Smith and is retailed in most economics textbooks) goes like this.

(1)   Once upon a time all exchange of goods was via barter, the direct exchange of one commodity for another.

(2)   Barter was problematic because it required a 'double coincidence of wants'. For a barter transaction between A and B to go through, A must not only want what B is offering but also have what B wants – and symmetrically for B.

(3)   Transactions are greatly eased if there exists some particular commodity that everyone is willing to accept in exchange, confident in the knowledge that they'll be able to pass it on in the next transaction.

(4)   So people decide, via some sort of 'social convention', to designate some commodity as the money-commodity. This can take a variety of forms (insert list of weird and wonderful 'monies' from world history).

(5)   Eventually, however, civilized societies settle on precious metal (gold and/or silver) as the money-commodity. The precious metals are inherently suitable for the job: they have a high ratio of value to weight (so money doesn't have to be too cumbersome); they are divisible and fusible (so one can make money in handy denominations); and they are (somewhat) durable.

(6)   Originally, the money-commodity is used 'raw'. This carries the inconvenience that its amount has to be assessed (by weighing, probably) in each transaction. The state comes along and performs the useful function of coinage: the precious metals are stamped into coin, hence certifying weight and fineness. Coins are discrete and can now 'pass by tale' (by counting).

(7)   Of course, step 6 is not an unalloyed blessing since it opens up the possibility of debasement of the coinage by a state greedy for revenue, but on balance it's worth it.

Note that the state appears on the scene late in the day, contributing a refinement to what is already a reasonably functional monetary system. The aboriginal system emerges spontaneously from interactions among a population of free and equal traders seeking to make economic life easier for themselves. Note also that, while nothing rules out lending and borrowing of the money-commodity, debt obligations play no role in the account.

In addition, the 'value of money' in this account is derivative of the value of the money-commodity, a commodity that has a cost of production and is in demand in its own right. What happens in debasement of the coinage? The state certifies that a certain coin contains a specified weight of precious metal. But then they mint new, adulterated coins. At first the debased coin passes at its previous value, but once people realize that it no longer contains the full measure of precious metal it is necessarily devalued to reflect its true metallic content.

Clearly this theory has some work to do in explaining monetary systems of the current type, where money takes the form of 'worthless' paper notes (and entries in bank ledgers). This sort of system is conceived as an innovation of the last century or so, representing a substantial break with previous monetary history.

The alternative account – Chartalism or the State Theory of Money – is a very different story.[3] Here, the state and debt play a key role from the start and the value of coin (where coins are used) is relatively independent of the value of the substance of which they are composed. On this view, the state gets to decide what counts as money by stipulating what it will accept in payment of tax obligations, and the value of this money in exchange depends on the proportion between (a) the state's issue of money and (b) the level of tax obligations imposed on the population. That is, the state can *make* coin of a certain sort valuable by requiring that citizens pay their taxes in this coin – provided, of course, that it is in a position to enforce its tax policy and to prevent forgery of the coin.[4] Prevention of forgery may be aided by making the coin out of a valuable substance but there's no inherent connection between the value of coin as money and its value as metal.

Reading further in a standard textbook, one finds an account of 'the three functions of money'.

(1)   Medium of exchange: money is used as an intermediary in the exchange of other commodities that are of primary interest to the traders.
(2)   Unit of account: prices, debts and so on are denominated in the monetary unit.
(3)   Store of value: people can store their wealth in the form of money.

---

[3] Leading proponents of this theory today include Wray (2004), Ingham (2004) and Forstater (2003). Their work builds on a tradition established by Knapp (1973) and Innes (1913).

[4] The classical economists were not unaware of this general idea. Adam Smith noted it in passing but did not develop it: 'A prince who should enact that a certain proportion of his taxes should be paid in a paper money of a certain kind might thereby give a certain value to this paper money...' (Smith, 1974: 428). Ricardo argued that debasement of the coinage did not necessarily produce a corresponding devaluation, provided the state could maintain its monopoly of coinage.

Of these three, the medium of exchange function is taken as logically primary. Once a definite medium of exchange is established it obviously makes sense to denominate prices in units of that medium, otherwise one would always have to be translating. And if the medium of exchange is durable it automatically provides a means of 'storing value' in the interval between transactions (though it's not unique in that respect and other assets may be better for storing value long term).

On the Chartalist view, however, money's function as unit of account is primary: the monetary unit denominates the citizen's debt to the state. This in itself represents an important development of a more primitive situation, in which the citizen's obligation takes the form of the requirement to serve as a soldier or otherwise provide direct labour services. You don't have to serve in the army (in time of peace) if you can satisfy your tax obligation in coin of the realm. But how do you get those coin? Minted by the state, they initially pass into circulation in payment to those who *do* provide services directly to the state (e.g. soldiers). So if I'm not a soldier but am to acquire coin, I need to sell something to a soldier – or to someone who has sold something to a soldier, there can be many layers of indirection. Thus the coin come to function as a means of exchange in the civil economy. In that role they may take on a life of their own, to some degree, but the ultimate guarantee of their value remains the fact that they are uniquely acceptable in discharge of citizens' tax-debt to the state. (The corollary is that if the state crumbles, so does its money. This is the most basic explanation of hyperinflation.)

We have expressed the Chartalist argument in terms of coin but that was just for ease of exposition. Given effective anti-forgery technology, specially printed pieces of paper would serve just as well as the embodiment of the unit of account. And given appropriate computer systems, special digital records on devices such as hard drives could also do fine. We'll see what such computer systems would have to look like in 12.3.

11.2.1   *Historical evidence for the State Theory*

We're unlikely ever to know 'exactly' when and how money first developed, but proponents of the State Theory have been able to marshal a good deal of historical evidence in favour of their view.

Prior to the issue of coinage, particular commodities acted as a unit of account in the payment of taxes and for extended systems of barter. Polanyi *et al.* (1957) describes this process in early Mesopotamia where trade transactions were entered into accounts in units of shekels, these being equivalently quantities of barley or silver. But it does not follow that payments were actually made in barley or silver. Rather the common unit of account allowed the mutual settling of debts in barter transactions. In international trade, weights of metal seem to have been used in the settlement of payments.

There is an important difference between coins and quantities of silver denominated in some standard of weight. As we said above, coins 'pass by tale'; that is, the value of a purse of coins is determined by counting them, multiplying by their denominations and summing the total. Precious metal, on the other hand, is valued by weight. These weights have to be verified on each transaction if one party is not to be defrauded. But the hypothesis that coins arose just as a means of providing standard weights of gold or silver does not fit well with the numismatic evidence.

Early coinage was far from being a standardized weight of gold or silver. The first coins were issued by Lydia in the seventh century BC. These were of a standard weight – the *stater*, roughly 220 grams – but, rather than being of pure gold, were made of electrum, an alloy of gold, silver and copper (Bolin, 1958). The addition of copper meant that they still looked golden, instead of the whitish look that a simple gold/silver alloy would have had. If they were supposed to be standard ingots of pure gold, then the Lydian state was defrauding its public. Further, if their purpose was to facilitate commodity exchange in the markets of the Kingdom, why were they so heavy and valuable? Why were they worth a month's subsistence (Carradice and Price, 1988)?

The alternative explanation is that they were used for the payment of taxes due to the Crown, the Chartalist view. The early Lydian *stater* were far too costly for day to day transactions, but a month's subsistence would be a plausible minimal unit of annual tax.

Wray's account of the matter encompasses state-money from ancient times to nineteenth century England.

> Originally, the money liability was always in terms of a unit of account as represented by a certain number of grains of wheat or barley. In fact, all the early money units were weight units for grain – the mina, the shekel, the lira, the pound. Once the state has imposed the tax liability, the taxed population has got to get hold of something the state will accept in payment of taxes. This can be anything the state wishes: It can be clay tablets, hazel-wood tallies, iron bars, or precious metal coins. This, in turn, means the state can buy whatever is offered for sale merely by issuing that thing it accepts in payment of taxes. If the state issues a hazel-wood tally, with a notch to indicate it is worth 20 pounds, then it will be worth 20 pounds in purchases made by the state so long as the state accepts that same hazel-wood stick in payment of taxes at a value of 20 pounds. And that stick will circulate as a medium of exchange at a value of 20 pounds even among those with no tax liability so long others need it to pay taxes.

Drawing on Innes, Wray further explicates what exactly the English 'tally' was:

> A tally was simply "a stick of squared hazel-wood, notched in a certain manner to indicate the amount of the purchase or debt", with the name of the debtor and the date of the transaction written on two opposite sides of the stick (Innes, 1913: 394). After notching, the stick was split down the middle in such a way that the notches were cut in half. The split was stopped about an inch from the base, with the longer piece (called the stock, from which

our term "capital stock" derives) retained by the creditor, with the "stub" (a term still used as in "ticket stub") held by the debtor. The two pieces of the tally would be matched later (most significantly at the time of settlement) to verify the amount of the debt. Importantly, governments spent by raising a "tallia divenda" on the exchequer, issuing tallies for payment for goods and services delivered to the court (after 1670, wooden tallies were supplemented by paper "orders of the exchequer", although tallies were still held in the English House of Commons until 1834).

Wray (2004)

Forstater notes that the essential interdependence of state and money is particularly clear in the history of empires, when the imperial power is faced with the task of 'monetizing' an economy from scratch. On conquering Africa, the Europeans met the problem that

> if the subsistence base was capable of supporting the population entirely, colonial subjects would not be compelled to offer their labor-power for sale. Colonial governments thus required alternative means for compelling the population to work for wages. The historical record is clear that one very important method for accomplishing this was to impose a tax and require that the tax obligation be settled in colonial currency. This method had the benefit of not only forcing people to work for wages, but also of creating a value for the colonial currency and monetizing the colony. In addition, this method could be used to force the population to produce cash crops for sale. What the population had to do to obtain the currency was entirely at the discretion of the colonial government, since it was the sole source of the colonial currency.

(Forstater, 2003)

If the State Theory is correct, that means that the period of the Gold Standard (on and off, between the seventeenth and nineteenth centuries) – under which the monetary value of gold currencies was quite closely related to the metallic value of gold – is not the historic norm, from which the world abruptly departed in the twentieth century, but the exception that demands special explanation.

11.3   Monetary relations and records

A monetary system sets up a binary relation

$$\{x \text{ is credited with } y : x \in \text{juridical subjects}, y \in \text{integers}\}$$

associating with each juridical subject an integer number.[5] Each historical form of money represents a step in the development of the technologies of record which support this binary relation.

---

[5] We use the term *relation* in the strict logical sense of a set of tuples defining the extent of a logical predicate. See Digression 11.3.

Digression 11.1 Coins and Abaci

We have already discussed the abacus as a sort of computing machine (see section 4.2). Reckoning – that is, calculating with coins – worked on the same principle. Coins were moved about on a reckoning table, or reckoning cloth laid on a table, to effect the calculation, as shown in the Figure below (intermediate rows denote 5 of the unit on the row below).

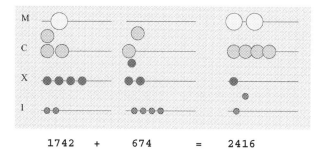

In a similar way the movement of physical coins between people's pockets acted to record changes in their respective wealth.

With the spread of algorithmics, using decimal numerals instead of Roman notation, calculation became a matter of manipulating and re-writing symbols on a slate or on paper. This allowed bank ledgers to record people's wealth in a purely symbolic way, and to register changes in wealth without any need for physical movement of coin-tokens. It also allowed for the representation of negative numbers, either by the prefix '−' or by the use of column notation in double-entry book keeping.

There has been a close relationship between the spread of banking and changes in calculating techniques.

Coins maintain the relation by possession. The number associated with each individual is encoded in the coins they carry. Coin, however is an imperfect technology of record as it can only record positive numbers. You cannot have minus £50 in your pocket. Coins and paper money are token-based methods of record keeping. They are *abacic*, in that they correspond to abacus-based systems of calculation. A change of state in the system of record is achieved by the physical movement of tokens – see Digression 11.1.

Tallies, double-entry account books, decks of punched cards and computerized relational databases are more sophisticated monetary technologies, able to associate with a legal person either a credit state or a debit state. Tallies are a specialized token system of record. The other technologies are *algorithmic* in the sense described in section 4.2. A change of state is achieved by the writing down or recording of symbols.

A key concern of all monetary technologies is their integrity of record: they must provide some protection against falsification. It is in this light that the use of precious metal for coins should be seen. States have always enacted severe penalties for the fraudulent issue of coin, but penalties would be ineffective if the issue of fraudulent coin is made too easy. Beyond legal prohibitions on forgery, state coin had two distinct protection mechanisms.

First, the coin is made by stamping from a master, one of the basic copying technologies described in section 3.3.3. Unless one has access to the master it is difficult to make accurate copies of the coin. In principle one could make passable copies by replicating the master: take an impression of the coin, use this to make a mould, and from that cast a new die. Until the invention of iron-casting, this process was technically infeasible since dies made from softer castable metals like bronze would not have the toughness required to stamp out coin. Note also that there are three copying stages between the coin used as a model and the new forged coins. Errors in copying accumulate exponentially so it is very difficult to get forgeries of acceptable quality. The remaining forgery techniques were to hand carve a new die, or to use an existing coin to make negative moulds from which coin could be cast rather than stamped. These are relatively expensive processes and would not be worthwhile for the production of low denomination coinage. For high denomination coinage they would be feasible.

Second, while low denomination coins were made from copper or copper alloys, and protected against forgery by the method above, high denomination coins required additional protection. This could be arranged by making them from expensive materials like gold and silver. Provided that the nominal value of the coins was not greatly in excess of the value of the metal they contained, this policy reduced the forger's incentive. The use of gold or silver is not essential to money tokens, as is shown by the abandonment of precious metals in favour of paper money printed using sophisticated techniques that make it difficult to copy. The use of bullion was in effect a low-tech anti-forgery expedient.

11.3.1   *Appropriation of surplus by the state*

As the state commutes taxes in kind to money taxes it moves from the direct appropriation of the surplus product to its indirect appropriation, mediated by the money symbol. In levying a money tax, the state symbolically asserts its right to a portion of of society's labour. When it spends the tax money purchasing goods and labour, it performs a real appropriation of a surplus product. Civil society then acts as an intermediary, transferring labour from those who paid the tax to those who provide the actual services to the state.

The state, of course, predates societies in which commodity production is general, and it has a primordial power to appropriate part of society's labour time. In the early empires of Mesopotamia and Egypt, or the later Inca empire, this appropriation was performed directly. All peasants had a duty to provide either time or crops to the state. Some of the crops would be consumed by priests or state officials, another portion would be stockpiled against drought and redistributed to the working population in times of scarcity. This form of economy was termed *redistributive* by Polanyi. Such a system requires the development of information technology – systems of writing down and recording numbers. Thus the Mesopotamian civilizations developed cuneiform numbers and later developed writing. The Incas developed *quipu*, a numerical notation based on knotted strings.

Such systems of record had to

- keep track of physical stocks of crops held by the state or temples;
- keep track of the deliveries made by individuals and groups subject to tribute deliveries; and
- track the tribute obligations of such groups.

All of these tasks require standardized systems of measurement and a reliable arithmetic technology. The state had to be able to associate numbers with tax-payers and types of products. It had to be able to measure the grain delivered. It had to be able to add up tribute delivered by groups to know what total it had in stock, hence a reliable technique for adding large numbers was needed. In order to determine if a group had met their tribute obligations, a technique of subtraction was required, taking away their deliveries from their obligations.

The Sumerian civilizations developed a sophisticated system of written numerals, using a place notation similar to that we use today. The key difference was the number base. Our place notation, deriving originally from India, uses base 10, the Sumerians used base 60. Place notation is concise and allows large numbers to be readily manipulated. It was also a written notation, lending itself to the recording of tables of tax deliveries. Without this technology for recording and processing information the social complexity of the early empires would not have been feasible. In all but the simplest social systems, social relations are embodied in information technology. Without a technique for recording debts, the social relation of creditor/debtor cannot persist. Without a means of measuring land and recording ownership, the relation of landlord to tenant cannot exist.

In Mesopotamia, different subjects of the empire would deliver different crops depending on their circumstances. Some might deliver barley, some dates, some dried fish. It was necessary to determine if a farmer delivering a basket of dates and three *gur* of barley had met his tax obligations. The solution was, first, to define the tax obligation in terms of barley and, second, to establish a set of 'exchange rates' whereby deliveries of other goods could be converted to their barley-equivalent. The *gur* – the standard volumetric unit of barley, about 300 litres – then became the unit in which deliveries of other products were measured. The *gur* of barley had an equivalent in silver, the shekel, defined as silver to the weight of 240 grains of barley. It appears that this then became the basis for a purely accounts-based monetary system. The shekel/*gur* was never issued as a coin, it existed only as entries in accounting records on clay tablets. This notional

1 gur barley	for 1 shekel silver
3 litres best oil	for 1 shekel silver
1.2 litres vegetable oil	for 1 shekel silver
1.5 litres pig fat	for 1 shekel silver
40 litres of bitumen	for 1 shekel silver
6 minas wool	for 1 shekel silver
2 gur salt	for 1 shekel silver

Figure 11.1 Opening section of Esnunna Law Code (Postgate, 1992).

quantity of barley then acted as a generalized way of measuring values and obliga-tions (see Figure 11.1). From regulating obligations to the state, it moved to being the unit in which credit relations between private individuals were expressed.

Such a system of credit-based accounting, involving a place-based number system and algorithmic calculation, required a literate and numerate class of scribes. If you are to become proficient in a place-based number system you need to spend childhood years learning your tables by rote. This is a hard enough task using base 10. With a base 60 number system it would probably have been more difficult. A naive estimate indicates that the size of the tables to be learnt is 36 times as great as for our school children. This overestimates the task, however, since the Babylonian number system is better seen as an alternating base 10, base 6 system, which gives rise to patterns that can be more easily learnt than those of a pure base 60 system. Nonetheless, to operate an accounting-based monetary system required an expensively educated class that was lacking in the petty kingdoms and city states where coinage was first introduced. Coins allowed monetary relations to operate in societies which lacked this class of numerate scribes.

11.4   Money space, an illustration

As we said above, any monetary system must maintain a binary relation between juridical subjects and sums of money. This binary monetary relation can be written as a table:

Subject	Shekels
Adad	7
Dagon	12
Ninki	200
Inanna	18
Hanish	23
TOTAL	260

There has to be some form of persistent store that can hold the state of this relation through time. Clay tablets served well, as do modern computer disks, but coins also work. Coins are self-registering and self-accumulating. The physical presence of coins in a purse records a number. The possession of the purse associates it with a juridical subject. The state of the monetary system is then encoded in the totality of such records – be they current account tablets, current account database relations or purses in people's pockets.

Besides storing the state of the subject–money relation at a point in time, a monetary system needs a mechanism by which the system of records can be updated when a *transaction* occurs. The transaction is the basic unit of change whereby the state of a monetary system evolves through time. Transactions are inherently atomic, indivisible events. A basic transaction must update two people's records, leaving the totals unaffected. Continuing the example above, a payment of 13 from Ninki to Adad yields a new state of the system:

Subject	Shekels
Adad	20
Dagon	12
Ninki	183
Inanna	18
Hanish	23
TOTAL	260

Such a transaction can be performed in several ways:

(1) In a system based on coins (or other portable tokens such as banknotes), the transaction is acheived via hand-over. The physical conservation of the coins ensures the atomic, conservative character of the transaction.

(2) If the relation is stored on some erasable and rewritable medium – like the old 'slate' used by shopkeepers to keep track of credit to customers, or a modern magnetic disk – then one follows this algorithm:

(a) Add 13 to the total listed for Adad.
(b) Rub out Adad's total.
(c) Write down the new total, 20.
(d) Subtract 13 from Ninki's total.
(e) Rub out Ninki's total.
(f) Write down Ninki's reduced total, 183.

This sounds simple enough, but when computers are used a great deal of trouble has to be taken to ensure the atomicity of such transactions. We take up this issue in section 12.3.

(3) In a system based on permanent records such as paper or clay tablets, one has to add a new record detailing the transaction:

Payer	Payee	Amount
Ninki	Adad	13

Each transaction requires the storage of a new record. The balance associated with each individual then has to be obtained by adding up all of the extant transaction records.

One consequence of moving from an account-based monetary system to coinage was decentralization. Accounting requires that the records of transactions are concentrated in a few centres such as palaces or clearing houses. Coins can be dispersed around the population at large. They were a flexible, low-tech, decentralized monetary technology that allowed monetary relations and the commodity economy to spread rapidly. According to Ingham (2004) the Macedonian and later Roman empires were important vehicles for this spread.

As we have said, a disadvantage of coins is that they can only record positive numbers. The recording of debt therefore required supplementary documents. Some debts arise from private transactions and others are due to the state (the obligation to pay taxes). A person's total position with respect to the state is now encoded in two distinct forms: the coins that they hold, and the tax obligation written down in the tax collector's records. We can thus extend our previous type of relations with an extra table – tax obligation – and an extra row to represent the state. With this apparatus we can illustrate the mechanism noted by Forstater, whereby an economy is monetized by a conquering power (see section 11.2.1). Our imagined monetary system bears some resemblance to Nigeria in 1905, after its conquest by Lugard and incorporation into the British Empire.

Step 0 The initial state of the system: a clean slate, no money and no tax obligations.

Agent	Coin	Tax obligation
State	0	0
Alande	0	0
Tunde	0	0
Femi	0	0
TOTAL	0	0

Step 1   The first step is for the state to mint coin.

Agent	Coin	Tax obligation
State	9	0
Alande	0	0
Tunde	0	0
Femi	0	0
TOTAL	9	0

Steps 2 and 3   The state employs Femi in the Royal West African Frontier Force for some months and pays him 7 coins (step 2). It then announces that everyone will have to pay a poll tax of 2 coins (step 3). The state system can now be described by the relation:

Agent	Coin	Tax obligation
State	2	6
Alande	0	−2
Tunde	0	−2
Femi	7	−2
TOTAL	9	0

Alande and Tunde hear that they must pay a poll tax in the new coin. They also hear that if they fail to pay the district commissioner will have them publicly flogged. They are keen to get hold of coins.

Step 4   A. and T. offer to sell Femi food in exchange for coins. Femi buys the food and we have the situation:

Agent	Coin	Tax obligation
State	2	6
Alande	3	−2
Tunde	2	−2
Femi	2	−2
TOTAL	9	0

Step 5   The day of reckoning arrives.[6] Taxes are due. Coin is accepted by the collectors in cancellation of tax debts due on that day. This gives us a situation described by:

Agent	Coin	Tax obligation
State	8	0
Alande	1	0
Tunde	0	0
Femi	0	0
TOTAL	9	0

Femi has spent all his money and is available for hire again. Tunde has sold part of his crop and covered his debt. Alande has sold somewhat more of her crop and is left holding a coin; she is now in a position to continue operating as a trader. From the standpoint of the new colonial monetary economy Alande is richer than she started, but in fact she has given up useful food for a copper disc of limited practical use. In real terms she has been impoverished, yet she has made a social advance: holding the King's coin, she partakes indirectly in the power and authority of the King. With coin she can command the labour of her fellows. She buys kola nuts for her stall. By itself this purchase looks a very emblem of reciprocity, free and voluntary exchange. But behind it, driving it, is coercion and fear of the tax collector.

We can now identify the basic circuit of money:

King → Lackey → Subject → ... → Subject → King

We can also identify the primitive operations that describe or change the state of a monetary system. These are the *signature* of money:[7]

(1)   *Holding(agent x → money)* This function specifies the holding of money by agent x. The social system will have various ways of encoding this holding.

(2)   *Pay(agent x, agent y, money m)* a payment by x to y of an amount of money m. This operation follows the constraint that the total holding of money by x and y remains constant, and that $Holding(x)_{\text{pre}} = Holding(x)_{\text{post}} + m$, where the subscripts indicate the situation prior to and after the operation. This is a conservative operation.

---

[6] The notion of the 'day of reckoning' reflects the apotheosis of the state – God as the supreme tax collector, an imaginary projection of the god-kings of the Roman, Hellenistic and earlier empires.

[7] We borrow the term 'signature' from type theory, where it describes the collection of basic operations supported by a type (Goguen and Meseguer, 1982).

(3)   *Mint(money m)* This operation increases the holding of money by the state by m, or in other words $Holding(state)_{pre} = Holding(state)_{post} - m$. This is a non-conservative operation.

Note that taxation is not a distinct operation in this signature. From the standpoint of the state of the money system, taxation is just another payment. Its special, enforced character is invisible in the space of money as such. It is only when we consider a more comprehensive space, commodity–money space, that tax payments stand out as special.

11.4.1   Seigniorage

In a monetary economy the state has two ways of gaining access to real labour resources. It can levy a tax in money and spend the money, buying labour or commodities, or it can simply mint and spend new money. The latter process is called seigniorage. Taxation and seigniorage are mutually interdependent. Unless there is an initial minting of money, no tax in money can be levied. On the other hand if no taxes are levied, the money will be valueless and the state will be unable to appropriate real resources with its coin.

In a 'natural' economy the appropriation of resources by the state is direct, and is constrained by its political ability to coerce property owners into handing over goods, and also to coerce subjects into performing labour services. With the invention of money, the appropriation of a surplus splits into two: a symbolic appropriation of coins as tax goes alongside a real appropriation, by purchase, of labour time and commodities. The real appropriation then appears as something equitable and voluntary. The coercive aspect of the process occurs entirely in the realm of symbols – rendering unto Caesar that which is Caesar's.

Coercion remains bounded by political ability. Taxation, whether in money or in kind, meets resistance. But because there is a split between the real and symbolic domains, seigniorage can act as a wedge to force them apart. A state can, within limits, appropriate more labour than it can raise symbolically as tax. Taxation is by nature a recurrent process: it provides an annual stream of 'symbolic labour' to be spent on real labour. In principle, seigniorage is a one-off event needed to start the tax process going (as in the example laid out above). In the year the coins are minted, the Crown can purchase more than it taxes. The opportunity for seigniorage, however, presents a constant temptation for states whose tax-raising power is weak, for minting coin is politically easier than raising taxes. Taxation is always specific and explicit – certain people are obliged to pay certain amounts under certain conditions – while appropriation via seigniorage is general and diffuse – everybody finds that their coin will buy a little less than before.

Appropriation via seigniorage is made easier by the fact that the issue of coin has to be a continuous process anyway. There are several reasons for this.

First, there is always a certain loss of coin due to accident or wear and tear. The subject's accidental loss is the Crown's gain. If a coin falls in a river, a record that services have been performed for the Crown goes with it. If taxes are to be met, the Crown must issue a new coin, and the subjects must perform new services to get it. This means that a certain level of seigniorage is built into the system – that which derives from the *information loss* caused by the imperfections of coin as a technology of record.

Second, some additional minting is required to keep pace with the growth in the value of commodity circulation. As more people are drawn into commodity production – due to population growth, the expansion of the state, or because previously 'natural' economic processes become commodified – then more coin is required to sustain this trade.

Third, hoarding withdraws coin from circulation. Many hoards are eventually lost, either for ever or to be found by archaeologists centuries later. Leaving those aside, the effect of hoarding is very similar to that of outright loss of coin, from the standpoint of the state. If a hoarder puts away 100 coins a year into a hoard, then unless this is offset by other people dissipating their hoards the Crown can issue an extra 100 coins per year. Any net hoarding by the population allows a corresponding rise in the annual issue of coin.

The consequence of a higher issue is more seigniorage – real appropriation of labour and services by the Crown. But the money-form hides this – both from holders of money and from some economists who should know better. Open an elementary economics textbook and you read that money serves as a store of value. Hoarders believed this, but it is fundamentally an illusion. A miser with 1000 pennies under the floor has not stored up value, he has buried the ghost of value departed.[8] The King issued pennies in return for real value, namely work. Like as not, they were born as soldier's pay. Then the work of soldiering, like winter's snow, vanished leaving no material residue. What the miser stored was information, a number that assigned to him a tiny fraction of the power royal. If he spends his hoard he commands the labour of others. But if all hoarders try to do this at once, they find themselves competing with the regular purchasers of labour and commodities. Prices go up. The social power represented by each coin falls.

In time of famine hoards are spent: the hoarders are able to grab a larger share of a diminished crop; starvation is redistributed. Real social provision against famine depends on a real accumulation of value in the form of corn in granaries, not coin in boxes.

11.5   Commodity–money space

We now extend our representation to include both commodities and money. Again we can use a table to summarize the position of our system in state space. Our new table will have a column for money followed by a column for each type of commodity.

---

[8] See the discussion of ghosts in Digression 11.2.

Digression 11.2 Money and the illusion of Pepper's ghost

In Victorian times there was a popular stage illusion known as Pepper's ghost. On a gloomy stage a ghostly, floating figure would appear, its ethereal yet living qualities revealed by the fact that it was at once animated and transparent. The ghost was in fact the image of an actor in the wings, reflected off a sheet of plate glass placed at 45° to the audience.

The ghostly and illusory properties of money and credit derive from the fact that our views of them are projections of a partially hidden stage – one on which every entity has its mirror image (to every credit a hidden debit, to every visible coin a hidden tax). It is perhaps fitting that an age when working lives were ruled by money and credit as never before should have developed an obsession with ghosts, mediums and spirits.

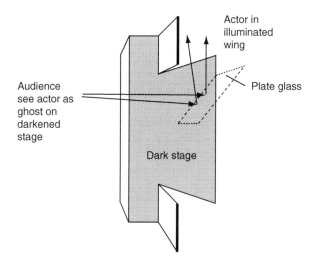

How the 'Pepper's ghost' illusion was performed
(we are looking at the stage from above)

The left-hand panel in Table 11.1 shows the initial holdings of coin and commodities by the agents in our little society. Suppose Femi buys 6 kola for 3 coins from Alande. This can be decomposed into two sub-operations:

Pay(Femi, Alande, 3)   move the money
Transfer(Alande, Femi, Kola, 6)   move the goods

Transfers conserve the commodity being transferred. After both of these operations we have the situation shown in the right-hand panel of Table 11.1.

Table 11.1 Agents' holdings of money and commodities

Agent	Coin	Cassava	Kola		Agent	Coin	Cassava	Kola
State	2	0	0		State	2	0	0
Alande	0	6	6	→	Alande	3	6	0
Tunde	0	2	5		Tunde	0	2	5
Femi	7	0	0		Femi	4	0	6

In commodity exchange such operations occur in matching pairs. In the case of taxation the payment is unilateral, with no corresponding transfer of goods. Note that in the example above we have not explicitly represented the prices of commodities; we will look at this in more detail in the following section.

11.5.1 Exchange is value-conserving

We have asserted that the operations of payment and commodity transfer are conservative, in the sense that they leave the amount of money and commodities unchanged. We will now examine what it means to say that commodity exchange – that is, linked pairs of monetary payment and commodity transfer – are in addition *value-conserving*.

In science it is often worth questioning, problematizing, the obvious. It seems self-evident that if Chantelle has a car, three chairs and a table we can add up the values of these assets to obtain her total worth; and we can do the same for Briony, who owns a table, 4 chairs and a washing machine (Table 11.2).

So Chantelle is £768 richer than Briony. All this is perfectly obvious to anyone in a commercial society like ours. But why exactly do these arithmetic operations work, and what are we doing when we thus compare two people's wealth? From a mathematical point of view, Chantelle and Briony possess *vectors of assets*. For Chantelle this vector is $(1, 1, 3, 0)$ denoting 1 car, 1 table, 3 chairs, 0 washing machines. For Briony it is $(0, 1, 4, 1)$. These vectors define positions in wealth space. When we compare their relative wealth we are deciding what 'distance' separates them in terms of wealth.

Table 11.2 Figuring agents' wealth

Chantelle		Briony	
Car	£900		
Table	£50	Table	£50
Chairs 3 at £12	£36	Chairs 4 at £12	£48
		Washing machine	£120
Total	£986		£218

This problem of measuring distance arises in many domains:

(1) We want to measure the distance that you would have to walk between two street corners in Manhattan.
(2) We want to know the distance 'as the crow flies' between two hilltops given their map coordinates.
(3) Given three variants of a conserved gene from chimpanzees, gorillas and humans, we wish to determine which two are closest.

Each of these examples uses distance in a different sense and for each there are appropriate mathematical techniques to work out the answer. An important property of all distances is that they are non-negative numbers, so the procedures used to measure distance must ensure that we don't get negative results. A mathematical method of measuring a distance is referred to as a *metric*.

Manhattan distance: On the regular street grid of New York, the walking distance between two street corners is just the sum of the distances along the two axes with which the streets are aligned (Figure 11.2). Whether you chose a simple route or try to zig-zag, you end up going the same distance. If the starting and finishing points are (a, b) and (x, y) the walking distance is $|a - x| + |b - y|$. The use of absolute values ensures that the result is positive because $|x - a| = |a - x| \geq 0$.

As the crow flies, or Euclidean distance: Over street grids offering us no shortcuts, birds fly freely. Where we have to walk 3 miles East and 4 North, pigeons fly only 5 diagonal miles. We calculate diagonal distance as the positive square root of the sum of the squared distances along the axes: $5 = \sqrt{3^2 + 4^2} = \sqrt{9 + 16}$. For points (a, b) and (x, y) the formula is $\sqrt{(a - x)^2 + (b - y)^2}$.

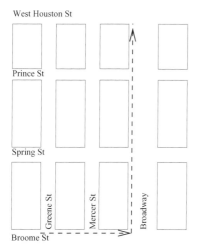

Figure 11.2 A walk in Manhattan.

Genetics and Hamming distance: DNA can be represented computationally as strings drawn from the alphabet A, T, C, G, where the letters correspond to the 4 bases that encode the information in a DNA molecule. Proteins can be represented as similar strings drawn from a larger alphabet representing the amino acids in their sequence. A simple measure of the distance between two DNA or amino acid sequences is simply to count the places along the sequence where the letters disagree. For example the following amino acid sequences differ in 26 places.

```
MKPGRLASIALAIIFLPMAVPAHAATITITMTNLVISPTEVSAKVGDTI
MKAGAKIRLSWLAALALMAAPAAAATIEVTIDKLVPSPATVEAKVGTDI
~*************    *    *    ** ***    *  ** *
```

The number of places where the sequences differs gives us a measure called the Hamming distance. Hamming (1950) invented it when trying to rank the seriousness of errors in digital codes. The measure is useful because it identifies the number of point mutations required to change one code into another.

Commodity value distance: Given the two vectors representing Chantelle and Briony's assets, $\mathbf{c} = (1, 1, 3, 0)$ and $\mathbf{b} = (0, 1, 4, 1)$, what mathematical formula can we use to obtain the distance, d, between their respective net worth? A suitable formula is:

$$d = |\sum_{i=1}^{4} \mathbf{p}_i(\mathbf{c}_i - \mathbf{b}_i)| \tag{11.1}$$

where $\mathbf{p}$ is the price vector, namely (900, 50, 12, 120) as in Table 11.2. That is, we take the signed difference between the two agents' holdings of each asset, $\mathbf{c}_i - \mathbf{b}_i$, multiply by the appropriate price, $\mathbf{p}_i$, and add up. We then take the absolute value of the result to produce a non-negative measure.

Notice that commodity-value distance is not Euclidean – no squaring was carried out – and neither is it Manhattan distance since we took the signed, not the absolute, difference in the amounts of each commodity held by the agents. Surprisingly, it turns out that the resulting metric is similar to one that occurs in physics when dealing with the conservation of energy. Suppose that instead of $\mathbf{b}$ and $\mathbf{c}$ being vectors of commodities, they represent the height and kinetic energy of two flying balls. Then equation (11.1) would give us the difference between their total energies (kinetic plus potential).

Is this significant? Perhaps. Marx said that in *Capital* he was trying to elucidate the 'laws of motion' of capitalism, thereby implicitly relating the study of capitalism to physics. He devoted considerable space to analysing the logic of commodity exchange. In this context the fact that net worth has the same metric as the conservation of energy may well be relevant.

The law of energy conservation constrains the paths that flying balls follow. If we threw a ball on the moon, where there is no atmospheric resistance, then at each instant the ball will have combination of height and velocity that causes its total energy to be unchanged (Figure 11.3).

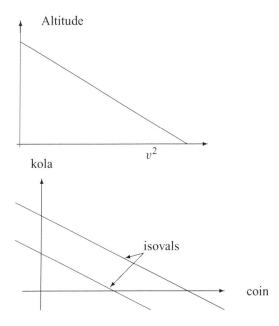

Figure 11.3 Points of equal net worth (isovals) in the space of commodities and money have the same form as points passed through in the phase space of altitude and velocity squared by a falling body.

If value were just a matter of providing an ordering or ranking of combinations of goods, then a Euclidean, or indeed any other, metric would pass muster. It is some additional property of the system of commodity production that imposes this specific metric characteristic of a system governed by a conservation law. This fits in nicely with the labour theory of value, where social labour would be the embodied substance conserved during exchange relations. So far, however, this is merely a formal argument: the form of the phenomena is *consistent* with a conservation relation. To justify our formulation fully we depend on the arguments presented in chapter 6.

Spatial metrics are so much part of our mode of thought that to imagine a different metric is conceptually difficult. Most of us have difficulty imagining the curved space–time described by relativity theory, Euclidean metrics being so ingrained in our minds. Conversely, when looking at commodities, a non-Euclidean metric is so ingrained that we have difficulty imagining a Euclidean commodity space.

But it is worth the effort of trying to imagine a Euclidean commodity space. By bringing to light the implicit contradictions of this idea, we get a better idea of the underlying reasons why value takes the particular form that it does.

In a commodity-value space of order 2, Euclidean 'isovals' take the form of circles centered on the origin. In higher-order spaces, they take the form of spheres or hyper-spheres. (We assume in all cases that some linear scaling of the axes is permitted to convert them into a common set of units.) Let us suppose that the economic meaning of these isovals is that given any pair of points **p**, **q** on an isoval, the bundle of commodities represented by **p** will be exchangeable as an equivalent with the bundle represented by **q**.

If the state of an economic agent is described by her position in this space, then the set of permissible moves that can be made via equivalent exchanges is characterized by unitary operators on commodity vector space. The set of equivalent exchanges of **p** is $\{|\mathbf{p}|\,\mathbf{u}$ such that $|\mathbf{u}| = 1\}$, i.e. the radius-preserving rotations of **p**. Mathematically, this is certainly a consistent system.[9]

But economically, such a system would break down. It says that I can exchange one, appropriately defined, unit of kola for one unit of coin, or for any equivalent combination such as ($\frac{1}{\sqrt{2}}$ coin, $\frac{1}{\sqrt{2}}$ kola). But then what is to stop me carrying out the following procedure?

(1)   Exchange my initial 1 unit of kola for $\frac{1}{\sqrt{2}}$ coin plus $\frac{1}{\sqrt{2}}$ kola.

(2)   Now sell my $\frac{1}{\sqrt{2}}$ coin for kola, giving me $\frac{1}{\sqrt{2}}$ kola.

(3)   Add my two bundles of kola together, to give a total of $\frac{2}{\sqrt{2}} = \sqrt{2}$ of kola in total.

I end up with more kola than I had at the start, so this cannot be a set of equivalent exchanges. The second step is illegal within the context of the Euclidean metric, since it involves operating upon one of the coordinates independently. But in the real world, commodities are physically separable, allowing one component of a commodity bundle to be exchanged without reference to others. It is this physical separability of the commodities that makes the observed metric the only consistent one.

The existence of a commodity-producing society, in which the individual components of the wealth held by economic agents can be independently traded, selects out of the possible value metrics one consistent with the law of value. In a society in which commodity bundles could not be separated into distinct components, and exchange obeyed a Euclidean metric, the labour theory of value could not hold – but that is not the world we live in.

11.6   The logical properties of financial transactions

We have already said that accounts-based monetary systems are capable of recording both positive and negative amounts of money. This is required to represent debt.

---

[9] A very similar model is used in one of the standard formulations of quantum theory to describe possible state transformations (von Neumann, 1955).

Suppose that starting from the initial holdings

Agent	money	kola	total
A	1d	0d	1d
B	0d	4d	4d
totals	1d	4d	5d

agent A buys 2d of kola from agent B.[10] Since A only has 1d in money to pay for it, the transaction leaves the following holdings:

Agent	money	kola	total
A	−1d	2d	1d
B	2d	2d	4d
totals	1d	4d	5d

We see that the totals for both money and kola are conserved, and the total assets of each person do not change. Sale on credit may still be considered a conservative operation, but only if we abstract from physical coinage. If money were just coin then we have a puzzle. There was initially only one penny in circulation, but after the sale agent B has two pennies. Where has the extra penny come from? The state has not issued a coin, so who created it?

The new penny is balanced by a new negative penny held by agent A. The positive and negative new pennies constitute a debt-relation between the two agents. Since coins can only represent positive numbers, this implies some ancillary system of record-keeping to encode debt. We came across this with the tables recording tax obligations and coin holding in section 11.4. There we represented the relationship between the state and individuals as a table with two columns, one showing the coin that people held and the other their tax debts. Implicitly, the tax debts were recorded in government ledgers.

There's an important difference, however. Tax debts originate in a fundamentally coercive, non-conservative operation, an enforced obligation to pay. The creation of private debt – as in the example of a sale on credit – is a fundamentally equitable or conservative operation.

---

[10] 2d means 2 pence worth. The small denomination coin circulating in colonial Nigeria were pennies. The suffix 'd', used to denote pennies in the British imperial monetary system, was a relic from the Roman imperial monetary system standing for Denarius, the basic silver coin of Rome. The Denarius transmuted into the Penny in the early middle ages.

The non-conservative operations associated with debts are

(1)   the formation of tax debts to the state; and
(2)   The levying of interest on existing private debts, which increases the indebtedness of the original debtor.

    Because of these cases it turns out to matter a good deal that debt operations do not follow the same symmetry and conservation laws as commodity exchanges. Debt formation has its own symmetries, but these are not inherently conservative ones.

11.6.1   Relative movements caused by loans

Consider Figure 11.4. This shows what happens when two agents, Ajit (A) and Rakesh (R), engage in mutual loans. The vertical axis measures coins held and the horizontal axis measures their mutual indebtedness. In each half of the diagram Ajit starts out with 1 coin and Rakesh starts with 6 coins. At the beginning, as they have no mutual debts, both agents lie on the vertical axis.
    Consider the situation where Rakesh lends one coin to Ajit, shown in the upper half of the figure. Ajit and Rakesh move along their isovals in opposite directions. Since they both remain on their isovals, it is clear that there is no alteration in the net worth of either. At the beginning Rakesh has a net worth of 5 coins richer than Ajit. He is still 5 coins richer after the loan has been made – on the assumption that Ajit will not default.
    Although their net worths do not change, it looks as if this operation brings the two agents closer together. Indeed, in Euclidean space it does. They are initially 5 coin apart, but after the loan, applying the Euclidean distance formula,

$$\delta(A'', R'') = \sqrt{(1 - (-1))^2 + (5 - 2)^2} = \sqrt{13} \approx 3.6055$$

they are closer. If on the other hand we look at the differences in Ajit and Rakesh's net worth, they are still 5 apart. More surprisingly their Manhattan distance stays the same:

$$\delta_m(R'', A'') = |1 - (-1)| + |5 - 2| = 5$$

    Now look at the lower part of Figure 11.4, which depicts the situation of Ajit lending 1 coin to Rakesh. Again the two agents move along their budget lines in opposite directions, but in this case the loan seems to move them further apart. This is obviously the case in Euclidean space, but the interesting thing is that they are also further apart in Manhattan space.

$$\delta_m(R'', A'') = |-1 - 1| + |7 - 0| = 9$$

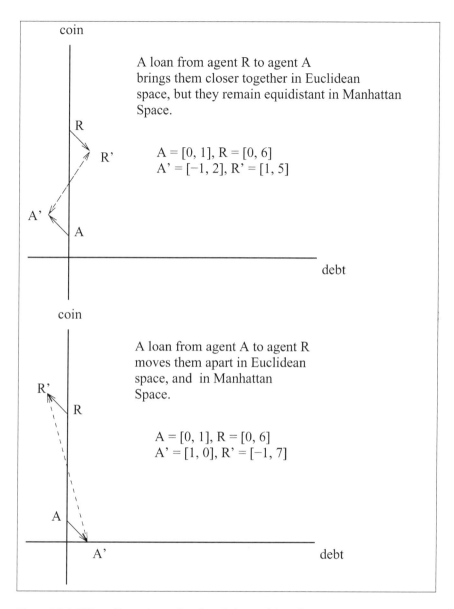

Figure 11.4 Effect of loans in moving the relative position of agents.

The rule for small loans, made by moneylenders who start out with much more money than the person they are lending to, is that the loan does not alter the Manhattan separation of the agents: the two agents are the same distance apart after the loan as before. On the other hand, if an agent with a small amount of cash lends to an agent who initially has much more cash, we find that the agents

---

Digression 11.3   Relations

In this chapter we use the word relation in the sense in which it is used in formal logic and *relational algebra*, the branch of mathematics used in computer databases.

The concept of a relation is closely related to that of a *predicate*, a statement regarding a place-holder object or objects which yields a true or false result depending on how the places are filled. For instance the predicate $\{F(x) : x$ is a dog$\}$ gives the result 'true' if x = Fido, 'false' if x = Mount Everest. This is an example of a unary or one-place predicate. An example of a two-place predicate is $\{G(x, y) : x < y\}$. In this context the symbol '$<$' (less than) is termed a relational operator. Relational algebra extends this idea to say that the *relation* 'less-than' is the set of all ordered pairs of numbers (x, y) such that $x < y$. We can conceptualize this as an infinite table

1	2
2	3
17	203
−9	−1
⋮	⋮

In other cases relations may yield a finite table. The relation 'x is a known satellite of y and y is an inner planet of our solar system' gives

Moon	Earth
Phobos	Mars
Deimos	Mars

Tables or relations can have more than two columns. We saw this with the table:

$$T = \begin{array}{l|ccc} & \textit{Agent} & \textit{Coin} & \textit{Tax} \\ \hline & \textbf{State} & 2 & 6 \\ & \text{Alande} & 0 & -2 \\ & \text{Tunde} & 0 & -2 \\ & \text{Femi} & 7 & -2 \end{array}$$

The relation encoded by T is: 'x has y coins and is due to receive z in tax'. When we *project* a relation we drop one or more columns from the table, as in

$$T' = \begin{array}{l|cc} & \textit{Agent} & \textit{Coin} \\ \hline & \textbf{State} & 2 \\ & \text{Alande} & 0 \\ & \text{Tunde} & 0 \\ & \text{Femi} & 7 \end{array}$$

Digression 11.3 (*continued*)

This is what we mean when we say that money, as conventionally understood, is a projection of an underlying relation. The notion of projection in this context comes from the way that a camera obscura projects or throws an image of three dimensional objects onto a flat surface. The key is dimensional reduction: a space of high dimension is represented in a lower dimensional one. Such projections involve a loss of information and can give rise to illusions; one only has to think of Escher to realize how tricky a two dimensional projection can be.

move apart in Manhattan space. This latter sort of loan might seem improbable at first sight, but it is just what happens when an individual or a company makes a deposit with their banker. But does this movement apart in Manhattan space have any practical significance?

Surely in the real world we deal with differences in net worth, not Manhattan distances between people. Since differences in net worth are unchanged, why worry about Manhattan distances? Because the Manhattan distance points to something of huge social significance. Why should a poor person lend to a rich person in the first case? Surely this would be a rare exception?

So it was in precapitalist society, but with capitalism it becomes the rule. Name the rich person 'Banker', and it becomes clear. Whenever we deposit money in the bank we lend to someone much richer than us. The growing Manhattan distance between us and the bank that this produces, measures the increasing social power of the banker.

Consider the theoretical entity that is termed the 'money supply'. This has various definitions, but is typically taken to be the sum of notes and coin in circulation along with the total of all current account deposits with the banks. At one level this seems obvious and unexceptionable since a deposit in my bank allows me to buy commodities using a cheque or debit card just as I could with coins or paper money. At this empirical level bank deposits can obviously function as a means of purchase, and seemingly should be counted in the money supply.

However a moment's thought indicates that when we talk of a 'money supply' we are using a metaphor. We are making an analogy between the supply of some ordinary commodity (say, petroleum) and money. But the two things are very different. Petroleum is something physical, it has mass. A supply of oil has a characteristic dimension, which we use to measure it. The world supply of oil would be expressed as x million barrels per day. In terms of dimensional analysis it is expressed in units of mass per unit time.

The money supply as conventionally measured is very different: it is measured in $ or £. We have argued above that such monetary units indirectly measure the amount of work that a social agent has done for the state. The transfer of monetary tokens allows agents who have done work for the state to transfer symbols representing this work to other people who use them to meet their tax obligations. It is thus evident that the money supply differs from a conventional supply in a number of respects:

(1)   It does not measure the rate at which something is produced over time. Its measure has no time dimension, thus it is not a supply in the normal sense of a flow of things.

(2)   Money is not a substance, it has no mass, instead it is a technology of record. As such it is information – or more properly, what we call money is a projection, in the strict relational sense, of an information structure. We have seen that holdings of coin by the public constitute one column of a relation between subjects and the state. The other column holds individual tax debts. This column is 'hidden' in the sense that it takes the form of covert records held by the exchequer.

The illusion that money is a substance, which is implied by the term *money supply*, arose from a particular stage in its technological evolution. When the state of the monetary information structure is partly encoded by people's holdings of coins, these coins, which encode but one column of the monetary relation, were seen as money itself. Money was misidentified as a self-sufficient substance. We should understand instead, that what exists is a relation, initially between the state and its subjects, later extending to credit relations between its subjects, whose partial projection appears as coin.

12 Banking and capital

12.1 Bank credit

In precapitalist economies lending was almost exclusively from rich to poor, and the rich lent out their own money (Itoh and Lapavitsas, 1999: ch. 3) In capitalist economies rich banks still lend to people who are much poorer, but the banks in turn borrow money from their depositors. The process of depositing money with banks is the crucial step in the creation of net credit.

Three crucial innovations are introduced by capitalist banking:

(1)   The acceptance of deposits.
(2)   The establishment of a system of mutual debt clearing.
(3)   The issue of loans denominated in the liabilities of the bank.

These are tied to the creation of an independent system of records and ledgers recording the debit/credit position of bank customers. Bank accounts, either as paper ledgers or as computer databases, are an algorithmic system of record that allow debt relations to be held in a relatively centralized fashion.

At an abstract theoretical level we can conceive of the mutual debts of agents in the economy as registered in a giant matrix, D. This is a square matrix, with n rows and columns, one for each agent; it therefore contains n^2 numbers. This is fine as a conceptual tool, but in a real society such an entity can only exist if there is a technology capable of supporting it.

If there are 100 million (10^8) people in an economy, the D matrix would contain 10^{16} numbers. This is impractical. But most of the people in an economy never meet one another, never trade, and never build up direct mutual debts. This means that the D matrix is *sparse* – that is, most of its elements are zero. Sparse matrices can be recorded compactly, since the zeros never have to be written down. For instance the matrix

$$D = \begin{bmatrix} 0 & 0 & 0 & 5 & 0 & 2 \\ 0 & 0 & 0 & 0 & 0 & 0 \\ 0 & 0 & 0 & 0 & 0 & 7 \\ -5 & 0 & 0 & 0 & 0 & 0 \\ 0 & 0 & 0 & 0 & 0 & -9 \\ -2 & 0 & -7 & 0 & 9 & 0 \end{bmatrix}$$

Table 12.1 The D matrix stored as a ternary relation

Debtor	Creditor	Amount
4	1	5
6	1	2
6	3	7
5	6	9

is sparse and can be more compactly represented by a *relation*, as shown in Table 12.1, which records each debt only once and lists the row and column numbers in the D matrix of the various creditors and debtors. We have replaced a matrix containing 36 numbers with a relation containing 12 numbers.

In this example agent 6 is acting as proto-banker: this agent has borrowed from agents 1 and 3 and lent to agent 5.

But the relation we have shown is global, tabulating the totality of debt relations between all of the agents. Agent 6 could keep a simpler private relation recording its account balances with its customers as shown in Table 12.2.

The relation is reduced to two columns since the bank knows that it is one party to all of the debts. If we assume that a large part of debt relations in a capitalist society take the from of loans to or from banks or other deposit takers, then these can be modelled by two-column relations of the sort above. Indeed this is more or less how they now exist in the relational databases of the banks.

Other trading organizations who have credit relations with a large number of customers can use similar techniques to record their debt relations with their trading partners. Since most of these trading partners will be private individuals who do not have the resources to maintain elaborate systems of account, the stored debt relations will largely be held by firms. Overall we can assume that the bulk of all the debt relations in society can be modelled by such binary (two column) relations.

Given this representation, the storage space required to record the information grows in proportion to the number of non-zero debts that actually exist, rather than in proportion to the number of potential debts, as would be the case with the full D matrix. We can express the required storage as the product of two terms, $n \cdot d$, where n is the number of people and d the average number of other agents with whom a person has debts. We would expect that as an economy grows d will

Table 12.2 A bank need only store credit information as a binary relation

Customer	Amount
1	2
3	7
5	-9

rise, but the rate of growth will be relatively slow, both with respect to time and with respect to the growth of the population.

The development of the banking system led to the growth of a specialized branch of the division of labour associated with the maintenance, storage, and updating of credit relations. These were typically recorded on paper in an indelible fashion. Such records leave an audit trail of previous balances in the ledger books. But this is not an essential feature of private credit relations. They can also be recorded in the same way as subjects' credit with the state – by the physical holding of tokens. At various times private individuals, firms and municipalities have issued coin-like tokens. Typically these would be given as change for higher denomination royal money in small purchases. A grocer might issue his own farthings as change for state pennies. Other tradesmen in the neighbourhood would accept them, accumulate them and periodically have them redeemed in royal money by the issuer (Berry, 1988).

This practice continued on a larger scale from the 18th century with the issue of paper banknotes by private banks. In return for a deposit of coin, the banks would issue paper notes, which, like tradesmen's tokens, were redeemable in royal money by anyone who presented them to the bank. The practice died out in England during the nineteenth century but Scottish and Northern Irish banks continue to issue their own private banknotes in this way. Such tokens are an abacic rather than algorithmic system of record. They record a binary relation of indebtedness between the bank and other economic agents who physically hold the notes. Changes in this relation are brought about by physically handing over banknotes to another agent – a process analogous to physically moving the beads on an abacus to change the number it records.

In English we retain the word 'banknote' to refer to paper money issued by the state bank, but nowadays such notes are better seen as an extension of the coinage system. This reflects the history of paper money. The successful issue of paper money in the West was pioneered in Britain where capitalist economy was most advanced. The Bank of England started to issue paper money in 1694 followed by the Bank of Scotland in 1695. Whereas the latter existed primarily to finance private trade the Bank of England was owned by private shareholders but its main function was to make loans to the Crown. The Crown could pay for purchases using notes that the Bank issued and would in return accept notes on the Bank issued as payment for taxes. This went alongside the process by which the Bank would issue notes to customers in return for coin deposits. Over time the Bank of England became a state-owned bank and its issue of notes became functionally indistinguishable from the issue of coin by the mint.

State paper money proper was invented much earlier in China. About one thousand years ago the Song dynasty had established an effective system of paper money.

In 1161, the Southern Song government essentially replaced its bronze coin standard with a new paper money system known as huizi. Regional huizi

Digression 12.1   Paper money in socialist economies

Our discussion has been about the institution of paper money under capitalism. Twentieth-century socialist economies also used paper money. Why did this exist and what caused it to circulate? Socialist states did not obtain their revenue from general taxation as capitalist ones did. Instead, their revenues came from the profits of state owned industry. It was the need of citizens to pay taxes that had forced Pounds, Dollars, Yen and D-Mark to circulate in the West. Since this need was absent in the USSR, why did the Rouble circulate?

The invention of money allowed states to separate the real appropriation of a surplus product from its symbolic appropriation as tax. Socialist states were the direct real appropriators of the social product, and as such had no need for money taxes. Money wages acted, instead, as a method for distributing the social product. Roubles circulated because state shops accepted them for purchase of consumer goods.

The Rouble was not a universal instrument of purchase like the Dollar. Rouble accounts did not entitle state enterprises to purchase arbitrary means of production except where these transfers had already been authorized by the Plan.

The Rouble could in principle have been replaced by notes indicating that the bearer had performed a given number of hours labour for society. That this did not occur was probably due to the continued existence of wage differentials, albeit small when compared to Western income differentials.

---

currencies also proliferated in the Southern Song, and even in petty transactions the xiaoping coin was replaced by a two-cash coin known as zheher.

(von Glahn, 2004)

In this context it is worth noting that the monetary theories of European economists like Ricardo, Marx and Menger are parochial. They take it as given that money must be made of a precious metal. In doing so they ignore the history of money in China. There money had frequently been made entirely of base metals such as bronze and iron, and, by the Song period, even this had been in large measure replaced by printed paper currency. The keys to this were:

(1)   The availability of paper (at a time when Europe was still using parchment derived from animal skin).
(2)   Knowledge of printing.
(3)   The existence of a large state with a professional salaried civil service, which enabled the government to ensure that its money circulated by virtue of accepting it for tax payments.

According to von Glahn's account, the principle that the value of money is determined by the monetary authority, irrespective of the use value of the substance employed as money, was a fundamental tenet of classical Chinese monetary analysis (von Glahn, 1996: 23–47).

This would make it seem that the predominance of metallist doctrines in Europe is a reflection of the long period of European barbarism and disunity between the fall of the Carolingian empire and the establishment of the EU. During this period states were small, and for much of the time lacked a professional salaried civil service. Their tax collecting apparatus was poor and they were not able to so effectively enforce the circulation of national coinage unless it was backed by gold that could be used in internal European trade between the petty states. This local and temporary historical phenomenon was universalized in metallist doctrines.

The first European banknotes, however, were quite different from Chinese paper money. Instead of just meeting the needs of the state they arose to meet the needs of capital. To understand this one needs to understand the signature of capital.

12.1.1   *The signature of capital*

The notion of capital as having a signature comes from Marx. He characterized the process of buying and selling commodities as having the signature $C \to M \to C$, indicating that an agent starts off with a commodity (C), sells it for money (M) and then uses the money to purchase another commodity. He then contrasted this with the signature of capital, $M \to C \to M'$, where M' represents an augmented sum of money, $M' > M$.

> The direct form of the circulation of commodities is C–M–C, the transformation of commodities into money and the re-conversion of money into commodities: selling in order to buy. But alongside this form we find another form, which is quite distinct from the first: M–C–M, the transformation of money into commodities, and the re-conversion of commodities into money: buying in order to sell. Money which describes the latter course in its movement is transformed into capital, becomes capital, and, from the point of view of its function, already is capital. ...
>
> Now it is evident that the circulatory process M–C–M would be absurd and empty if the intention were, by using this roundabout route, to exchange two equal sums of money, £100 for £100. The miser's plan would be far simpler and surer: he holds on to his £100 instead of exposing it to the dangers of circulation. ...
>
> The complete form of this process is therefore M–C–M′, where $M' = M + \Delta M$, i.e. the original sum advanced plus an increment. This increment or excess over the original value I call 'surplus-value'. The value originally

advanced, therefore, not only remains intact while in circulation, but increases its magnitude, adds to itself a surplus-value, or is valorized. And this movement converts it into capital.

(Marx, 1976: 250–2)

The merchant, having converted $M \rightarrow M'$, will want to build on his success, turning his M' back into commodities to sell again. The signature of capital thus implies a process of exponential growth

$$M \rightarrow C \rightarrow M' \rightarrow C' \rightarrow M'' \rightarrow C'' \rightarrow M'''$$

If the whole class of merchants are doing this it implies that over time there must be an exponential growth in the sum of money in their hands.

The thrust of the previous chapter was to argue that money is a technology of record, that it is essentially information about social power. As an information structure there is no inherent obstacle to its exponential growth. When a place number system is used – whether binary, decimal or the old Babylonian base 60 system – the size of the number that can be recorded grows exponentially with the number of digits. But if a token number system such as gold coin is used to encode social power, exponential growth is a problem. It implies an exponential rise in the mass of gold, an altogether more difficult matter. As shown in Table 12.3, the annual rate of gold stock growth has been around 1.5 per cent per annum for the last 100 years. The rate of growth was about half that during the nineteenth century, and was lower still prior to the discovery of the Californian fields in the 1840s. Were gold coin the only form of money in which capital could accumulate, the circuit $M \rightarrow C \rightarrow M' \rightarrow C' \rightarrow M''$ would have been limited to very low rates of return on capital. The signature of capital was incompatible with gold money. It demanded new monetary technologies, the first of which was the paper banknote. It was no harder to print a £50 banknote than a £5 banknote.

Table 12.3 Growth of the world gold stock 1840 to 2000

Period	Stock (million troy oz.)	Annual growth (per cent)
1840–1850	617.9	0.27
1851–1875	771.9	0.89
1876–1900	953.9	0.85
1901–1925	1430.9	1.64
1926–1950	2130.9	1.61
1951–1975	3115.9	1.53
1976–2000	4569.9	1.54

Not all of this stock would have been available for use as coin, decorative and other uses absorbing the rest. Calculated from data on annual production from Gold Fields Mineral Services Ltd.

12.1.2   *Cash and credit payments*

At the end of the week workers have to be paid, the firms' products have to be sold, and stocks of raw materials must be replenished. This involves a vast number of atomic transactions each of which is, taken by itself, value-conserving. In reality of course they do not all take place at the end of the week, that is just a pedagogic simplification. However, we can partition the set of atomic transactions into three groups:

(1)   Transactions between capitalists.
(2)   Payments of wages by capitalists.
(3)   Purchases of consumer goods by workers.

With regard to payments between capitalists, an Iron Master taking delivery of coal, for instance, would typically write a bill of exchange, a private certificate of debt, promising to pay within 30 or 90 days.

Payment of wages, on the other hand, would generally have to be made in cash. At times capitalists have tried to pay wages in the form of tokens which are redeemable only at company stores, but legislation by the state, eager to maintain its monopoly of coinage if not to defend the rights of workers, tended to put a stop to this. Payment in cash represents a transfer from the safes of capitalists to the pockets of their employees, with a corresponding cancellation of wage debts. At the end of the week, the wage debt has been cleared to zero, and there has been an equal and compensating movement of cash.

Workers then spend their wages on consumer goods. For the sake of simplicity we assume that there is no net saving by workers so that in the course of the week all of the money they have been paid is spent. This implies that immediately after payday the money holdings of the workers were equal to one week's wages. If wages are paid in coin this sets a lower limit to the quantity of coin required for the economy of function.

When workers spend their wages on consumer goods they transfer money only to those firms who sell consumer goods – shopkeepers, inn-keepers and so on. We can expect these firms not only to make up the money they had spent paying wages, but to retain a surplus. The final sellers of consumer goods will end up with more money than they paid out in wages. From this extra cash, they can afford to redeem the bills of exchange that they issued to their suppliers.

In the absence of bank credit, suppliers of manufactured consumer goods would be entirely dependent for their cash-flow on money arriving when the bills of exchange, in which they had been paid, were eventually redeemed by shopkeepers and merchants. The payment situation facing sellers of raw materials was even more indirect: they could not be paid unless the consumer goods manufacturers – the weavers, potters, and millers – had sufficient cash to redeem bills of exchange issued for yarn, coal, grain, etc.

The process of trade between capitalists leads to the build-up of inter-firm debt. We suggest that the total volume of inter-firm debt that could be stably supported would have been some multiple of the coinage available after allowing for that needed to pay wages. If one takes the aggregate of all firms the ideal signature of this process can be represented as:

$$M \rightarrow [C \Rightarrow (C + \Delta C)] \rightarrow M + \Delta M$$

where $[C \Rightarrow (C + \Delta C)]$ represents the production process, which generates a physical surplus of commodities after the consumption needs of the working population has been met. If there is no new issue of coin by the state then the ΔM cannot be 'real money', rather it must be in the form of bills of exchange and other inter-firm credit.

For the capitalist class considered as a whole this should not be a problem since the ΔM is secured against the accumulated commodity surplus ΔC. There is a net accumulation of value as commodities, and accounting practice allows both the debts owed to a firm and the stocks of commodities held by the firm to be included in the value of its notional capital. As the process of accumulation proceeds in this way the ratio of commercial debt to real money will rise. If the period for which commercial credit is extended remains fixed (say, at 90 days), then a growing number of debts will be falling due each day. If these must be paid off in cash then a growing number of firms will have difficulty meeting their debts.

The mechanism of commercial credit works in the circulation between capitalists but fails in the consumer goods market since wages are still paid in cash. Let us indicate a commodity movement by $\rightarrow$, a payment of money by $\Leftarrow$, and the issue of a bill of exchange by $\leftarrow$. We therefore denote a sale by bill of exchange as $\overset{\rightarrow}{\leftarrow}$ and a sale for cash as $\overset{\rightarrow}{\Leftarrow}$. For the economy as a whole we have the sequence

$$\text{factory} \; \overset{\rightarrow}{\leftarrow} \; \text{Wholesaler} \; \overset{\rightarrow}{\leftarrow} \; \text{shop} \; \overset{\rightarrow}{\Leftarrow} \; \text{worker} \; \overset{\rightarrow}{\Leftarrow} \; \text{factory}$$

The weakness is the way in which credit transactions ($\overset{\rightarrow}{\leftarrow}$) were interrupted by cash transactions ($\overset{\rightarrow}{\Leftarrow}$). This gave rise to an asymmetry in the credit/debt position of different sections of firms. The retailers, selling against cash, would have liabilities in bills of exchange that would exceed bills in their favour. For wholesalers, the credit and debit bills would be in rough balance, while for the manufacturers, bills in their favour would predominate. The ΔM of the overall accumulation process became embodied in this balance of bills of exchange in favour of manufacturers.

There's no problem if the economy is in a steady state, but there is a problem if the economy is to undergo exponential growth.

12.1.3   *How much money is needed?*

Consider the probability that an individual firm will be unable to meet its debts. Let us first normalize the assets, liabilities and cash of firms with respect to their turnover. We assume that, normalized to turnover, a firm's expected gross

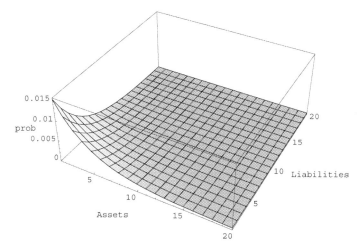

Figure 12.1 Probability surface for a form's assets and liabilities, normalized to turnover.

assets and gross liabilities in terms of commercial credit will follow a negative exponential distribution with a probability density of the form:

$$f(D) = Ke^{-\frac{D}{t}} \qquad (12.1)$$

where D is debt, t is turnover, and K is a normalization constant, chosen such that area under the curve equals 1.[1] The same distribution is assumed to apply to the debts owed to the firm. There is thus a two dimensional probability surface relating assets to liabilities as shown in Figure 12.1.

We can use this surface to represent the distribution of firms along the creditor/debtor axis, as shown in Figure 12.2.

Note that while the probability density peaks where the firm has zero gross commercial debts and zero gross assets, the probability of such a situation is actually very small. The density falls off steeply on either side. We now have to consider two questions.

(1) How much of the debt will be falling due each month?
(2) How likely is it that a firm will have insufficient cash to meet its debts at the end of the month?

Clearly, the longer the period, p, for which commercial credit is extended, the smaller will be the amount of debt falling due each month. If it were the custom

---

[1] This is of course the Gibbs–Boltzmann distribution discussed in Chapter 13. The actual distribution may be either this or a power law; the argument that follows is robust in either case.

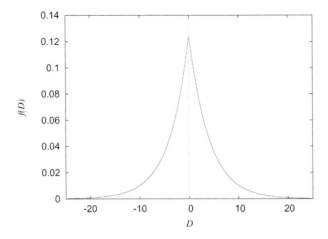

Figure 12.2 Plot of the probability distribution for firms along the gross debt/gross credit axis with respect to commercial debts outstanding. This is composed of two distinct curves, one for debts and one for assets. The plot is zero-centered due to the symmetry of the commercial debt relationship. Note that while this distribution has a sharp peak, a plot of *net* debt position would show a Gaussian distribution. If we were to plot separate curves for the retail and manufacturing sectors, we would see the former skewed to the left and the latter skewed to the right.

to extend 90-day credit then $1/3$ of the debt will fall due each month, as opposed to all of it in the case of a 30-day commercial credit rule.

In order to work out how likely it is that a firm will have too little money to pay its debts we need some account of the distribution of money balances across firms. We take this from the Social Architecture model, presented in chapter 13 (see Figure 13.10 in particular). In this model the probability of a firm's having money holding x is given by the Pareto distribution:

$$P(x) \propto \left(\frac{x}{m}\right)^{-(\alpha+1)} \tag{12.2}$$

where m is the average money holding of a firm and $\alpha \approx 1.4$. Using this we can plot the probability surface $g(D, x)$ relating debts D to cash holdings x (Figure 12.3).

A firm with net debt D is unable to meet its bills if the net repayment on this debt exceeds its current cash balance. The net repayment can be written as $R = D/p$ where p is the period on commercial loans. Thus the probability of a firm's defaulting will be given by

$$P(\text{default}) = \int_{-\infty}^{0} \int_{0}^{\infty} g(D, x) \cdot I\left(\frac{D}{p} > x\right) dx \, dD \tag{12.3}$$

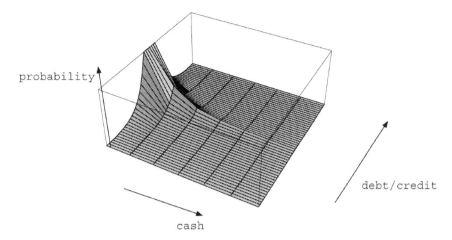

Figure 12.3 Plot of $g(D, x)$, the probability distribution for firms along the net debt/credit axis with respect to cash holdings.

where $I(\cdot)$ is the indicator function, which takes on the value 1 if the condition in parentheses holds, otherwise 0. The shape of the surface $g(D, x)$ depends on the amount of money in circulation. The greater the average amount of money held by firms, relative to turnover, the smaller the probability of default. This is illustrated in Figure 12.4.

It is important to note that what is being considered here is purely stochastic bankruptcy due to cash-flow fluctuations. It is quite aside from bankruptcies that may occur due to economic inefficiency or increases in costs. This is bankruptcy that can hit perfectly viable firms due to random fluctuations in indebtedness.

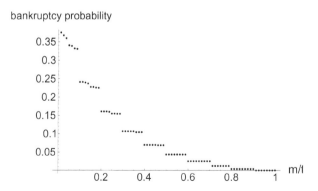

Figure 12.4 Plot of the fraction of firms going bankrupt per period against the ratio of mean money holding, m in equation 12.2, to mean turnover, t in equation 12.1. The evaluation was based on a 3-month period for commercial loans. The steps in the curve are the result of 'binning' as the functions were evaluated on a discrete grid.

12.2   The necessity of paper money

Let us summarize the argument so far. We know that the signature of capital implies an increase in the values of commodities being traded over time. We also know from the historical record of gold production that the rate of increase of gold stocks was relatively low, certainly much lower than one would expect capital stocks to grow. This implies that the ratio of cash to commodity turnover would tend to fall in an economy using gold for its coinage. In consequence, an increasing fraction of capitals would have insufficient cash holdings to meet the liabilities falling due each month, and would therefore become bankrupt.

This mechanism provided a basic engine of commercial crises under the gold standard and, in the absence of other innovations to replace gold money, would have limited the rate of growth of capital to the rate of growth of the gold stock. Note that this argument applies to the proportionate growth, not the absolute growth, of the gold and capital stocks. From Table 12.3 we know that the world gold stock rose by about 154 million oz in the 25 years from 1851 to 1875. At that time the price of gold in terms of UK currency was £2.87 per oz, being determined by the weight of metal in a gold sovereign coin. The gold mined during that period was thus worth £441 million, an annual increase of about £17 million. Did this mean that the total world capital accumulation in those years could only have been £17 million per annum?

No. It means that the annual growth in monthly turnover that could be supported by a gold currency would have been limited to around £($p \times 17$) million, where p was a constant determined by the period of commercial loans.[2] We would expect from the labour theory of value that the aggregate value of turnover would increase along with the population producing commodities. As more people became engaged in commodity production – due to both increase in population and the demise of the 'natural' peasant economy in favour of production for the market – there would have been a proportionate rise in the turnover of commodities on the capitalist world market. While the absolute increase in turnover supported by gold would be some multiple of the actual gold production, the *percentage* increase in turnover would still have been limited by the low percentage increase in gold stocks. It would have been, that is, had the banking system not been able to create alternative means by which commercial debts were paid.

We have already shown how the process of banks accepting deposits in coin and making loans in coin will create net credit, hence increasing the Manhattan distance between agents. The issue of banknotes accelerates this process enormously. Suppose Mr Lang made a deposit of £100 in coin with the Bank of Scotland in 1696. If the bank were then to make a loan of £90 in coin to Mr Strang, there would be a creation of net credit as we showed above. But what the bank actually did was much more dramatic. It used the £100 as a reserve against which it made loans of several hundred pounds in its own banknotes. These

---

[2] The stock of capital taking the form of plant and machinery could have grown more rapidly than this, depending, among other things, on the depreciation period of capital equipment.

notes were redeemable on demand against royal coin, but because of the greater convenience of paper money the bank could count on only a small fraction of the notes actually being redeemed on any banking day. This was termed fractional reserve lending.

Deposits and withdrawals by customers are the result of multiple independent circumstances. As such they have a noisy character analogous to the 'shot noise' discussed in section 3.3.3. Recall that shot noise (due to the discrete photon nature of light) set a limit to the information-capture accuracy of any camera or photo-sensor. Recall too that shot noise was proportional to the square root of the mean number of photons arriving at each sensor during the exposure period of the camera. As a result shot noise falls as a proportion of the total signal the more photons we can capture. A similar principle applies to banking. The more customers that a bank has, the smaller will be the proportionate variation in the withdrawals from day to day.

Look at Figure 12.5. The horizontal axis shows the number of customers and the vertical axis the highest proportion of the bank's deposits withdrawn in any week over a 20-year period. As the number of customers rises, the variation in the amount withdrawn in any week falls, and so too does the maximum withdrawal that can be expected. A very small bank would have to keep all its deposits in the safe as an insurance against having to pay them out, but a bank with 20,000 customers might never (under normal conditions) see more than 3.4 per cent of its cash deposits withdrawn in any week. A bank with that number of customers could safely issue as loans 20 times as much in paper banknotes as the coin that it held in its vaults, safe in the knowledge that the probability of it ever having to pay out that much in one day was vanishingly small.

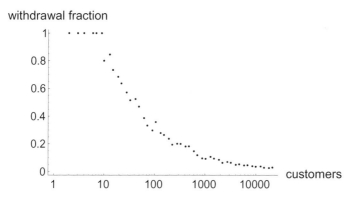

Figure 12.5 Plot of the largest fraction of a bank's deposits withdrawn in a single day over a 20 year period as the number of customers rises. The plot comes from a simulation in which it was assumed that a customer might withdraw any sum up to their maximum deposit, and that customers were as likely to make deposits as withdrawals. The slightly irregular nature of the trace reflects the underlying stochastic properties of such a simulation.

This creation of new paper money by the banks was the secret behind the signature of capital, $M \rightarrow C \rightarrow M' \rightarrow C' \rightarrow M''$. Unlike the creation of token money by the state, or the issue of gold coin, there was no unproductive withdrawal of value in the form of seigniorage or mining costs. Loans in bank money were made to capitalists (group A) who were expanding their business. With these loans group A either directly purchased, or through wage payments financed the sale of, the surplus produced in the workshops of other established capitalists (group B). The surplus product sold by group B was thus on the one hand converted into money (phase $C \rightarrow M + \Delta M$), and at the same time became new capital for group A (phase $\Delta M \rightarrow \Delta C$). This money creation was distinct in its effects from the Chinese state's creation of paper money. In the latter case the money first appears as a purchase of commodities by the state. While this would still create money profits for the merchants who sold to the state, the surplus so purchased was consumed by the state rather than becoming capital.

We are here considering bank money in its initial historical form, prior to the widespread use of chequeing accounts or even more modern forms like debit cards. These modern forms have their own technical preconditions, which we shall discuss later, but the *Ur*-form allows us to understand much of what followed.

The first thing to notice is that bank money is derivative from state money. Bank notes or chequeing accounts are denominated in state money, and they ultimately gain currency through being redeemable in state money. The banks lack an independent coercive power analogous to the state's power to tax. The second thing to notice is the crucial importance of size. Unless a bank reaches a certain threshold number of customers it will be unable to operate a system of fractional reserve lending. In order to pass this threshold the Bank of England, the Bank of France and the Bank of Scotland were initially given Royal monopolies.

Figure 12.5 makes it clear that a big bank had much more money-issuing ability than a small one. The larger the number of customers a bank had, the smaller the proportionate variation in its weekly withdrawals, and hence the smaller the proportionate reserve it was forced to maintain. This would be reflected in larger banks' being more profitable, since a higher proportion of their assets would be in the form of loans on which they earned interest, as opposed to than cash which earned them nothing.

The curve in Figure 12.5 comes from a simulation in which the probability of each customer making a deposit or withdrawal is independent: customers are assumed not to 'collude' in making withdrawals. This is normally the case but if the bank's credit is impugned then customers can cease to act independently. A panic can set in, leading to a run on the bank. Because a small bank faced greater proportionate variations in its weekly withdrawals, its credit would be less secure than that of larger banks, and bank failures would be more frequent among small banks.

The combined effects of these two factors led to a process of gradual centralization of banks, with the larger and more profitable ones taking over the smaller.

A crucial factor in creating a large customer base was the creation of a branch network. Initially banks would have a single office in the capital city; only later did they develop a branch network. So long as the private issue of banknotes was their main form of money creation, notes issued in the capital could circulate among merchants in outlying towns, and distance would slow down demand for these notes to be redeemed. Suppose the Bank of Prudence had only one branch in the capital, as had the Bank of Temperance. Each issued its own banknotes, which were redeemed only when they were presented at the bank's head office. These notes would circulate mainly in the capital, but some would go the rounds in the main provincial towns. If the Bank of Prudence opened branches in Gloucester, Chester, Bolton, Halifax, etc., it gained several advantages:

- By opening a multitude of branches it obtained more depositors and thus increased its loanable capital stock.
- The increase in the number of customers reduced the variation in its weekly withdrawals and allowed it to operate with smaller reserves.
- Some of its depositors would have made their deposits, not in cash, but with the notes of its rival the Bank of Temperance. The Bank of Prudence would return these to the head office of the Temperance to be redeemed. This would increase the rate at which Bank of Temperance notes were cashed, forcing it to hold higher reserves.

There were thus strong competitive pressures forcing the establishment of regional, provincial or national networks of bank branches.

We will now go on to look at two topics:

(1) The way in which the technology of information processing has contributed to the spread of bank money.
(2) How probabilistic arguments can be used to analyse the formation of a rate of interest.

12.3 Banking technology

The existence of a network of branches, when combined with the fast transport provided by the new railways, allowed the next phase in the evolution of bank money, namely cheques.

Payment by drafts on Merchant Banks was a much older practice, dating back to the middle ages. International merchant companies – primarily Italian – would arrange payments in, say, Florence against a bill issued, for example, by their Paris office. This payment system grew out of the practice of issuing commercial bills of exchange, and was used primarily to finance international trade. The nineteenth century establishment of dense branch bank networks allowed chequeing transactions to penetrate into general domestic commerce between capitalists.[3] The development of a system for transferring bank deposits via cheque marks a general social transition between abacic and algorithmic calculation. With banknotes, the social wealth relation subsisted in the physical placement of notes: whose pocket were they in? With cheque accounts it subsists in the ledgers of the banks. The establishment of such accounts meant that the banks had to build up an information processing machine – in the first instance a machine of flesh, brain, paper and ink. The routine processing of this information became a major branch of the division of labour and generated a whole social stratum of bank clerks devoted to its operation.

The basic operations being performed by this social computer were payments between accounts. Cash payment had been a simple movement of coin. With cheques it looks almost as simple, you hand a cheque to the shop to make your payment. But this physical handover only acquires meaning when supported by an interpretation mechanism provided by the banking system. A cheque is a *record volant*, a Cartesian of the form (bank $\otimes$ payee $\otimes$ sum $\otimes$ payer) written out in longhand as:

National Commercial Bank

Pay *William Sydney* the sum of £*10*

                                                    James Ross

---

A cheque $(x \otimes a \otimes n \otimes b)$ is in effect a procedure call on the banking system to perform the action

---

Atomic
procedure   *cash* $((x \otimes a \otimes n \otimes b))$

---

if	Account$[b] > n$	**then**	
	Account$[a]$	$\leftarrow$	Account$[a] + n$
	Account$[b]$	$\leftarrow$	Account$[b] - n$

By *atomic* we mean that the operation is all or nothing. It is impermissible for one account to be updated but not the other. Even with modern computer technology, performing such atomic updates is not trivial. One has to write code to 'lock out' any other programs which might be making changes to accounts while the update occurs. The problem is complicated by the fact that more than one bank is involved (which is glossed over in the algorithm above). The actual process of cashing a cheque involves handing it into your own bank. Let's say William Sydney banks with the British Linen Bank; then he'd hand the cheque in

---

[3] Bank accounts did not spread to the mass of the working class population until the late twentieth century.

to his branch of that bank. But it is drawn on the National Commercial Bank. We must thus fill in more detail in the algorithm:

Atomic	
procedure	cash $(y, (x \otimes a \otimes n \otimes b))$

---

if	x.Account[b] > n	**then**	
	y.Account[a]	$\leftarrow$	y.Account[a] +n
	x.Account[b]	$\leftarrow$	x.Account[b] −n

We see that a's account at bank y is credited and b's account at bank x is debited. Nowadays these accounts would be held on different computers, and the update involves what is termed a distributed atomic transaction. It took a considerable period of development before such transactions could be performed reliably using electronic computers (Bernstein *et al.*, 1980; Traiger *et al.*, 1982).

Consider how this worked in the days of ink and paper, when the 'computers' that held the accounts were systems of clerks and ledgers. The cheque we were looking at instructed the National Commercial to pay money to Mr Sydney. If Sydney went to the offices of the National Commercial they could just hand over cash and debit Mr Ross's account. But the National Commercial could not directly modify Sydney's account since that was recorded in the ledgers of the British Linen. (Sydney could cash the cheque at the National Commercial then carry the cash round to his own bank and pay it in, but then what's the point of the cheque?)

If Sydney handed the cheque into his branch of the British Linen bank, they could easily credit his account, but would want to know that Ross had the funds to meet it. If Ross's account were at the same bank, the updating clerk could turn to Ross's page and verify that he was sufficiently in credit. But his record is held by another company, so the procedure was to update update Sydney's record provisionally, and send the cheque to the National Commercial to *clear*. The provisional update would be cancelled were the National Commercial to return the cheque as invalid.

Clearing referred to the process by which, at a central place, the different banks exchanged the cheques drawn against them and computed the net inter-bank monetary transfers that resulted. Babbage, ever a keen observer of the technical details of economic interchange, described the London Clearing House.

In a large room in Lombard Street, about thirty clerks from the several London bankers take their stations, in alphabetical order, at desks placed round the room; each having a small open box by his side, and the name of the firm to which he belongs in large characters on the wall above his head. From time to time other clerks from every house enter the room, and, passing along, drop into the box the checks due by that firm to the house from which this distributor is sent. The clerk at the table enters the amount of the several checks in a book previously prepared, under the name of the bank to which they are respectively due.

Four o'clock in the afternoon is the latest hour to which the boxes are open to receive checks; and at a few minutes before that time, some signs of increased activity begin to appear in this previously quiet and business-like scene. Numerous clerks then arrive, anxious to distribute, up to the latest possible moment, the checks which have been paid into the houses of their employers.

(Babbage, 1832: Sec. II, ch. 13)

Note the incentives here: a banker who's in possession of cheques payable to his own customers and drawn on other banks has an interest in clearing those cheques as fast as possible. The clearing will augment his reserves, but he probably won't credit his customers' accounts right away. Thus he benefits from a 'float', a little wedge on which he can make some interest. Anyway, resuming Babbage's account:

At four o'clock all the boxes are removed, and each clerk adds up the amount of the checks put into his box and payable by his own to other houses. He also receives another book from his own house, containing the amounts of the checks which their distributing clerk has put into the box of every other banker. Having compared these, he writes out the balances due to or from his own house, opposite the name of each of the other banks; and having verified this statement by a comparison with the similar list made by the clerks of those houses, he sends to his own bank the general balance resulting from this sheet, the amount of which, if it is due from that to other houses, is sent back in bank-notes.

At five o'clock the Inspector takes his seat; when each clerk, who has upon the result of all the transactions a balance to pay to various other houses, pays it to the inspector, who gives a ticket for the amount. The clerks of those houses to whom money is due, then receive the several sums from the inspector, who takes from them a ticket for the amount. Thus the whole of these payments are made by a double system of balance, a very small amount of bank-notes passing from hand to hand, and scarcely any coin.

(Babbage, 1832: Sec. II, ch. 13)

Technology changed. The mid-nineteenth century brought the electronic transfer of funds by telegraph, but behind this modernity stood the armies of clerks calculating and updating records by hand. The Morse impulses still had to be translated into paper and ink. Up till the 1960s banks still closed their doors at three to allow the manual tallying up of accounts.

Modern electronic bank money required two critical inventions: the programmable electronic computer described in section 5.2 and, less obviously, the random access disk drive.

The first electronic computers used a bewildering variety of memory devices. Turing (1937) had famously proposed his tape marked with symbols, a sort of halfway house between the punched paper tape that was used by contemporary telex machines and the squared paper used by mathematicians or school children. When he came to collaborate on the Colossus (Hodges, 1983), it was paper tape that he used as the storage medium. Paper tape was relatively cheap, and it could hold data in a persistent fashion; it didn't need constant energy input to remember things. But tape, whether magnetic or paper, is a *sequential* store. In order to read the 100th character on the tape one must first read the other 99. The first generation of computers was constrained to the use of sequential stores. As one alternative to paper, it was found that a television tube could be used as a sequential memory: charge deposited by the cathode ray on the screen during one scan persisted long enough to be detected on the next scan (Lavington, 1978, 1980). Acoustic delay lines were another early alternative, but both of these were volatile stores. The information had to be constantly refreshed if it was to be remembered. Such stores are obviously unsuitable for bank records.

During the 1920s and '30s there had been a fairly extensive development of business automation based on punched cards. These had been invented to hold census data, with a record card being punched for each person recorded in the census. Decks of cards could then be fed through sorting machines that would select cards if they bore a particular pattern of holes. Tabulating machines could then calculate and print totals from the sorted cards. This technology had diffused from census-taking to stock-control applications. For instance, shoes were distributed to shops with a punched card in each shoe-box. When the shoes were sold, the shop retained the the card and returned it at the end of the day to the supplier's warehouse. By feeding the returned cards through sorters and tabulators the warehouse could ensure that appropriate replacement shoes were dispatched the next day, and that the total bill for each shop was computed.

During the 1950s and '60s companies such as IBM and ICL that had originally been active in the manufacture of punched card machines moved into the computer market, extending the power of the tabulators with simple stored program computers. But these card and tape technologies were still not well adapted to accounting operations. To understand why, let us first look at how a Turing machine could have been used to update bank accounts.

Turing's original description of his machine allowed for only a single memory tape, but theorists have subsequently proposed Turing machines with two or more tapes. We'll assume that the National Commercial Bank has a three-tape machine. In this scenario the bank keeps its accounts on tapes and each evening, when the day's transactions are over, it feeds in yesterday's tape to tape head 1 and places a blank tape on head 2. On head 3 it places a tape onto which all pay-in slips and outgoing cheques have been transcribed. The idea is that at the end of its work, the Turing machine will have produced on tape 2 an updated ledger in which all the accounts originally listed on tape 1 have been debited or credited by appropriate cheques found on tape 3. We assume that both the transcribed cheques and the

---

Digression 12.2   A Turing machine program to update bank ledgers

---

(1)   Output a start-of-record character to tape 2, and read in the start-of-record characters from tapes 1 and 3. If instead of a start-of-record character on tape 1 we got an end-of-file character, stop. If instead of a start-of-record on tape 3 there is an end-of-file character, goto state 8.

(2)   Copy the entire record from tape 1 to tape 2, then rewind tape 2 to the start of the record.

(3)   Read in the first digit from tapes 3 and 2. If they match goto state 4 otherwise goto state 7.

(4)   Repeat step 3 another 5 times and then go to state 5.

(5)   We have now ascertained that the cheque is to debit the current account and we have written a copy of the account number to tape 2. Read in the amount from the cheque on tape 3 and the current balance from tape 2 and write the result of debiting the account to tape 2. Then go to state 6.

(6)   Rewind tape 2 to the first digit of the current account number and goto state 1. We are now ready to process the next cheque on tape 3.

(7)   (a) Rewind tape 2 back to the character immediately after the *previous* start-of-record marker.

    (b) Skip tape 3 forward to the character after the *next* start-of-record.

    (c) Goto state 3.

(8)   We get here if we have scanned the whole of tape 3 for a cheque affecting the current account on tape 1.

    (a) Rewind tape 3 to the start.

    (b) Skip forward to the next record on tape 1.

    (c) Move tape 2 forward till we come to a blank space.

    (d) Goto state 1.

---

account records start with a 6 digit account code. The program for the machine is outlined in Digression 12.2.

As the digression shows, a Turing machine would be quite capable of doing banking transactions, but it would be very slow. For each account on tape 1 it has to read the whole of tape 3, searching for cheques that relate to that account. Its running time will be proportional to NC where N is the number of accounts and C the number of cheques.

The computers of the early 1960s were only slightly more powerful than this. In addition to multiple tapes, they had a small number of words of auxiliary working store into which the records of a few accounts could have been read. Suppose a machine had sufficient working store to handle 100 account records. It could read in 100 accounts from tape 1 in a block and then search the whole of tape 3 for updates to these accounts before writing the updated block of accounts to tape 2. Such a machine would have a running time proportional to $NC/100$, obviously much faster than a pure Turing machine with no auxiliary working store. Despite the acceleration, the time-order of the process, $O(NC)$, is still the same. This formula, pronounced 'order NC', means that the running time is proportional to the product of the number of cheques and the number of accounts. Suppose that in the early 1960s a small US bank had an IBM 1400, which could read 1,000 records a second from its tapes. The following table shows the time it would have taken to process different numbers of accounts and cheques.

Accounts	Cheques	Seconds	hr:min:sec
10,000	1,000	1,000	00:16:40
50,000	5,000	25,000	06:56:40
100,000	10,000	100,000	17:46:40

The technical change which made electronic banking possible came when IBM introduced the world's first magnetic hard disk for data storage. RAMAC (or Random Access Method of Accounting and Control) offered unprecedented performance by permitting random access to any of the million characters distributed over both sides of 50 two-foot-diameter disks. Produced in San Jose, California, IBM's first hard disk stored about 2,000 bits of data per square inch and had a purchase price of about $10,000 per megabyte.[4] As the original IBM sales literature stated:

> Information is stored magnetically on a stack of 50 disks which rotate continuously at 1,200 RPM. Each metal disk is two feet in diameter and is coated on each side with a magnetic material. The face of a standard disk contains 100 tracks, in each of which 600 digits may be stored. In double capacity disk files there are 200 information tracks on each disk face. Thus, standard memory file capacity is six million digits and the double capacity Model 2 IBM 355 disk storage unit can store 12 million digits. Up to four random access memory units may be used in a RAMAC 650 system.

> In each memory file there are three electronically-controlled access arms containing magnetic heads. They read and write the information contained on the rotating disks. They act independently of each other, but each arm can be directed to any track in the file. As a result, there can be simultaneous seeking of three different records and information constantly is available for processing.

The development of random access disks gave rise to the relational databases which provide the material embodiment of modern money. Once monetary relations were encoded in relational databases, it was a relatively simple step to develop Switch Cards and electronic payments.

---

[4] Today an 80 gigabyte hard drive can be bought for about $40, or about one-twentieth of a cent per megabyte of storage.

Card payment systems originated with Diner's Club and American Express, which were closed loop payment systems. A single firm acted to pay the merchants, bill customers and manage accounts. Initially the process was paper-based, with the cards being used to make records on carbon paper stubs. With Visa cards, multiple banks became involved as franchisers. The Visa payment system was thus open-loop, in that different firms were responsible for crediting merchants and billing customers – the process being an extension of the prior cheque clearing mechanisms. There was still a manual processing phase of data entry from the sales stubs, but the data was processed electronically from that point on. Switch or electronic payment cards allow automation of the entire process.

The process of going from coin, to banknotes, to Switch cards and relational databases is one of increasing abstraction. With each step, the symbolic or formal character of money becomes more apparent. With coin, it still appears as if the metallic substance is crucial. The illusion persists at one remove with banknotes, which for years appeared to be promises to pay coin.[5] They thus could be thought of as symbols for which the real referent was coin. With relational databases the illusions are stripped off, and the logical essentials of money as a technology of record are revealed.

12.4   The interest rate

We will now discuss a hypothesis for the formation of the rate of interest which we will later use when looking at the determinants of investment. Our hypothesis uses probabilistic arguments to set a floor to interest rates.

(1)   The cost to a bank of making a loan is related to the likelihood that the reserves left after the loan will be too small to cover fluctuating withdrawals. If failure occurs the bank may lose its capital.

(2)   From a 'micro' point of view the cost is also determined by the amount of interest that a bank has to pay on the capital that it borrows, but that is a recursive definition of interest.

(3)   The fixed point is provided by (1) since this does not presuppose the existence of the rate of interest which it seeks to explain.

Consider the random variable W which is the maximal excursion of reserves from their mean position during a year, due to deposits and withdrawals by customers. Figure 12.6 illustrates this. We may normalize the distribution so that one standard deviation of W is 1,000,000, as might be the case with a small bank of the nineteenth century. With reserves at 3 standard deviations of W, we know from the tabulation of the normal distribution that the probability of bank failure in any given year would be about 0.001. If reserves fell to 2,000,000 or 2 standard

---

[5]   British bank notes still bear the inscription, 'I promise to pay the bearer on demand...' – but nobody takes that as meaningful any more. US notes state the sober truth: 'This note is legal tender for all debts, public and private.'

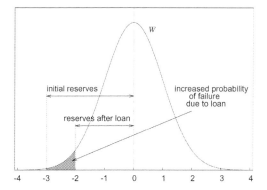

Figure 12.6 The distribution, W, which represents the greatest excursion from a bank's mean reserve position. The scale is both in standard deviations and in millions. If the bank initially has reserves of 3 million then a loan of 1 million will increase the probability that withdrawals exceed reserves.

deviations then the probability of failure would rise to about 0.02. Suppose the banker had a capital of 5,000,000, which he would lose if the bank failed. In that case if he started with reserves of 3 million, making a loan of 1 million would have an expected cost of $(0.02 - 0.001) \times 5,000,000$ or 95,000. This expected cost sets a lower limit on the interest it would be rational for the banker to charge for the loan, namely 9.5 per cent in this example. For safety's sake he would be likely to charge more than this.

The lower rational limit to the interest charged would vary with

(1) The banker's capital: the more of his own capital is invested in the bank the more he stands to lose on failure.
(2) The size of the loan, since this determines the reserve position after making the loan.
(3) The size of the bank reserves measured in standard deviations of W (σ_W). The larger the reserves relative to W the lower the cost of making the loan.

Since the interest charged will be proportional to the loan, for small loans it follows that the rational floor to the rate of interest should be proportional to the slope of the normal curve at its intersection with the current level of reserves, measured in terms of σ_W.

We cannot go from this to deducing what the actual rate of interest would be as a function of the ratio of reserves to deposits. For a start, the preceding argument has been about a rational floor to the rate of interest on the assumption that the banker is lending his own cash. If the marginal loan is made out of money for which the banker is himself having to pay interest, the interest that the banker himself pays would have to be added to this floor for him not to expect a loss.

A further factor is that the expected loss, if the marginal loan turns out to be the last straw that breaks the bank at some future date, is proportional to the banker's own capital. The ratio of the banker's capital to the deposits he has accepted will, over the population of banks, be another random variable.

Beyond this we have to add the effects of ignorance. It is a conceit of economic theory to assume perfect knowledge (or knowledge of probability distributions in the present case). Nineteenth-century bankers were probably ignorant of the work of Gauss on the normal distribution, and even had they understood it they may not have had good enough records to accurately measure σ_W. We can expect that the actual rate of interest charged by banks will be randomly distributed with a mean somewhat above the rational floor, but with some bankers lending below their rational floor. Those that do lend below run the risk of failure, but this is a risk rather than a certainty. We might expect, however, that even if the bankers were not aware of a precise relationship between reserves and failure probability, trade folklore would convey to them the need to get anxious as the ratio of reserves to deposits fell. This anxiety would be reflected in higher interest rates, and there would thus still be an inverse relationship between the reserve to deposit ratio and the interest rate.

If reserves are exogenously determined, the interest rate will then vary as a result of the endogenous creation of bank money – either negotiable deposits, or issues of bearer notes in return for deposits. For the economy as a whole we would expect the interest rate to be a non-linear increasing function of the ratio of deposits to bank reserves.

12.5   Dominance of the financial sector

Why does the financial sector come to be so dominant in mature capitalist economies like Britain? What causes it to replace manufacturing as the bedrock of the economy? It is often supposed that the role of the financial sector is to fund investment. Savings are meant to be channelled through the banks, investment trusts and the stock market into firms that want to carry out investment in new capital stock. This process obviously does occur, but it is by no means obvious why, in the face of continuing improvements in information processing technology, the sector which carries out this channeling of funds should come to absorb a larger and larger portion of national resources, and appear to contribute an increasing share of national income.

Channelling funds is manipulation of information. The 'funds' are records kept by the banking system and their channelling is a sequence of transfers between records. The records have long ago moved from paper to computer databases. The power of computers has improved by leaps and bounds. One would have thought that the labour required to manage this system would have declined. The mechanization of agriculture eliminated the peasantry, but computers have not laid waste to the City of London. Why? The key to this paradox is to realize that despite the modern jargon of a financial services 'industry' that offers financial 'products' to customers, the financial sector is not a productive industry in the

Figure 12.7 Flows into and out of the financial sector.

normal sense. Its structural position in capitalistic information flows ensures its continued command over resources despite changes in technology that would decimate any other industry.

Consider Figure 12.7, which shows in summary form the flows of funds into and out of the financial sector. Savings by individual capitalists, by firms, and also from the pension schemes of employees, enter the system. Funding flows out to firms carrying out capital investment, and also to the state to fund the public debt. However money also flows out as costs, in other words the income of the financial sector itself. This comprises wages of its employees, the bonuses it pays, the distributed dividends of financial companies, and the costs of buildings and equipment that the sector uses. We denote savings by S, bonuses and costs by B and funding of investment by I. The residual, δ, is made up by the change in the money balances of the financial sector itself: $\delta = S - B - I$. We wish to explain why B tends to rise as a share of national income over time.

We have argued (section 14.3.4) that the real rate of return on capital tends to decline over the course of capitalist development. If the rate of interest does not fall at a corresponding rate then the level of voluntary borrowing and stock-issues by firms will decline, since a diminishing portion of firms will be making enough profits to cover the rate of interest. However the level of savings will not necessarily decline at a corresponding rate.

The level of saving via employees' pension schemes changes relatively slowly (although recently British firms have been trying to reduce such schemes). We showed in chapter 13 that the distribution of income in capitalist societies will be highly uneven: a large proportion of income goes to a small part of the population. People with very high incomes tend to save a good deal, and a decline in the rate of profit on capital will not alter this. It just means that the book value of the assets of those on very high incomes rises. So savings going into the financial system will not decline. The slack can be taken up in three ways.

(1)   A build up in the reserves of the financial sector, δ in our equation.
(2)   An increase in borrowing by the state.
(3)   A rise in the income/costs of the financial sector itself.

We can view these as the short-, medium- and long-term consequences respectively. The immediate consequence of a fall in I relative to S will be that the reserves of financial institutions rise. If a bank gets more deposits than it makes loans, then its cash reserves rise. But financial institutions will have a target for the proportion of their assets that they wish to keep as cash. This target will vary over time and in response to conditions on the stock market, but their immediate response to a rise will be to attempt to shift cash into other assets.

A fall in investment by non-financial companies does often lead to a rise in state borrowing. During recessions the state takes in less tax while expenditure on social security climbs; more state bonds become available as assets, thus allowing the financial sector to limit the growth of its cash balances. But in the longer term there are political pressures to limit government budget deficits. The position of the dollar as an international reserve currency has allowed the US government great leeway in the accumulation of public debt but the EU Stability Pact imposes much more stringent limits on European states.

Although over the longer term the growth of public debt has been constrained, financial institutions can still balance their portfolios by bidding up the prices of assets. Share prices and land prices will rise until the financial sector reaches its desired cash reserve ratio. Although real capital investment may be sluggish, this is hidden from savers. They see the book price of their holdings in investment trusts, etc., rise.

There remains a conceptual problem here. A rise in the aggregate book price of shareholdings is a *stock* phenomenon (measured in £ billion), but the variables I and S denotes *flows* (£ per year). One cannot redress an imbalance between the flows of savings and investment by a change in stock prices, there has to be a corresponding outflow of funds. Closure is provided by the charging practices of the investment funds. These typically charge a management fee assessed as a fixed proportion of the assets they manage, for example 0.5 per cent per year. As average asset prices rise so too do management fees. The income of the financial sector then rises to ensure that $B \approx S - I$. There is an inbuilt tendency for the 'costs' of the financial sector to absorb uninvested surplus value.

In a young capitalist economy like contemporary China the financial sector really does transfer funds into productive capital investment. It allows hundreds of millions of workers to be employed in the construction of capital assets, while recording the claims on those assets held by individual capitalists. In an old capitalist country like Britain, the financial sector increasingly abandons its role of 'intermediation' and becomes a consumer of the surplus product. The vast bureaucracy of finance administers ever more distant claims on real assets, and as the share of the population constructing these real assets fell, the costs of administration rose. From one generation to the next, millions of people shifted from making real capital goods to administering claims. While the steelworks of Motherwell and Redcar yielded to the wrecker's crane, the glass towers of Canary Wharf rose. This is the reality behind our famous shift from a productive to a service economy.

Burgeoning bonuses made City financial analysts the second highest paid group of employees, after CEOs. Their *average* salaries in 2005 were £80,000 a year. Such largesse generated in its wake new servant classes – nannies, cleaners, restaurant workers. Openings grew for every trade that caters to luxury: lifestyle consultants, designers, home decorators, etc. House prices escalate. Television became obsessed with house makeover shows and guides to property speculation.

This vast cost was unproductive. Although it grew at the very point when the original social function of the financial sector atrophied, this was not obvious. Bonuses were a form of self-affirmation; they seemed a testament to productivity. In reality they were an inadvertent side effect of economic conditions way beyond the control of their recipients.

Part III
Class distribution of income

13 A probabilistic model of the social relations of capitalism

13.1 Introduction

The dominant social relation of production within capitalism is that between capitalists and workers. A small class of capitalists employ a large class of workers organized within firms of various sizes that produce goods and services for sale in the marketplace. Under normal circumstances capitalist owners of firms collect revenue and workers receive a share of the revenue in the form of wages.

Over the last hundred years or more the number and type of material objects and services processed by capitalist economies have significantly changed, but the social relations of production have not. Marx (1976) proposed the distinction between the forces of production and the social relations of production to convey this idea. The existence of a social relationship between a class of capitalists and a class of workers mediated by wages and profits is an invariant feature of capitalism, whereas the types of objects and activities subsumed under this social relationship is not.

The social relations of production constitute an abstract, but nevertheless real, enduring social architecture that constrains and enables the space of possible economic interactions. These social constraints are distinct from any natural or technical constraints, such as those due to scarcities or current production techniques. Many economic models describe relations of utility between economic actors and scarce commodity types (i.e., actor to object relations studied under the rubric of neoclassical economics), or theorize relations of technical dependence between material inputs and outputs. But here we want to do something different and entirely abstract from these relations. Instead we'll examine relations of social dependence mediated by economic value. The basic parts of the economic model developed in this chapter are therefore quite simple, consisting solely of economic actors and money. The aim is to concentrate as far as possible on the economic consequences of the social relations of production alone, that is on the enduring social architecture, rather than particular and perhaps transitory economic mechanisms, such as particular markets, commodity types and industries. As the worker–capitalist social relation is dominant in developed capitalism the model abstracts from land, rent, states and banking.

In what follows we describe a dynamic, computational model of the social architecture of capitalism. It uses a small set of assumptions about capitalist property relations, but, when we simulate it on a computer, we find that it replicates some of the most important empirical features of modern capitalism. The computer serves as a logical test-bed, and simulation allows us to explore the complex consequences of our simple assumptions. It allows us to say if important large scale features of a capitalist economy follow necessarily from its most basic social relationships.

The features of capitalism that we want to recreate are:

(1)   The structural division of society into a small employing class and a large employed class (see section 13.3.1).
(2)   The class distribution of income both between the employing and employed class (see section 13.3.2), and also the distribution of individual incomes.
(3)   The distribution of sizes of capitals/firms with a small number of large firms and a large number of small firms (see section 13.3.4).
(4)   The way in which the growth rates of firms cluster around the mean growth rate (see section 13.3.5).
(5)   The rate at which firms die or go bankrupt (see section 13.3.6).
(6)   The distribution of GDP growth rates and recessions (see section 13.3.7 and 13.3.8).

For each of these criteria we will examine the predicted statistical structures derived from the computational model and compare these to what is known about the statistical properties of the corresponding real-world data. Our aim is to see if a formal model of the social relations of capitalism can predict what we know about the statistical properties of capitalist economies. This way we'll begin to understand what features of capitalism are necessary consequences of the way economic activity is socially organized. For instance, we will see that extreme income inequality is a necessary feature of capitalist social relations. This does not mean that we should accept this as a natural feature of economic life. There can be many kinds of political response to this scientific fact: accept the necessity of extreme income inequality (pro-capitalist), try to alleviate it within the current social relations (reformist), or accept the necessity of changing the social relations that give rise to it (anti-capitalist). But whatever the favoured political response the economic model we develop in this chapter indicates there are powerful and enduring market forces that continually generate income inequality, whatever the subjective intentions of politicians.

13.2   A dynamic model of the social relations of production

The elements of the model are a set of N economic actors each of whom has a sum of cash at their disposal. This sum may fall to zero, but in the model we assume that nobody actually gets into debt. We do not concern ourselves with the process by which the state issues money therefore the total money in the economy is a constant. We assume all transactions are in cash, there are no cheques, credit cards, etc in use. Each actor is either an employee, an employer or is unemployed. So the model consists merely of a set of people, each of whom has a sum of money. The simulation keeps track of who their employer is, if any.

All the actors in the economy are naturally partitioned into three mutually exclusive classes: an employing or capitalist class, if they employ one or more other actors, an employee or working class, if they have an employer, and an unemployed class, if they are neither an employee or employer. We assume an actor cannot belong to more than one class, but an actor may change classes over time.

The structure of a firm is simply an employer and their employees. Firm ownership is limited to a single capitalist employer: there are no stocks or joint ownership.

Although the total number of actors is fixed this can be interpreted as a stable workforce in which individuals enter and exit the workforce at the same rate. An actor, therefore, represents an abstract role in the economy, rather than a specific individual. At each instant of simulated time t the model has a state S_t. The evolution through time of this state, $S_t \rightarrow S_{t+1}$, is determined by a set of predominantly random transition rules, which are applied at each time step. Processes that involve subjective indeterminacy (e.g., deciding to act in a given period) or elements of chance (e.g., finding a buyer in the marketplace) are modelled by selection from a bounded set according to a given probability distribution. Often the chosen distribution is uniform in accordance with Bernoulli's Principle of Insufficient Reason, which states that in the absence of knowledge to the contrary assume all outcomes are equally likely.[1]

The model considers a pure capitalist economy in isolation from non-capitalist sectors. The assumption of a finite set of actors differs from Marx's assumption of the existence of a latent reserve army of potential workers in the non-capitalist sector (e.g., domestic and subsistence agricultural workers) that may enter the capitalist sector and regulate the wage at a conventional level (Foley and Michl, 1999).

Next we shall describe the rules that control how the actors interact with each other.

13.2.1 The active actor

Each actor in the economy performs actions on average at the same rate, which is modelled by allowing each actor an equal chance to act in a given time period. Note however that an actor may act multiple times in a given period, or not at all. The following rule selects an *active actor* who subsequently has the opportunity to perform economic actions. The unit of time is interpreted as a single month of real time, and therefore each actor is active on average once each month.

---

[1] More generally, each uniform distribution can be considered as a default functional parameter of the model, which may be replaced with a different distribution that has empirical support.

Actor selection rule : (Stochastic).

(1)   Randomly select an actor a according to a uniform probability distribution.

13.2.2   Employee hiring

The labour market is modelled in a simple manner. All unemployed actors seek employment, and all employers hire if they have sufficient *ex ante* funds to pay the average wage. The wage interval, $\omega = [w_1, w_2]$, is a fixed, exogenous parameter to the model. Wages are randomly chosen from the wage interval according to a uniform distribution; hence the average wage is $\langle w \rangle = (w_1 + w_2)/2$.

Hiring of employees by firms is controlled by a hiring rule:

Hiring rule : (Stochastic).

(1)   If actor a is unemployed then:
   (a) Form the set of potential employers, H, consisting of all non-employees.
   (b) Select an employer, $c \in H$, according to a probability function that weights potential employers by their wealth.
   (c) If c's cash holdings m_c exceeds the average wage, then c hires a.

The hiring rule allows all non-workers to potentially hire employees, including hiring by other unemployed individuals to form new firms, but the chances of hiring favour those employers with greater wealth, a stochastic bias that represents the tendency of firm growth to depend on accumulation of capital out of current profits (Kalecki, 1954). But the stochastic nature of the rule reflects the innumerable concrete reasons why particular firms are willing and able to hire more workers than others. Note that the rule does not imply that workers know the money holdings of potential employers, only that the wealthy firms probably hire more people.

13.2.3   Expenditure on goods and services

Each actor spends its income on goods and services produced by firms. But the particular purchases of an individual actor are not modelled. Instead, they are aggregated into a single amount that represents the actor's total expenditure for the month. The total expenditure can represent multiple small purchases, a single large purchase, or a fraction of a purchase amortized over several months: the interpretation is deliberately flexible. Absent a theory of consumption patterns the only relevant information is that expenditure is constrained by the amount of money an actor has. For simplicity assume that the amount spent is bounded by the actor's coin endowment on a randomly selected day. A *consumer actor* is selected to spend its income but the spent income is not immediately transferred to firms. Instead, it is added to a pool of market value that represents the currently available sum of consumer expenditures, which firms compete for.

Expenditure rule : (Stochastic).

(1) Randomly select a consumer *b* other than the current actor *a* according to a uniform distribution.
(2) Randomly select an expenditure amount, *m*, according to a uniform distribution, from the budget set by *b*'s cash holding.
(3) Transfer the *m* cash from *b* to the available pool of market value, *V*.

This rule controls the expenditure of all consumers, whether workers, capitalists or unemployed. Clearly, a rich actor is more likely to spend more.

Different classes spend for different reasons, in particular workers normally spend their incomes on consumption goods, whereas capitalists not only consume but invest. The payment of wages is treated separately, and therefore capitalist expenditure is interpreted as expenditure on non-wage goods, such as capital goods or personal consumption. The expenditure rule is also implicitly a saving rule as in a given period the probability of an actor spending all its wealth is low.

13.2.4 Interaction between firms and the market

To simplify matters assume that all means of production are controlled by capitalist owners and therefore individual actors are unable to produce. Self-employment is ignored in this model: productive work resulting in saleable goods or services is performed only by actors within firms.

Each firm produces some collection of use-values that it attempts to sell in the marketplace. But individual commodity types and sales are not modelled. Instead, the total volume of a firm's sales in a given period are disaggregated into *market samples*, which are transfers of money from marketplace to seller, representing multiple separate transactions, or fractions of a single large transaction. At this level of abstraction the mapping from market samples to actual material exchanges is ignored and assumed to be arbitrary.

Under normal circumstances a firm expects that a worker's labour adds a value to the product that is bound from below by the wage. A firm's markup on costs reflects this value expectation, which may or may not be validated in the market. Obviously, there are multiple and particular reasons why a worker adds more or less value to the firm's total product, most of which are difficult to measure, as partially reflected in the large variety of contested and negotiable compensation schemes.

We will model the relationship between concrete labour and value-added by assuming that a firm randomly samples the market once for every employee. The firm samples per employee to reflect the fact that each worker potentially adds value, but samples randomly to reflect contingency and subsume the range of possibilities, from slackers to Stakhanovites, or from replaceable administrators to irreplaceable film stars. This is a weak formulation of the law of value (Marx,

1976; Rubin, 1973; Wright, 2008b), which implies that, absent profit-equalizing mechanisms and rents, there is a statistical tendency for the value of a firm's product to be linearly related to the amount of social labour-time expended on the product.

Each firm therefore samples the market to gain revenue for every worker employed. In an idealized freely competitive economy there is a tendency for particular production advantages to be regularly adopted by competing firms, including the removal of scarcities due to employment of particular kinds of skilled labour. We can therefore assume that the determinants of the value-added per worker are statistically uniform across firms. The statistical variation can be interpreted as representing transient differences in the productivity of different concrete labours.

Although different workers may be more or less productive the value realized from their labour is constrained by the overall level of demand in the market. The value-added by an active worker to the firm's product is represented by a transfer of money from the current available market value V. The actual value received in money-form depends on the prevailing market conditions, and mismatches between value and exchange-value, or more plainly, costs and revenue, determine whether firms are rewarded with profits for performing socially-necessary labour.

The revenue received from the market is the legal property of the capitalist owner. Capitalist owners therefore accrue revenue via market sales that represent the social utility of the efforts of their workers. All these abstractions are expressed in the following market sample rule:

Market sample rule : (Stochastic).

(1)   If a is not unemployed then:
   (a)   Randomly select a revenue amount m from the interval $[0, V]$ according to a uniform distribution (V is reduced by m).
   (b)   If actor a is an employee then transfer m coins to the employer (hence the employers cash is increased by m).
   (c)   Alternatively, if actor a is a capitalist owner, then transfer m coins to actor a (hence the employers cash is also increased by m).

In either case the transferred coins are counted as firm revenue. In the first case we are modelling the way that a worker contributes to the firm's income, in the second we are modelling the way that capitalist owners also contribute to firm revenue by their work. We are assuming that the expected contribution of an employee or employer to the firms revenue will be the same. This, of course, applies only to the expected contribution: the individual contributions of actors will vary randomly. In a real economy higher motivation might make non-absent employers contribute more per day than their employees. But we ignore this for simplicity.

The money received may represent value embodied in many different kinds of products and services that are sold in arbitrary amounts to arbitrary numbers of buyers. The market sample rule abstracts from the details of individual market transactions and may be interpreted as modelling the aggregate effect of a dynamic random graph that links sellers to buyers in each market period. The stochastic nature of the rule subsumes innumerable reasons why particular firms enjoy particular revenues: the only constraints are that revenue received is determined by the available value in the marketplace, and that a firm with more employees will on average sample the market on more occasions than a firm with fewer employees, a bias justified by the law of value.

A firm may enjoy a sequence of high value samples of the market, which can be interpreted as the result of a competitive advantage, for example, highly productive workers or advanced capital equipment. However, each sample is independent, hence we abstract from the possibility that the value-added by workers in the same firm is correlated over a time period.

13.2.5   Employee firing

If the revenue received by a firm is insufficient to pay the wage bill then the employer must reduce costs and fire employees. This is captured by the following firing rule:

Firing rule : (Deterministic).

(1)   If actor *a* is an employer, then determine the number of workers to fire, *u*, according to the rule that no workers are fired if the *ex ante* wage bill is payable from the firm's current money holdings (the wage bill is calculated from the average wage and the number of employees). Otherwise, the firm's workforce is reduced to a size such that the wage bill is payable.

(2)   Select the *u* actors from the set of employees, according to a uniform distribution, and fire them.

In this model there are no skill differences therefore each actor is identical. It does not matter which particular workers are fired, simply the amount, and so the particular individuals to fire are chosen randomly. Note the asymmetry between hiring and firing: hiring occurs one individual at a time at a frequency determined by the number of unemployed actors, whereas firing may occur in bulk at a frequency determined by the number of firms. Just as new firms may form when two actors enter an employee-employer relationship, existing firms may cease trading when all employees are fired and the capitalist owner enters the unemployed class.

13.2.6   Wage payment

Employers pay wages according to the following rule, which implements the transfer of value from capitalist to worker.

Wage payment rule : (Stochastic).

(1)   For each actor e that a employs

    (a) transfer w in cash from a to e, where w is selected from the discrete interval $[w_1, w_2]$ according to a uniform distribution. (If employer a has insufficient funds to pay w then w is selected from the employer's current cash holdings according to a uniform distribution.)

In reality wages are not subject to monthly stochastic fluctuations. A more elaborate model would introduce wage contracts between employer and employee that fix the individual employee's wage for the duration of employment. But in the aggregate, for example in terms of the total wage bill on average payable by a firm, or wage and profit shares in national income, the existence of monthly fluctuations in individual wages is not significant, and allows a considerable simplification of the model.

13.2.7   Historical time

Finally, the above rules are combined and repeatedly executed to simulate the functioning of the economy over time. The following simulation rule orders the possible economic actions:

Simulation rule: Allocate M/N in cash to each of the N actors; that is we set all actors to have equal wealth at the start. Also set all actors to be initially unemployed.

(1)   Execute the actor selection rule to select the active actor a.
(2)   Execute the hiring rule.
(3)   Execute the expenditure rule that augments the available market value with new expenditure.
(4)   If a is associated with a firm, execute the market sample rule that transfers m in cash from the market to the firm owner.
(5)   Execute firing rule.
(6)   Execute wage payment rule.

The application of this simulation rule can generate a variety of events. For example, if the active actor is unemployed it may get hired by an existing firm, or with lower probability form a new small firm with another unemployed actor. An employed active actor will generate a market sample for its employer, which generates revenue bound by the available market value, itself a function of the stochastic spending patterns of other actors. If the active actor is a capitalist owner of a firm it may decide to fire employees if current revenues do not cover the expected wage bill. If all employees are fired then the firm ceases trading.

Otherwise, the wage bill is paid, augmenting the spending power of the working class, which on the next cycle will affect the available market value that firms compete for, and so on.

A period of one month is defined as the N applications of the simulation rule. This means that on average wages are paid once per simulated month.

One month rule :

(1) Execute the simulation rule.
(2) Repeat N times.

The rule is executed N times to allow each of the N actors an opportunity to act. But clearly this does not guarantee that each actor will in fact act within the month: some actors may act more than once, others not at all. This introduces a degree of causal slack that is intended to model the fact that in real economies events do not occur with strict regularity. In addition, the repeated random selection of active actors during a simulated month breaks any symmetries that might be introduced if actors are selected in a regular order. In reality, economic actions occur both in order and in parallel and this causal chaos is modelled by noisy selection.

A period of one year, which is the accounting period, is defined as 12 applications of the one month rule. The model is therefore given a notional time scale loosely linked to real time via the empirical fact that on average wages are paid once each month.

The set of rules discussed above, along with three parameters – the total cash in the economy M, the total number of actors, N, and the fixed wage interval ω – constitute a dynamic, computational model of the social architecture (SA) of capitalist production.

13.3   Results

Over the last 20 years it has become apparent that very simple computational models can generate complex behaviours (Wolfram, 2002). The rules of the computational model described here are also simple, yet the dynamic behaviour they generate is rich and complex.

The total number of coins, M, and the total number of actors, N, on condition that $M \gg N$, appear to act as scaling parameters and do not affect the relative dynamics, unlike the wage interval parameter. The computational rules do not refer to absolute numbers of coins or actors, hence a doubling of both leaves wealth per actor unchanged. Similarly, increasing the number of coins scales the overall wealth and income levels, all other things being equal. As opposed to this, if the number of actors is very small the model behaves qualitatively differently. But real economies are composed of millions of people, so we do not examine such edge cases.

The computational rules refer to the absolute wage, and hence changes to the wage parameter affect the emergent dynamics. In all reported results, $N = 1000$

and $M = 100000$, so that the average wealth in the economy is 100 coins. On *a posteriori* grounds the wage interval is set to $\omega = [10, 90]$; hence, the minimum wage is 10 coins, the average wage 50 coins, half the mean wealth in the economy, and the highest possible wage never exceeds the mean wealth. This results in an almost equal split of national wealth between the two classes, and is designed to be in agreement with the general predictions of Farjoun and Machover.

When we start the simulation running, it very rapidly organizes itself into a stochastic equilibrium. In this equilibrium, while individual economic variables fluctuate, the probability distributions of these variables do not change over time. The simulation does not settle to a motionless equilibrium but converges to a dynamic equilibrium of ceaseless motion and change.

Unless stated otherwise the model was allowed to run for 100 simulated years.

13.3.1   Class distribution

The social stratification generated by capitalist economies is a complex phenomenon with systematic causal relations to the dominant social relations of production. In reality the social relations of production are more complex than the relations in the SA model (actors may receive combinations of wage and property income and therefore belong to more than one economic class, some actors are self-employed, others receive the majority of their income from rent, many people work for governments rather than private enterprises, and so forth). In consequence, some work is required to map empirical data on social stratification to the more basic categories employed here. It is equally clear, however, that the class of capitalists is numerically small, whereas the class of workers, that is those actors who mostly rely on wage income for their subsistence, constitute the vast majority of the population. The SA model should reflect this empirical fact.

Figure 13.1 is a group of histograms showing class sizes generated by the model collected over the duration of the simulation. The number of workers, capitalists and unemployed are normally distributed. The normal distributions summarize a dynamic process of individual social mobility, where actors move between classes during their imputed lifetimes, occurring within a stable partition of the population into two main classes – a small employing class and a larger employed

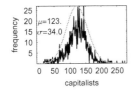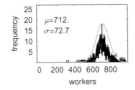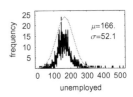

Figure 13.1 Class distributions: histograms of the number of actors in each economic class with a constant bin size of 1. The smooth lines are fitted normal distributions. On average approximately 71.2 per cent of the population are workers, 12.3 per cent are capitalists employing one worker or more, and the remaining 16.6 per cent are unemployed.

class. Fluctuations in class sizes are evidently mean-reverting, reflecting stable and persistent class sizes, given the pre-specified and constant wage interval. The unemployment rate is higher than is usually reported in modern economies, but published measures of unemployment typically under-report actual unemployment. For example many people who might work but are not eligible for unemployment benefits are not counted, whereas here all non-employed actors are considered unemployed. In addition, there is no concept of self-employment. In conclusion, the SA model self-organizes into a realistic partition of the working population into a minority of employers and a majority of employees.

13.3.2 Class distribution of income

GDP (which we label X) is the sum of revenues received by firms during a single year. Firms pay the total wage bill, W, from this revenue. Hence the total value of domestic output is divided into a share that workers receive as wages, $X_w = W/X$, and the remainder that capitalists receive as profit, $X_p = 1 - X_w$. Advanced capitalist countries publish national income accounts that allow wage and profit shares to be calculated, which reveal some characteristic features. Shares in national income have remained fairly stable during the twentieth century, despite undergoing yearly fluctuations. For example, the profit share, normally lower than the wage share, is between 0.25 to 0.4 of GDP, although it occasionally can be as high as 0.5.[2]

In the model we compute the wage share as $X_w = W/X$ where W is the total wages paid during the year, and X is the total firm income during the year. Figure 13.2 is a plot of the shares in national income generated by the model. The profit share is generally lower than the wage share, and the yearly fluctuations are normally distributed about long-term stable values. Ignoring differences of definition, and for the purposes of a rough and ready comparison, the model generates an average profit share of 0.45, which compares well to the empirical data. The model therefore reproduces the empirical situation of fluctuations about a long-term stable mean, and additionally the profit and wage shares have realistic values, although it is an open question whether suitably de-trended fluctuations are normally distributed in capitalist economies.

13.3.3 Disaggregated income distributions

The income shares produced by the model can be disaggregated and measured at the level of individuals in order to understand income differentiation within classes.

---

[2] See the calculations of Foley and Michl (1999) for the US, UK and Japan spanning a period of over 100 years. Other authors place the wage share nearer to $\frac{1}{2}$, for example on average 0.54 between 1929 and 1941 for the USA (Kalecki, 1954); similar figures are given in chapters 3 and 8 of Farjoun and Machover (1983).

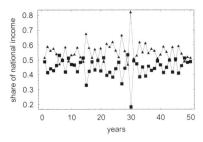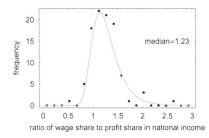

Figure 13.2 Wage and profit shares in national income. The LHS graph is a representative time series of the fluctuating shares in national income. GDP, denoted X, is the sum of revenues received by firms during a single year. The solid triangles are the wage share, X_w, which represents the sum total of wages paid to the working class, W, divided by GDP, $X_w = W/X$. The solid squares are the profit share, X_p, which represents the sum total of profits received by the capitalist class divided by GDP, $X_p = 1 - (W/X)$. The wage share fluctuates around a mean of 0.55 and the profit share fluctuates around a mean of 0.45. The RHS graph is a histogram of the ratio $W/(1 - W)$. The smooth line is a fitted probability distribution of a ratio of two normal variates, which indicates that fluctuations of shares in national income are normally distributed around long-term stable means.

The empirical income distribution is characterized by a highly unequal distribution of income, in which a very small number of households receive a disproportionate amount of the total. For example, using wealth as an indicator of income, in 1996 the top 1 per cent of individuals in the US owned 40 per cent of the total wealth (Levy and Solomon, 1997). The higher, property-income, regime of the income distribution can be fitted to a Pareto (or power) distribution.[3] The lower, or wage-income, regime, which represents the vast majority of the population, is usually fitted to a lognormal distribution (Souma, 2000; Montroll and Shlesinger, 1983; Badger, 1980) but recently some researchers report that an exponential (Boltzmann–Gibbs) distribution better describes the data (Nirei and Souma, 2003b; Dragulescu, 2002; Dragulescu and Yakovenko, 2002). Plotting the income distribution as a complementary cumulative distribution function (ccdf) in log–log scale reveals a characteristic 'knee' shape at the transition between the two regimes (Matteo *et al.*, 2004; Dragulescu, 2002; Dragulescu and Yakovenko, 2002; Souma, 2000; Nirei and Souma, 2003b). The functional form of the income distribution is stable over many years, although the parameters seem to fluctuate within narrow bounds. For example, for property income, the power-law, $P(x) \propto x^{-(\alpha+1)}$, has a value $\alpha = 1.3$ for the UK in 1970 (Levy and Solomon, n.d.), $\alpha = [1.1, 1.3]$ for Australia between 1993 and 1997 (Matteo *et al.*, 2004), $\alpha = 1.7$ for US in 1998 (Dragulescu, 2002), on average $\alpha = 1.0$

---

[3] This is confirmed by many authors: see Levy and Solomon (1997); Matteo *et al.* (2004); Levy and Solomon (n.d.); Dragulescu (2002); Nirei and Souma (2003a); Souma (2000); Nirei and Souma (2003b).

Digression 13.1 Power-law distributions

Many man-made and naturally occurring phenomena, including city sizes, incomes, word frequencies, and earthquake magnitudes, are distributed according to a power-law distribution. A power-law implies that 'small occurrences' are extremely common, whereas 'large occurrences' are extremely rare. The exponential (or Boltzmann–Gibbs) distribution also has this characteristic, that large energy values are very rare. So how do the two distributions differ?

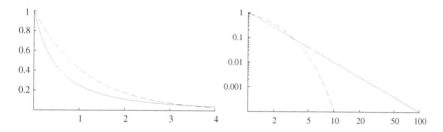

Look at the two graphs above. The graph on the left shows a power-law (solid) and an exponential distribution (dashed) in linear scale. The two distributions appear similar: the probability of high values tends to decrease. But the graph on the right tells a different story. It shows the same distributions but plotted in log-log scale and extended beyond $x = 4$. In log-log scale the exponential distribution is a curve that drops off sharply. But the power-law distribution is a straight-line that continues well beyond the exponential. This is why the power-law distribution is sometimes described as having a 'heavy tail'. A heavy tail implies that extreme 'large occurrences' may still occur with some probability. So if personal wealth is governed by a power law it means that there are more very rich people than there would be if wealth is governed by an exponential distribution. Far out in the heavy tail there are a small number of individuals who enjoy enormous personal wealth.

for post-war Japan (Nirei and Souma, 2003a), and $\alpha = [0.5, 1.5]$ for US and Japan between 1960 and 1999 (Nirei and Souma, 2003b). In sum, the income distribution is asymptotically a power-law with shape parameter $\alpha \approx 1.0$, and this regime normally characterizes the top 1 to 5 per cent of incomes.

The two-parameter lognormal distribution

$$P(x) = \frac{1}{x\sigma\sqrt{2\pi}} \exp(\frac{-(\log\frac{x}{m})^2}{2\sigma^2}) \tag{13.1}$$

where m is the median and $\beta = 1/\sqrt{2\sigma^2}$ is the Gibrat index, can describe the remaining 95 per cent or so of incomes. For example, for post-war Japan, the

Gibrat index ranges between approximately $\beta = 2.25$ and $\beta = 3.0$ (Souma, 2000). In contrast, if the lower income range is fitted to an exponential law

$$P(x) \propto \lambda \exp^{\lambda x} \tag{13.2}$$

then by analogy with a perfect gas, from which the Boltzmann–Gibbs law originates, λ is interpreted as an average economic 'temperature', which should be close to the average wealth in the economy, adjusting for the effects of the Pareto tail.

The SA model is in close qualitative and quantitative agreement with all these empirical facts. It also explains why there are two major income regimes, and provides a candidate explanation of why the distribution of low incomes is sometimes identified as either lognormal or exponential.

Figure 13.3 is a plot of the stationary income ccdf generated by the model. It reproduces the characteristic 'knee' shape found in empirical income distributions. The 'knee' is formed by the transition from the lower regime, consisting mainly of the wealth of the working class and owners of small firms, to the higher regime, consisting mainly of the wealth of the capitalist class. The knee occurs at around $P(M \geq m) = 0.1$, which means the power-law regime holds for at most 10 per cent of incomes.

Figure 13.4 splits the income distribution according to class. The capitalist distribution has a long tail, qualitatively different from the worker distribution, which is clustered around the average wage.

Figure 13.5 is a plot of the lower regime of the income distribution in log-linear scale fitted to a lognormal distribution with Gibrat index $\beta = 1.42$.

Figure 13.6 is a plot of the property-income regime in log–log scale. The straight line fit indicates that higher incomes asymptotically approach a power-law

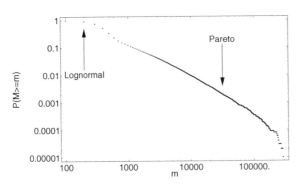

Figure 13.3 The complete income distribution plotted as a ccdf in log–log scale. The data is binned at a constant size of 1. Note the characteristic 'knee' shape, a feature found in empirical distributions. The transition from the lognormal to the Pareto regime occurs between $P(x) = 0.1$ and $P(x) = 0.01$, which means that under 10 per cent of incomes follow the Pareto law.

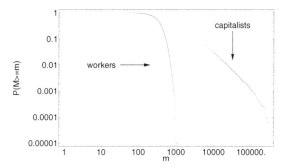

Figure 13.4 The class components of the income distribution plotted as ccdfs in log–log scale. Note the long tail of the capitalist income distribution. Worker income is clustered around the average wage.

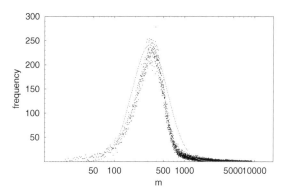

Figure 13.5 The lower regime of the income distribution plotted in log-linear scale. The solid line is a fit to a lognormal distribution. The approximately lognormal distribution results from a mixture of wage income and small employer income.

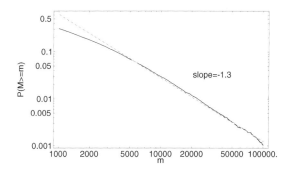

Figure 13.6 The power law regime of the income distribution plotted as a ccdf in log–log scale. The straight line is a fit to the power (Pareto) law, $P(x) \propto x^{-(\alpha+1)}$, where $\alpha = 1.3$.

distribution of the form $P(x) \propto x^{-(\alpha+1)}$, with $\alpha = 1.3$. The two income regimes are consequences of the two major sources of income in capitalist societies, that is wages and profits, and the overall income distribution is a mixture of two qualitatively different distributions. The lower regime is fitted better by a lognormal distribution rather than an exponential. The lognormal distribution, in this model, is not the result of stochastic multiplicative process, which is the explanation often proposed, but results from a mixture of normally distributed wage incomes and the profit-income of small firm owners. It is an open question whether the lognormal distribution found in empirical data can be similarly explained by the combined effect of income from employment and the income of small employers.

At first glance it appears that the model contradicts empirical evidence that the lower income regime is exponentially distributed. But if the stationary distribution of money holdings (i.e., instantaneous wealth) is measured, rather than income, a different picture emerges, which may help explain the lack of consensus in empirical studies. Wealth in our model can be measured by the total money held by each actor at the end of the year.

Figures 13.7 to 13.10 are plots of the stationary money ccdf generated by the model. Figure 13.7 reproduces the characteristic 'knee' shape found in empirical income distributions. But in this case the lower regime is characterized by an exponential (or Boltzmann-Gibbs) distribution. The transition between regimes occurs approximately in the middle of the ccdf corresponding to a situation in which the total wealth in the economy is distributed approximately evenly between the classes.

Figure 13.9 plots the workers' money distribution in log-linear scale. The straight line fit reveals an exponential distribution of the form $P(x) = \lambda \exp^{\lambda x}$, where $\lambda = 0.017$, which is reasonably close to the average wealth in the economy, $\lambda = N/N = 0.01$ (Dragulescu and Yakovenko, 2002). Figure 13.10 plots the capitalists' money distribution in log–log scale. The straight line fit reveals a power-law distribution with similar exponent to that of income.

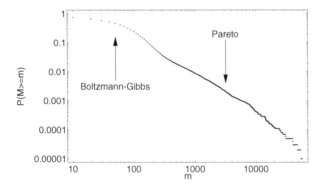

Figure 13.7 The complete money distribution plotted as a ccdf in log–log scale. The transition from the Boltzmann-Gibbs to Pareto regime occurs in the middle of the ccdf. The data is binned at a constant size of 1.

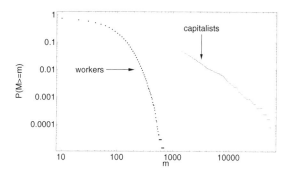

Figure 13.8 The class components of the money distribution plotted as ccdfs in log–log scale. Note the long tail of the capitalist money distribution.

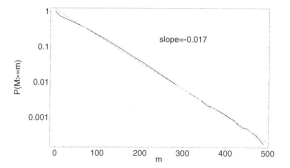

Figure 13.9 A section of the workers' money ccdf plotted in linear–log scale. The straight line is a fit to the exponential (Boltzmann-Gibbs) law, $P(x) = \lambda e^{\lambda x}$, where $\lambda = 0.017$.

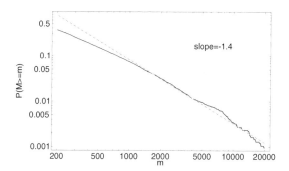

Figure 13.10 A section of the capitalists' money ccdf plotted in log–log scale. The straight line is a fit to the power (Pareto) law, $P(x) \propto x^{-(\alpha+1)}$, where $\alpha = 1.4$.

The higher income and wealth regimes are qualitatively identical, but the lower income and wealth regimes are qualitatively distinct. Measuring the lower end of income yields a lognormal distribution, whereas measuring the lower end of wealth yields an exponential. Income depends solely on monies received during an accounting period, whereas wealth depends on both income and spending patterns. The differences between the empirical studies could be due to differences in whether the measures employed are primarily income measures or wealth measures.

The lognormal and power-law fits are only approximations to the true distributions, and we do not embark on a full analysis of the income distribution here. However, a few brief points can be made. A popular explanation of the power-law tail of the income distribution is that it arises from an underlying stochastic multiplicative process, often thought to model the geometric growth of capital invested in financial markets (Nirei and Souma, 2003b,a; Reed, 2000, 2001; Levy and Solomon, n.d., 1997; Bouchaud and Mézard, 2000). The importance of financial markets in determining capital flows and hence capitalist income is undeniable. But the model developed here shows that an income power-law can arise from industrial capital invested in firms, absent financial markets that support capital reallocation between industries or between capitalists. Capitalist income, in this model, is not derived from investment in portfolios that provide a return, but is composed of the sum of values added via the employment of productive workers.

It is remarkable that the model's simple rules generate detailed income distributions in close agreement with reality. It seems very likely, therefore, that the fundamental reason for the observed income distribution in capitalism is due to the way firm revenue is distributed: as wages to workers, and profits to capitalist owners. There are two major ways of getting money in capitalism: by working, or by employing. Hence there are two, qualitatively distinct income regimes, the negative exponential for the majority, and the Pareto for the few.

13.3.4 *Firm size distribution*

Axtell (2001) analysed US Census Bureau data for US firms trading between 1988 and 1997 and found that the firm size distribution followed a special case of a power-law known as Zipf's law, and this relationship persisted from year to year despite the continual birth and demise of firms and other major economic changes. During this period the number of reported firms increased from 4.9 million to 5.5 million. Gaffeo *et al.* (2003) found that the size distribution of firms in the G7 group over the period 1987-2000 also followed a power-law, but only in limited cases was the power-law actually Zipf. Fujiwara *et al.* (2004) found that the Zipf law characterized the size distribution of about 260,000 large firms from 45 European countries during the years 1992–2001. A Zipf law implies that a majority of small firms coexist with a decreasing number of disproportionately large firms.

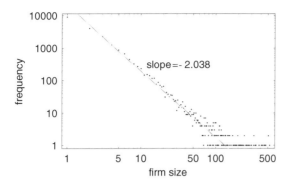

Figure 13.11   Firm size distribution: histogram of firm sizes by employees in log–log scale with a constant bin size of 1. The straight line is an ordinary least squares regression of the data and represents a power-law distribution $P(x) \propto x^{-(\alpha+1)}$ with exponent $\alpha = 1.038$ for data collected over 15 simulated years. Axtell (2001) reports $\alpha = 1.059$ from data of approximately 5.5 million U.S. firms in 1997. The special case $\alpha = 1$ is known as the Zipf distribution.

Firm sizes in the SA model are measured according to the number of employees they have. The model also replicates the empirical firm size distribution. Figure 13.11 is a histogram of firm sizes. The straight line is a fit to the power-law:

$$P(x) \propto x^{-(\alpha+1)} \tag{13.3}$$

For data collected over a relatively short time period, such as 15 simulated years, α approaches 1.0. The special case $\alpha = 1.0$ is Zipf, and hence the firm size distribution generated by the model is consistent with the empirical data. Data collected over shorter periods follows a power-law with exponent that deviates from 1.

The largest US firm in 1997 had approximately 10^6 employees from a total reported workforce of about 10^7 individuals (Axtell, 2001). Therefore, the largest firm size should not exceed about $1/10$th of the total workforce. Figure 2 shows that, with low but non-zero probability, a single firm can employ over half the workforce, representing a monopolization of a significant proportion of the economy by a single firm, which is clearly unrealistic. A possible reason for the over-monopolization of the economy is the assumption that firms have a single capitalist owner, which conflates capital concentration with firm ownership. In reality, large firms normally have multiple owners and individual capitalists own multiple firms. Further, there are many technical reasons why particular firms do not grow beyond a certain size that are ignored in this model. A final point is that the probability of monopoly within the period of observation decreases with the number of actors; hence, if the simulation were run with $N = 10^7$ actors (which is not possible due to insufficient computational resources) then it is unlikely that a single firm would employ half the workforce. Gaffeo *et al.* (2003) note that firms are distributed more equally during recessions than during expansions, which accounts for the yearly deviations from Zipf. We have not tested this relationship in the SA model.

13.3.5 Firm growth

Stanley *et al.* (1996) and Amaral *et al.* (1997a) analyzed the log growth rates of publicly traded US manufacturing firms in the period 1974–93 and found that growth rates, when aggregated across all sectors, appear to robustly follow a Laplace (double exponential) form. This holds true whether growth rates are measured by sales or number of employees. More precisely, if the annual growth rate is $r = \ln(\frac{s_{t+1}}{s_t})$, where s_t is the size of a firm in year t, then for all years the probability density of r is consistent with an exponential decay:

$$f(r) \propto e^{-|\frac{r-\alpha}{\beta}|} \tag{13.4}$$

with some deviation from the Laplace distribution at high and low growth rates resulting in slightly 'fatter wings' (Lee *et al.*, 1998; Amaral *et al.*, 1997b, 2001). Bottazzi and Secchi (2003) replicate these findings and report a Laplace growth distribution for Italian manufacturing firms during the period 1989–96.

We can measure firm growth in the SA model in terms of the change in the number of employees or in sales from year to year. The model generates log annual growth rates for firms that are consistent with a Laplace distribution, whether growth is measured in terms of sales or number of employees. Figure 13.12 plots log growth rates in log-linear scale and reveals the characteristic 'tent'

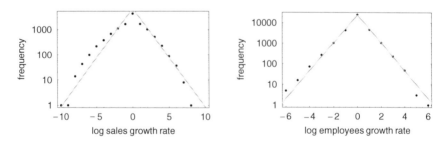

Figure 13.12 Firm size growth rate distribution: histogram of the log growth rates of firms per simulated year in linear–log scale with a constant bin size of 1. The LHS graph shows growth rates of firm sales. The RHS graph shows growth rates of employees. The solid lines are OLS regressions of the data and represent a Laplace (double-exponential) distribution $P(x) \propto e^{-|(x-\alpha)/\beta|}$. Many researchers report that log growth rates of sales and employees of US and Italian firms follow a Laplace distribution (Lee *et al.*, 1998; Bottazzi and Secchi, 2003; Stanley *et al.*, 1996; Amaral *et al.*, 1997a,b, 2001; Fabritiis *et al.*, 2003).

shape signature of a symmetric exponential decay. In the SA model there is no net growth in population or in monetary stocks, this means that the mean rate of growth of a firm will be zero. There is some deviation from a Laplace distribution for firms with shrinking sales, which may be due to noise or represent some non-accidental property.

The replication of the empirical Laplace growth distribution suggests that the social relations of production may play an important role in constraining the dynamics of firm growth. Lee *et al.* (1998); Fabritiis *et al.* (2003); Amaral *et al.* (2001, 1997b); Stanley *et al.* (1996) note that the standard deviation (std) of growth rates decreases as a power law with size, that is, $\ln \sigma(r) \sim -\beta \ln r$, where $\beta \approx 0.15$. The SA model does not replicate this finding given the specified wage interval. In fact, $\ln \sigma(r)$ appears to increase as a power law with size, although the data is quite noisy. However, the exponent of the power law is sensitive to the wage parameter, and it is possible to replicate the empirical relationship at lower average wages. Explanations of the relationship between growth variation and size assume that firms have internal structures such that increased size lessens market risk (Amaral *et al.*, 2001, 1997b), which contrasts with the simple firm structure employed in this model. Axtell (1999), for example, presents an actor-based model of the life-cycle of firms that replicates the Zipf size distribution, Laplace growth rates and power-law scaling of the std of growth. In Axtell's model firms have a richer internal structure compared to firms in this model.

13.3.6 *Firm deaths*

Cook and Ormerod (2003) report that the distribution of US firm deaths per year during the period 1989 to 1997 is closely approximated by a lognormal distribution, and note that the number of deaths varies little from year to year with no clear connection to recession or growth.

We can measure the number of firm deaths per month in the simulation. A firm dies if it fires all its employees. Demises per month are measured rather than per year in order to avoid bucketing the data. Figure 13.13 is a histogram of firm deaths per month with a fitted lognormal distribution. It shows that the model generates a distribution of firm deaths that is approximated by a lognormal distribution and is therefore consistent with empirical findings.

According to Cook and Ormerod the average number of firms in the US during the period 1989 to 1997 was 5.73 million, of which on average 611,000 died each year. So roughly 10 per cent of firms die each year. In the simulation on average 18 firms die each month and therefore on average 216 firms die each year, a figure in excess of the 123 firms that exist on average. So although the distribution of firm deaths is consistent with empirical data, the rate at which firms are born and die is much higher than in reality. This is not too surprising when it is considered that the model entirely abstracts from the material nature of the goods and services processed by the economy and any persistent demand for them. In this model firms compete by playing a game of chance that models the unpredictability of a competitive economy. But the complete absence of the

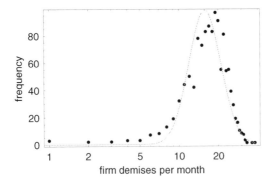

Figure 13.13 Firm deaths distribution: Histogram of firm deaths per simulated month in log-linear scale with a constant bin size of 1. The solid line is a fit to the lognormal distribution. Cook and Ormerod (2003) report that the distribution of US firm deaths per year during the period 1989 to 1997 is closely approximated by a lognormal distribution.

material side of the economy results in an unrealistic level of volatility in market interactions. The SA model must therefore be extended to include causal relations between the social architecture and the forces of production. Clearly there is a limit to what may be deduced from consideration of the social relations of production alone.

13.3.7 GDP growth

Gross Domestic Product (GDP) measures the value of gross production at current prices, including consumption and gross investment. Lee *et al.* (1998) and Canning *et al.* (1998) analyse the GDP of 152 countries during the period 1950–52 and find that the distribution of GDP log growth rates is consistent with a Laplace distribution, and therefore conclude that firm growth and GDP growth are subject to the same laws (Lee *et al.*, 1998).

The GDP in the SA model is measured using total firm income. Growth rates are measured year on simulated year. Empirical measurements of GDP must be detrended to remove the effects of inflation but this is unnecessary when measuring GDP in the model due to the assumption of a fixed amount of money.

Figure 13.14 plots log GDP growth rate for the simulated economy in log-linear scale. The data is noisy but consistent with a Laplace distribution when sampled over a period of 100 years so for clarity figure 13.14 contains data from an extended run of 500 years. The characteristic tent shape indicates that the SA model is consistent with the Laplace distribution of GDP growth.

Delli Gatti *et al.* (2005) present an actor-based model of the life-cycle of firms that replicates the Zipf size distribution and Laplace growth rates of firms and aggregate output (GDP). They show that the power-law of firm size implies that growth is Laplace distributed and also that small micro-shocks can aggregate into

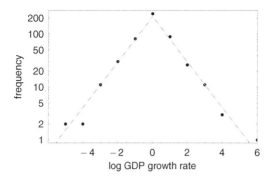

Figure 13.14 Rescaled GDP growth rate distribution: histogram of the log growth rate of GDP in linear–log scale with a constant bin size of 1. The solid lines are OLS regressions of the data and represent a Laplace (double-exponential) distribution $P(x) \propto e^{-|(x-\alpha)/\beta|}$. Lee *et al.* (1998) report that log GDP growth rates of 152 countries during the period 1950–92 follow a Laplace distribution.

macro-shocks to generate recessions. Firms in their model are not disaggregated into employees and employers and market shocks are exogenous, whereas in this model firms are composed of individuals and are subject to endogenous shocks that are the consequence of the competition for a finite amount of available market value, itself a product of income flows.

13.3.8 Duration of recessions

Wright (2005a), reinterpreting empirical data presented by Ormerod and Moun-field (2001), concludes that the frequency of the duration of economic recessions, where a recession is defined as a period of shrinking GDP, follows an exponential law for 17 Western economies over the period 1871–1994. Recessions tend not to last longer than 6 years, the majority of recessions last 1 year, and for the US the longest recession has been only 4 years (Ormerod, 2002).

The SA model, in which recession begins when the GDP falls and ends when it ceases to fall, is in close agreement with these empirical findings. Figure 13.15 is a histogram of the frequency of the duration of recessions collected over a period of 500 simulated years. The functional form of the frequency of duration of recessions is exponential, $f(d) \propto \lambda \exp^{-\lambda d}$, with $\lambda = 1.22$, which compares to a value of $\lambda = 0.94$ for the empirical data (Wright, 2005a). The value of λ is the average duration of a recession. Also, the duration of recessions in the model ranges from 1 to 4 simulated years.

Ausloos *et al.* (2004) subsequently analysed a more comprehensive set of GDP data and concluded that overall the distribution of recessions follows a power-law, not an exponential law, although the matter is not entirely settled. Ormerod and Mounfield argue that economic management often prevents recessions lasting more than one year, but if they do last longer, then subjective expectations of

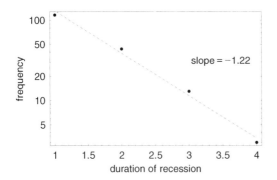

Figure 13.15 Recession duration distribution: Histogram of the frequency of the duration of recessions in log-linear scale with a constant bin size of 1. The solid line is a fit to an exponential distribution, $f(d) \propto \lambda \exp^{-\lambda d}$, with exponent $\lambda = 1.22$, representing an average recession duration of 1.22 simulated years.

growth become depressed and recessions may then occur on all scales of duration, resulting in a power-law. They propose that the distribution is not determined by a common set of causal factors for all durations, but instead there is a 'breakdown of scaling' for recessions of short duration. The SA model does not include the subjective expectations of economic actors, and therefore it is an open question whether the introduction of expectations to the model could more closely replicate the empirical data.

13.3.9   *Rate-of-profit distribution*

Farjoun and Machover (1983) propose that the proportion of industrial capital (out of the total capital invested in the economy) that finds itself in any given rate-of-profit bracket will be approximated by a gamma distribution by analogy with the distribution of kinetic energy in a gas at equilibrium. The gamma distribution is a right-skewed distribution. Wells (2001) examined the distribution of profit rates defined in a variety of ways of over 100,000 UK firms trading in 1981 and found right-skewness to be prevalent, but did not investigate their functional form.

In reality capitalist owners of firms invest in both variable capital (wages) and constant capital (commodity inputs to the production process and relatively long-lasting means of production) and the rate of profit is calculated on the total capital invested (Okishio, 1990). The SA model abstracts from the forces of production and capitalists invest only in variable capital. Capitalists also spend income in the marketplace and this expenditure could be interpreted as either consumption or investment in constant capital, but to theoretically ground the latter interpretation the model would need to be extended to include a determination of the distribution of ratios of constant to variable capital across firms. Rather than introduce the material side of the economy, which properly belongs to future substantive

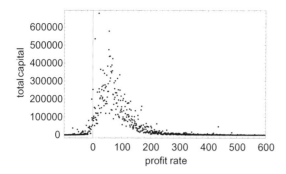

Figure 13.16 Capital-weighted rate-of-profit distribution: Histogram of amount of capital invested that generated a given percentage profit rate within a simulated year. The data is collected over the duration of the simulation and binned at a constant size of 1. The average profit rate is 80.5 per cent and the median profit rate is 64 per cent (on average 1 coin invested returns 1.8 coins). Wells (2001) measured the profit rate distribution of over 100,000 UK firms trading in 1981 and found that the distribution was right-skewed.

extensions of the model, the rate of profit in the simulation is calculated on variable capital alone and hence will exceed real-world rates.

The profit-rate distribution in the model is measured according to:

Profit rate measure: After each year calculate the profit rate for each firm trading at the close of the year. The profit rate, p_i, of firm i is defined as

$$p_i = 100 \left(\frac{r_i}{w_i} - 1 \right)$$ (13.5)

where r_i is the total revenue received during the year and w_i is the total wages paid during the year.

Figure 13.17 graphs the amount of capital that returned a given profit within a year. Consistent with empirical research the distribution is highly right-skewed. Wells (2001) reports that if the rate-of-profit is weighted according to number of firms, rather than capital invested, the distribution is also right-skewed and very similar in overall character, although less noisy. Figure 11 graphs the firm-weighted distribution from the simulation. It is also right-skewed, like the capital-weighted distribution, but considerably less noisy.

13.4 A note on methodology

The empirical coverage of the SA model is broad although the model can be formally stated in a small number of simple economic rules that control the dynamics. The model compresses and connects a large number of empirical facts

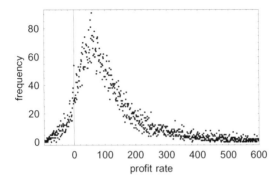

Figure 13.17 Firm-weighted rate-of-profit distribution: Histogram of number of firms that generated a given percentage profit rate within a simulated year. The data is collected over the duration of the simulation and binned at a constant size of 1. Wells (2001) measured the firm-weighted profit rate distribution of over 100,000 UK firms trading in 1981 and found that, similar to the capital-weighted rate-of-profit, the distribution was right-skewed, although less noisy.

within a single causal framework. Our aim in this chapter was to show how the social relations of production peculiar to capitalism, that is how humans relate to each other as workers and capitalists in order to produce the things they need, has a pervasive and determinate effect on many of the macro-level properties of capitalism. We can extend this modelling approach in many ways, and there are many aspects of the simulation that we could further measure and analyse, and so this chapter represents only a starting point.

The enormous benefit of exploring computational models of phenomena is that the complex dynamic consequences of a set of causal rules can be automatically and correctly deduced by running a computer program that performs a computational deduction. In this case the deduction is from micro-economic social relations to emergent, macro-economic phenomena. But the reasons why a set of causal rules necessarily generate the observed dynamic consequences may initially be opaque precisely because a computer simulation is required to perform the deduction. This is why computational modelling is not an alternative to deductive mathematical modelling but is connected to it. To give just one example, within the parameter space explored, the SA model generates fluctuations in national income about long-term stable means. But it requires a mathematical deduction to understand why this necessarily occurs. The computational model demonstrates that in principle such a deduction may be produced and its basic elements and assumptions will correspond to those of the computational model. Of course, a deductive proof may be more or less difficult to construct even if known to be possible. So one use of computational modelling is to more easily identify candidate theories, which may then be further analysed to generate explanations in the form of mathematical deductions or natural language explanations, the aim being to understand why the dynamic consequences are logically necessary. An example of the potential of this approach is the deduction of a candidate functional form for the distribution of industrial profit, which for the interested reader is discussed in appendix D. Contrast this situation to a purely deductive approach, in which the investigator may only explore candidate theories that are directly amenable to mathematical deduction. This methodology is unnecessarily restrictive, particularly if the system presents difficult analytic challenges.

The fact that the empirical distributions considered emerge from the social relations of production alone suggests that some of the striking phenomena of a capitalist economy depend not so much on specifics but on very general and highly abstract structural features of that system. In consequence, existing theories may be looking in the wrong place for economic explanations, or at least introducing redundant considerations. Given this possibility, it is worth making a few comments to contrast the approach taken in this paper to standard approaches.

The basic elements of this model differ from standard economic models. Standard competitive equilibrium models, or neoclassical models, normally take as their starting point an ontology of rational actors that maximize self-interest in a market for scarce resources (Debreu, 1959). Attention is focussed on determining the equilibrium exchange ratios of commodity types, which are solutions to a set of simultaneous, static constraints. Historical time is absent, so equilibrium states are logically rather than causally derived, and typically money is not modelled. Neo-Ricardian models, in contrast, take as their starting point an ontology of technical production relations between commodity types that define the available material transformations that economic actors may perform. The production of commodities by means of commodities (Sraffa, 1960) results in a surplus product that is distributed to capitalists and workers (Pasinetti, 1977). Despite many essential differences, there are some important similarities between neo-classical and neo-Ricardian models. For example, prices in neo-Ricardian models are also exchange ratios determined by solutions to static, simultaneous constraints. Similarly, historical time is absent, so there is no causal explanation of how or why a particular configuration of the economy arose. Money only plays a nominal not a causal role. There are clear differences between, on the one hand, neo-classical and neo-Ricardian ontologies, and, on the other, the basic ontology of the model developed here. Most obvious is that commodity types and rational actors are absent. Instead, the model emphasizes precisely those elements of economic reality that neo-classical and neo-Ricardian theories tend to ignore, specifically actor-to-actor relations mediated by money, which unfold in historical time, and result in dynamic, not static, equilibria. At a high level of abstraction, and at the risk of over simplification, neo-classical models theorize scarcity constraints, neo-Ricardian models theorize technical-production constraints, whereas this model theorizes the dynamic consequences of social constraints, which are historically contingent facts about the way in which economic production is socially organized.

There is a large and longstanding literature on the failings of standard general equilibrium theory to describe economic reality. But there are deep and enduring sociological reasons why standard economic theory is resistant to criticism and persists largely unchanged. Nonetheless, the model we have described in this chapter constitutes constructive proof that the standard ontology is redundant for forming explanations of the macroeconomic phenomena we have surveyed. This is not to deny that some other, perhaps more concrete issues, may require consideration of purposive activity for their explanation and hence the introduction of rational actors, or require consideration of technical production constraints and hence the introduction of commodity types. Rather, the claim is that, for the empirical aggregates considered, there is no need to perform the standard reduction of political economy to psychology and the technical conditions of production, and further, that the dominant causal factors at work are not to be found at the level of individual behaviour, nor are they to be found at the level of technical-production constraints, but are found at the level of the social relations of production, which constitute an abstract, but nevertheless real, social architecture that constrains the possible actions that purposive individuals may choose between, whether optimally or otherwise. This is why the actors in this model probabilistically choose between possible economic actions constrained only by their class status and current money endowments, an approach that is closer to the Classical conception of political economy of Smith, Ricardo and Marx, in which individuals are considered to be representatives of economic classes that have definite relations to each other in the process of production. The social architecture, in particular the wage-capital social relation, dominates individuals, who, although free to make local economic decisions, do so in a social environment neither of their own choosing or control.

As we discussed in Chapter 7 the method of abstracting from the mechanics of individual rationality, and instead emphasizing the particle nature of individuals, is valid because the number of degrees of freedom of economic reality is very large. This allows individual rationality to be modelled as a highly simplified stochastic selection from possibilities determined by an overriding social architecture. The quasi-psychological motives that supposedly drive individual actors in the rational actor approach can be ignored because in a large ensemble of such individuals they hardly matter.

13.5   Essential and inessential properties of capitalism

Our aim was to begin to understand the economic consequences of the social relations of production considered in isolation and develop a model that included money and historical time as essential elements. The theoretical motivation for the approach is grounded in Marx's distinction between the invariant social relations of production and the varying forces of production. Capitalism does change over time, but the existence of the social role of worker and capitalist are an unchanging and defining feature of it.

The model of the social relations of production replicates some important empirical features of modern capitalism, such as (i) the tendency toward capital concentration resulting in a highly unequal income distribution characterized by a lognormal distribution with a Pareto tail, (ii) the Zipf or power-law distribution of firm sizes, (iii) the Laplace distribution of firm size and GDP growth, (iv) the exponential distribution of recession durations, (v) the lognormal distribution of firm deaths, and (vi) the gamma-like rate-of-profit distribution. Also, the model naturally generates groups of capitalists, workers and unemployed in realistic proportions, and business cycle phenomena, including fluctuating wage and profit shares in national income. The good qualitative and in many cases quantitative fit between model and empirical phenomena suggests that the theory presented here captures some essential features of capitalist economies, demonstrates the causal importance of the social relations of production, and provides a basis for more concrete and elaborated models.

A final and important implication is that the computational deduction outlined in this paper implies that some of the features of economic reality that cause political conflict, such as extreme income inequality and recessions, are necessary consequences of the social relations of production and hence enduring and essential properties of capitalism, rather than accidental, exogenous or transitory.

14 Understanding profit

'...the difficulty which has hitherto troubled the economists, namely to explain the falling rate of profit'

(Marx, 1971: 230)

The argument in chapter 12 can be summarized as follows. The essential signature of capital as a form of information is the process $M \rightarrow C \rightarrow M'$ in which money expands exponentially. We have argued that this was inhibited so long as the technology of record supporting money was the use of gold or silver coin. This constraint was removed through the development of the banking system in which the technology of record was first replaced by paper and ink and then by computer disks. But a complex social phenomenon like profit has multiple levels of causality. The ability of the monetary technology to support it is only one such level. One can look at the causes of profit in several ways:

(1)   From the standpoint of the social architecture of capitalism as in chapter 13. In this case the occurrence of profit is seen as being caused by the property relations according to which the product belongs to capitalists, whose employees have no property claim on it. The use of computer simulation indicates that these assumptions alone will suffice to generate realistic functional forms for the structure of incomes in society.

(2)   From the standpoint of monetary technology, as in chapter 12.

(3)   From the standpoint of production technology. This is the approach that was taken by economists such as Sraffa (1960), Okishio (1961) and Roemer (1982).

(4)   From the standpoint of necessary and surplus labour-time, as in Marx (1976). We will argue below that this approach passes over, via dimensional analysis, to an examination of the role of demography in the evolution of profit rates.

(5)   From the standpoint of macroeconomic flows of expenditure, as pioneered by Kalecki (1954).

14.1   Sraffa: profit and the technology matrix

In section 10.4 we introduced the idea of an input–output table. We brought this in to explain how one could estimate labour values. In 1960 Sraffa showed how a sufficiently detailed input–output table could be seen as determining the entire price and profit structure of an economy, provided that one crucial simplifying assumption is made.

He starts out by considering a simple self-reproducing economy producing wheat and iron. Each of these goods are used both for the sustenance of the workers and as inputs to the agricultural and industrial production processes. 280 quarters of wheat and 12 tons of iron are used to produce 400 quarters of wheat; while 120 quarters of wheat and 8 tons of iron go to produce 20 tons of iron. In schematic form we have

Input		*Output*
280 qr. wheat + 12 t. iron	$\rightarrow$	400 qr. wheat
120 qr. wheat + 8 t. iron	$\rightarrow$	20 t. iron

All outputs are consumed either as wages or as means of production. Sraffa argues that there is a unique set of prices which ensures that each industry can buy enough inputs to continue producing at the current scale. In this case the net output of industry 1 – namely, 120 quarters of wheat – must exchange for the net output of industry 2, 12 tons of iron. This establishes an exchange rate of 10 quarters of wheat to one ton of iron.

With two commodities there is only one exchange ratio. With n different commodities there would be $n-1$ exchange ratios. With n commodities we would have n input–output equations.

$$A_a p_a + B_a p_b + \cdots + N_a p_n = A p_a$$
$$A_b p_a + B_b p_b + \cdots + N_b p_n = B p_b$$
$$\vdots \qquad \qquad \vdots$$
$$A_n p_a + B_n p_b + \cdots + N_n p_n = N p_n$$

where A means the total output of commodity A, B_a means the amount of commodity B used up in industry A, and p_a is the price of commodity A. Sraffa supposes that one of the commodities is used as the standard of value – let's say this is gold. The price of gold in terms of itself is obviously 1, so we are left with $n-1$ unknowns. It might appear that we have more equations than unknowns, but the total quantity of each good occurs twice – once among the inputs and once among the outputs – so any one of the equations can be inferred from the sum of the others. It follows that we have only $n-1$ independent equations, and thus the set of prices is uniquely determined.

Sraffa then went on to consider what will happen if there is a surplus product. The immediate effect is to make the equations independent of one another, since it is no longer the case that the input and output quantities are equal. In general

$$\sum_{i=a}^{n} A_i \leq A \tag{14.1}$$

This would appear to make prices indeterminate. To compensate, he introduces a new constraint, assuming that all industries earn the same rate of profit, r. This allows him to obtain a new system of price equations:

$$(A_a p_a + B_a p_b + \cdots + N_a p_n)(1 + r) = A p_a$$
$$(A_b p_a + B_b p_b + \cdots + N_b p_n)(1 + r) = B p_b$$
$$\vdots \qquad \vdots$$
$$(A_n p_a + B_n p_b + \cdots + N_n p_n)(1 + r) = N p_n$$

These n equations simultaneously determine all $n - 1$ relative prices and the rate of profit. It is relatively easy to show that if the productivity in any industry rises – so that either its output goes up for the same inputs or it uses less inputs for the same outputs – this will lead to rise in the rate of profit. Given the assumption of an equal rate of profit, any technically advantageous invention in a given sector will raise the rate of profit for the economy as a whole. But Sraffa shows that this only holds if every output is also used as an input by other industries. Luxury goods industries, whose output does not feed back into production, are different. He divided industries into two sectors:

(1) the *basic* sector, made up of those industries whose output is a direct or indirect input to every other industry; and
(2) the *non-basic* sector, which includes 'luxury goods' (good which enter no production process) and goods that are only used as inputs in other non-basic industries.

An improvement in productivity in the basic sector will raise the rate of profit. An improvement in a non-basic sector will leave the rate of profit unchanged. If the manufacture of bombs becomes more efficient, for example, bombs get cheaper but here will be no knock-on effect to raise the general productivity of the economy.

Up to this point Sraffa has treated the goods consumed by workers as part of the necessary inputs to a production process. For instance, his iron industry used up wheat to feed its workers. Once one recognizes that workers are paid money wages rather than getting paid in kind, there is an additional variable to

Table 14.1 Physical input–output table of economy with a surplus

	Iron	Corn	Labour	Output	Surplus
iron	440	1100	110	825	185
corn	100	500	50	2250	550
silk	100	100	20	1000	1000
totals	640	1700	180		

deal with: the wage rate, w. To handle this he extends his input–output table, including labour inputs, L_i, as an additional column:

$$(A_a p_a + B_a P_b + \cdots + N_a p_n)(1 + r) + L_a w = A p_a$$
$$(A_b p_a + B_b P_b + \cdots + N_b p_n)(1 + r) + L_b w = B p_b$$
$$\vdots \qquad \vdots$$
$$(A_n p_a + B_n P_b + \cdots + N_n p_n)(1 + r) + L_n w = N p_n$$

We then have n equations and $n + 1$ variables, which implies that the system has one degree of freedom. If one fixes either the wage rate or the rate of profit 'from the outside', the system becomes determined.

Table 14.1 shows an example of an economy with a surplus. Sraffa was able to show that there is an inverse relationship between profits and wages: as wages rise, profits fall as shown in Figure 14.1. At the point where wages are high enough for workers to purchase the whole net product profits will be zero. This is hardly surprising. More interesting is the result he obtained for the maximal rate of profit – that is, the rate of profit that would obtain were wages to fall to zero.

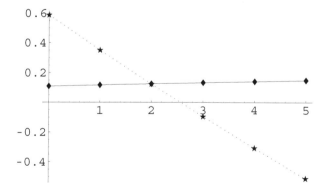

Figure 14.1 How the rate of profit (dotted line) falls as the wage rises, wages being expressed in tons of iron. The solid line shows the change in the price of corn expressed in tons of iron as the rate of profit and wage rate change. The graph is based on the model economy shown in Table 14.1.

To arrive at the maximal rate of profit Sraffa introduces what he calls the Standard System. This is made up of part of the output of each of the industries in the basic sector. Specifically, the industries of the basic sector are scaled in such a way as to ensure that the ratios in which outputs are produced is the same as the ratios in which the inputs are used. Sraffa argued that every economy contains a Standard System, which can be discovered by

(1)   discarding all non-basic industries, and
(2)   scaling back those basic industries whose share of the output mix exceeds their share of the input mix.

Table 14.2 shows the result of applying this rule to the economy introduced in Table 14.1. We first discard the silk industry as non-basic. Then, observing that the ratio of iron to corn in the output was $825/2250 = 11/30$ but the ratio of iron to corn in the input of the basic sector was $540/1600 = 11/32$, less than $11/30$, we scale back the iron industry until the iron–corn ratios are equal in the input and the output at $1/3$. This gives the Standard System shown in Table 14.2.

In the Standard System we can express the maximum profit rate, R, in terms of the physical expansion rate of the economy. Recall that commodities occur in the input vector in the same proportions as they occur in the output vector. Thus, whatever the relative prices of the various commodities, the ratio of the total money value of the collection of output commodities to the total value of the input will be $(1+R)$, the same as the physical expansion rate if all the surplus were re-invested. Note that the value of $R = 0.5$ obtained in Table 14.2 is not exactly the same maximal rate of profit as we observed in Figure 14.1. This is because the profit rate in the figure was expressed in terms of iron as the numeraire. Since the relative prices of commodities changes with the rate of profit (see the corn price in Figure 14.1) no single commodity can act as a stable numeraire for measuring prices or profit rates. Sraffa showed that the only reliable numeraire would be the Standard Commodity – that is, a 'basket' of basic commodities in which each commodity appears in the proportion in which it enters the Standard System. This weighting, alone, will precisely compensate for the fluctuations in relative prices that occur as the rate of profit changes. The maximal rate of profit when measured in this weighted bundle is then equal to the physical expansion rate R.

Table 14.2 Example of a Sraffian Standard System. Note that the iron/corn ratios in both input and output are $1/3$ and the ratio of the total output to the total input is $3/2$. This gives an expansion rate of $R = 0.5$

	Iron	Corn	Labour	Output
iron	400	1000	100	750
corn	100	500	50	2250
totals	500	1500	150	

Sraffa's analysis has a number of very interesting implications, but it also suffers from some weaknesses. As we noted in chapter 6, an initial conclusion that other economists drew was that Sraffa had shown that the labour theory of value espoused by the classical economists was redundant (e.g. Steedman (1981)). Sraffa had been able to derive all prices and the rate of profit in an economy from just the technology matrix and the wage rate. Although Sraffa discussed the feasibility of deriving labour-values from the technology matrix, his price theory did not rely on such values. His assumption of equal rates of profit in every industry amounted to assuming that labour inputs had no independent causal effect on prices. But this is just an assumption, and one should see Sraffian price theory as being conditional on this assumption. It amounts to saying, *if* we assume an equal rate of profit across the economy, what conclusions can we draw? We have already argued that from the standpoint of the theory of value, it is necessary to think of the rate of profit as a non-degenerate random variable, not a uniform magnitude (chapter 10).

14.1.1   Technical change and the rate of profit

Sraffa's conclusions regarding the determinants of the average level of profit still stand. He shows that profit levels can be seen as deriving from two types of cause: overall technical productivity, which sets the maximal profit rate, R; and the struggle between labour and capital over the wage rate, which sets the actual average rate of profit, $r \leq R$. In particular, he has shown that technological advances will raise profit rates only if they occur within the basic sector (confirming Ricardo's argument to this effect). In his first examples Sraffa treated the real wage consumed by workers as part of the necessary inputs to the production process. He then says that in practice wages are made up of a necessary component, required to ensure the workers' survival, and a surplus component, over which capital and labour contend. If one treats the necessary component of the real wage as part of the productive inputs to all branches of production, then the definition of the basic sector becomes more general. It can now be defined as all those industries whose output is directly or indirectly necessary to reproduce the working population.

From this concept of the basic sector and Standard System it is easy to see why a technical change which increases the rate of profit in a single industry above the economy-wide average will tend to raise the overall rate of profit, as originally argued by Okishio (1961). Okishio made the assumption of a fixed real wage. In Sraffian terms, this is equivalent to assuming a zero surplus component of the wage, in which case wage-goods can be included among the productive inputs. Under this assumption Okishio's rate of profit is equivalent to Sraffa's R. Suppose that technical change occurs in a single industry. If the change is to be profitable to the individual firm it must involve either a reduction of at least one input for unchanged output, or must increase outputs with the same inputs. Either of these effects will reduce the inputs required to produce the output of the basic sector, and thus increase R.

14.1.2   Computers and the productivity paradox

As we have said, technological advances in non-basic sectors such as banking, the manufacture of executive jets, or warship construction will not affect the average rate of profit. This may have relevance to the much discussed 'productivity paradox' of computer technology (Brynjolfsson, 1993). The paradox stems from the fact that economists have had the greatest of difficulty in detecting any significant increase in economic productivity stemming from the use of computers. The discussion of the productivity paradox has taken place by economists working within the framework of neoclassical economic theory. This framework, which Sraffa was criticizing in his work, assumes that output is determined by an exponential production function of the general form:

$$Y = AL^a \cdot K_1^b \cdot K_2^c$$

where Y is the money value of output, A is a scale factor, L is the labour input, K_1 is the stock of computer capital goods, K_2 the stock of non-computer capital goods, and a, b and c are constants. This model differs from Sraffa's in that it is nonlinear. More significantly, the Sraffian model measures all inputs and outputs in physical terms whereas the neoclassical model measures them in money terms. From the Sraffian point of view the measurement of capital in money is a serious flaw since the valuation of commodities depends upon the distribution of income between labour and capital (Foley, 2003). One cannot hope to measure the 'productivity' of aggregations of capital goods, since the valuation of these aggregations is itself a function of the class distribution of income.

From a classical standpoint the notion of productivity measured in money terms was ill-defined. The only context in which one could define productivity was as the inverse of labour values – an increase in productivity being equivalent to a fall in the labour required to make goods. Sraffa added to this concept the idea of the productivity of the basic sector measured in terms of its own inputs. One could in principle measure R for different years and see if it has gone up after the introduction of computer technology. Since there were many other technical changes at the same time, it would be hard to say whether such an increase in R might have stemmed from computer technology or from other innovations. Beyond this point though, the concept of the basic sector may provide another reason why productivity gains due to computers are so hard to discover: if computers are primarily used in non-basic sectors, Sraffian theory predicts that their use will leave R unchanged.

14.2   Kalecki: profit and monetary flows

Sraffa approached profit from the standpoint of the capacity of the economy to produce a physical surplus. An alternative approach, based on the sort of analysis presented in chapter 12, looks at the way the accounting identities imposed by commodity sales constrain the overall level of profit. Such a model for the determination of profits was given by Kalecki (1954). He showed that in an abstract capitalist economy with only two classes, no government sector, and subsistence wages, aggregate profits is determined by the sum of capitalist consumption and investment.

The basic argument is of disarming simplicity. First, from a macroeconomic point of view, aggregate income and aggregate expenditure are necessarily equal. In each and every transaction in which money changes hands in exchange for goods or services, this flow of money is expenditure from one party's point of view, and income from the point of view of the other party. Income and expenditure are really just two ways of looking at the same transfer of money. This proposition is enshrined in modern National Income accounting.

Now, in a simplified economy as described above (no government sector, no foreign trade), there are only two categories of income, namely wages (W) and profits (P). And there are just three categories of expenditure, namely workers' consumption (C_w), capitalists' consumption (C_c) and investment (I). We may therefore write

$$W + P = C_w + C_c + I \tag{14.2}$$

If the workers do not save then $C_w = W$ and we get

$$P = C_c + I \tag{14.3}$$

That is, aggregate profit is necessarily equal to the sum of capitalists' expenditure on consumer goods and investment. It remains to assign a causal interpretation to equation 14.3. Kalecki's insight was that capitalists cannot simply 'decide' on their incomes. They may plan or hope for a certain income, but what they actually receive is out of their control. On the other hand, they do decide on their expenditures. These expenditures may be more or less closely related to their income in the previous period, but the possibility of spending on credit, or of drawing down or running up money balances, allows room for discretion. But if capitalists get to decide their expenditures, and if the sum of these expenditures necessarily equals profit, it follows that the expenditures by the capitalists *determine* profit. As Kalecki put it, capitalists 'get what they spend'.

The above analysis can easily be extended to a less simplified economy. If we have a government that taxes and spends then its tax revenue, T, must be counted as an additional form of income (and wages and profits should be accounted after-tax) and its spending, G, has to be added to the expenditure side. Equation (14.2) then becomes

$$W + P + T = C_w + C_c + I + G$$

If foreign trade goes on, then we must allow for an additional category of spending on the output of the home economy, namely the trade balance or net exports

(exports minus imports), NX. This component of spending may be negative, if the country in question runs a trade deficit.[1] So the full form of the equation is

$$W + P + T = C_w + C_c + I + G + NX$$

or

$$P = C_c + I + (G - T) + NX - (W - C_w) \tag{14.4}$$

In relation to the simplest Kaleckian model, we find that profit is augmented by government deficit spending $(G - T)$ and net exports, but is reduced to the extent that workers save $(W - C_w)$.

This sort of analysis is extremely useful in the analysis of the business cycle. It shows very clearly the effects of capitalists' own expenditures, government fiscal policy, workers' saving, and the trade balance on the level of profits. It is not difficult to see how a cumulative movement may occur. For example, if capitalists become uncertain regarding the future profitability of their investments they may cut their expenditures. If this cut is not balanced by an increase in government deficit spending, an increase in net exports, or a reduction in workers' saving, then profits will fall, 'justifying' the capitalists' pessimistic forecast and likely leading to a further fall in their expenditures. And similarly in the upswing, when optimism leads to high capitalist expenditures and therefore high profits, encouraging yet higher expenditures. In this chapter, however, we are mainly focused on the long-run behaviour of the rate of profit, which is exposed more clearly by an analysis that runs in terms of labour-time. We develop this in the next section.

14.3   Demographics and the long-run rate of profit

What does the rate of profit tells us? It tells us something about the potential rate of expansion of capital stock. It sets an upper limit on the rate of expansion – the rate of capital growth that will be achieved if all profit is reinvested. From Sraffa's notion of the Standard System, the rate of profit tells us something about the rate of material expansion of the productive base of the economy.

The focus of the following analysis is be on how this rate of expansion will change over time, if capital actually is reinvested. We also examine the circumstances under which capital might be reinvested, and the consequences of capital not being reinvested.

---

[1] Imports must be entered with a negative sign for the following reason: we assumed above that each act of expenditure generates income to the same value (implicitly, in the home economy). But spending on imports does not produce income in the home economy, it generates income for somebody in another economy. If we were doing our accounting on a world scale net exports would drop out, since planet earth neither imports nor exports any commodities.

14.3.1 The mathematics of profit and labour time

If we approach the time-evolution of the rate of profit from the standpoint of capital accumulation, then the issue becomes simpler. Initially we will assume that all measurements are performed either in labour hours, or – what amounts to the same thing – in a monetary unit whose labour-time equivalent does not change from year to year. Using this approach we will derive an equation for the time-evolution of the rate of profit and show that the rate of profit tracks towards a long-run value which depends on the rate of growth of the working population along with the fraction of profit that is reinvested.

To begin with, consider the implications of taking a labour-time perspective on the question of profit. Profit can be measured as a flow of labour value, in which case its units are person hours per annum, which in dimensional terms is just persons since the division hours/annum gives a scalar. Thus the annual flow of profit when measured in labour terms corresponds to a certain number of people – the number of people whose direct and indirect output is materialized in the goods purchased out of profits.

The capital stock of a nation is, in these terms, a quantity expressed in millions of person years. And the rate of profit is then:

$$R = \frac{\text{Millions of workers whose product is bought by profits}}{\text{Millions of worker years represented by the capital stock}}$$

The evolution of R then depends on how rapidly the capital stock is built up compared to the growth rate of the number of workers producing the surplus that corresponds to profit. (Note that we now re-using the symbol R for the value-rate of profit – this is not the same as Sraffa's R in section 14.1.)

Let us represent the total profit or surplus value as a given share of the economy's net output (we consider the effects of a change in this share later).[2] We will write this share as $(1 - w)$, where w is the share of wages and salaries. Now, the concept of 'net output' requires some clarification. First, since we are working in terms of labour hours, the gross output of the economy is measured by the total hours worked, which we'll write as L. To get the net output we need to subtract from the total hours worked the number of hours required to maintain the capital stock. This includes 'physical' depreciation, whereby part of the existing capital stock, K, wears out each year. We assume that depreciation occurs at a constant rate, δ, so that δK hours must be spent in maintaining the capital stock in physical terms. But, since we are measuring capital stock in terms of labour-hours embodied, there is an additional factor to be taken into account. Namely, if the productivity of labour is increasing over time, at some proportional rate g, then a given physical collection of commodities will come to embody a declining number of labour-hours. Call this effect *devaluation* of the capital stock.

---

[2] At the level of abstraction of this argument, we are not distinguishing the components of surplus value – profit of enterprise, rent and interest – but rather treating the entire surplus as 'profit'.

To maintain the capital stock in *value terms* (worker years embodied), the physical capital stock must be expanded. We can then write the following expression for net output:

$$L - (g + \delta)K$$

That is, net output equals gross output minus the sum of depreciation and devaluation of the capital stock.

Writing S for total profit, we then have

$$S = (1 - w)(L - (g + \delta)K) \tag{14.5}$$

We next examine the growth of the capital stock. This is given by gross investment ('source') minus the sum of depreciation and devaluation ('sink'). Gross investment we take to be a proportion, λ, of total profit. That is,

$$\dot{K} = \lambda S - (g + \delta)K \tag{14.6}$$

where $\dot{K}$ is shorthand notation for the time-derivative of the capital stock, dK/dt.[3]

Now the rate of profit (in labour-time terms) is the ratio of the surplus, S, to the capital stock, K:

$$R = \frac{S}{K} \tag{14.7}$$

Using equation (14.5) to substitute for S, we get

$$R = \frac{(1 - w)(L - (g + \delta)K)}{K} = (1 - w)\left(\frac{L}{K} - (g + \delta)\right) \tag{14.8}$$

If the wage-share in net output, w, remains constant (along with g and δ), then the time-derivative of the rate of profit is given by

$$\dot{R} = (1 - w)\frac{d(L/K)}{dt} \tag{14.9}$$

---

[3] Note that since we have defined λ as the ratio of *gross* investment to S, and S is defined as a fraction of net output, it is possible in principle to have $\lambda > 1$. (This could happen if the capitalists fully cover depreciation and devaluation, and at the same time plough all of the surplus into new investment.)

That is, the change in the profit rate over time is a fraction of the change in the ratio of labour to capital stock. Via basic calculus,

$$\frac{d(L/K)}{dt} = \frac{1}{K}\dot{L} - \frac{L}{K^2}\dot{K} = \frac{L}{K}\left(\frac{\dot{L}}{L} - \frac{\dot{K}}{K}\right)$$

We will assume that the total labour performed per year changes at a proportional rate n (that is, $\dot{L}/L = n$). In addition we infer from (14.6) that

$$\frac{\dot{K}}{K} = \frac{\lambda S - (g + \delta)K}{K} = \lambda R - (g + \delta)$$

It follows that

$$\dot{R} = (1 - w)\frac{L}{K}(n - \lambda R + (g + \delta)) \tag{14.10}$$

Here we have an expression for the time-evolution of the value-rate of profit in terms of the basic parameters of the system. Under what condition is the rate of profit unchanging (i.e. $\dot{R} = 0$)? Given that the wage share, w, must lie between 0 and 1, and that total hours worked, L, must be positive, the required condition is that $n - \lambda R + (g + \delta) = 0$. That is,

$$R^\star = \frac{n + g + \delta}{\lambda} \tag{14.11}$$

where $R^\star$ is the value of R that yields $\dot{R} = 0$. This is the *steady-state* rate of profit – the rate which, once attained, will persist over time.

It is easy to show that the steady-state rate of profit, $R^\star$, is an *attractor* for the actual rate of profit. Suppose that at some point in time R is greater than $R^\star$. Since R enters equation (14.10) with a negative coefficient, namely $-\lambda(1-w)L/K$, this means that $\dot{R}$ will be negative, or in other words the rate of profit will be falling. By the same token, if $R < R^\star$ the rate of profit will be rising.

Equation 14.11 shows that the long-run rate of profit is positively related to the growth rate of population (strictly speaking, total hours worked), the growth rate of labour productivity, and the rate of depreciation of the capital stock. It is inversely related to the proportion of the surplus that is reinvested. Note, however, this this long-run rate does not depend on the wage share in net output, w. If w were changing continuously over time this would require a modification to equation 14.9, but

- the long run rate of profit is independent of w so long as w is constant (that is, it makes no difference to $R^\star$ whether w equals 0.1 or 0.9); and

- if w does change progressively over time, its change is nonetheless bounded. If the wage share falls over time (the rate of surplus value rises) it can't fall below 0, so the ultimate effect is limited.

To get a sense of what the above analysis implies let's consider a simplified case, where we set both depreciation and the growth of labour productivity to zero. In that case equation (14.11) becomes

$$R^\star = \frac{n}{\lambda}$$

That is, the long-run rate of profit is simply a multiple of the population growth rate, that multiple being larger, the smaller is the fraction of the surplus that is reinvested. If 100 per cent of the surplus is reinvested, the steady-state rate of profit just equals the population growth rate. This brings out the key role of historical demography in the long-run evolution of the rate of profit.

14.3.2   *Growth of the workforce, growth of productivity*

Once the argument is on this terrain one has to ask what determines the rate of growth of the working population. Two factors are clearly important, the natural rate of population growth and the evolution of the fraction of the total population that is employed in wage labour under capitalist relations of production. Economies undergoing transition from peasant farming to capitalist industry typically have a rapid rate of growth of the working population from both factors. The birthrate tends to be high and at the same time infant mortality falls. This gives a rapid rate of natural population increase. At the same time the fraction of the population employed as wage labourers rises, giving a high compounded rate of growth of the employed population.

In a mature capitalist economy things are different. Although infant mortality continues to fall this is offset by a falling birth rate, which in many advanced capitalist economies falls below replacement level. At the same time the share of capitalistically employed wage labour in the population tends to reach a plateau or even to fall. The result is a relatively stagnant or declining capitalistically employed population.

If we assume that the rate of growth of the employed population is fixed then the effect is that the actual rate of profit tends towards some multiple of the rate of growth of the employed population, the multiple depending on the percentage of profit that is reinvested. In Figure 14.2 we start out with a rate of profit of 33 per cent and have the population growing at 3 per cent a year. Half of all profits are reinvested. The rate of profit tends towards 6 per cent, as this is the only rate of profit at which the rate of growth of the capital stock will equal the rate of growth of the population. It is the latter that constrains the rate of growth of value production.

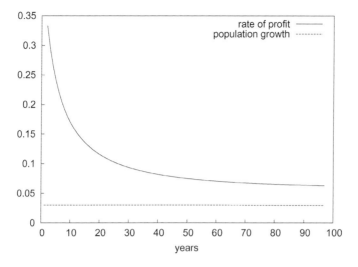

Figure 14.2 Evolution of the profit rate under constant population growth.

If we take a more realistic model as shown in Figure 14.3, where the rate of growth of the population declines with time, then the rate of profit chases the rate of population growth downwards.

The examples above assume a constant rate of surplus value of 50 per cent (that is, $w = \frac{2}{3}$). If technology is improving and the productivity of labour is increasing, this amounts to assuming that real wages are rising over time: a constant wage

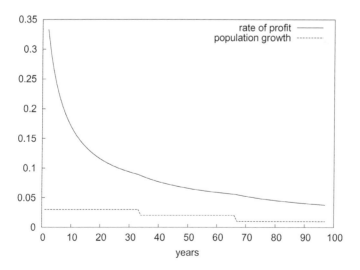

Figure 14.3 Evolution of the profit rate given declining population growth. The rate of profit declines further than in Figure 14.2.

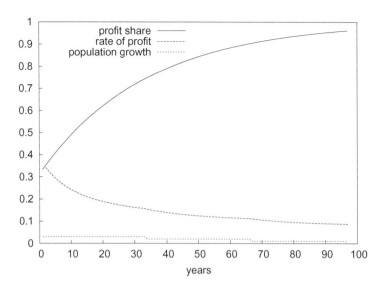

Figure 14.4 Evolution of the profit rate given declining population growth and constant real wages. The rate of profit declines despite the increasing share of profit in output (the top curve).

share of $^2/_3$ of the national income will correspond to a rising real standard of living. Okishio's 1961 paper assumed that real wages were constant. This corresponds to a gradually increasing profit share in national income. Figure 14.4 models this process. We here assume that the productivity of labour grows at 3 per cent a year, while real wages remain constant. Under these circumstances the wage share will fall by 3 per cent a year. (That is, w in year t equals w in year $t - 1$ divided by 1.03.) Observe that the rate of profit still falls.

Investment in new plant and equipment is often associated with improvement in production techniques and hence a reduction in the labour-content and price of capital goods. Under these circumstances the existing of stock of capital capital will be devalued. This has two contrary effects on the rate of profit. On the one hand the devaluation of capital slows down the growth of the capital stock, which tends to mitigate any decline in the profit rate (see equation 14.6). On the other hand, devaluation produces a loss on the capital account which directly reduces profits (equation 14.5).

The simulation shown in Figure 14.5 shows the relatively complex effects which emerge when a change occurs in the pace of technical improvement. During years 1–14 and 55 onwards there are no improvements in productivity, but over years 15 to 54 labour productivity rises by 5 per cent a year.[4] Real wages are

---

[4] To make the effect on the graph more apparent we have also set the depreciation rate, δ, to 2 per cent over this period. Other than that, physical depreciation of the capital stock is ignored in these simplified examples.

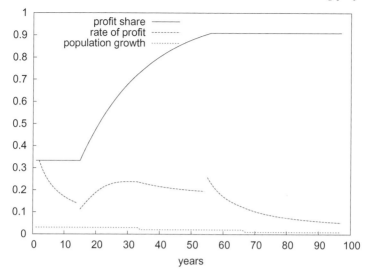

Figure 14.5 Evolution of the profit rate given declining population growth and technical improvement. From years 15 to 55 there is a 5 per cent improvement in labour productivity. Other years see no improvement.

assumed to be held constant, so the wage share falls and the profit share rises during the period of growth in productivity. In year 15 the rate of profit drops sharply because of induced devaluation of capital. But for the following 15 years the rate of profit rises. This is due to the combined effect of slower growth of the capital stock and a rise in the profit share. The rate of profit subsequently settles into a declining trend because of the slowdown in population growth.

As we showed earlier (equations 14.9 and 14.11), the rate of profit R^*, towards which the actual rate of profit tends in the Figures above, is the only one at which the ratio of current labour to the labour embodied in the capital stock is stable. If the rate of profit is higher then the organic composition is driven up; if it is lower, then the organic composition falls. This has the interesting implication that if an economy were to have a declining population – which, given trends in birth rates, is quite plausible for many capitalist nations – then the long-term profit rate might be zero or negative. To retain a positive profit rate with a declining workforce, the rate of improvement in labour productivity must be greater than the rate of shrinkage of the workforce.

14.3.3 *Monetary illusions*

The argument in Section 14.3.2 is formulated on the assumption that all accounting of profit and loss is done in value terms. In practice, of course, profits are calculated in terms of money, not labour values. The argument assumed that the value of money in terms of labour did not change over time. If the product of a day's labour sold for £1 in 1900, it would still sell for £1 in 1910, 1920,

1930,... But this is obviously false. Over time the value of money has gone down in two senses:

(1)   £1 bought less and less labour as the decades progressed.
(2)   The price of many, but not all, commodities tended to rise. Bread in Britain is about 15 times as expensive as it was 40 years ago.

We can measure the purchasing power of money in goods that it buys, or in labour it purchases. In both senses the value of money has fallen. Such inflation makes commerce *appear* more profitable. You have only to hold assets a while then sell, and you make a profit. Millions of house-owners know this. Inflation transfers resources from lenders to borrowers and can also hide a falling real rate of profit. Banks do notice that the money they are being paid back is worth less than when they lent it. They know the difference between real and money profits and compensate by charging more interest.

The same applies to other businesses. Their accountants distinguish between nominal profits arising from inflation and real profits. But how should they make the adjustment? Should they measure the value of money in terms of commodities or in terms of labour?

Official inflation is measured using a consumer price index. Such an index tracks the aggregate price of a 'shopping basket' of typical consumer purchases. An index of this sort tells you what wage increase is required to maintain a given standard of living, and so is more useful to trade union negotiators than to capitalists. Capitalists are more interested in the prices of labour and raw materials. Adam Smith said that money was the power to command the labour of others. The entrepreneur seeks this command over labour. He wants to 'grow the business', and this growth comes down either to having more employees or – what amounts to the same thing – indirectly employing more people via suppliers and subcontractors. Unless the business grows in these terms, the entrepreneur's social position has not improved. From the capitalist standpoint, the value-based accounting that we presented above is indeed the most appropriate. It is only when he deflates the monetary profit rate to get the value profit rate that the capitalist can measure the growth of his social power.

If a capitalist wants to go up in the world, he should watch his value rate of profit. If he does not want his absolute standard of living to decline, he should ensure that his money rate of profit is greater than price inflation.

Equation 14.12 showed how, for a representative capitalist, the growth of his power comes to be constrained by investment (λ), population growth (n), technical progress (g) and the rate of depreciation (δ). We can transform the attractor of the value rate of profit, $R^\star$, into an attractor for the monetary rate of profit, $R_M^\star$, by adding the rate of inflation in value terms, π_v, i.e., $R_M^\star = R^\star + \pi_v$. This π_v measures the annual price increase for a commodity bundle containing, say, 100 hours of labour. As labour productivity rises, the 100-hour bundle will get physically bigger at the rate g. Suppose that the cost of living, measured in the usual way by the aggregate price of a representative bundle of goods, is constant.

This means we have zero inflation in the ordinary sense of the word, but the rate of inflation in value terms is not zero: it is equal to g. The 100 hours corresponds to a larger bundle of goods, with a higher aggregate price. With ordinary price-inflation, π, at zero, $\pi_v = g$. If ordinary inflation is positive, this augments value-inflation, hence in general $\pi_v = g + \pi$. It follows that the attractor for the monetary rate of profit will be

$$R^\star_M = R^\star + \pi_v = \frac{n + g + \delta}{\lambda} + g + \pi \qquad (14.12)$$

Table 14.3 shows five possible scenarios to get a feel for the behaviour of the long-term value- and money-rates of profit. The scenarios are labeled by historical periods that have similar general features. Note that in the table $R^\star$ and $R^\star_M$ are not the actual rates of profit, but rather the limits towards which the rates of profit evolve. Scenario 1 represents a period of high inflation, high accumulation and slow population growth – for example, the UK in the late 1960s and early 1970s. The long-run money rate of profit, $R^\star_M$, is high but discounting the effect of inflation the underlying value-rate of profit is very close to g, the improvement in labour productivity.

Going back a century (Scenario 2), we have faster population growth, but a much lower rate of accumulation out of profits and, because of the deflationary effect of the gold standard, slightly declining money prices. The value- and money-rates of profit are close to each other and stand considerably higher than in Scenario 1 due to the slow pace of accumulation.

Scenarios 3 and 4 envisage a future European economy with a declining population, with the Euro managed so as to maintain a zero rate of price inflation, and assuming 3 per cent growth in labour productivity. Given relatively rapid accumulation, the value-rate of profit is approximately equal to the growth of labour productivity; if accumulation is slower the value-rate is higher. In both cases the money-rate exceeds the value rate by the growth of labour productivity.

Scenario 5 pertains to a rapidly emergent capitalist economy such as China in the early twenty-first century: the population is growing fast and the rate of investment is high. At the same time, the importation of advanced technology allows for much faster growth of labour productivity than can be attained in a

Table 14.3 The rate of profit: five scenarios. A depreciation rate of $\delta = 0.03$ is assumed in all cases

Scenario	n	g	λ	π	$R^\star$	$R^\star_M$	Comment
1	0.5%	2.25%	100%	8%	2.78%	13.03%	UK 1970
2	1.0%	2.00%	20%	−1%	15.15%	16.15%	UK 1870
3	−1.0%	3.00%	30%	0%	6.77%	9.77%	Europe 2020
4	−1.0%	3.00%	70%	0%	2.90%	5.90%	Europe 2020, high accum.
5	5.0%	10.00%	100%	0%	15.03%	25.03%	China 2000

mature capitalist economy. The long-run profit rate is therefore high despite the rapid pace of accumulation.

14.3.4   *A tendency for the rate of profit to fall?*

Smith, Ricardo and Marx all held the view that the rate of profit would tend to fall in the course of capitalist development. However, each offered a different reason for this thesis.

Smith thought that as capital accumulated, and the supply of commodities expanded, there would be increased competition between the capitalists to sell their wares, which would drive down both prices and the rate of profit. Ricardo rejected this argument. In modern terminology, he accused Smith of confusing microeconomics with macroeconomics. It's true, at the microeconomic level, that if capitalists expand the production of some particular commodity, while the demand for that commodity remains unchanged, then its price will fall and so will the rate of profit in that line of production. But if the capitalists collectively expand the production of all commodities, at the macroeconomic level, one cannot assume that demand remains unchanged. With higher employment and higher wages (due to the increased demand for labour), accompanied by greater orders for capital goods, demand must expand along with supply. But then there's no necessity for prices or profits to fall.

Ricardo's own case for a falling rate of profit hinged on increasing costs in agriculture. As population expanded it would be necessary to bring less fertile land into cultivation, and/or to farm the best land more intensively. The result would be a rise in the labour-time required to produce basic foods ('corn' or wheat, in Ricardo's day), and hence a rise in the price of food. Profits would be put under a double squeeze: on the one hand wages would have to rise to cover the increased cost of subsistence for the workers; on the other, rent would increase since the rent on any given piece of land is equal to the wedge between the cost of production at the margin (i.e. on the worst land in use) and the cost of production on the land in question. This wedge will grow as progressively less fertile land comes to be cultivated.

Ricardo's argument is logically valid, but one of his factual premises has proved false. He thought that improvement in agricultural productivity, due to the application of science and technology, would be at best a mitigating factor, slowing the inevitable rise in the cost of food. In fact, to date we have managed to do better than that. The most basic index of the huge increase in agricultural productivity is the declining percentage of the workforce employed in agriculture. In the UK this fell from a large majority at the beginning of the nineteenth century to 22 per cent at mid-century, to 10.7 per cent in 1891, and to 7.8 per cent in 1911 (Thompson, 1993).

That leaves Marx. Writing at a time when the ongoing increase in the productivity of labour in agriculture had become readily apparent, Marx did not subscribe to Ricardo's prognosis. His basic argument concerned the balance between the organic composition of capital (i.e. roughly speaking, the capital–labour ratio) and the rate of surplus value (i.e. the division of the working day between the 'necessary labour' required to maintain and reproduce the workforce and the 'surplus labour' that produces the goods purchased out of profit, rent and interest). Marx thought that (a) the organic composition tends to rise as capital accumulates, which of itself reduces the rate of profit (basically, by increasing the denominator), but also (b) the rate of surplus value tends to rise as the productivity of labour increases, which of itself raises the rate of profit. It might then seem that the net outcome for the rate of profit is indeterminate, but Marx had the intuition that the rising organic composition would ultimately win out. This intuition is borne out by the 'demographic' model we developed above.

Unfortunately, Marx presented two arguments regarding the falling rate of profit, one correct and one fallacious. The fallacious one attracted a good deal of attention from the 1960s onward, hence obscuring the real issue. So it is necessary to disentangle the two. The problematic argument of Marx's runs as follows.

(1)   Each individual capitalist has an incentive to introduce new technology to cut his costs (true).
(2)   The bias in such new technology will tend to be to increase the capital–labour ratio (probably true).
(3)   In the short run, this will increase the profits of the innovating capitalist, who is able to sell his product at the 'old' price while having a reduced cost of production (true).
(4)   When the new technique becomes generalized, the effect is to raise the economy-wide organic composition of capital (true, if point 2 is correct).
(5)   And this will lower the general rate of profit (false).

Marx's argument has an air of paradox: a policy which raises the rate of profit for each capitalist, considered individually, nonetheless ends up having the effect of lowering the overall rate of profit. That a proposition of economic theory seems paradoxical is not in itself an argument against that proposition, but in this case the paradoxical claim is not sustainable. As we said in section 14.1, it can be shown on the basis of Sraffian input–output analysis that Marx's argument is incorrect. If a new technique of production raises the rate of profit for an individual capitalist at the current vector of prices (and wages), then the generalization of that technique is bound to raise, not lower, the economy-wide rate of profit provided that the real wage remains unchanged; Okishio (1961) was the first to notice this point.

It is important to notice, however, that the point at issue between Marx and Okishio – couched in terms of 'choice of technique' – slides past the historical–demographic argument given above. Marx claims that individual capitalists will choose capital-intensive techniques which, once they are generalized, will have the effect of lowering the overall rate of profit; and Okishio refutes him. But the increase in capital-intensity (organic composition) that occurs in the historical progress towards the steady-state rate of profit, R^*, is not a matter of 'choice of technique'; rather, it is an inevitable consequence of a pace of accumulation of capital which exceeds the rate of growth of the population engaged in wage labour.

The only way out of this 'trap' for the rate of profit is that capital accumulation itself slows to match population growth. Or in other words, the scenarios shown in Figures 14.3 and 14.4 will never occur. How plausible is this idea? Not very, according to the studies cited in the following section.

Before proceeding to the historical evidence, it may be worth offering one more perspective on the theoretical argument. In the model we presented above there are two aspects to the 'falling rate of profit'.

(1) If capitalist economies 'start out' with a relatively small stock of capital (as they surely must) then they will initially have a relatively high rate of profit. But over the decades, as capital is accumulated, the organic composition of capital will rise and the rate of profit will decline towards its steady-state level, the $R^\star$ given in equation (14.11).

(2) The steady-state rate of profit will itself fall over historical time, if the rate of population growth tends to fall, as we have seen in the developed economies over the last century or so.

The only long-term offsets to a declining rate of profit are those which have the effect of raising $R^\star$, namely

• an increase in the rate of growth of labour productivity, g;
• an increase in the rate of depreciation, δ; and
• a reduction in the investment ratio, λ.

We leave aside here the possibility of an increase in the population growth rate, n, which is not under the control of capitalists, and we may as well dismiss δ on the same grounds. That leaves productivity growth and the investment ratio. Naturally, capitalists would prefer to have faster rather than slower growth of labour productivity, but historically it seems that something like 3 per cent is the maximum sustainable rate (maybe more like 2 per cent) – other, that is, than in the case of newly emerging capitalist economies which are able, for a certain time, to increase productivity at a faster pace by playing 'catch up' (see the China scenario in Table 14.3). Which leaves the investment ratio. Capitalists can halt the tendency for the rate of profit to fall by ceasing to accumulate capital – but then, in effect, they cease being capitalists. They may still be exploiters, consuming the surplus product created by the productive workforce, but if capitalists stop accumulating it seems that their days must be numbered: who needs a rooster that won't crow, or a capitalist that won't accumulate?

14.3.5   *Historical evidence*

There is evidence that over periods of decades in individual economies the rate of accumulation has exceeded the rate of population growth and that as a consequence the organic composition of capital has risen Cockshott *et al.* (1995), Edvinsson (2003, 2005).

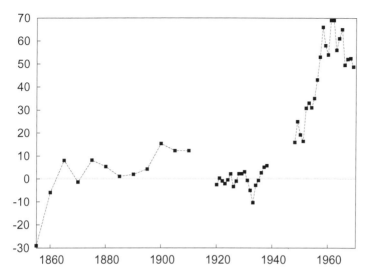

Figure 14.6 Accumulation of capital as a percentage of profit in the UK, 1855–1969.

In the UK the migration from country to town was effectively complete 100 years ago. As the proletarian population became more stable and hereditary, trades union organization spread and strikes and labour disputes became more common. It became harder for employers to expand their workforce at the old level of wages. This process was already underway in the Belle Époque just before the first world war, a period that saw the rapid spread of general trades unions. Earlier unions had been craft-based, organizing skilled labour. It now proved possible to organize unions among the the bulk of the working class, not just an aristocracy of skilled artisans.

The dynamic interaction of industrial capital and the banks polarizes capital and precipitates out a class of rentiers. By the late Victorian era this process was well underway. A capitalist class whose grandfathers had been the pioneering cotton masters or iron masters of the industrial revolution had been transformed into a rentier class. Where frugality and accumulation had once been their watchwords, they now increasingly aped the lifestyles of their former political enemies, the landed aristocracy. Fortunes were spent constructing stately homes in the country and on employing retinues of domestic servants. With so much going on luxury consumption, less was left for investment. The late Victorian rate of investment was low: typically, less than 15 per cent of profit was reinvested in new plant and equipment within the UK (see Figure 14.6). In consequence the organic composition of capital remained low, and rate of profit did not decline significantly, in the late Victorian period (Figure 14.7).[5]

---

[5] Figures 14.6 and 14.7 are constructed from Tables 3.1 and 3.2 in Cockshott *et al.* (1995).

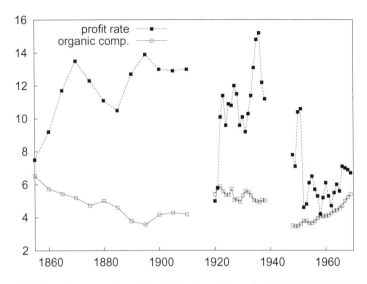

Figure 14.7 Organic composition of capital and profit rate in the UK, 1855–1969.

Again during the inter-war period, recession meant that capital accumulation was relatively slow. It was not until the period after 1945 that rapid capital accumulation, along with slow population growth, produced a substantial decline in profitability.

David Zachariah has computed what the steady-state rate of profit in the UK and Japan should have been if the theory in this chapter is correct. As in section 14.3.1, the profit rate is defined as $R = S/K$, where S is the total net profit, computed by subtracting wages, W, and depreciation, δK, from the Gross Domestic Product, Y. That is, $S = Y - W - \delta K$. The steady-state rate of profit is given by equation (14.11) above. The actual and steady-state rates are compared in Figure 14.8. It can be seen the the actual rate of profit closely follows the steady-state rate – with a time lag, as one would expect.

Edvinsson shows data for Sweden indicating that over a prolonged period there had been a significant rise in the organic composition of capital and a fall in the rate of profit. Duménil and Lévy (2002) show that there was a prolonged decline in profit rates in the USA in the postwar period (see Figure 14.9).

Table 14.4 Rising organic composition of capital, manufacturing and mining in Sweden (Edvinsson, 2003: table 7.5)

	Average 1871–1900	*Average 1971–2000*	*Change*
$c/(s+v)$	184%	305%	66%
$s/(s+v)$	34%	21%	−38%
s/c	19%	7%	−61%

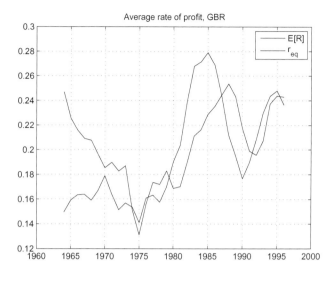

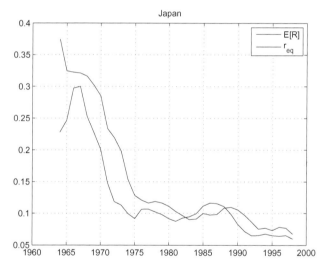

Figure 14.8 The evolution of the equilibrium rate of profit predicted by the theory in this chapter and the rate of profit observed in the UK and Japan (Zachariah, 2008).

14.3.6 *The Okishio critique revisited*

Many people have interpreted Okishio's critique of Marx to mean that the sort of historical trends discussed above ought not to have occurred. Since they did occur, we are led to believe that there must be some premises in his argument that are not an accurate reflection of the way capitalist economies actually work.

Broad profit rate: Six sectors (prfall)

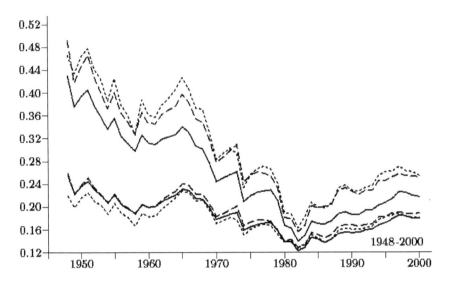

Figure 14.9 Evolution of the profit rate in the USA (Duménil and Lévy, 2002).

One source of weakness in the Okishio theory is the assumption of an equalized rate of profit. This rate of profit is used as a benchmark against which possible improvements in productivity are measured. We have argued that this assumption is unrealistic. Actual profit rates show a wide dispersion (Table 10.5), wider than the dispersion in the rate of surplus value for instance. The general rate of profit is not a given *datum* for an individual firm. A firm knows what its own rate of profit last year was, and it knows what the interest rate is, but the 'general rate of profit' is difficult to measure and is of interest mainly to economic statisticians.

The process by which equilibration of profit rates is supposed to come about was originally invoked by classical economists in the context of comparing processes such as the maturation of wine and forestry, which had turnover times of several years, with corn-growing which had an annual turnover period. The argument was that capital would be invested in low-turnover activities only if it yielded the same return as in normal agriculture. This argument may have some plausibility when applied to activities such as the production of vintage wine, where the rate of technical change is low and decades or centuries can be allowed for the establishment of relative prices, but it is less clear that it can be invoked where there is rapid technical change. In this case the time taken to establish equilibrium can be longer than the lifespan of the technology. This is especially true in certain industries with a very high capital–labour ratio, ones which are particularly relevant to the question at hand. Consider the Victorian railways. Here was an entirely new technology requiring huge capital investment. The lifetime of the capital in the form of bridges, embankments and stations would be a century or more. The railway booms resulted in over-capacity, which led to line closures by the early twentieth century. But before the capital invested in railways could depreciate to the level at which it would yield an equilibrium rate of return, the whole technology was superseded by road transport. The sort of equilibrium that is required for the Okishio theorem can be so long in coming that the industry has died before it is relevant.

One can distinguish three rates that might act as benchmarks for a capitalist contemplating new investment:

(1)   the statistical average rate of profit;
(2)   the average rate of return on equities; and
(3)   the rate of interest available from the banks.

We have ruled out item 1 as a practical guide, what about the rate of return on equities? This rate is certainly more accessible, since there are well developed stock markets that make such data available. This makes it a more plausible investment benchmark.

Suppose we have a static working population, and the rate of return on equities is equal to the general rate of profit. And suppose that any net investment in fixed capital would lead to a lower return on capital than allowed by the equity market. That is, in Okishio's terms, no 'viable' labour-saving techniques are available.[6] Firms will thus tend to select only capital-saving technical innovations. This implies that firms, taken as a whole, will need no net infusion of capital, so there should be zero net issue of new equities. If the rentier class as a whole is content to carry out no net saving then the situation is stable. But this is unlikely. If the rentiers attempt to accumulate capital by investing in shares, the net effect will be to bid up the price of equities, given that no new equities are being issued. The effect of this is to depress the rate of return on equities. This will affect the discount rate used in assessing investment projects. Previously unprofitable ones will seem profitable. New equities will be issued and the proceeds invested. Given that the population is static, this will raise the organic composition of capital and depress the real rate of profit.

Similar considerations apply to the interest rate. If rentiers wish to accumulate assets in the form of bonds, and if capitalist enterprises are not issuing bonds to finance new investment on the grounds that such investment will lower the rate of profit, then the price of bonds will be bid upwards, which corresponds to a reduction in the interest rate. Just as with equities, this will make previously unprofitable investments seem profitable.

---

[6]   A 'viable' technique is one which raises the profitability of the firm that introduces it, taking the current vector of prices and wages as given. As noted above, Okishio argues that if a technique is viable in this sense, its generalization must raise the economy-wide rate of profit so long as the real wage remains constant.

The weakness in Okishio's argument stems from a fundamental failing of the entire 'price of production' school: they tend to elide the distinction between the formation of a general rate of return on financial assets and the formation of a uniform rate of profit on real invested capital. The former tendency will be much stronger than the tendency towards a uniform rate of profit on real capital stock. Stocks of capital goods held by companies originated as manufactured commodities with a price and a corresponding accounting book-value. This book-value may be written down due to depreciation, or written up due to inflation, but at heart the valuation of real capital remains grounded in commodity prices. In contrast the stock market valuation of a company represents the discounted present value of its anticipated future earnings. If the company owns readily saleable capital assets, these can set a lower bound on its share price – below this price takeovers by asset strippers become likely. Even allowing for this constraint, share prices have great flexibility and respond rapidly to changes in reported profits. These fast changes in the nominal valuation of companies can create the illusion that the rate of profit in different industries is narrowly clustered around an average profit rate.

Part IV

Information and coordination

15 Hayek, information and knowledge

The fact that the present authors have, on balance, a positive view of the economic work of Karl Marx will not have escaped the reader. Although this book, with its grounding in the physical and information sciences, is by no means a work of orthodox Marxism, its presentation of economic issues is certainly influenced by Marx and the school of economics that follows him. Examination of the economics of information is, however, more associated with a very different school of economics, that of Hayek. Friedrich August von Hayek (1899–1992) was an Austrian economist and political philosopher, noted for his defense of liberal democracy and free-market capitalism against socialist and collectivist thought in the mid-twentieth century. Hayek's ideas acquired a practical relevance from their political adoption, first by the Thatcher government in Britain in the 1980s and later by post-Soviet governments in Russia and Eastern Europe. We consider that he made fundamental errors in his analysis of economic information – errors which, when they became the basis for practical policy, had catastrophic effects on economic co-ordination and performance.

Whereas the present authors strongly believe in the applicability of the methods of natural science to the study of social phenomena, Hayek (1955) was concerned to distinguish radically between the two domains of investigation. In the natural sciences, advances involve recognizing that things are not what they seem. Science dissolves the immediate categories of subjective experience and replaces them with underlying, often hidden, causes. The study of society, on the other hand, has to take as its raw material the ideas and beliefs of people in society. The facts studied by social science

> differ from the facts of the physical sciences in being beliefs or opinions held by particular people, beliefs which as such are our data, irrespective of whether they are true or false, and which, moreover, we cannot directly observe in the minds of people but which we can recognize from what they say or do merely because we have ourselves a mind similar to theirs.
>
> (Hayek, 1955: 28)

He argues that there is an irreducible subjective element to the subject mater of the social sciences which was absent in the physical sciences.

> [M]ost of the objects of social or human action are not "objective facts" in the special narrow sense in which the term is used in the Sciences and contrasted to "opinions", and they cannot at all be defined in physical terms. So far as human actions are concerned, things *are* what the acting people think they are.
>
> (Hayek, 1955: 26–27)

His paradigm for the social or moral sciences is that society must be understood in terms of people's conscious reflected actions, it being assumed that people are constantly consciously choosing between different possible courses of action. Any collective phenomena must thus be conceived of as the unintended outcome of the decisions of individual conscious actors.

This imposes a fundamental dichotomy between the study of nature and of society, since in dealing with natural phenomena it may be reasonable to suppose that the individual scientist can know all the relevant information, while in the social context this condition cannot possibly be met.

We believe that Hayek's objection is fundamentally misplaced. Even Laplace, who is famously cited as an advocate of determinism, argued that although the universe was in principle predictable to the smallest detail, this was in practice impossible because of limited knowledge and that thus science had to have recourse to probability theory. Certainly since Boltzmann it has been understood how collective phenomena arise as 'unintended' or emergent outcomes of a mass of uncoordinated processes. Our work in chapter 7 shows how the law of value arises in a similar way. But we did not have to model consciousness on the part of the economic actors to get this result.

In Hayek's view, there were two knowledge forms: scientific knowledge (understood as knowledge of general laws) versus 'unorganized knowledge' or 'knowledge of the particular circumstances of time and place'. The former, he says, may be susceptible of centralization via a 'body of suitably chosen experts' (Hayek, 1945: 521) but the latter is a different matter.

> [P]ractically every individual has some advantage over others in that he possesses unique information of which beneficial use might be made, but of which use can be made only if the decisions depending on it are left to him or are made with his active cooperation.
>
> (Hayek, 1945: 521–22)

Hayek is thinking here of 'knowledge of people, of local conditions, and special circumstances' (Hayek, 1945: 522), e.g., of the fact that a certain machine is not fully employed, or of a skill that could be better utilized. He also cites the sort of specific, localized knowledge relied upon by shippers and arbitrageurs. He claims that this sort of knowledge is often seriously undervalued by those who consider general scientific knowledge as paradigmatic. But this leaves out of account whole layer of knowledge that is crucial for economic activity, namely knowledge of specific technologies, knowledge captured in designs, knowledge captured in software.[1] Such knowledge is not reducible to general scientific law (it is generally a non-trivial problem to move from a relevant scientific theory to a workable industrial innovation), but neither is it so time- or place-specific that it is non-communicable. The licensing and transfer of technologies in a capitalist context shows this quite clearly. It also misses out the tendency of capitalist society to capture even human knowledge in objective form:

> Once a worker's knowledge is captured as structural capital, you can then do away with the worker. In industrial capitalism the worker's surplus labor was expropriated, but you had to retain the worker as long as you wanted to make use of his labor. The worker still owned his labor power, and sold it for his wages. But in the new economy, knowledge is both labor and the means of production, both of which are expropriated and turned into structural capital for the exclusive use of the corporation. Thus, intellectual capital can be totally alienated from the worker. Not only is the value of the labor stolen, but the labor itself.
>
> (Harris, 1996)

Hayek's notion of knowledge existing solely 'in the mind' is an obstacle to understanding. It is by now all but universal practice for firms to keep records of their inputs and outputs in the form of some sort of computer spreadsheet. These computer files form an image of the firm's input–output characteristics, an image which is readily transferable.[2]

Further, even the sort of 'particular' knowledge which Hayek thought too localized to be susceptible to centralization is now routinely centralized. Take his example of the information possessed by shippers. In the 1970s American Airlines achieved the position of the world's largest airline, to a great extent on the strength of their development of the SABRE system of computerized booking of flights (Gibbs, 1994). Since then we have come to take it for granted that either we will be able to tap into the Internet to determine where and when there are flights available from just about any A to any B across the world. Hayek's appeal to localized knowledge in this sort of context may have been appropriate at the time of writing, but it is now clearly outdated.

15.1   Inadequacy of the price form

Prices, according to Hayek, provide the telecoms system of the economy. But how adequate is this telecoms system and how much information can it really transmit?

---

[1] It would be anachronistic to accuse Hayek of not seeing knowledge in software, but in his day knowledge already existed in the control programs for automatic machines, for instance pianola rolls.

[2] Admittedly, such an image does not of itself provide any information on how, for instance, a particularly favorable set of input–output relations can be *achieved*, only that it is *possible*.

While insisting that very specific, localized knowledge is essential to economic decision making, Hayek clearly recognizes that the 'man on the spot' needs to know more than just his immediate circumstances before he can act effectively. Hence there arises the problem of 'communicating to him such further information as he needs to fit his decisions into the whole pattern of changes of the larger economic system' (Hayek, 1945: 525) How much does he need to know? Fortuitously, only that which is conveyed by prices. Hayek constructs an example to illustrate his point:

> Assume that somewhere in the world a new opportunity for the use of some raw material, say tin, has arisen, or that one of the sources of supply of tin has been eliminated. It does not matter for our purpose and it is very significant that it does not matter which of these two causes has made tin more scarce. All that the users of tin need to know is that some of the tin they used to consume is now more profitably employed elsewhere, and that in consequence they must economize tin. There is no need for the great majority of them even to know where the more urgent need has arisen, or in favor of what other uses they ought to husband the supply.
>
> (Hayek, 1945: 526)

Despite the absence of any such overview, the effects of the disturbance in the tin market will ramify throughout the economy just the same.

> The whole acts as one market, not because any of its members survey the whole field, but because their limited individual fields of vision sufficiently overlap so that through many intermediaries the relevant information is communicated to all.
>
> (*ibid.*)

Therefore the significant thing about the price system is 'the economy of knowledge with which it operates' (Hayek, 1945: 526–7). He drives his point home thus:

> It is more than a metaphor to describe the price system as a kind of machinery for registering change, or a system of telecommunications which enables individual producers to watch merely the movement of a few pointers, as an engineer might watch the hands of a few dials, in order to adjust their activities to changes of which they may never know more than is reflected in the price movements.
>
> (Hayek, 1945: 527)

He admits that the adjustments produced via the price system are not perfect in the sense of general equilibrium theory, but they are nonetheless a 'marvel' of economical coordination. (*ibid.*)

Hayek's example of the tin market bears careful examination. Two preliminary points should be made.

First, the market system does manage to achieve a reasonable degree of coordination of economic activities. The 'anarchy of the market' is far from total chaos. In the end, through the fluctuation of prices the law of value acts. Fluctuations of prices about values do function to regulate the allocation of labour between branches of production.

Second, even in a planned economy there will always be scope for the disappointment of expectations, for projects that looked promising ex ante to turn out to be failures and so on. Failures of coordination are not confined to market systems.

That said, it is nonetheless clear that Hayek grossly overstates his case. In order to make rational decisions relating to changing one's usage of tin, one has to know whether a rise in price is likely to be permanent or transient, and that requires knowing *why* the price has risen. The current price signal is never enough in itself. Has tin become more expensive temporarily, due, say, to a strike by the tin miners? Or are we approaching the exhaustion of readily available reserves? Actions that are rational in the one case will be quite inappropriate in the other.

Prices *in themselves* provide adequate knowledge for rational calculation only if they are at their long-run equilibrium levels, but of course for Hayek they never are. On this point it is useful to refer back to Hayek's own theory of the trade cycle (Hayek, 1935; Lawlor and Horn, 1992; Cottrell, 1994), in which the 'misinformation' conveyed by disequilibrium prices can cause very substantial macroeconomic distortions. In Hayek's cycle theory, the disequilibrium price that can do such damage is the rate of interest, but clearly the same sort of argument applies at the micro level too. Decentralized profit-maximizing responses to unsustainable prices for tin or RAM chips are equally capable of generating misinvestment and subsequent chaos.

At minimum, prices may be said to carry information regarding the terms on which various commodities may currently be exchanged, via the mediation of money (so long as markets markets clear, which is not always the case). It does not follow, however, that a knowledge of these exchange ratios enable agents to calculate the profitability, let alone the social usefulness, of producing various commodities. A commodity can be produced at profit if its price exceeds the sum of the prices of the inputs required to produce it, using the production method which yields the least such sum, but the use of current prices in this calculation is legitimate only in a static context: either prices are unchanging or production and sale take zero time. Hayek, of course, stresses constant change as the rule, so he is hardly in a position to entertain this sort of assumption. Whether production of commodity x will in fact prove profitable or not depends on future prices as well as current prices. And whether production of x currently appears profitable depends on current expectations of future prices.

If we start from the assumption that prices will almost certainly not remain unchanged in future, how are agents supposed to form their expectations?

One possibility is that they are able to gather sufficient relevant information to make a definite forecast of the changes that are likely to occur. This clearly requires that they know much more than just current prices. They must know the process whereby prices are formed, and form forecasts of the evolution of the various factors (at any rate, the more important of them) that bear upon price determination. Hayek's informational minimalism is then substantially breached. A second possibility is that described by (Keynes, 1936: ch. 12): agents are so much in the dark on the future that, although they are sure that some (unspecified) change will occur, they fall back upon the convention of assuming that tomorrow's prices will equal today's. This enables them to form a conventional assessment of the profitability of producing various commodities, using current price information alone; but the cost of this approach (from the standpoint of a defender of the efficiency of the market) is the recognition that those ex ante assessments will be regularly and perhaps substantially wrong.

Prices do convey objective information about the social costs of production: through the noise of their fluctuations the signal of value shines through. Because of this they may well function as a regulator of production. Divergence of prices from values can serve to attract labour resources into an industry (when price is above value) or repel labour (when price is below value). It is one thing to recognize that this is possible, another to assess its importance in regulating the economy. Posted prices are not the only telecoms system the economy has. Actual orders for commodities are another. Firms set prices and then get orders which are specified in quantities. If a business manager paid attention only to the prices she sold things at and ignored the quantities being ordered, the firm would not survive long.

A priori one can not say whether the price system or the quantity system is more significant in regulating the economy. One has to know how flexible firms actually are in adjusting their prices in response to sales and then to compare this with how often they adjust their actions in response to changes in orders. Consider a supermarket, how many price adjustments does it make in a day compared to the number of new quantitative orders it places with its warehouse? Or a TV factory: how often does the factory respond to orders with a change in price, and how often by adjusting the current level of production? Or consider a design engineer deciding what components to use in a new set-top box for digital TV. Should the engineers base their choice solely on component price, or should they take into account information such as availability, the stocks held by suppliers, the existence of second sources?

The relative importance of the price channel and the quantity channel in inter-firm communication is an open question. One could answer it either by empirical studies of business practice or by multi-agent simulations similar to those described earlier in the book, extended to incorporate input–output tables coding the flows between industries. Given such a model one could vary the rules used by firms in responding to orders and examine the consequences. Initial investigations by one of the authors seem to indicate that systems which place excessive reliance upon price signals can be subject to catastrophic instabilities. Fluctuations in deliveries can lead to key industries collapsing and the whole economy shutting down.

15.1.1 Information loss

Hayek is certainly right to say that prices involve 'economy of information', since the process by which a price is formed is entropy-reducing. If we consider an input–output table such as Table 10.1, we see that it is a square matrix. A full input–output table of an economy with n products would contain n^2 numbers. But the prices of these products can be encoded in a vector of only n distinct numbers. If we assume that the entropy of interconnection of an economy H_I is encoded in the input–output table, then the entropy of the price vector, H_P, grows according to the law

$$H_P \approx \sqrt{H_I}$$

We will see later that this treatment somewhat overestimates the entropy of inter-connection, but it is clear that there is a very substantial reduction of information going on here. How then can such a reduced information structure function to regulate the economy? How can it work if it allows 'individual producers to watch merely the movement of a few pointers'?

We will leave aside for now the relative importance of the price and quantity channels in economic information flows, and concentrate on how a single vector of prices might act as a regulator for a complex matrix of inter-sectoral flows. There seem to be two basic reasons why it could work.

(1)   The universality of human labour means that it is possible to associate with each commodity a single scalar number – price – which indirectly represents the amount of labour that was used to make it. Deviations of relative prices from relative values can then allow labour to move from where it is less socially necessary to where it is more necessary. But this is only possible because all economic activity comes down in the end to human activity. Were that not the case, a single indicator would not be sufficient to regulate the consumption of inputs that were of fundamentally different dimensions. It is only because the dimension of all inputs is ultimately labour – direct or indirect – that prices can regulate activity.

(2)   Another answer lies in the computational tractability of systems of linear equations.

Consider the method that we gave in section 10.4.1 for computing the labour values of commodities from an input–output table. We made an initial estimate of the value of each commodity and then used the table to produce successively more precise estimates. What we have here is an iterative functional system where we repeatedly apply a function to the current value vector to arrive at a new value vector. Because the mapping is what is termed a *contractive affine transform* the functional system has an attractor to which it converges.[3] This attractor is the system of labour

---

[3]   For a discussion of such systems see (Barnsley, 1988: ch. 3).

values. The system must constitute a contractive transform because any viable economy must have a net surplus product in its basic sector. Hence an initial error in the estimate of the value of an input commodity is spread over a larger quantity of the commodity on output and thus with each iteration the percentage error declines.

A variant of the process that we described algorithmically in section 10.4.1 is carried out in a distributed manner in a real economy as prices are formed. Firms add up wage costs and the costs of other commodity inputs, add a mark-up, and set their prices accordingly. This distributed algorithm, which is nowadays carried out by a combination of people and company computers, is structurally similar to the one we described. It, too, constitutes a contractive affine transform which converges on a price vector. Empirical evidence indicates that the price vector that it converges on lies somewhere between the vector of labour values and the vector of Sraffian prices. The exact attractor is not relevant at this point, what is relevant is that the iterative functional system has a stable attractor. It has such an attractor because the process of economic production can be well approximated by a piecewise contractive linear transform on price or value space. If production processes were strongly nonlinear, so that the output of (say) corn were a polynomial such as

$$C_{out} = aC_{in} + bC_{in}^2 + dC_{in}^3 + dL + eL^2 + fL^3 + gI + hI^2$$

with C representing corn, L labour and I iron, then the iterative functional system would be highly unstable, and the evolution of the entire price system would be chaotic and unpredictable. Prices would then be useless as a guide to economic activity. For the instability of such systems see Becker and Dorfler (1989) or Baker and Gollub (1990).

Neither of the two factors above is specific to a market economy. Labour is the key universal resource in any society prior to full robotization. By the full version of the Church–Turing thesis, if a problem can be solved by a distributed collection of human 'computers', then it can be solved by a Universal Computer. If it is tractable for a distributed collection of humans it is also algorithmically tractable when calculated by the computers of a socialist planning agency. The very factors which make the price system relatively stable and useful are the factors which make socialist economic calculation tractable. Computing the labour value of each product is tractable,[4] hence labour values could be used as a basis for pricing in a planned economy, transmitting basically the same information as is transmitted in prices.

Having argued that the centralized processing of much economic information is tractable, we now consider its desirability. When economic calculation is viewed as a computational process, the advantages of calculation on a distributed or

---

[4] See Cockshott and Cottrell (1993); also see sections 5.5.2 and 15.3.

decentralized basis are far from evident; the question hinges on how a multiplicity of facts about production possibilities in different branches of the economy interrelate. The interrelation of facts is, partially, an image in the field of information of the real interrelation of the branches of the economy. The outputs of one activity act as inputs for another: this is the *real* interdependence. In addition, there are *potential* interactions where different branches of production function as alternative users of inputs.

It is important to distinguish the two types of interaction. The first represents real flows of material and is a static property of a snapshot of the economy. The second – the variation in potential uses for goods – is not a property of the real economy but of the phase space of possible economies. The latter is part of the economic problem insofar as this is considered to be a search for optimal points within this phase space. According to neoclassical economic theory, the evolution of a real market economy – the real interdependencies between branches – provides the search procedure by which these optima are sought. The economy describes a trajectory through its phase space. This trajectory is the product of the trajectories of all of the individual economic agents, with the individual agents deciding upon their next position on the basis of the information they get from the price system.

Following up on Hayek's metaphor of the price system as telecoms system or machinery for registering changes, the market economy as a whole acts as a single processor.[5] A single processor, because at any one point in time it can be characterized by a single state vector that defines its position in the phase space of the economic problem. Moreover, this processor operates with a very slow cycle time, since the transmission of information is bounded by the rate of change of prices. To produce an alteration in prices, there must be a change in the real movement of goods (we are abstracting here from the small number of highly specialized futures markets). Thus the speed of information transmission is tied to the speed with which real goods can be moved or new production facilities brought on line. In sum, a market economy performs a single-threaded search through its state space, with a relatively slow set of adjustments to its position, the speed of adjustments being determined by how fast the real economy can move.

Contrast this now with what can potentially be done if the relevant facts can be concentrated, not in one place – that would be impossible – but within a small volume of space. If the information is gathered into one or more computing machines, these can search the possible state space without any change in the real economy.

Here the question of whether to concentrate the information is very relevant. It is a basic property of the universe that no portion of it can affect another in less time than it takes for light to propagate between them. Suppose one had all the

---

[5] If we take neoclassical theory in its own terms the processor would have to be an analogue processor, since the maths of neoclassical theory is cast in terms of real variables. According to Velupillai (2003) this fundamentally undermines many of its conclusions.

relevant information spread around a network of computers across the country. Assume any one of these could send a message to any other. Suppose that this network was now instructed to simulate *possible* states of the economy in order to search for optima. The evolution from one simulated state to another could proceed as fast as the computers could exchange information regarding their own current state. Given that electronic signals between them travel at the speed of light this will be far faster than a real economy can evolve.

But the speed of evolution will be much faster still if we bring all of the computers into close proximity to one another. Massively parallel computers attempt to place all the processors within a small volume, thereby allowing signals moving at the speed of light to propagate around the machine in a few nanoseconds, compared to the hundredths of a second required for telecoms networks. Hence, in general, if one wishes to solve a problem fast, the information required should be placed in the smallest possible volume.

It may be objected that the sheer scale of the economic problem is such that although conceivable in principle, such computations would be unrealizable in practice (Hayek, 1955; Nove, 1983).[6] Given modern computer technology this is far from the case, as we show in section 15.3. However neoclassical economists and the Austrian school have a very different concept of equilibrium from us. Our concept is of statistical equilibrium as discussed in section 7.1.2. Statistical equilibrium is not a point in phase space, but a region defined by a set of specific values for certain macroscopic variables, compatible with a very large set of microscopic conditions. The concept of equilibrium with which Hayek was familiar was that of a mechanical equilibrium, a unique position in phase space at which all forces acting on the economy come into balance. Arrow and Debreu (1954) supposedly established the existence of this sort of equilibrium for competitive economies, but as Velupillai (2003) showed, their proof rested on theorems that are only valid in non-constructive mathematics.

Why does it matter whether Arrow used constructive or non-constructive mathematics? Because only constructive mathematics has an algorithmic implementation and is guaranteed to be effectively computable. But even if a mechanical economic equilibrium can be proven to exist and it can be shown that there is an effective procedure by which this can be determined – i.e., the equilibrium is in principle computable – there is still the question of its computational tractability. What complexity order governs the computation process that arrives at the solution?

Suppose that an equilibrium exists, but that all algorithms to search for it are NP-hard, that is, the algorithms may have a running time that is exponential in the size of the problem. This is just what has been shown by Deng and Huang

---

[6] The specific reference to Hayek is to note 37 on pp. 212–13 of *The Counter-Revolution of Science*. Here Hayek appeals to the judgment of Pareto and Cournot, that the solution of a system of equations representing the conditions of general equilibrium would be practically infeasible. This is worth emphasizing in view of the tendency of Hayek's modern supporters to play down the computational issue.

(2006). Their result might at first seem to support Hayek's contention that the problem of rational economic planning is computationally intractable. In Hayek's day, the notion of NP-hardness had not been invented, but he would seem to have been retrospectively vindicated. Problems with a computational cost that grows as $O(e^n)$ soon become astronomically difficult to solve. We mean astronomical in a literal sense. One can readily specify an NP-hard problem that involves searching more possibilities than there are atoms in the universe before arriving at a definite answer. Such problems, although in principle finite, are beyond any practical solution.

But this knife cuts both ways. On the one hand it shows that no planning computer could solve the neoclassical problem of economic equilibrium. On the other it shows that no collection of millions of individuals interacting via the market could solve it either. In neoclassical economics, the number of constraints on the equilibrium will be proportional, among other things, to the number of economic actors n. The computational resource constituted by the actors will be proportional to n but the cost of the computation will grow as e^n. Computational resources grow linearly, computational costs grow exponentially. This means that a market economy could never have sufficient computational resources to find its own mechanical equilibrium.

It follows that the problem of finding the neoclassical equilibrium is a mirage. No planning system could discover it, but nor could the market. The neoclassical problem of equilibrium misrepresents what capitalist economies actually do and also sets an impossible goal for socialist planning.

If we dispense with the notion of mechanical equilibrium and replace it with statistical equilibrium we arrive at a problem that is much more tractable. The simulations described in chapter 9 show that a market economy can rapidly converge on this sort of equilibrium. But as we have argued above, this is because regulation by the law of value is computationally tractable. This same tractability can be exploited in a socialist planning system. Economic planning does not have to solve the impossible problem of neoclassical equilibrium, it merely has to apply the law of value more efficiently.

15.1.2 Prices, efficiency and 'know how'

It is one of the progressive features of capitalism that the process of competition forces some degree of convergence upon least-cost methods of production (even if the cost in question is monetary cost of production, which reflects social cost in a partial and distorted manner). Hayek reminds us, and rightly so, that this convergence may in fact be far from complete. Firms producing the same commodity (and perhaps even using the same basic technology) may co-exist for extended periods despite having quite divergent costs of production. If the law of one price applies to the products in question, the less efficient producers will make lower profits and/or pay lower wages.

The question arises whether convergence on best practice could be enforced more effectively in a planned system. This may be the case. If all workers are paid at a uniform rate for work done, it will be impossible for inefficient producers to mask their inefficiency by paying low wages. Indeed, with the sort of labour-time accounting system advocated elsewhere (Cockshott and Cottrell, 1989, 1993), differentials in productive efficiency will be immediately apparent. Not only that, but there should be a broader range of mechanisms for eliminating differentials once they are spotted. A private firm may realize that a competitor is producing at lower cost, but short of industrial espionage may have no way of finding out how this is achieved. Convergence of efficiency, if it is attained at all, may have to wait until the less efficient producer is driven out of business and its market share usurped by more efficient rivals. In the context of a planned system, on the other hand, some of the managers or technical experts from the more efficient enterprises might, for instance, be seconded as consultants to the less efficient enterprises. One can also imagine – in the absence of commercial secrecy – an economy-wide wikipedia on which the people concerned with operating particular technologies, or producing particular products, share their tips and tricks for maximizing efficiency.

15.2   Information flows under market and plan

One of Hayek's most fundamental arguments is that the efficient functioning of an economy involves making use of a great deal of distributed information, and that the task of centralizing this information is practically impossible.

In what follows we attempt to put this argument to a quantitative test. We compare the information transmission costs implicit in a market system and a planned system, and examine how the respective costs grow as a function of the scale of the economy. Communications cost is a measure of work done to centralize or disseminate economic information: we will use the conceptual apparatus of algorithmic information theory (Chaitin, 1999) to measure this cost.

Our strategy is first to consider the dynamic problem of how fast, and with what communications overhead, an economy can stabilize. We will demonstrate that this can be done faster and at less communications cost by the planned system. We consider initially the dynamics of convergence on a fixed target, since the control system with the faster impulse response will also be faster at tracking a moving target.

Consider an economy $E = [\mathbf{A}, \mathbf{c}, r, w]$ with n producers each producing distinct products using technology matrix $\mathbf{A}$, with a well defined vector of final consumption expenditure $\mathbf{c}$ that is independent of the prices of the n products, an exogenously given wage rate w and a compatible rate of profit r. Then there exists a possible Sraffian solution $e = [\mathbf{U}, \mathbf{p}]$ where $\mathbf{U}$ is the commodity flow matrix and $\mathbf{p}$ a price vector. We will assume, as is the case in commercial arithmetic, that all quantities are expressed to some finite precision rather than being real numbers. How much information is required to specify this solution?

The argument that follows is relatively insensitive to the exact way we have specified the starting condition from which a solution is to be sought. This is because we consider convergence in information space. Recall that we have in section 10.3 expressed scepticism about the existence of a uniform rate of profit r

as assumed in Sraffian theory. We are not concerned with showing that a capitalist economy does converge towards a solution, that can be left to the neoclassical and neo-Ricardian economists. Whether or not such a convergence tendency actually exists, let us concede that it does for the sake of the current argument.

Assuming that we have some efficient binary encoding method and that $I(s)$ is a measure in bits of the information content of the data structure s using this method, then the solution can be specified by $I(e)$, or, since the solution is in a sense given in the starting conditions, it can be specified by $I(E) + I(p_s)$ where p_s is a program to solve an arbitrary system of Sraffian equations. In general we have $I(e) \leq I(E) + I(p_s)$. In the following we will assume that $I(e)$ is specified by $I(E) + I(p_s)$.

Let $I(x|y)$ be the conditional or relative information (Chaitin, 1987) of x given y. The conditional information associated with any arbitrary configuration of the economy, $k = [\mathbf{U}_k, \mathbf{p}_k]$, may then be expressed relative to the solution, e, as $I(k|e)$. If k is in the neighbourhood of e we should expect that $I(k|e) \leq I(k)$. For instance, suppose that we can derive $\mathbf{U}_k$ from $\mathbf{A}$ and an intensity vector $\mathbf{u}_k$ which specifies the rate at which each industry operates then

$$I(k|e) \leq I(\mathbf{u}_k) + I(\mathbf{p}_k) + I(p_u)$$

where p_u is a program to compute $\mathbf{U}_k$ from some $\mathbf{A}$ and some $\mathbf{u}_k$. Since $\mathbf{U}_k$ is a matrix and $\mathbf{u}_k$ a vector, each of scale n, we can assume that $I(\mathbf{U}_k) > I(\mathbf{u}_k)$.

As the converges on a solution the conditional information required to specify it will shrink, since $\mathbf{u}_k$ starts to approximate to $\mathbf{u}_e$.[7] Intuitively we only have to supply the difference vector between the two, and this will require less and less information to encode, the smaller the distance between $\mathbf{u}_k$ and $\mathbf{u}_e$. A similar argument applies to the two price vectors $\mathbf{p}_k$ and $\mathbf{p}_e$. If we assume that the system follows a dynamic law that causes it to converge towards a solution then we should have the relation $I(k_{t+1}|e) < I(k_t|e)$.

Now construct a model of the amount of information that has to be transmitted between the producers of a market economy in order to move it towards a solution. Make the simplifying assumptions that all production process take one time step to operate, and that the whole process evolves synchronously. Assume the process starts just after production has finished, with the economy in some random non-equilibrium state. Further assume that each firm starts out with a given selling price for its product. Each firm i carries out the following procedure.

(1) It writes to all its suppliers asking them their current prices.
(2) It replies to all price requests that it gets, quoting its current price $\mathbf{p}_i$.
(3) It opens and reads all price quotes from its suppliers.

---

[7] Note that this information measure of the distance from equilibrium, based on a sum of logarithms, differs from a simple Euclidean measure, based on a sum of squares. The information measure is more sensitive to a multiplicity of small errors than to one large error. Because of the equivalence between information and entropy it also measures the conditional entropy of the system.

(4) It estimates its current per-unit cost of production.
(5) It calculates the anticipated profitability of production.
(6) If this is above r it increases its target production rate $\mathbf{u}_i$ by some fraction. If profitability is below r a proportionate reduction is made.
(7) It now calculates how much of each input j is required to sustain that production.
(8) It sends off to each of its suppliers j, an order for amount $\mathbf{U}_{ij}$ of their product.
(9) It opens all orders that it has received and totals them up.

    (a) If the total is greater than the available product it scales down each order proportionately to ensure that what it can supply is fairly distributed among its customers.
    (a) It dispatches the (partially) filled orders to its customers.
    (a) If it has no remaining stocks it increases its selling price by some increasing function of the level of excess orders, while if it has stocks left over it reduces its price by some increasing function of the remaining stock.

(10) It receives all deliveries of inputs and determines at what scale it can actually proceed with production.
(11) It commences production for the next period.

Experience with computer models of this type of system indicates that if the readiness of producers to change prices is too great, the system could be grossly unstable. We will assume that the price changes are sufficiently small to ensure that only damped oscillations occur. The condition for movement towards solution is then that over a sufficiently large ensemble of points k in phase space, the mean effect of an iteration of the above procedure is to decrease the mean error for each economic variable by some factor $0 \le g < 1$. Under such circumstances, while the convergence time in vector space will clearly follow a logarithmic law – to converge by a factor of D in in vector space will take time of order $\log_{1/g}(D)$ – in information space the convergence time will be linear because of the logarithmic nature of information measures. Thus if at time t the distance from equilibrium is $I(k_t|e)$, convergence to within a distance ϵ will take a take a time of order

$$\frac{I(k_t|e) - \epsilon}{\delta \log(\frac{1}{g})}$$

where δ is a constant related to the number of economic variables that alter by a mean factor of g each step. The convergence time in information space, for small ϵ, will thus approximate to a linear function of $I(k|e)$ which we can write as $\Delta I(k|e)$.

We are now in a position to express the communications costs of reducing the conditional entropy of the economy to some level ϵ. Communication takes place at steps 1, 2, 8 and 9c of the procedure. How many messages does each supplier have to send, and how much information must they contain?

Letters through the mail contain much redundant pro-forma information; we will assume that this is eliminated and the messages reduced to their bare essentials. The whole of the pro forma will be treated as a single symbol in a limited alphabet of message types. A request for a quote would thus be the pair $[R, H]$ where R is a symbol indicating that the message is a quotation request, and H the home address of the requester. A quote would be the pair $[Q, P]$ with Q indicating the message is a quote and P being the price. An order would similarly be represented by $[O, \mathbf{U}_{ij}]$, and with each delivery would go a dispatch note $[N, U_{ij}]$ indicating the actual amount delivered, where $U_{ij} \leq \mathbf{U}_{ij}$.

If we assume that each of n firms has on average m suppliers, the number of messages of each type per iteration of the procedure will be nm. Since we have an alphabet of message types (R, Q, O, N) with cardinality 4, these symbols can be encoded in 2 bits each. We will further assume that $(H, P, \mathbf{U}_{ij}, U_{ij})$ can each be encoded in binary numbers of b bits. We thus obtain an expression for the communications cost of an iteration of $4nm(b + 2)$. Taking into account the number of iterations, the cost of approaching the equilibrium will be $4nm(b + 2)\Delta I(k|e)$.

Let us now contrast this with what would be required in a planned economy. Here the procedure involves two distinct procedures, that followed by the (state-owned) firm and that followed by the planning bureau. The model of socialist economy we are describing is roughly that given in Lange (1938) or Cockshott and Cottrell (1993). The firms do the following:

(1) In the first time period:

    (a) They send to the planners a message listing their address, their technical input coefficients and their current output stocks.

    (b) They receive instructions from the planners about how much of each of their output is to be sent to each of their users.

    (c) They send the goods with appropriate dispatch notes to their users.

    (d) They receive goods inward, read the dispatch notes and calculate their new production level.

    (e) They commence production.

(2) They then repeatedly perform the same sequence replacing step 1a with:

    (a) They send to the planners a message giving their current output stocks.

The planning bureau performs the complementary procedure:

(1) In the first period:

    (a) They read the details of stocks and technical coefficients from all of their producers.

    (b) They compute the equilibrium point e from technical coefficients and the final demand.

(c) They compute a turnpike path (Dorfman *et al.*, 1958) from the current output structure to the equilibrium output structure.

(d) They send out for firms to make deliveries consistent with moving along that path.

(2) In the second and subsequent periods:

(a) They read messages giving the extent to which output targets have been met.

(b) They compute a turnpike path from the current output structure to the equilibrium output structure.

(c) They send out for firms to make deliveries consistent with moving along that path.

We assume that with computer technology the steps b and c can be undertaken in a time that is small relative to the production period (see section 15.3).

Comparing the respective information flows, it is clear that the number of orders and dispatch notes sent per iteration is invariant between the two modes of organization of production. The only difference is that in the planned case the orders come from the center whereas in the market they come from the customers. These messages will again account for a communications load of $2nm(b+2)$. The difference is that in the planned system there is no exchange of price information. Instead, on the first iteration there is a transmission of information about stocks and technical coefficients. Since any coefficient takes two numbers to specify, the communications load per firm will be: $(1 + 2m)b$. For n firms this approximates to the $nm(b + 2)$ that was required to communicate the price data.

The difference comes on subsequent iterations, where, assuming no technical change, there is no need to update the planners' record of the technology matrix. On $i - 1$ subsequent iterations, the planning system has therefore to exchange only about half as much information as the market system. Furthermore, since the planned economy moves on a turnpike path to equilibrium, its convergence time will be less than that of the market economy. The consequent communications cost is $2nm(b + 2)(2 + (i - 1))$ where $i < \Delta I(k|e)$.

The consequence is that, contrary to Hayek's claims, the amount of information that would have to be transmitted in a planned system is substantially lower than for a market system. The centralized gathering of information is less onerous than the commercial correspondence required by the market. Hayek's error comes from focusing on the price channel to the exclusion of the quantity channel. In addition, the convergence time of the market system is slower. The implication of faster convergence for adaptation to changing rather than stable conditions of production and consumption are obvious.

In addition, it should be noted that in our model for the market, we have ignored any information that has to be sent around the system in order to make payments. In practice, with the sending of invoices and receipts, the clearing of cheques, and so on, the information flow in the market system is likely to be several times as high as our estimates. The higher communications overheads of market economies are reflected in the numbers of office workers they employ, which in turn leaves its mark on the architecture of cities – as witnessed by the skylines of Moscow and New York in the 1980s.

15.3 The argument from dynamics

Does Hayek's concentration on the dynamic aspect of prices – price as a means of dynamically transmitting information – make any sense?

In one way it does. In section 10.2 we showed that the information content of a price in the UK was less than 14 bits. If we consider today's price of a cup of coffee as an example, then yesterday's price was probably the same. If the price changes only once a year, then for 364 days the only information that it conveys is that it has not changed. The information content of this, $- \log_2 \frac{364}{365}$, is about 0.0039 of a bit. Then when the price does change its information content is $- \log_2 \frac{1}{365} + b$ where b is the number of bits to encode the price increase. For a reasonable value of the increase, say 10 pence, the whole amounts to some 12 bits. So on the day the price changes, it conveys some 3000 times as much information as it did every other day of the year.

So it is almost certainly true that most of the information in a price series is encoded in the price changes. From the standpoint of someone observing and reacting to prices, the changes are all-important. But this is a viewpoint internal to the dynamics of the market system. One has to ask if the information thus conveyed has a more general import. The price changes experienced by a firm in a market economy can arise from many different causes, but we have to consider which of these represent information that is independent of the social form of production.

We can divide the changes into those that are direct results of events external to the price system, and those which are internal to the system. The discovery of new oil reserves or an increase in the birth rate would directly impinge upon the price of oil or of baby clothes. These represent changes in the needs or production capabilities of society, and any system of economic regulation should have means of responding to them. On the other side, we must count a fall in the price of acrylic feed stocks and a fall in the price of acrylic sweaters among the second- and third-order internally generated changes consequent upon a fall in oil prices. In the same category would go the rise in house prices that follows an expansion of credit, any fluctuation in share prices, or the general fall in prices that marks the onset of a recession. These are all changes generated by the internal dynamics of a market system, and are as such irrelevant to the consideration of non-market economies.

Hayek is of course right that the planning problem is greatly simplified if there are no changes, but it does not follow from this that all the changes of a market economy are potential problems for a planned one. If we assume that the economy retains some form of market for consumer goods, as proposed by Lange, to provide information on final requirements then the process of deriving a balanced plan is tractable.

Let us take a very simple example, an economy with 4 types of goods which we will call bread, corn, coal and iron. In order to mine coal, both iron and coal are used as inputs. To make bread we need corn for the flour and coal to bake it. To grow the corn, iron tools and seed corn are required. The making of iron itself demands coal and more iron implements. We can describe this as a set of four processes:

1 ton iron	← 0.05 ton iron + 2 ton coal + 20 days labour
1 ton coal	← 0.2 ton coal + 0.1 ton iron + 3 days labour
1 ton corn	← 0.1 ton corn + 0.02 ton iron + 10 days labour
1 ton bread	← 1.5 ton corn * 0.5 ton coal + 1 days labour

Assume, following Lange (1938), that the planning authorities have a current estimate of consumer demand for final outputs. The planners start with the required net output. This is shown on the first line of Table 15.1. We assume that 20,000 tons of coal and 1000 tons of bread are the consumer goods required.

The planners first estimate how much iron, corn, coal, and labour would be directly consumed in producing the final output: 2000 tons of iron, 1500 tons of corn and 4500 additional tons of coal. They then add the intermediate inputs to the net output to get a first estimate of the gross usage of goods. Since this estimate involves producing more iron, coal and corn than they at first allowed for, they repeat the calculation to get a second estimate of the gross usage of goods. Each time they repeat the process they get different total requirement of iron, coal corn and labour, as shown in Table 15.1.

Does this confirm the claim that the equations necessary for socialist planning are unsolvable? Not at all. The answers differ each time round, but the differences between successive answers get smaller and smaller. Eventually – after 20 attempts in this example – the planners get a consistent result: if the population is to consume 20,000 tons of coal and 1000 tons of bread, then the gross output vector must be 3708 tons of iron, 34896 tons of coal and 1667 tons of corn.

Table 15.1 Convergence of gross production on that required for the final net product

Step	Iron	Coal	Corn	Bread	Labour	
0	0	20000	0	1000	0	Net output
1	2000	24500	1500	1000	61000	1st estimate of gross usage
2	2580	29400	1650	1000	129500	
3	3102	31540	1665	1000	157300	
4	3342	33012	1666	1000	174310	
⋮	⋮	⋮	⋮	⋮	⋮	
18	3708	34895	1667	1000	196510	
19	3708	34895	1667	1000	196515	
20	3708	34896	1667	1000	196517	20th estimate of gross usage

Is it feasible to scale this up to the number of goods produced in a real economy? While the calculations would be impossibly tedious to do by hand, they are readily automated. Table 15.1 was produced by running the computer algorithm given in Appendix C. If detailed planning is to be feasible, we need to know:

(1) How many types of goods an economy produces.
(2) How many types of inputs are used to produce each output.
(3) How fast a computer program running the algorithm would be for the scale of data provided in (1) and (2).

Table 15.2 illustrates the effect of running the planning algorithm on a cheap personal computer of 2004 vintage. We determined the calculation time for economies whose number of industries ranged from one thousand to one million. Two different assumptions were tested for the way in which the mean number of inputs used to make a good depends on the complexity of the economy.

It is clear that the number of direct inputs used to manufacture each product is only a small fraction of the range of goods produced in an economy. It is plausible that as industrial complexity develops, the mean number of inputs used to produce each output will also grow, but more slowly. In the first part of Table 15.2 it is assumed that the mean number of inputs (M) grows as the square root of the number of final outputs (N). In the second part of the table the growth of M is assumed to follow a logarithmic law.

It can be seen that calculation times are modest even for very big economic models. The apparently daunting million-equation foe yields gracefully to the modest home computer. The limiting factor in the experiments is computer memory. The largest model tested required 1.5 Gigabytes of memory. Since the usable data space of a P4 processor is at most 2 Gigabytes, larger models would have required a more advanced 64-bit computer.

Table 15.2 Timings for applying the planning algorithm in Appendix C to model economies of different sizes. Timings were performed on a 3 Ghz Intel Zeon running Linux, with 2 GB of memory

	Industries N	Mean Inputs M	CPU Time (seconds)	Memory required
$M = \sqrt{N}$	1,000	30	0.1	150KB
	10,000	100	3.8	5MB
	40,000	200	33.8	64MB
	160,000	400	77.1	512MB
	320,000	600	166.0	1.5G
$M \approx \log N$	1,000	30	0.1	150KB
	10,000	40	1.6	2.4MB
	100,000	50	5.8	40MB
	1,000,000	60	68.2	480MB

The experiment went up to 1 million products. The number of industrial products in the Soviet economy was estimated by Nove (1983) to be around of 10 million. Nove believed this number was so huge as to rule out any possibility of constructing a balanced disaggregated plan. This may well have been true with the computer technology available in the 1970s, but the situation is now quite different. A single PC could compute a disaggregated plan for a small economy like Sweden in a couple of minutes.

Suppose we want to plan a continental scale economy. It might have 10 million products. Let us assume that the average number of direct inputs required to produce each output is 2000. On the basis of Table 15.2 this would require a computer with 80 Gigabytes of memory, costing Euro 6000 at 2006 prices. Using a single 64-bit processor of 2006 vintage the computation would take of the order of an hour.

The algorithm we have presented is for a single processor, but the problem lends itself well to parallelization. A Beowulf cluster of PCs, costing perhaps Euro 40,000, could probably cut the compute time to under 10 minutes. More sophisticated algorithms capable of allocating fixed capital stocks have comparable complexities and running times (Cockshott, 1990; Cockshott and Cottrell, 1993).

The compute time required is sufficiently short for a planning authority, should it so wish, to be able to perform the operation on a daily basis. In performing this calculation the planners arrive at the various scales of production that the market economy would operate at were it able to attain equilibrium. Faced with an exogenous change, the planners can compute the new equilibrium position and issue directives to production units to move to it. This real economic motion will involve the physical movement of goods, laying of foundations, fitting out of buildings, and so on, and will therefore take some considerable time.

We then have two times, the time of *calculation* and the time of *physical adjustment*. The key difference between the market system and a planned system is that under planning the calculation phase can be done in short order on a digital computer while in the market system – even if we make the most favourable assumptions about its ability to adjust stably to equilibrium – the individual iterations of the calculation will take a time proportional to the physical adjustment time.

Part V
Appendices

Appendix A

The law of value: proofs

Proof of lemma 1. Substituting (9.4) into (9.7) and considering a single sector gives:

$$\dot{a}_j = \psi \gamma M \left(b_j - a_j \sum_{k=1}^{L} \frac{l_k b_k}{c_k a_k} \right) \tag{A.1}$$

which is coupled with:

$$\dot{b}_j = -\omega N \left(\frac{a_j}{l_j} - \frac{1}{c_j} \right) \tag{A.2}$$

Setting $\dot{\mathbf{a}} = \dot{\mathbf{b}} = \mathbf{0}$ yields the unique equilibrium point of the system. (A.2) implies $a_j = l_i/c_j$ and (A.1) implies $a_j = b_j$ as $\sum_{k=1}^{L} b_k = 1$. This solution is valid and unique for economies with reproduction coefficient $\eta = 1$, such that the equalities $\sum_{k=1}^{L} a_k = \sum_{k=1}^{L} b_k = \sum_{k=1}^{L} l_k/c_k = 1 = \eta$ hold. $\qquad \square$

Proof of lemma 2. The non-linear sum in (A.1) can be eliminated as follows. Summing over all sectors:

$$\sum_{j=1}^{L} \dot{a}_j = \sum_{j=1}^{L} \left[\psi \gamma M \left(b_j - a_j \sum_{k=1}^{L} \frac{l_k b_k}{c_k a_k} \right) \right]$$

but given that

$$\sum_{j=1}^{L} a_j = 1 \Longrightarrow \dot{a}_1 + \dot{a}_2 + \ldots + \dot{a}_L = 0$$

then

$$\sum_{j=1}^{L} \left[\psi \gamma M \left(b_j - a_j \sum_{k=1}^{L} \frac{l_k b_k}{c_k a_k} \right) \right] = 0 \Longrightarrow \gamma M \sum_{j=1}^{L} \left[\psi b_j - a_j \sum_{k=1}^{L} \frac{l_k b_k}{c_k a_k} \right] = 0$$

As $\gamma M \neq 0$ then

$$\sum_{j=1}^{L} \psi b_j = \sum_{j=1}^{L} a_j \sum_{k=1}^{L} \frac{l_k \, b_k}{c_k \, a_k}$$

Recalling that $\sum_{j=1}^{L} a_j = 1$ and $\sum_{j=1}^{L} b_j = 1$ then

$$\sum_{j=1}^{L} \frac{l_j \, b_j}{c_j \, a_j} = 1$$

Substitution into (A.1) yields a linear form of the labour equation:

$$\dot{a}_j = \psi \gamma M (b_j - a_j) \tag{A.3}$$

A change of variables, $x_j = a_j - \frac{l_j}{c_j}$ and $y_j = b_j - \frac{l_j}{c_j}$ translates the equilibrium point to the origin. Given that $\dot{\mathbf{x}} = \dot{\mathbf{a}}$ and $\dot{\mathbf{y}} = \dot{\mathbf{b}}$ the transformed linear system is:

$$\dot{\mathbf{x}} = \psi \gamma M (\mathbf{y} - \mathbf{x})$$
$$\dot{\mathbf{y}} = -\omega N \mathbf{X} \mathbf{l}$$

where $\mathbf{X}$ is the L by L diagonal matrix with (i, i) entry equal to x_i and the (i, j) $(i \neq j)$ entry zero.

The x_j and y_j represent production and income errors respectively. Consider the function

$$V : \mathbb{R}^{2L} \to \mathbb{R}$$

$$V(x_1, \ldots, x_L, y_1, \ldots, y_L) = \frac{1}{2 \psi \gamma M} \sum_{j=1}^{L} x_j^2 + \frac{1}{2 \omega N} \sum_{j=1}^{L} l_j y_j^2$$

that associates a scalar error measure with each possible state of the simple commodity system. In fact, V defines an error potential.

Global stability is now deduced by Lyapunov's direct method (e.g. see Brauer and Nohel (1989)). V is positive definite as $V(\mathbf{0}) = 0$ and $V(\mathbf{x}) > 0$ for $\mathbf{x} \neq \mathbf{0}$. Hence, V is a Lyapunov function. V is now shown to be strictly decreasing on all state trajectories:

$$V^* = \frac{\partial V}{\partial x_1} \dot{x}_1 + \frac{\partial V}{\partial x_2} \dot{x}_2 + \ldots + \frac{\partial V}{\partial x_L} \dot{x}_L + \frac{\partial V}{\partial y_1} \dot{y}_1 + \frac{\partial V}{\partial y_2} \dot{y}_2 + \ldots + \frac{\partial V}{\partial y_L} \dot{y}_L$$

$$= \frac{1}{\psi \gamma M} \sum_{j=1}^{L} x_j \dot{x}_j + \frac{1}{\omega N} \sum_{j=1}^{L} l_j y_j \dot{y}_j$$

Substituting for $\dot{x}i$ and $\dot{y}_i$ gives

$$
\begin{aligned}
V^* &= \sum_{j=1}^{L} x_j(y_j - x_j) - \sum_{j=1}^{L} x_j y_j \\
&= \sum_{j=1}^{L} x_j y_j - \sum_{j=1}^{L} x_j^2 - \sum_{j=1}^{L} x_j y_j \\
&= -\sum_{i=j}^{L} x_j^2 \\
&\leq 0
\end{aligned}
$$

with $V^* = 0$ only when $\mathbf{x}^* = \mathbf{0}$. In other words, as time progresses the simple commodity system always follows an error-reducing trajectory that approaches the origin. By Lyapunov's Theorem the equilibrium point is asymptotically stable. Stability properties for linear systems are global. Therefore the equilibrium point is globally asymptotically stable. □

Derivation of equation (9.12).   The exchange value is given by

$$
\langle \epsilon_j \rangle = \frac{\langle p_j \rangle}{\lambda} = \frac{\gamma M}{\lambda N} \frac{b_j}{a_j} l_j = \frac{b_j}{a_j} l_j
$$

Rearrange to give $b_j = a_j \langle \epsilon_j \rangle / l_j$ and substitute into equation (A.3):

$$
\begin{aligned}
\dot{a}_j &= \psi \gamma M (b_j - a_j) \\
&= a_j \left(\frac{\langle \epsilon_j \rangle}{l_j} - 1 \right) \psi \gamma M
\end{aligned}
$$

□

Appendix B

The law of value: experimental details

The **SCE** is defined to have reached a state of statistical equilibrium when the rate of change (sampled every 1000 time steps) of the labour value/market price vector correlation is lower than a small threshold. When this convergence condition is met the simulation continues for a further 5000 time steps in order to sample the stationary distributions. (An alternative convergence condition is to check when the rate of change of entropy of every commodity price distribution is lower than a small threshold, but this was not tried). An upper-limit of 200,000 time steps is set in case convergence is not achieved within a reasonable time period. In almost every cases convergence is reached before the upper-limit. Market clearing rule M_1 cycles until there are either no buyers or no sellers for every commodity. With a large number of actors the clearing loop takes a prohibitively long time, therefore, in practice, an upper limit of the maximum number of transaction attempts per actor is set. Once the number of maximum transactions is reached the actor is neither a buyer nor seller for any commodity. This can be interpreted as a 'time limit' on the market period.

Table B.1 Labour value/market price correlations from random samples of the **SCE**, with parameter settings N:200, L:n ($n = 3, \ldots, 10$), M:500, R:20, C:2. Each parameter setting is sampled 10 times. Results are rounded to 2 decimal places. The current implementation runs out of memory when the number of commodities exceeds 10 (and is also prohibitively slow). If $L \to N$ (i.e. the number of commodities approaches the number of actors) then the economy is unlikely to sustain production rates and correlations will decrease.

L	3	4	5	6	7	8	9	10
corr.	1.0	0.99	0.98	0.96	0.98	0.88	0.96	0.96
	0.99	1.0	0.99	0.97	0.98	0.97	0.96	0.99
	0.98	0.94	0.99	0.99	0.97	0.94	0.96	0.96
	0.98	0.99	0.93	0.99	0.95	0.97	0.97	0.91
	0.99	0.99	0.99	0.99	0.94	0.91	0.86	0.92
	0.96	0.84	0.99	0.93	0.98	0.99	0.95	0.95
	1.0	0.95	0.99	0.99	0.96	0.93	0.95	0.98
	0.99	0.97	1.0	0.98	0.96	0.94	0.94	0.95
	1.0	0.96	0.96	0.95	0.95	0.94	0.93	0.99
	1.0	1.0	0.95	0.97	0.95	0.95	0.99	0.93
mean	**0.99**	**0.96**	**0.98**	**0.97**	**0.96**	**0.94**	**0.95**	**0.95**

Appendix C

A simple planning program

The following algorithm performs the planning calculations that are presented in Chapter 15.

```
program plan ;
type
    good = (iron, coal, corn, bread, labour);
    consv = array [good] of real ;
const
    usage: array [good ,1..3] of real = ((0.05, 2.0, 20.0),
    (0.2, 0.1, 3.0),
    (0.1, 0.02, 10.0),
    (1.5, 0.5, 1.0),
    (0, 0, 0));
    inputs: array [good ,1..3] of good = ((iron, coal, labour),
    (coal, iron, labour),
    (corn, iron, labour),
    (corn, coal, labour),
    (corn, coal, labour));
    demand: consv = (0, 2e4, 0, 1e3, 0);
var
    Let used, previous ∈ consv;
procedure calcstep; (see below)
var
    Let l ∈ integer;
begin
    used ← demand;
    previous ← 0;
    writeln(iron, coal, corn, bread, labour);
    write(round(used));
    for l ← 1 to 20 do
        calcstep;
end.
```

The following preocedure performs one step of the plan-balancing by adding up the ingredients used to make the previous step of the iteration.

```
procedure calcstep ;
var
      Let i, k ∈ good;
      Let j ∈ integer;
      Let temp ∈ consv;
begin
      temp ← 0;
      for i ← iron to labour do
            for j ← 1 to 3 do
            begin
                  k ← inputs_{i,j};
                  temp_k ← temp_k + (used_i - previous_i) × usage_{i,j};
            end ;
            previous ← used;
            used ← used + temp;
            write(round(used));
      end ;
```

Appendix D
Profits in the SA model

The SA model provides the opportunity to deduce an analytical form for the industrial rate-of-profit distribution given additional assumptions on capital investment. As a step toward this goal an approximation to the firm-weighted rate-of-profit distribution in the SA model is now derived.

Consider a single firm that trades for a single year and has an average size of s employees during this period. The firm samples the market on average $12s$ times during a year. This is a simplification, as during a year, firms are created and destroyed, and therefore do not necessarily interact with the marketplace over the whole year. The value of each market sample, M_i, is a function of the instantaneous money distribution, which is mixture of exponential and Pareto forms. Assume each M_i is independent and identically distributed (iid) with mean μ_m and variance σ_m^2. During a month the same employee may be repeatedly selected, or not selected, due to the causal slack introduced by rule **1M**. Therefore the value generated per employee per month, V_i, is some function f of M_i independent of the firm size s. Simplifying further to avoid detailed consideration of the distribution of market samples per employee, assume that $f(x) = x + v$, where v is a constant. Hence each V_i is idd with mean $\mu_1 = \mu_m + v$ and variance $\sigma_1^2 = \sigma_m^2$. By the Central Limit Theorem the sum of the firm's market samples in a year, which constitutes the total revenue, R, can be approximated by a normal distribution $R = \sum V_i \approx N(\mu_r, \sigma_r^2)$, where $\mu_r = 12s\mu_1$ and $\sigma_r^2 = 12s\sigma_1^2$.

The firm's total wage bill for the year, W, is the sum of $12(s-1)$ individual wage payments, ω_i. Note that the capitalist owner does not receive wages. Each ω_i is iid according to a uniform distribution, $\omega_i \sim U(\omega_a, \omega_b)$, with mean $\mu_2 = (\omega_a + \omega_b)/2$ and variance $\sigma_2^2 = (\omega_b - \omega_a)^2/12$. By the Central Limit Theorem the wage bill, W, can be approximated by a normal distribution $W = \sum \omega_i \approx N(\mu_w, \sigma_w^2)$, where $\mu_w = 12(s-1)\mu_2$ and $\sigma_w^2 = 12(s-1)\sigma_2^2$.

Define the ratio of revenue to the wage bill as $X = R/W$ and assume that R and W are independent. X is the ratio of two normal variates and its pdf is derived by the transformation method to give:

$$f_X(x \mid s) = \frac{\exp\left[-\frac{1}{2}(\frac{\mu_r^2}{\sigma_r^2} + \frac{\mu_w^2}{\sigma_w^2})\right]}{4\pi k_1^{3/2}} \times$$

$$\left(2\sigma_r\sigma_w\sqrt{k_1} + \exp^{\Lambda(x)}\sqrt{2\pi}(1 + \Phi(\sqrt{\Lambda(x)}))(\mu_w\sigma_r^2 + x\mu_r\sigma_w^2)\right)$$

$$(D.1)$$

where

$$k_1 = \sigma_r^2 + x^2\sigma_w^2$$

$$\Lambda(x) = \frac{(\mu_w\sigma_r^2 + x\mu_r\sigma_w^2)^2}{2\sigma_r^2\sigma_w^2(\sigma_r^2 + x^2\sigma_w^2)}$$

$$\Phi(x) = \frac{2}{\sqrt{\pi}}\int_0^x \exp^{-t^2} dt$$

(D.1) is the pdf of the rate-of-profit conditional on the firm size s. The unconditional rate-of-profit distribution can be obtained by considering that firm sizes are distributed according to a Pareto (power-law) distribution:

$$f_S(s) = \frac{\alpha\beta^\alpha}{s^{\alpha+1}}$$

where α is the shape and β the location parameter. Firm sizes in the model range between 1 (a degenerate case of an unemployed worker) to a maximum possible size N. Therefore the truncated Pareto distribution

$$g_S(s) = f_S(s \mid 1 < S \le N) = \frac{f(s)}{F(N) - F(1)} = \frac{s^{-(1+\alpha)}\alpha}{1 - N^{-\alpha}}$$

where

$$f(s) = F'(s)$$

is formed to ensure that all the probability mass is between 1 and N. By the Theorem of Total Probability the unconditional distribution $f_X(x)$ is given by:

$$f_X(x) = \int_2^N f_X(x \mid s)g_S(s)\, ds \tag{D.2}$$

where the range of integration is between 2 and N as firms of size 1 are a degenerate case that do not report profits. Expression (D.2) defines the $g_S(s)$ parameter-mix of $f_X(x \mid S = s)$. The rate-of-profit variate is therefore composed of a parameter-mix of a ratio of independent normal variates each conditional on a firm size s that is distributed according to a power-law. Writing (D.2) in full yields:

$$f_X(x) = \int_2^{\cdot N} \frac{\exp\left[-6\left(\frac{s\mu_1^2}{\sigma_1^2} + \frac{(s-1)\mu_2^2}{\sigma_2^2}\right)\right]}{2\pi\,\Theta^{3/2}(x)} \times$$

$$\left(k_2\sqrt{\Theta(x)} + \sqrt{6\pi}\,\Psi(x)\exp\left[\frac{6\Psi^2(x)}{k_2^2\Theta(x)}\right]\right) \times$$

$$\left(1 + \Phi\left(\frac{\sqrt{6}\Psi(x)}{k_2\sqrt{\Theta(x)}}\right)\right)\frac{s^{-(1+\alpha)}\alpha}{1 - N^{-\alpha}}\,ds \qquad (D.3)$$

where

$$
\begin{aligned}
k_2 &= \sqrt{s\sigma_1^2}\sqrt{(s-1)\sigma_2^2} \\
\Theta(x) &= s\sigma_1^2 + (s-1)x^2\sigma_2^2 \\
\Psi(x) &= (s-1)s(\mu_2\sigma_1^2 + x\mu_1\sigma_2^2)
\end{aligned}
$$

(D.3) is the pdf of $X = R/W$ but the rate-of-profit in the simulation is measured as $P = 100\,(X - 1)$. The pdf of P is therefore a linear transform of X:

$$f_P(x) = \frac{1}{100}f_X\left(1 + \frac{x}{100}\right) \qquad (D.4)$$

(D.4) defines a distribution with 6 parameters: (i) the mean employee market sample μ_1, (ii) the variance of the employee market sample σ_1^2, (iii) the mean wage μ_2, (iv) the wage variance σ_2, (v) the Pareto exponent, α, of the firm size distribution, and (vi) the number of economic actors N.

(D.4) is solved numerically to compare the distribution of the theoretically derived variate P with the profit data generated by the SA model. The values of the parameters are measured from the simulation. In this particular case $\mu_1 = \mu_m + v \approx 50 + v$, $\sigma_1^2 = \sigma_m^2 \approx 55000$, $\mu_2 \approx 50$, $\sigma_2^2 \approx 533.3$, $\alpha \approx 1.04$ and $N = 1000$. The best fit is achieved with $v = 25$ coins. Figure D.1 plots the pdf $f_P(x)$ with the rate-of-profit frequency histogram of Figure 13.17 and shows a reasonable fit between the derived distribution and the data.

With some further work the 6-parameter distribution $f_P(x)$ could be fitted to empirical rate-of-profit measures and compared against other candidate functional forms. Although (D.4) ignores effects due to capital investment the interpretation of the parameters μ_1, σ_1^2, μ_2 and σ_2^2 can be extended to refer to the means and variances of revenue and cost per employee (Wright, 2004). A testable

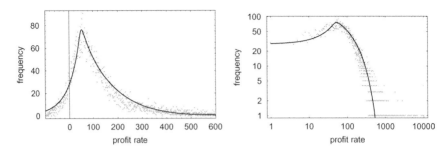

Figure D.1 Theoretical fit to the firm-weighted rate-of-profit distribution. The solid lines
plot the theoretical pdf $f_P(x)$ scaled by a constant in the frequency axis. The
RHS graph plots the function and data in log-log scale and extends the range of
the plot to the super-profit range. All profits in excess of 10000 are truncated,
which accounts for the outlier at the maximum profit rate.

consequence of the SA model is the conjecture that the empirical rate-of-profit
distribution will be consistent with a parameter-mix of a ratio of normal variates
with means and variances that depend on a firm size parameter that is distributed
according to a power law.

References

Althusser, L. and É. Balibar (1970) *Reading Capital*, London: New Left Books.

Amaral, L. A. N., S. V. Buldyrev, S. Havlin, H. Leschhorn, F. Maass and M. A. Salinger (1997a) 'Scaling behavior in economics: I. empirical results for company growth', *Journal de Physique I France* 7: 621–633.

Amaral, L. A. N., S. V. Buldyrev, S. Havlin, P. Maass, M. A. Salinger, H. E. Stanley and M. H. R. Stanley (1997b) 'Scaling behavior in economics: the problem of quantifying company growth', *Physica A* 244: 1–24.

Amaral, L. A. N., P. Gopikrishnan, V. Plerou and H. E. Stanley (2001) 'A model for the growth dynamics of economic organizations', *Physica A* 299: 127–136.

Ammon, K. (1993) 'An automatic proof of Gödel's incompleteness theorem', *Artificial Intelligence* 61(2): 291–306.

Arrow, K. J. and G. Debreu (1954) 'Existence of an equilibrium for a competitive economy', *Econometrica* 22(3): 265–290.

Asimov, I. (1950) *I Robot*, New York: Gnome Press.

Ausloos, M., J. Miskiewicz and M. Sanglier (2004) 'The duration of recession and prosperity: does their distribution follow a power or an exponential law?', *Physica A* 339: 548–558.

Axtell, R. L. (1999) 'The emergence of firms in a population of agents: local increasing returns unstable Nash equilibria, and power law size distributions'. CSED working paper No. 3.

———— (2001) 'Zipf distribution of U.S. firm sizes', *Science* 293: 1818–1820.

Babbage, C. (1832) *The Economy of Machinery and Manufactures*, London: C. Knight.

Bachelard, G. (1970) *La philosophie du non: essai d'une philosophie du nouvel esprit scientifique*, Paris: Presses Universitaires de France.

Badger, W. W. (1980) 'An entropy-utility model for the size distribution of income'. In B. J. West (ed.), *Mathematical Models as a Tool for Social Science*, pp. 87–120, New York: Gordon and Breach.

Bak, P., S. F. Nørrelykke and M. Shubik (1999) 'Dynamics of money', *Physical Review E* 60: 2528–2532.

Baker, G. L. and J. P. Gollub (1990) *Chaotic Dynamics*, Cambridge: Cambridge University Press.

Barnsley, M. (1988) *Fractals Everywhere*, Academic Press.

Becker, K. H. and M. Dorfler (1989) *Dynamical Systems and Fractals*, Cambridge: Cambridge University Press.

Bennett, C. H. (1988) 'Logical depth and physical complexity'. In R. Herken (ed.), *The Universal Turing Machine: a Half Century Survey*, Oxford: Oxford University Press.

Bernstein, P. A., D. W. Shipman and J. James B. Rothnie (1980) 'Concurrency control in a system for distributed databases (SDD-1)', *ACM Trans. Database Syst.* 5(1): 18–51.

Berry, G. (1988) *Seventeenth Century England: Traders and their Tokens*, London: Seaby.

Bolin, S. (1958) *State and Currency in the Roman Empire to 300 A.D.*, Stockholm: Almqvist and Wiksell.

von Bortkiewicz, L. (1907) 'Wertrechnung und Preisrechnung im Marxschen System', *Archiv fur Sozialwissenschaft und Sozialpolitik* XXV.

Bottazzi, G. and A. Secchi (2003) 'Explaining the distribution of firms growth rates'. LEM Papers Series 2005/16, Laboratory of Economics and Management, Sant'Anna School of Advanced Studies.

Bouchaud, J.-P. and M. Mézard (2000) 'Wealth condensation in a simple model of economy', *Physica A* 282: 536–545.

Brillouin, L. (1951) 'Maxwell's demon cannot operate: Information and entropy', *Journal of Applied Physics* 22: 334–337.

Brynjolfsson, E. (1993) 'The productivity paradox of information technology', *Commun. ACM* 36(12): 66–77.

Burrows, M. and D. Wheeler (1994) 'A block sorting lossless data compression algorithm'. Technical Report 124, Digital Equipment Corporation.

Canning, D., L. A. N. Amaral, Y. Lee, M. Meyer and H. E. Stanley (1998) 'Scaling the volatility of GDP growth rates', *Economics Letters* 60: 335–341.

Capek, K. (1999) *Four Plays*, London: A&C Black.

Carradice, I. and M. Price (1988) *Coinage in the Greek World*, London: Seaby.

Chaitin, G. J. (1987) *Information, Randomness and Incompleteness*, Singapore: World Scientific.

——— (1999) 'Information and randomness: A survey of algorithmic information theory'. In *The Unknowable*. New York: Springer.

Chakraborti, A. and B. K. Chakrabarti (2000) 'Statistical mechanics of money: how saving propensity affects its distribution', *The European Physical Journal B* 17: 167–170.

Church, A. (1936) 'An unsolvable problem of elementary number theory', *American Journal of Mathematics* 58: 345–363.

Cockshott, P., L. Mackenzie and G. Michaelson (2008) 'Physical constraints on hypercomputation', *Theoretical Computer Science (A)*. To appear.

Cockshott, P. and G. Michaelson (2007) 'Are there new models of computation? Reply to Wegner and Eberbach', *The Computer Journal* 50(2): 232.

Cockshott, P. and K. Renfrew (2004) *SIMD Programming Manual for Windows and Linux*, New York: Springer.

Cockshott, W. P. (1990) 'Application of artificial intelligence techniques to economic planning', *Future Computing Systems* 2: 429–443.

Cockshott, W. P. and A. Cottrell (1989) 'Labour value and socialist economic calculation', *Economy and Society* 18: 71–99.

——— (1993) *Towards a New Socialism*, Nottingham: Spokesman.

——— (1997) 'Labour time versus alternative value bases: a research note', *Cambridge Journal of Economics* 21: 545–549.

——— (2003) 'A note on the organic composition of capital and profit rates', *Cambridge Journal of Economics* 27: 749–754.

——— (2005) 'Robust correlations between prices and labour values: a comment', *Cambridge Journal of Economics* 29(2): 309–316.

Cockshott, W. P., A. F. Cottrell and G. Michaelson (1995) 'Testing Marx: some new results from UK data', *Capital and Class* 55: 103–129.

Cook, W. and P. Ormerod (2003) 'Power law distribution of the frequency of demises of US firms', *Physica A* 324: 207–212.

Cottrell, A. (1994) 'Hayek's early cycle theory re-examined', *Cambridge Journal of Economics* 18: 197–212.

Cottrell, A. and P. Cockshott (1993) 'Calculation, complexity and planning: the socialist calculation debate once again', *Review of Political Economy* 5(1): 73–112.

Cottrell, A., G. Michaelson and P. Cockshott (2008) 'Cantor diagonalisation and planning', *International Journal of Unconventional Computing*. To appear.

Davies, R. (1989) *Service in the Roman Army*, Edinburgh: Edinburgh University Press.

Debreu, G. (1959) *Theory of Value: An Axiomatic Analysis of Economic Equilibrium*, New Haven: Yale University Press.

Delli Gatti, D., C. Di Guilmi, E. Gaffeo, G. Giulioni, M. Gallegati and A. Palestrini (2005) 'A new approach to business fluctuations: heterogenous interacting agents, scaling laws and financial fragility', *Journal of Economic Behavior & Organization* 56(4): 489–512.

Deng, X. and L. Huang (2006) 'On the complexity of market equilibria with maximum social welfare', *Information Processing Letters* 97(1): 4–11.

Dick, P. K. (1968) *Do Androids Dream of Electric Sheep?*, Grenada.

DiVincenzo, D. (1995) 'Quantum computation', *Science* 270: 255–261.

Dorfman, R., P. Samuelson and R. Solow (1958) *Linear Programming and Economic Analysis*, New York: McGraw Hill.

Dragulescu, A. A. (2002) *Applications of Physics to Economics and Finance: Money, Income, Wealth, and the Stock Market*. Ph.D. thesis, Department of Physics, University of Maryland. http://arXiv.org/abs/cond-mat/0307341.

Dragulescu, A. A. and V. M. Yakovenko (2000) 'Statistical mechanics of money', *The European Physical Journal B* 17: 723–729.

—— (2002) 'Statistical mechanics of money, income and wealth: a short survey'. http://arXiv.org/abs/cond-mat/0211175.

Duménil, G. (1983) 'Beyond the transformation riddle: a labor theory of value', *Science and Society* 47(4): 427–450.

Duménil, G. and D. Lévy (2002) 'The profit rate: where and how much did it fall? Did it recover? (USA 1948–2000)', *Review of Radical Political Economics* 34(4): 437–461.

Edvinsson, R. (2003) 'A tendency for the rate of profit to fall'. Presented at the economic-historical meeting in Lund.

—— (2005) *Growth, Accumulation, Crisis: With New Macroeconomic Data for Sweden 1800–2000*. Ph.D. thesis, Stockholm University.

Fabritiis, G. D., F. Pammolli and M. Riccaboni (2003) 'On size and growth of business firms', *Physica A* 324: 38–44.

Farjoun, E. (1984) 'Production of commodities by means of what?' In E. Mandel and A. Freeman (eds.), *Ricardo, Marx, Sraffa*, London: Verso.

Farjoun, E. and M. Machover (1983) *Laws of Chaos, a Probabilistic Approach to Political Economy*, London: Verso.

Farmer, J. D., M. Shubik and E. Smith (2005) 'Is economics the next physical science?', *Physics Today* 9(58): 37–42.

Feigenbaum, E. A. (2003) 'Some challenges and grand challenges for computational intelligence', *J. ACM* 50(1): 32–40.

Feynmann, R. P. (1999) 'Simulating physics with computers'. In A. J. G. Hey (ed.), *Feynmann and Computation: Exploring the Limits of Computers*, pp. 133–153, Cambridge, MA: Perseus Books.

Fisher, D. (1963) *The Epic of Steel*, New York: Harper and Row.

Foley, D. K. (1982) 'The value of money, the value of labor power, and the Marxian transformation problem', *Review of Radical Political Economics* 14(2): 37–47.

———— (1983) 'On Marx's theory of money', *Social Concept*, pp. 5–19.

———— (2003) 'Sraffa's legacy', *Cambridge Journal of Economics* 27(2): 225–238. Available at http://ideas.repec.org/a/oup/cambje/v27y2003i2p225-238.html.

Foley, D. K. and T. R. Michl (1999) *Growth and Distribution*, Cambridge, MA: Harvard University Press.

Forstater, M. (2003) 'Taxation: A secret of colonial capitalist (so-called) primitive accumulation'. Technical Report 25, Center for Full Employment and Price Stability.

Frisch, U. B., B. Hasslacher and Y. Pomeau (1986) 'Lattice gas automata for the Navier Stokes equation', *Physical Review Letters* 56: 1505–1508.

Fujiwara, Y., C. D. Guilmi, H. Aoyama, M. Gallegati and W. Souma (2004) 'Do Pareto-Zipf and Gibrat laws hold true? An analysis with European firms', *Physica A* 335: 197–216.

Gaffeo, E., M. Gallegati and A. Palestrini (2003) 'On the size distribution of firms: additional evidence from the G7 countries', *Physica A* 324: 117–123.

Gibbs, W. W. (1994) 'Software's chronic crisis', *Scientific American* 271: 86–95.

von Glahn, R. (1996) *Fountain of Fortune: Money and Monetary Policy in China, 1000–1700*, Berkeley: University of California Press.

———— (2004) 'Revisiting the Song monetary revolution: a review essay', *International Journal of Asian Studies* 1: 159–178.

Gode, D. and S. Sunder (1993) 'Allocative efficiency of markets with zero intelligence traders: market as a partial substitute for individual rationality', *Journal of Political Economy* 101: 119–137.

Gödel, K. (1962) *On Formally Undecidable Propositions of Principia Mathematica and Related Systems*, Edinburgh: Oliver and Boyd.

Goguen, J. A. and J. Meseguer (1982) 'Completeness of many-sorted equational logic', *SIGPLAN Not.* 17(1): 9–17.

Grossman, H. (1977) 'Marx, classical political economy and the problem of dynamics', *Capital and Class* 2: 32–55.

Hales, T. C. (2001) 'The honeycomb conjecture', *Discrete and Computational Geometry* 25: 1–22.

Hamming, R. W. (1950) 'Error-detecting and error-correcting codes', *Bell Sys. Tech. J.* 29: 147–160.

Harris, J. (1996) 'From Das Capital to DOS Capital: A look at recent theories of value'. Technical report, Chicago Third Wave Study Group.

Hayek, F. A. (1935) *Prices and Production*, London: Routledge.

———— (1945) 'The use of knowledge in society', *American Economic Review* 35: 519–530.

———— (1955) *The Counter-Revolution of Science*, New York: The Free Press.

Hodges, A. (1983) *Alan Turing: the Enigma*, New York: Touchstone.

Huffman, D. A. (1952) 'A method for the construction of minimum-redundancy codes', *Proceedings of the I.R.E.* 40(9): 1098–1102.

Hutchinson, T. (1988) *Before Adam Smith, The Emergence of Political Economy, 1662–1776*, Oxford: Oxford University Press.

Ingham, G. (2004) *The Nature of Money*, Cambridge: Polity.

Innes, A. M. (1913) 'What is money?', *Banking Law Journal* 30: 377–408.

Ispolatov, S., P. L. Krapivsky and S. Redner (1998) 'Wealth distributions in asset exchange models', *The European Physical Journal B* 2: 267–276.

Itoh, M. and C. Lapavitsas (1999) *Political Economy of Money and Finance*, Basingstoke: Macmillan.

Jevons, W. S. (1871) *Theory of Political Economy*, London: Macmillan.

Kalecki, M. (1954) *Theory of Economic Dynamics*, New York: Rinehart.

Kapur, J. N. (1989) *Maximum Entropy Models in Science and Engineering*, Wiley Eastern.

Kapur, J. N. and H. K. Kesavan (1992) *Entropy Optimization Principles with Applications*, Academic Press.

Keynes, J. M. (1936) *The General Theory of Employment, Interest and Money*, London: Macmillan.

Khinchin, A. I. (1949) *Mathematical Foundations of Statistical Mechanics*, New York: Dover.

Kim, E. and G. H. Whitesides (1995) 'The use of minimal free energy and self-assembly to form shapes', *Chem. Mat.* 7: 1257–1264.

Kleene, S. C. (1935) 'General recursive functions of natural numbers', *American Journal of Mathematics* 57.

Kliman, A. (2007) *Reclaiming Marx's "Capital"*, Lanham, MD: Lexington Books.

Kliman, A. J. (2002) 'The law of value and laws of statistics: sectoral values and prices in the US economy, 1977–97', *Cambridge Journal of Economics* 26(3): 299–311. URL http://cje.oxfordjournals.org/cgi/content/abstract/26/3/299.

Knapp, G. F. (1973) *The State Theory of Money*, New York: A. M. Kelley.

Krause, U. (1982) *Money and Abstract Labour*, London: Verso.

Kuhn, T. (1970) *The Structure of Scientific Revolutions*, Chicago: University of Chicago Press.

Landauer, R. (1961) 'Irreversibility and heat generation in the computing process', *IBM Journal of Research and Development* 5: 183–191.

Lange, O. (1938) *On the Economic Theory of Socialism*, University of Minnesota Press.

Lardner, D. (1834) 'Babbage's calculating engines', *Edinburgh Review* 59: 263–327.

Lavington, S. (1980) *Early British Computers*, Manchester: Manchester University Press.

Lavington, S. H. (1978) 'The Manchester Mark I and Atlas: A historical perspective', *Commun. ACM* 21(1): 4–12.

Lawlor, M. S. and B. L. Horn (1992) 'Notes on the Sraffa–Hayek exchange', *Review of Political Economy* 4.

Lee, Y., L. A. N. Amaral, D. Canning, M. Meye and H. E. Stanley (1998) 'Universal features in the growth dynamics of complex organizations', *Physical Review Letters* 81(15): 3275–3278.

Levy, M. and S. Solomon (1997) 'New evidence for the power-law distribution of wealth', *Physica A* 242: 90–94.

——— (n.d.) 'Of wealth power and law: the origin of scaling in economics'. http://citeseerx.ist.psu.edu/viewdoc/summary?doi=10.1.1.53.6822.

Lifshitz, E. M. and L. P. Pitaevskiĭ (1993) *Physical Kinetics*, New York: Pergamon Press.

Marciszewski, W. (2002) 'Hypercomputational vs. computational complexity: A challenge for methodology of the social sciences', *Free Market and Computational Complexity. Essays in Commemoration of Friedrich Hayek (1899-1992). Series: Studies in Logic, Grammar and Rhetoric* 5: 18.

Marshall, A. (1890) *Principles of Economics*, London: Macmillan.

Marx, K. (1971) *Capital*, vol. 3, Moscow: Progress Publishers.

——— (1973) *Grundrisse*, Harmondsworth: Penguin/New Left Review.

——— (1976) *Capital*, vol. 1, Harmondsworth: Penguin. Translated by Ben Fowkes.

——— (1988) *Marx and Engels Collected Works*, vol. 43, Moscow: Progess Publishers.

Matteo, T. D., T. Aste and S. T. Hyde (2004) 'Exchanges in complex networks: income and wealth distributions'. In F. Mallamace and H. E. Stanley (eds.), *The Physics of Complex Systems: New Advances and Perspectives.* Amsterdam: IOS Press.

Maxwell, J. C. (1875) *The Theory of Heat*, London: Longman.

McConnell, C. R. and S. L. Brue (1996) *Economics: Principles, Problems, and Policies*, New York: McGraw-Hill, 13 edn.

Michaelson, G. and P. Cockshott (2006) 'Constraints on hypercomputation'. In A. Beckmann, U. Berger, B. Lowe and J. V. Tucker (eds.), *Logical Approaches to Computational Barriers: Second Conference on Computability in Europe, CiE 2006, Swansea, UK*, no. 3988 in LNCS, pp. 378–387. Springer.

Minsky, M. (1967) *Computation: Finite and Infinite Machines*, Englewood Cliffs, NJ: Prentice-Hall.

Mirowski, P. (1989) *More Heat Than Light: Economics as Social Physics, Physics as Nature's Economics*, Cambridge: Cambridge University Press.

Montrell, E. W. and M. F. Shlesinger (1982) 'On $1/f$ noise and other distributions with long tails', *Proceedings of the National Academy of Sciences of the USA* 79: 3380–3383.

Montroll, E. W. and M. F. Shlesinger (1983) 'Maximum entropy formalism, fractals, scaling phenomena, and 1/f noise: tale of tails', *Journal of Statistical Physics* 32: 209–230.

Mueth, D. M., H. M. Jaeger and S. R. Nagel (1998) 'Force distribution in a granular medium', *Physical Review E* 57: 3164–3169.

Murphy, J. P. (2006) 'Cantor's diagonal argument: an extension to the socialist calculation debate', *Quarterly Journal of Austrian Economics* 9(2): 3–11.

Nagel, E. and J. R. Newman (1959) *Gödel's Proof*, Routledge and Kegan Paul.

von Neumann, J. (1955) *Mathematical Foundations of Quantum Mechanics*, Princeton, NJ: Princeton University Press.

Nirei, M. and W. Souma (2003a) 'Income distribution and stochastic multiplicative process with reset events', *Lecture Notes in Economics and Mathematical Systems* 531: 161–170.

——— (2003b) 'Income distribution dynamics: a classical perspective'. mimeo.

Norretranders, T. (1998) *The User Illusion*, Harmondsworth: Penguin.

Nove, A. (1983) *The Economics of Feasible Socialism*, London: George Allen and Unwin.

Ochoa, E. M. (1989) 'Values, prices, and wage–profit curves in the US economy', *Cambridge Journal of Economics* 13: 413–429.

Okishio, N. (1961) 'Technical change and the rate of profit', *Kobe University Economic Review*, 7: 86–99.

——— (1990) 'Constant and variable capital'. In J. Eatwell, M. Milgate and P. Newman (eds.), *The New Palgrave – Marxian Economics*, pp. 91–103, New York and London: Norton.

Ormerod, P. (2002) 'The US business cycle: power law scaling for interacting units with comple internal structure', *Physica A* 314: 774–785.

Ormerod, P. and C. Mounfield (2001) 'Power law distribution of the duration and magnitude of recessions in capitalist economies: breakdown of scaling', *Physica A* 293: 573–582.

Pashukanis, E. B. (1989) *Law and Marxism: A General Theory*, London: Pluto Press.

Pasinetti, L. L. (1977) *Lectures on the Theory of Production*, New York: Columbia University Press.

Petrovic, P. (1987) 'The deviation of production prices from labour values: some methodolog and empirical evidence', *Cambridge Journal of Economics* 11: 197–210.

Polanyi, K., C. Arensberg and H. Pearson (1957) *Trade and Market in the Early Empires*, New York: Free Press.

Porter, A. W. (1946) *Thermodynamics*, London: Methuen.

Postgate, J. N. (1992) *Early Mesopotamia: Society and Economy at the Dawn of History*, London: Routledge.

de Prony, G. (1824) 'Notice sur les grandes tables logarithmique'. Technical report, L'Academie Royal Des Sciences, Paris.

Rae, J. (1965) *Life of Adam Smith*, New York: A. M. Kelley.

Reed, W. J. (2000) 'The Pareto law of incomes – an explanation and an extension'. Mimeo.

———— (2001) 'The Pareto, Zipf and other power laws', *Economics Letters* 74: 15–19.

Ricardo, D. (1951) *Principles of Political Economy and Taxation*, Cambridge: Cambridge University Press. Volume 1 of *The Works and Correspondence of David Ricardo*, edited by Piero Sraffa.

Roemer, J. E. (1982) *A General Theory of Exploitation and Class*, Cambridge, MA: Harvard University Press.

Rubin, I. I. (1973) *Essays on Marx's Theory of Value*, Black Rose Books. Russian edition 1928.

Samuelson, P. (1972) *The Collected Scientific Papers of Paul A. Samuelson*, vol. III, Cambridge, MA: The MIT Press.

Saygin, A., I. Cicekli and V. Akman (2000) 'Turing test: 50 years later', *Minds and Machines* 10(4): 463–518.

Sedgewick, R. and P. Flajolet (1996) *An Introduction to the Analysis of Algorithms*, Addison-Wesley.

Shaikh, A. M. (1984) 'The transformation from Marx to Sraffa'. In E. Mandel and A. Freeman (eds.), *Ricardo, Marx, Sraffa – the Langston Memorial Volume*, pp. 43–84, London: Verso.

———— (1998) 'The empirical strength of the labour theory of value'. In R. Bellofiore (ed.), *Marxian Economics: A Reappraisal*, vol. 2, pp. 225–251, Macmillan.

Shannon, C. (1948) 'A mathematical theory of communication', *The Bell System Technical Journal* 27: 379–423 and 623–56.

Shaw, P., P. Cockshott and P. Barrie (1996) 'Implementation of lattice gases using FPGAs', *Journal of VLSI Signal Processing* 12(1): 1251–1256.

Shubik, M. (1997) 'Time and money'. In W. B. Arthur, S. N. Durlauf and D. A. Lane (eds.), *The Economy as an Evolving Complex System II*, pp. 263–284, Reading, MA: Addison-Wesley.

———— (1999) *The Theory of Money and Financial Institutions*, Cambridge, MA: The MIT Press.

Smith, A. (1974) *The Wealth of Nations*, Harmondsworth: Penguin. Edited by Andrew Skinner.

Sobel, D. (1996) *Longitude: The True Story of a Lone Genius Who Solved the Greatest Scientific Problem of His Time*, Harmondsworth: Penguin.

Souma, W. (2000) 'Physics of personal income'. In H. Takayasu (ed.), *Empirical science of financial fluctuations: the advent of econophysics*, Tokyo: Nihon Keizai Shimbun. http://arxiv.org/abs/cond-mat/0202388.

Sraffa, P. (1960) *Production of Commodities by Means of Commodities*, Cambridge: Cambridge University Press.

Stanley, M. H. R., N. L. A. Amaral, S. V. Buldyrev, S. Havlin, H. Leschhorn, P. Maass, M. A. Salinger and H. E. Stanley (1996) 'Scaling behavior in the growth of companies', *Nature* 379: 804–806.

de Ste. Croix, G. E. M. (1981) *Class Struggle in the Ancient Greek World*, London: Duckworth.

Steedman, I. (1981) *Marx after Sraffa*, London: Verso.

Strand, S. (1979) *Machines: An Illustrated History*, Göteborg: AB Nordbok.

Szilard, L. (1964) 'On the decrease of entropy in a thermodynamic system by the intervention of intelligent beings', *Behavioral Science* 9: 301–310.

Tann, J. (1981) *Selected Papers of Boulton and Watt*, London: Diploma Press.

Thompson, F. M. L. (1993) *The Cambridge Social History of Britain, 1750–1950*, Cambridge: Cambridge University Press.

Traiger, I. L., J. Gray, C. A. Galtieri and B. G. Lindsay (1982) 'Transactions and consistency in distributed database systems', *ACM Trans. Database Syst.* 7(3): 323–342.

Tsoulfidis, L. and T. Maniatis (2002) 'Values, prices of production and market prices: some more evidence from the Greek economy', *Cambridge Journal of Economics* 26: 359–369.

Turing, A. M. (1937) 'On Computable Numbers, with an application to the Entscheidungsproblem', *Proceedings of the London Mathematical Society* 42: 230–265.

——— (1950) 'Computing machinery and intelligence', *Mind* LIX(236): 433–460.

Velupillai, K. (2003) 'Essays on computable economics, methodology and the philosophy of science'. Working Paper 0308, Università Degli Studi di Trento, Dipartimento di Economia.

Wannier, G. H. (1966) *Statistical Physics*, New York: Dover.

Wells, J. (2001) 'What is the distribution of the rate of profit?' Presented at the IWGVT mini-conference at the Eastern Economic Association.

Whately, R. (1832) *Introductory Lectures on Political Economy*, London: Fellows.

Whitehead, A. N. and B. Russell (1910–13) *Principia Mathematica*, Cambridge: Cambridge University Press.

Whitesides, G. H. (1995) 'Self-assembling materials', *Scientific American* 273: 146–149.

Wolfram, S. (2002) *A New Kind of Science*, Champaign, IL: Wolfram Media.

Wray, R. (2004) 'The credit money and state money approaches'. In *Credit and State Theories of Money: the contributions of A. Mitchell Innes*, pp. 79–98, Cheltenham: Edward Elgar.

Wright, I. (2004) 'A conjecture on the distribution of firm profit', *Economía: Teoría y Práctica* 20.

——— (2005a) 'The duration of recessions follows an exponential not a power law', *Physica A* 345: 608–610.

——— (2005b) 'The social architecture of capitalism', *Physica A: Statistical Mechanics and its Applications* 346(3-4): 589–620.

——— (2008a) 'Statistical mechanics of money'. URL http://demonstrations.wolfram.com/StatisticalMechanicsOfMoney/. From the Wolfram Demonstrations Project.

——— (2008b) 'The emergence of the law of value in a dynamic simple commodity economy', *Review of Political Economy* 20(3): 367–391.

Zachariah, D. (2006) 'Labour value and equalisation of profit rates', *Indian Development Review* 4(1): 1–21.

——— (2008) 'Determinants of the average profit rate and the trajectory of capitalist economies'. Presented at the conference on Probabilistic Political Economy, Kingston University, July 2008.

Index

abacus 75–6, 211, 235
algorithmics 76, 211
Althusser, Louis 7
Arrow, Kenneth 330
ASCII 44, 48, 85
Asimov, Isaac 112
Axtell, Robert 280, 281, 283

Babbage, Charles 1, 47, 64, 74–84, 109, 249
Bachelard, Gaston 30
banking technology 247–54
banknotes 215, 237, 238, 244, 246, 254
bankruptcy 154, 155, 243, 244, 264
banks: centralization of 246; creation of money by 155, 246; deposits and credit 233; recording of debt relations 233
bees: and entropy 27, 38; architects and 12; efficiency of 15–16
bitmap 53, 90
bits 31, 33, 90
Boltzmann, Ludwig 22, 24, 33, 42, 150, 322
Boltzmann–Gibbs distribution 141, 142, 144, 148–50, 153, 155, 159, 275
Bortkiewicz, Ladislaus von 130
Boulton, Matthew 10
Brillouin, Leon 33

Capek, Karel 109
capital: constant and variable 127; fixed and circulating 127; organic composition 128, 129, 135, 136, 184, 192, 196, 311; signature of 237–40, 244, 246, 292
capitalism: essential and inessential properties 290; social architecture of 263, 292; social relations of 263–91
Carnot, Sadi 19, 37

Chaitin, Gregory 39, 40, 42, 51, 105
Chaos theory 39
Church–Turing thesis 99–102, 328
classical political economy 1, 113–30
Clausius, Rudolf 21, 22
coin 206–8, 211, 212, 216, 237, 240, 245
commercial credit 240, 241
commercial crisis 244
commodity production 115
commodity–money space 220
complexity 38, 105–8, 330, 331
Compton's Mule 59
computers: and algorithmic information theory 40; and productivity paradox 298; Babbage's designs 82–84; efficiency of 37, 41; in banking 215, 249–54; see also Turing machines 85
conservation: of energy 144, 148, 149, 224; of money 140, 142, 146, 148, 150, 153, 155, 159
copying technologies 61–6
cotton spinning 58–61

Debreu, Gérard 134, 143, 289
debt: and default 242; and money 155, 207; and tallies 209; as negative money 153; as sparse matrix 233; as ternary relation 234; formation of 228–31; recording 213, 216, 226; to the state 208, 216, 218, 227
Delli Gatti, Domenico 284
delta-function distribution 150, 159
Difference Engine 82–4
digital electronics 69–73
digital paper 42, 45, 48
distribution: of income see income 292; of wealth, see wealth 292
Dragulescu, Adrian 140–2, 274, 278
Duménil, Gérard 172, 314

economic planning 325 and efficiency 332; and the law of value 331; feasibility of 107, 328, 338
economic subject 204–6
Edvinsson, R., 314
entropy; algorithmic and thermodynamic 56–7, 62; and printing technology 48; and production 48–53; and the distribution of money 151; Boltzmann's formula 22–4; conditional 51, 53, 189, 334; first introduced 20; maximization of 145; reduction via work 30
epistemological break 31
equilibrium and rate of profit 124; and the law of value 163; distribution of money 148; division of labour 169; general 134; mechanical 143, 160; statistical 136, 143–4, 160, 330; supply and demand 132, 133, 167; thermodynamic 24, 34, 149, 158
exchange value 115, 116, 126

Farjoun, Emmanuel 119, 136, 184–9, 191, 272, 286
Feynman, Richard 37
financial sector 256, 258
financial transactions 226–31
firms; death of 283–4; growth rate of 282–3; size distribution of 280–2; structure of 265
Foley, Duncan 172, 180, 203, 265, 298
Ford, Henry 54
Forstater, M., 210
Fuller, Buckminster 17
Fullerenes 17

Gödel, Kurt 100
genomics 73
Glahn, Richard von 237
gold 180, 206, 209, 210, 212, 237, 238, 244, 246
Gold Standard 210, 244

Halting Problem 101–2
Hamming distance 224
Hayek, F. A., 321–5, 327, 329, 331, 332, 337
hieroglyphs 45
Hilbert, David 100
Honeycomb Conjecture, 16
horsepower 10, 11, 85
horses, and human labour 11, 28, 110
Hume, David 114

ideal gas 144
income distribution of 146, 257, 264, 273–8, 298; of financial sector 258; sectoral 174–5
inequality 154, 257, 264, 291
information and market transactions 333–5; and property relations 66; and randomness 40, 43; and replicated parts 49–53; and telephony 31; cost of 41; mutual 189; paradoxes of, 43; processing of 85–108
information theory 30–46 algorithmic 39, 42; and computation 34; and economic dynamics 332–3; and the printing industry 49
Innes, Mitchell 209
input–output analysis 107–8, 192, 295, 327, 338
interest 228, 246, 250, 308
interest rate 257, 316–8; formation of, 254–6
iron-working 63

Jevons, W. S., 131

Kalecki, Michal 299–300
Keynes, J. M., 119, 187, 326
Khinchin, Aleksandr 147
Kliman, Andrew 131, 201
Knapp, Georg 207
Kolmogorov, Andrei 38, 40, 43, 105
Krause, Ulrich 181

labour as measure of value 117–9, 187; division of, 55, 77–8, 82, 115 in simulation model 167; intensification of 54; productivity of 47–73, 114; prolongation of 54; purposeful 19, 30; universality of 3, 123, 327
labour theory of value 119–23, 161, 182–3; critiques of 131–5, 201; emprirical evidence for 192–9; stochastic formulation 185
Landauer, Rolf 34–7
Landauer-energy 37
Lange, Oskar 335, 338
Laplace distribution 282–4, 291
lattice gas 25–7, 33
law of value 183, 322, 325, 331 in Marx 161–3; simulation of 163–72
Laws of Chaos 119, 184–8
Lévy, Dominique 314

Levy, Moshe 274
Locke, John 114
longitude 77
Lydian coinage 209

Machover, Moshe 119, 136, 184–9, 191, 272, 286
Mandelbrot set 39–40, 42
Manhattan distance, 223, 224, 228, 231, 244
Marshall, Alfred 132
Marx, Karl 1, 2, 74, 115, 224, 321; and falling rate of profit, 310; and the form of value 203; and the law of value 161–2; and transformation problem 184; architect and bee 12; on labour and labour-power 126; on the labour theory of value 125–30
Maxwell's demon 20–2, 33–4, 38, 48
Maxwell, James Clerk 20, 30, 33
mechanical equilibrium *see* equilibrium 292
MELT 131, 173, 174, 180
Mirowski, Philip 143
monetary technologies 210–12, 232
money: and the form of value 203; as information structure 238, 256; circuit of 218; conservation of 140, 148; distribution of 148–60; in Chinese history 235, 246; in colonial regimes 210, 216–18; in socialist economies 236; relations and records 210; signature of 218; state theory of 206–10; three functions of 207; *see also* gold 292
'money supply' 231

natural law tradition 114, 131
natural price 117, 123
navigation 76
neo-Ricardians 1, 131, 135, 184, 192, 289
Newcomen engine 8, 10
Newtonian dynamics 25
normal distribution 186, 189
Nove, Alec 107, 330, 340

Okishio, Nobuo 292, 297, 306, 311, 317

paper, production of 48
Pasinetti, Luigi 289
pensions 257
Pepper's ghost 221
photography 66–8

power-law distribution 275, 276, 278, 280, 290
prices and information 323–6; and the rate of profit 190–2; economy of information 324, 327; information content of 188–90; relationship to values 163, 171, 174, 188, 194–6, 326
prices of production 129, 130, 135, 136, 318
probabilistic approach 136, 161
probabilistic models 139–40
probability 139; and entropy 24; and the rate of interest 254; in information theory 32
'productivity paradox', 298
profit: macroeconomic determination of 298–300; monetary illusions 307–10; Sraffian theory of 293–7; *see also* rate of profit 292
Prony, Gaspard de 77–78
property relations 66, 69, 115, 205, 206, 264, 292

rate of interest *see* interest rate 292
rate of profit and historical demography 300–7; and technical change 297–8; computer simulations 304–7; equalization of, 124 191, 197, 316; falling tendency of 310–12; historical evidence 312–14; in money and value terms 129, 307; Okishio critique 315–18
Ricardo, David 1, 44, 118, 121–5, 130, 132, 133, 184, 297, 310
robots 108–12
Roemer, John 181, 292
Roman numerals 75
Rosetta stone 45
Rubin, I. I., 163, 174, 178, 180, 182
Russell, Bertrand 99

Samian ware 61–62
Samuelson, Paul 135, 136, 184
seigniorage 219–20, 246
sewing machines 55–6, 58
Shaikh, Anwar 136, 192, 194
'shot noise' 67, 245
simple exchange economy 140–3
Smith, Adam 1, 55, 77, 82, 113–21, 184, 187, 206, 310
Soviet economy 115, 236
Sraffa, Piero 107, 134–6, 199, 293–8
Standard System 296–7

statistical equilibrium *see* equilibrium 292
steam engine 7–10, 19, 20, 28, 36, 113
subject *see* economic subject 203
Sumer 213–6
surplus product 212, 236, 246, 258, 289, 294, 312, 328
surplus value 127–9, 238, 258, 301, 304, 311, 316
Szilard, Leo 33

tallies 209, 211
thermodynamic weight 24
thermodynamics 1, 19–28, 31, 56, 189
second law 19, 20, 22, 24, 28, 42, 45, 145
Thimonnier, Barthelemy 55
time-reversal symmetry 148, 156, 158
transformation problem 127, 129, 130, 190
trigonometric tables 77, 78
Turing machines 51, 89–105, 111; and banking 251; and markets 103
Turing, Alan 84, 89, 100, 110, 251

Universal Turing Machine 40, 41, 97–98
use value 69, 115, 116, 126

value: adding-up theory 117; calculation of 192–4, 327; conservation of 222–6; in Smith 115; marginalist theory of 131–3; measure of 116; the form of 203; *see also* labour theory of value 292

wages 54, 118, 119, 121, 123, 126, 127, 187, 192, 193, 195–197, 236, 239, 294, 295, 297, 299, 301, 306, 310, 314, 332
Walras, Léon 131
Watt, James 7–11, 19, 30, 31, 36, 37, 85, 113
wealth 47, 48, 58, 211, 222, 272, 276 distribution of 141, 143, 146, 149, 152, 159, 278, 280; store of 207
Whately, Richard 132
Whitehead, A. N., 99
work 1, 3, 7, 10, 19 and heat 19; James Watt on 7–11
Wray, Randall 207, 209

Zachariah, David 314
Zipf law 280, 281, 283, 284